KISSING COUSINS?

CHRISTIANS AND MUSLIMS FACE TO FACE

In a world marred by religious conflict, can Christians and Muslims discover more positive views of one another?

Bill A. Musk

MONARCH
BOOKS
Oxford, UK & Grand Rapids, Michigan, USA

First published in the UK in 2005 by Monarch Books
(a publishing imprint of Lion Hudson plc),
Mayfield House, 256 Banbury Road, Oxford, OX2 7DH.
Tel: +44 (0) 1865 302750 Fax: +44 (0) 1865 302757
Email: monarch@lionhudson.com
www.lionhudson.com

ISBN 1 85424 675 5 (UK)
ISBN 0 8254 6090 5 (USA)

Distributed by:
UK: Marston Book Services Ltd, PO Box 269,
Abingdon, Oxon OX14 4YN;
USA: Kregel Publications, PO Box 2607,
Grand Rapids, Michigan 49501.

British Library Cataloguing Data
A catalogue record for this book is available
from the British Library.

Book design and production for the publishers by Lion Hudson plc.
Printed in Malta.

All royalties from the sale of this book are assigned to

Urban Vision, a ministry of
Interserve
325 Kennington Road
London
SE11 4QH

Many people seem to think that distant relatives are the best kind to have.

Contents

Figures 7
Preface 11

Cousins Apart? 17
1. Living Godwards 19
Step-brothers in God 39

Comparable Cousins? 45
2. Voicing God's Concerns 47
3. Words Perfectly Spoken 84
4. And Who Exactly is God? 118
The Essential Ingredient 150

Uncomfortable Cousins? 153
5. "Befores" and "Afters" 155
6. Set Free or Set Fast? 187
7. Do It in Public? 219
Eastern Relatives 248

Competing Cousins? 253
8. A Tainted Past 255
9. Meeting Head-on 283
Helps Along the Way? 300

Cousins in Hope? 303
10. Dust and Divinity 305
11. Made-up Messiah 332
God For All 366

Kissing Cousins? 371
12. Delightful Kids 373

Appendices 395
1. Transliteration 397
2. An Introductory Bibliography 399
3. Glossary 409
4. Notes 419
5. Index 470

Figures

1. "Submission" and "rejection" in Arabic 25
2. "By faith" in Hebrews 11 30
3. Abram's male progeny 40
4. Different sons of Abraham 42
5. Significant dates in Muḥammad's life 48
6. Earliest revelations 51
7. Moses' calling to prophethood 53
8. Processes of inspiration 55
9. Revelation at Mount Sinai 56
10. The northern kingdom of Israel and the southern kingdom of Judah 58
11. Arabia 60
12. Tribes in Medina 61
13. Principles ordained in Meccan suras 63
14. Rules emanating from the Medinan period 64
15. Major battles during the Medinan period 67
16. Prophet Muḥammad's wives/concubines 72
17. Jesus as a second Moses in Matthew's Gospel 74
18. Suras given in Mecca and Medina 87
19. Margoliouth's description of "Meccan" and "Medinan" suras 88
20. The first caliphs 90
21. Significant codices of the Qur'ân consulted by Zaid ibn Thâbit 91
22. Seven "Readers" of the Qur'ân and their "Transmitters" 93
23. Examples of references to *tanzîl* or "sending down" in the Qur'ân 95

24. Books "sent down" by God to humankind 96
25. Revelation as portrayed in Islam and Christianity 100
26. Abrogated verses in the Qur'ân 105
27. Stories in the Qur'ân reflective of Jewish and Christian apocryphal material 108
28. *Hymn to Aten* and Psalm 104 110
29. Arab gods and goddesses 120
30. *Allâh*: local and cosmic 123
31. Names for God 125
32. Related Semitic words for "God" 126
33. El in Genesis 127
34. The "Beautiful Names" of God 136
35. Chapman's theological approach to Qur'ân and Bible 139
36. "God" and "Jesus" in Bible translations in languages spoken by Muslims 141
37. Continuity and discontinuity 145
38. Frankincense and myrrh 151
39. Continuity and discontinuity between Judaism and Christianity 156
40. "Trinity" in the Bible 164
41. Models for theologizing AD 150–400 165
42. Wrestling with "the Trinity" 168
43. Contrasting models of theologizing in Islam AD 800–1300 172
44. John Travis's spectrum of contextualized communities of believers in Christ 181
45. Contextualization and syncretism 185
46. From charismatic to dynastic leadership 191
47. Developing church: councils and splits 194
48. The ecumenical councils 195
49. Theological debates 196
50. Culture bloc and theological "flag" 197

51. Creed of Nicaea 199
52. Jesus Christ: divine and human 202
53. The "definition" of Chalcedon 204
54. Jewish Hasmonean power-holders 214
55. Roman power-holders 215
56. The "five pillars" of Islam 221
57. The changing face of British religiosity according to Callum Brown 230
58. Religion in Britain in the third millennium 231
59. "Values" of secular society 232
60. Mosque registration in Britain 239
61. Britons of Pakistani and Bangladeshi descent born in the United Kingdom 240
62. The Crusades 259
63. Spain in the seventh and eighth centuries 265
64. Significant events of the *Reconquista* 266
65. Spain in the twelfth century 269
66. Spain in the late fifteenth century 270
67. Mission imperative 283
68. Growing faith communities 284
69. Objectives of the Organization of the Islamic Conference 290
70. Collective Muslim "success" 292
71. Declaration by Muslim background, Christian believers in Egypt 295
72. Mystery in Islamic "Adam" and Christian "Christ" 308
73. "Man" and knowledge 309
74. Interpreting Romans 5:12 317
75. Serious sins and mild sins 321
76. Sins leading to capital punishment in Sinaitic and Islamic law 323
77. "Salvation" in Islam and Christianity 326

78. Hope in judgement? 328
79. “Man” in Qur’ân and Bible 330
80. Mary in the Qur’ân and in Christian apocryphal books 334
81. The annunciation in Qur’ân and Bible 336
82. Miracles of Jesus 338
83. Positive witness to Jesus in the Qur’ân 339
84. Negations about Jesus in the Qur’ân 341
85. Theories of non-crucifixion 344
86. Verses about Jesus’ death 347
87. Jesus in the *Gospel of Barnabas* 352
88. Christ as “Sign” in Qur’ân and New Testament 357
89. Saul’s credentials with God 367
90. Self-revealing God 369
91. Judaism, Islam and Christianity 376
92. Elaine Pagels’ “social history of Satan” in the four Gospels 387
93. Transliteration and pronunciation of Arabic alphabet 397
94. A summary of terms for relevant Jewish material 425
95. Targums 432
96. Muslims by ethnic group according to 2001 census 453
97. Sin as described in the Qur’ân 461

Preface

The couple standing, or more accurately swaying, on my doorstep intrigued me. As I live beside the church where I serve as a vicar, I am often approached for help by all manner of people. Apart from the occasional mentally disturbed person, most callers are seeking money for some emergency in their lives. As a church, we have had to come to a publicly stated policy of not disbursing money from the vicarage, but we do run a community larder. I offer callers gifts of food and other grocery items.

The couple ringing my doorbell on this occasion were people I had previously noticed around the parish. As I opened the door to them their behaviour quickly told me that they had both had too much to drink. The woman spoke before I had even greeted them. She delivered a rather slurred version of: "Hello vicar. We are kissing cousins." She then proceeded to recount their latest troubles and could I help them out please? A little while later I sent them on their way with food and other groceries while they called down God's richest blessings on me for assisting them.

"Kissing cousins." The phrase stayed with me and I have thought about it, on and off, for many months. The words conjure up contradictory connotations, positive and negative. Cousins are, of course, close relatives: not quite brothers and sisters, but much closer than, say, "second cousins". They are my father or mother's siblings' children – the same generation as myself, probably the same age as myself, and participators in the same family history as myself. Indeed, some well-known figures such as Charles Darwin, Albert Einstein and Texan rock-and-roll legend Jerry Lee Lewis are renowned for marrying their cousins. Cousins are "family", sharing blood affinity and genealogical history.

Yet should the "cousins" hovering on my vicarage doorstep be "kissing"? Although the law in England permits the marriage of first cousins, there remains for many people a strong hesitation about the rightness of such a possibility. There is something not quite healthy, something a bit risqué, about *kissing* cousins. In the United States of America today, about half the states of the union prohibit marriage between first cousins, while several more permit such marriages only under special circumstances. Cousins, it is often felt, should not be allowed to be that close. And, of course, the very ambiguity of the phrase raises the question – exactly how close are they? What does kissing include or exclude? Can anyone in our Western culture, cousin or not, just be kissing when they say they are "kissing"?

"Kissing cousins", then, is an ambiguous phrase. It is a phrase that conveys a sense of commonality, of shared experience, and the idea of being in the same family. It carries a warm sense of mutuality, evoking bonds that are deep and impervious to what may challenge them.

"Kissing cousins" also evokes negative thoughts and emotions. Feelings, perhaps, of disgust or at least of a sense of "not everything in this relationship is appropriate" may be raised by the phrase. The phrase also provokes as many questions as it answers – exactly what kind of relationship are we talking about here? How deep, how common, how intertwined?

Mulling over the thoughts raised by my doorstep encounter with two rather inebriated Londoners has led me to determine that "kissing cousins" is both a delightful and an ambiguous way of speaking about relationship.

Such is also my conclusion, or starting-point, concerning the relationship between Islam and Christianity. The two faiths seem to me to be like "kissing cousins". There is much that is delightful about their relationship. There exists a lot of commonality and a great deal of the sense of "being on the same side". Origins of the two communities go back a long way to a common ancestor – Abraham – or to a similar conviction about a sole, sovereign God. Muslims and Christians share a belief that the one God is creator and sustainer of the world. Moreover, both hold that God has revealed himself and his will to his human creation within that world. Human beings, for both faiths, are endowed with moral responsibility for their deeds. They have a duty of worship and obedience, the privilege of petition and the delicate responsibility for ordering the rest of creation. In both faiths, Jerusalem is venerated. Both communities practise weekly communal prayer. Muslims and Christians each recognize that a Day of Judgement is coming, on which every human will be held accountable for his or her life by God.

At the same time, however, there is tremendous distance between the two faiths. They may be related in terms of an original link to Abraham, but how they have developed from that common ancestor is totally different. They have discrete views of what relationship with God means, even of what God is like. They have alternative conceptions of "religion". "Worship" finds expression in contrasting human responses. Living with God means vastly different things to members of the different faiths.

And do they "kiss"? Well, in some ways, they have done and still do. There are some ways in which Muslims and Christians have related positively at different times to one another. Such positive relating, however, seems largely eclipsed by long episodes of negative relating. From a Muslim perspective, for example, the century and a half from AD 1800 saw their growing humiliation at the hands of an aggressive, colonizing, "Christian" West:

> scarcely a decade, indeed scarcely half a decade, passed without some Muslim area somewhere in Asia or Africa being lost to the Western Christian powers or Muslims fighting against the encroachment of these powers.[1]

In the West today, "Christians" are very conscious of an "Islamic threat" that excites strongly negative emotions:

> It is no longer possible today to use the word Islam before a Western audience without immediately conjuring up powerful imagery combining the strongly negative connotations of the terms *jihad*, holy war, terrorism, fanaticism, violence, oppression of women, polygamy, repudiation, the veil as the Islamic headscarf, the rejection of the West, the violations of human rights and so on.[2]

"Kissing cousins" conveys a whisper of wistfulness for the future as well as a somewhat ambiguous summary of bygone relationship. If followers of each faith could better understand where each religion is "coming from", maybe hope could be engendered for more positive relating and communicating across the gap between them. In this book, therefore, there is a strong element of looking back for the purpose of looking forward. Attitude-change is my major aim. Unravelling misconceptions hopefully renders more likely the possibility of truer understanding.

I could fairly be accused, in this book about religion, of glossing over complexities of theological view as they have developed within both the Islamic and the Christian traditions. My motive, in refraining from delving too deeply into such complexities, has been to avoid allowing my text to contract into multiple descriptions of Islamic or Christian theological positions. Rather, I have tried to illustrate – within both faiths – how theologies as they develop or find expression tend to be in reality as much about "power" or "clan loyalty" or "cultural difference", as about the "knowledge of God".

In line with this overarching concern for assessment at a broader level rather than detailed description, I have offered a lot of figures in the pages that follow. Sometimes it is easier to grasp the larger picture, especially in complex comparisons or in detailed arguments, via a simple summary. I accept that such summaries frequently constitute oversimplifications – sometimes of years of history or incredible details of theological negotiation – but I hope they may help give a broader sense of "how things interrelate" or may add up to convey an idea of progress, regress or whatever.

I have intentionally spiced the "heavy" material of the various chapters with more reflective interludes. Those interludes constitute a hesitant attempt to "do theology", to theologize. My aim in them is to ask questions of the biblical record that might impinge on how we look at relationships between Muslims and Christians. I have been provoked to such examination of scripture by my recent involvement with the Islamic Centre at Newbold Seventh Day Adventist College. Jerald Whitehouse, with other folk at Newbold, has planted an urgent question in my heart. If God really wants to include Muslims in his love and purposes, what kind of hints of his concern for them might be discerned within scripture? The interludes explore some of those hints and I am grateful to my Seventh Day Adventist friends for stimulating me to consider them.

Some readers might query the order in which I have offered my thoughts. After all, the issue of how Jesus Christ is assessed, for example, might reasonably be perceived as the primary matter at stake in Christian–Muslim relationships – at least from a Christian perspective. So why not parade it first? I have two major reasons. Firstly, I am not primarily concerned with presenting comparisons of Islamic and Christian doctrines. There are plenty of other helpful resources that proceed by comparing the two faiths' teachings about humankind, Christ, salvation and so on. My aim, in this book, is to shift comparison away from that kind of emphasis towards one in which parallels are discovered about how the two faiths have actually found expression on earth. Observing, for example, the different routes taken by the two faiths with regard to the relationship between the sacred and the secular helps us understand that both Christians and Muslims have wrestled (perhaps with not such dissimilar results in practice) with that perennial problem of how to live on behalf of God in a non-cooperative world. My second reason for "coming to Christ" at the end of the book, rather than at the beginning, is that I hope that the earlier chapters will have engendered in the reader a change of attitude, a "repentance" even. Such a stalling of previously held presuppositions might more readily lead to a hearing of my attempt at restating the Christian case in concepts more attuned to Muslim ears. For sure, the critical matter in any consideration of the two faiths' relationship is focused on their views of Jesus Christ. I hope I can make a case for abandoning a Christian view of Muslims as simply "rejecting" the Jesus of the Bible, and contribute to a proposition for beginning with where Muslims are at in their comprehension of Jesus and seeking to move them on from there. As I said above, attitude-change is my major aim in writing this book. If our Christian attitude towards Muslims can shift a bit, maybe theirs towards Jesus might also.

I have included fairly comprehensive notes as Appendix 4. Such notes often expand a detailed argument or quote in full a textual source being referred to in a chapter. They also, of course, give full references for quotations. I hope that the text is self-explanatory without them, but the reader may prefer to consult the notes as they are referenced in the text, in order better to grasp the full import of what I am trying to communicate.

This book has not been easy to research or write but it has been immensely fulfilling to grapple with. I am grateful to those upon whom I have tried out some of my ideas, especially Colin Chapman, Chawkat Moucarry and Silas Edmonds, and for their critiques and comments I thank them. The responsibility for any inadequacies of what is presented here, however, remains mine alone. The need for this kind of exposition was excited in me by a short course on "Understanding Islam" that I ran at Holy Trinity Church, Tulse Hill. The questions and discussions that arose during that course helped determine the kind of topics covered in these chapters. So to my congregation – thank you! It was Tony Collins who made the suggestion that I look at this subject. I am grateful to him and the team at Monarch Books for their willingness to place considered attempts at cross-faith relating in the public domain.

Bill A. Musk

Cousins Apart?

Chapter 1 Living Godwards

"This just does not add up!"

The sheikh looked at me with pity, stroked his beard, and gently declared: "But that is the truth!"

"The truth" is what Mustafa and I had been arguing about. The two of us had ended up at the home of the sheikh in order to come to some settlement of our conversation of the previous day. That conversation had arisen over Mustafa's bold statement that "Of course, Jesus (praise be upon him) was a Muslim." "Conversation" is probably too polite a word for what I had allowed to deteriorate into a haranguing match.

"Look Mustafa," I had started, secretly revelling in the intellectual advantage I discerned I had won for myself over my Muslim friend. "I went to Oxford University and studied modern history there. Listen! These are the facts ... Jesus was born somewhere around 3 BC. We have the records of Jewish and Roman historians to consult concerning the event. Even if we do not know the precise day or year, we know that Jesus was a real person who lived in the first century AD. He lived for about 33 years and then was executed. Jewish and Roman historians tell us that also. The details of his life we learn from the Gospels composed by Matthew, Mark, Luke and John. Those Gospels link in with many archaeological discoveries made in recent years – lots of the references in the Gospels to times or places can be validated. Jesus of Nazareth was a real person – "

"I agree," Mustafa interrupted. "Of course Jesus, son of Mary (praise be upon him) was a real person. Our Qur'ân speaks quite a bit about his remarkable birth and childhood. It also describes what happened when it looked as if he was going to be wrongly executed."

"Okay," I came back at him. "So you agree that Jesus lived in the first century AD?" I quickly checked the development of my argument,

confident of where I was leading my friend but wondering why Mustafa had conceded this important "fact" so quickly. "Mustafa," I continued, "Prophet Muhammad was born in AD *570. His revelations began in* AD *610. His exodus from Mecca to Medina took place in* AD *622." I looked hard at my sparring partner. "Prophet Muhammad lived over 500 years after Jesus Christ!"*

"Yes," agreed Mustafa, beaming. "The Prophet (praise be upon him) was born in AD *570. The* hijra *or exodus as you say occurred in* AD *622 and we Muslims date our calendar from that momentous event.* AD *622 in your calendar became* AH *1 in ours."*

"But Mustafa," I spelled out slowly and with overbearing pride, "if Prophet Muhammad was born in AD *570 and his revelations began in* AD *610 – there is no way that Jesus Christ, who lived 500 years before these events, could be a Muslim."*

"Brother Bill," smiled Mustafa, evidently with a great deal more equanimity than I was feeling by this point, "of course Jesus the Messiah lived 500 years before Prophet Muhammad (praise be upon them), but that doesn't alter anything in my argument. Jesus Christ was still a Muslim."

I felt I was banging my head against a brick wall. Could not the man accept the obvious conclusion of a simple argument? Then a brilliant thought came to me. "All right," I said, "let's go and ask a sheikh!"

"Fine!" responded Mustafa.

So today we found ourselves at the house of the sheikh of Mustafa's choice. I rehearsed my argument before him, a little more politely than the day before. The sheikh had smiled, nodded. He agreed with me that Jesus had lived 500 years before Prophet Muhammad –

"There, you see!" I turned to Mustafa, triumphant.

"But Jesus (praise be upon him) was certainly a Muslim," the sheikh continued, hardly noticing my aside to Mustafa. I was floored. The older, intelligent, well-read gentleman had sided with my Muslim friend against all the wisdom of an Oxford history graduate. I could not help exploding in frustration, "This just does not add up!"

Such is our starting-point in this introductory chapter. Christian and Muslim ways of looking at faith just do not add up. Each religious heritage proceeds from alternative ways of looking at life or history or reality. We may be using the same words or referring to the same people or events, but what we mean by what we say can be strangely different.

A consideration of how each of these two major world faiths came to be "named" illustrates such difference. What do Muslims and Christians mean by the terms "Islam" or "Christianity"? Struggling to reach some kind of understanding of alternative ways of looking at such basic concepts leads us to predict the delicate work of comparison that we shall need to explore in this book.

What's in a name?

> The Religion before God Is Islam ... (Sura 3:19)

> The disciples were first called Christians at Antioch. (Acts 11:26)

Islam "names" itself in its holy book, the Qur'ân. It gives itself its own identification. In words originating from God, it calls itself "Islam" (Sura 3:19). In so doing, Islam constitutes an exception to the rule, for most religions or religious communities of the world have first been named by human outsiders. "Christians", for example, were first designated as such by onlookers in Antioch (Acts 11:26). For a while the ascription was resisted by the insiders, who tended to refer to themselves as "followers of the Way" (Acts 24:14). Were they reluctant to accept the name "Christian" because that term implied that the disciples were "Christly"? After all, who would want to pretend that he was so like Jesus that he should share his name? "Hindus" were delineated as such by Muslims after the latter had invaded the Indian subcontinent (around AD 1000) – in fact, at the time, the term served to include those people later differentiated as Hindus, Jains, Buddhists and so on. "Hindu" really designated non-Muslim people in the newly conquered land. Most religions of the world were "named" by Europeans during the eighteenth and nineteenth centuries. "Buddhism", "Hinduism", "Taoism", "Sikhism", "Zoroastrianism", "Confucianism" – even "Mohammedanism" – were terms by which people in Europe categorized the religions of others.

Insiders belonging to those religious traditions, however, did not necessarily think in those kind of categories. In Chinese, for example, there is no singular term meaning "Confucian" or "Buddhist" or "Taoist". Even with the term "Christianity", it was only towards the end of the eighteenth century and well after the end of the Reformation period that the word came almost exclusively to carry the sense of a systematized religion. Prior to that, the terms more commonly used to refer to the commitment of Christians were "Christian faith" or "Christianness" or "Christlikeness".[3] It was during the Enlightenment process especially that the more systematic or propositional idea of "Christianity" as a system of beliefs developed.

Islam, unusually, names itself, but even then the word "Islam" appears only eight times in the whole Qur'ân. What is referenced by the name "Islam" is a "religion", a *dîn*:

> This day have I
> Perfected your religion [*dîn*]
> For you, completed
> My favour upon you,
> And have chosen for you
> Islam as your religion [*dîn*]. (Sura 5:4)

Dîn carries several senses. It can refer to personal piety and it can identify a discrete religious system. Often, in the Qur'ân, it includes a sense of evaluation as in *yawm al-dîn* (Day of Judgement, mentioned every time the *Fâtiḥa* or opening sura of the Qur'ân is recited). It also – perhaps most significantly – conveys the sense of "conforming to traditional customs". *Dîn* is a holistic kind of concept, carrying within its embrace a sense of far more than just a list of beliefs and duties that make a follower a Muslim. We shall develop our consideration of this holistic idea of religion in a minute when we look at the requirements of submission.

Interestingly, the Western world has only recently learned to refer to the Islamic faith as "Islam". In the Middle Ages, Europeans used to make reference to the sect or heresy of the Saracens, often pejoratively. Later, Tartars and Turks were included in the reference.[4] Thereafter, followers of the Islamic faith came to be known as "Mohammedans" or even as "Islams" – terms one can sadly still hear used today. The religion became known in the West as "Mohammedanism". Just as Christianity is named after Christ, so, it was assumed, "Mohammedanism" must be the appropriate title for the religion introduced by Muhammad.

Islam and *islâm*

When the Qur'ân names its own faith-holding as "Islam", what does it mean? As we have seen, the word occurs relatively few times. The word predominantly used for "faith" in the Qur'ân is *îmân*: this word occurs 45 times and its associated term for "man of faith" – *mu'min* – occurs more than five times as frequently as the word "Muslim". These "faith" words are descriptive of human action – they refer to people believing, men and women acting out their commitment. In other words, the Qur'ân presents God as being concerned with something people do, with the persons who do it, rather than with an abstract entity. In focus is the requirement for a "believer" to be a person of faith rather than just one who acquiesces to a set of religious propositions.

There has been considerable debate within the Islamic community concerning what the Qur'ân means by terms such as "faith", "believer", "unbelief", "unbeliever" and so on. Different definitions have emerged from within the various Islamic theological "schools". We need briefly to introduce those schools.

Three major theological schools are to be found within Sunnî Islam: those of Ashᶜari, Maturidi and Ḥanbal. Of these, the school of Ḥanbal is the most literalist. The Kharijîs – the extreme purists or "fundamentalists" of the Islamic theological world – have their own school. Two main schools of Muᶜtazilî theology exist – the Basrian and the Baghdadian – and Muᶜtazilî theologians may be either Sunnî or Shîᶜa. Their theological approach is strongly characterized by rationalism. Out of all the theological schools, the Ashᶜarite – most representative within

Sunnî Islam – and the Muᶜtazilite are probably the most significant. The earliest debates, around which different theological schools gradually developed, focused on four main issues: the nature of the divine attributes, and the relationships between predestination and free will, faith and works, and reason and authority. Chawkat Moucarry offers a helpful summary of the various Islamic theological schools in his recent book *The Search for Forgiveness*.[5] When it comes, then, to discovering definitions of "faith", "believer", and so on, we need to recognize that different Islamic theological schools offer varying emphases. For Kharijî theologians, for example, "faith" equates simply to obeying God's commands. For Sunnî Muslims of the Ḥanbalî school of theology, "faith" includes elements of internal trust, verbal confession and outward fulfilling of the pillars of Islam. For Murji'î theologians (including the Ashᶜarites), "faith" is primarily expressed in terms of knowing God, by which is meant submitting to him, exalting and worshipping only him. For such Murji'î theologians, good works in themselves are counted as secondary.[6] While acknowledging the variety of detailed description of what "faith" might involve, the fundamental point that I wish to make is that, within Islam, having or exercising faith is not primarily seen as intellectual assent to certain propositions. Rather it consists in a willed trust, in a reasoned submission, or in acts of obedience. Such a conception contrasts strongly with a Western view of "faith" as amounting primarily to acquiescence to certain dogmas or definitions.

In the Qur'ân, as we shall explore in detail (in chapter 3), God takes the initiative in "sending down" a revelation. That revelation is sent down for humankind to heed and obey – for humanity to submit to. "Submission" constitutes the essence of what Islam is about. *Aslama* is the Arabic verb that means "to submit", "to surrender oneself". It conveys the sense of accepting the obligation to obey God's command. Its opposite is *kafara*, meaning "to reject". A *kâfir* is someone who rejects God's call to submission, who remains indifferent to God or ignorant about him. That is why such a person is considered an infidel or unbeliever – he is saying "No!" to God (see Figure 1). He does not trust God, does not hold a right attitude towards his creator.

Figure 1
"Submission" and "rejection" in Arabic

Word	Grammar	Meaning
aslama	verb	to submit, to surrender oneself
islâm	verbal noun	submission
muslim	noun	a submitted person
kafara	verb	to reject
kâfir	noun	a rejecter

Kufr refers to that rejection, to "unbelief" in all its manifestations. The Arabic word *islâm* is a verbal noun, a noun describing something that someone does. It translates into English as "submission". It carries the sense of positive obedience. A Muslim is someone who wills to submit to God. The Qur'ân can therefore refer to a person's "*islâm*", to a person's "submission":

> They swear by God that they
> Said nothing (evil), but indeed
> They uttered blasphemy,
> And they did it after accepting
> Islam ... (Sura 9:74)

This verse conveniently contains both the word meaning "submit" and the word meaning "reject". The Arabic says literally that "they refused or rejected (*kafarû*) after their *islâm* ..." These people at one point submitted but then their later rejection may be deduced from their blasphemous behaviour. Sura 49:17 refers to "your *islâm*, your commitment". The concept of *islâm* in the Qur'ân is one of personal, active faith expressed in obedience. It does not primarily refer to an institution or religious system as such.

Here we need to mention capital letters! The Arabic language (like Hebrew) has no capital letters. When the Qur'ân talks about Islam, it is actually talking about *islâm*. Islam in that sense – the sense of *islâm* – existed long before Prophet Muḥammad, and long before the final shape it came to take in the faith-expression that Muḥammad oversaw. Such an assertion has big implications for the idea, commonly held, that Muḥammad "established" Islam. Did he really? And, if he did, in what sense did he establish this relatively recent religion? We shall explore such questions in chapter 2. For the moment, we need to recognize that, from a Muslim perspective, *islâm* is far older than what we all refer to as "Islam". The latter is in effect the institutionalized expression of the former as it came to find fulfilment under Muḥammad's apostleship. Mind you, his institutionalized expression of *islâm* as "Islam" is announced as the most faithful and mature rendering of the faith. After all, he was the seal of the prophets.

One way of gaining some insight into this way of thinking about faith/religion is via Süleyman Chelebi's famous song concerning the birth and life of Prophet Muḥammad. Chelebi was a contemporary of Chaucer, living at the Ottoman court of Sultan Beyazid. He died in AD 1421 and was buried at Bursa. He composed his *Mevlidi Şerif* or "Birth-song of the Prophet" to refute a teaching that Muḥammad was no greater than other prophets. Chelebi maintained that, to the contrary, Muḥammad is far superior to other prophets because with Muḥammad comes the fullness of all that God ever intended to communicate to humankind. In part of his poem, Chelebi traces how God's intention for the truest expression of appropriate apostleship passed, like a light, from one prophet to another until it came to its apotheosis in Muḥammad:

> When man was first by Allah's pow'r created,
> The ornament was he of all things living.
> To Adam came all angels in submission,
> A gesture oft, at God's command, repeated.
> On his brow first God set the Light of Prophets,
> Saying: This Light belongs to my Beloved.
> Long years that Light shone there, nor ever wavered,
> Until the prophet's earthly life was ended.
> Know that to Eve's brow next the Light migrated,

Remaining there through many months and seasons.
Then Seth received this sigil of Mustafa,
Which glowed more bright as year to year was added.
Thus Abraham and Ishmael received it –
My time would fail should all the line be counted.
From brow to brow, in linked chain unbroken,
The Light at last attained its goal, Muhammed.
The Mercy of the Worlds appeared, and straightway
To him the Light took wing, its journey ended.[7]

The song (in Turkish) is full of puns and clever rhymes, and clearly expresses this sense in which – all along – God has revealed via his prophets the response he wants human beings in each age to make towards himself in appropriate *islâm*. That response comes finally to be fully realized on earth in the life and faith of Prophet Muḥammad. The "Light" migrates to Muḥammad, the "Mercy of the Worlds", but it is a light that has been traceable within the whole line of prophets from Adam. True *islâm* has been required and sometimes offered throughout the various epochs of human history. I have described at the beginning of this chapter my argument with a Muslim cleric over whether Jesus Christ was a Muslim or not. My contention was that Jesus could not have been a Muslim because the "religion" of "Islam" came over 500 years after his birth, death and resurrection. The sheikh's contention was, of course, that Jesus was *muslim* because he was a true submitter to God. God accepted his *islâm*, just as long before he accepted the *islâm* of Abraham, Moses, David and all the other prophets.

Islam – here is our difficulty in English! – by which I mean *islâm*, comprises the essence and expression of what religion should be. It is about the active surrender by human beings of their lives and wills to God. It finds complete, full and correcting expression in the religion of Islam. This is the special noun – *islâm* – that the Qur'ân designates to the calling or worldview of those who are truly *muslim*. They are people caught up into what God has all along desired and willed. God's idea of religion is *islâm*. God is its author and provocateur. He places it on the agendas of peoples in different ages through prophets whom he raises up and uses. He conveys its essence by "sending down" books that communicate what it means, in his eyes, for humankind to be *muslim*. Islam then (in either sense!), as far as human beings find it impinging upon them, consists in their acknowledging that the divine creator has an original and abiding claim upon his creation. The important question, for any member of the human race, is not so much, "how can God become better known to me?" as "how may the human creation give itself to responding to God's prior claim upon it?"

The faith and "faith"

God's idea of religion, according to Islam, is *islâm*. I accept that such a way of conceptualizing is hard for Western children of the Enlightenment to grasp. As a result of that concentrated and revolutionary period of Western intellectual development, we Enlightenment children inherit a "narrowed" understanding of faith. "Believing" has been swiftly recast to emerge as the embracing of graspable, institutionally defined doctrines or practices. "Faith" has become synonymous with "the faith" as dogmatically or ecclesiastically defended. Westerners, as a consequence, want to delineate people of equivalent though different religious faith as "-ists" (Confucianists, Buddhists, etc.) belonging to "-isms" (Hinduism, Sikhism, etc.). "Religion", for us, amounts to the institutionalized formulation of discrete beliefs and practices: Christianity, Islam, Taoism and so on. When we speak of "Christianity" we mean the institutionalized religion as expressed in systems of belief and codes of practice. When we think of Islam, the easiest way for us to understand its make-up is by a consideration of "the five pillars" or "the six articles of belief" of that faith. There is nothing inherently wrong with that, and those pillars and articles of belief are proposed and defined within the Muslim community itself. They do not in themselves, however, take us very far in comprehending what "Islam" amounts to as a faith.

Actually, the potential sterility of looking at religion in this way is exemplified within our own Christian faith. Too much concentration on signing up to the "oughts" of a system leaves little heart for seeing beyond those norms. Jesus constantly highlighted the poverty of heart and mind that proceeds along such lines. He frequently challenged those contemporaries of his who assumed that because they owned a "kosher" religious allegiance, everything must be all right between them and God. There were, for example, "the Jews" of the gospel era who assumed that they were on the right side of God because Abraham was their father. "Is Abraham really your father?" questioned Jesus (John 8:39). There were the disciples who believed that being on Jesus' side meant inheriting places of power when his reign kicked in. "Not so," said Jesus. "Not everyone who says to me 'Lord, Lord!'... " (Matthew 7:21).

How can people like Enoch or Abraham or even Isaiah be said to have had a relationship with the Father through Christ? Well only, surely, by thinking about faith or relationship with God in a manner similar to the Islamic conceptualization of *islâm* and *muslim*. Such Old Testament characters were people whose hearts were evidently oriented towards God, individuals who knew a vital, saving relationship with *'elôhîm* or Yahweh. They certainly did not know, intellectually, about Jesus Christ, yet in a way they did know him, for he is the only way to the Father and the Father they did know. These ancient heroes received hints about Messiahship, about the essential requirement for some kind of dealing with human sin, about God providing a sacrifice even, but the lifeblood of their relationship with God was their *pistis*, their faith. "Faith" with a small "f": not "the faith" as in "Judaism" or "Christianity", but faith in the sense of active belief and ongoing trust in God.

The great Christian theologian Augustine reached an equivalent conclusion, though beginning from a different starting-point. Following Cyprian, he wanted to affirm that "outside the church there is no salvation" – the famous *extra ecclesiam, nulla salus* sentence! How did the believing saints of Old Testament times fit into that kind of scheme? Augustine was led to pronounce concerning Old Testament people of faith:

> For what is now called the Christian religion existed even among the ancients and was not lacking from the beginning of the

human race until 'Christ came in the flesh.' From that time, true religion, which already existed, began to be called Christian.[8]

Such people of Old Testament faith constitute the "great cloud of witnesses" (Hebrews 12:1) that surrounds those of us who are living and believing now. The living object of those Old Testament characters' faith (Jesus Christ) only came later in time, but the intention or the sureness or the ultimate realness of Christ's incarnation, death and resurrection has been guaranteed from eternity. Thus these heroes' faith may be assumed to be as active or sure as ours (see Figure 2). It is just that within the dimensions of space and time they could not have comprehended the details of how what they grasped by faith was going to be worked through. They certainly, however, read God's heart correctly.

When Jesus walked this earth, he sought mostly to reclaim and revolutionize the lost children of the house of Israel. The people who had come to rely on the premise that they belonged to the institutional faith – in this case Judaism – needed to recognize that such "belonging by birth" constituted no guarantee

Figure 2
"By faith" in Hebrews 11

Grasped by faith ...	Knew God as ...
that the universe was formed at God's command	creator
what constitutes an appropriate sacrifice	holy, needing appeasement
the avoidance of death's sting	victor over death
that the human predicament leads to judgement	judge and saviour
security (city without foundations) in God for land and progeny	giver of eternal security

of belonging essentially to God. It was an uphill struggle for Jesus to get such a message across: "He came to that which was his own, but his own did not receive him" (John 1:11)! Jesus was repeatedly and delightedly surprised by people from outside the Jewish religious system whose hearts leapt with faith towards God. Pride of place on his list of "faithful" acquaintances was given to a Roman centurion – a person hated by those of Jesus' own community who suffered from the swords of such representatives of the dominating imperial power. And there were other non-Jews who figured significantly – Samaritans, Syro-Phoenicians, Greeks and wise men from the east. As John reflects, "to all who needed him, to those who believed in his name, he gave the right to become children of God" (John 1:12).

The Apostle Paul found a way of rewriting Jewish religious history from a "faith" perspective. What mattered was not, he claimed, whether you were a Jew by birth or by physical circumcision. What mattered was whether you were a Jew by faith, by circumcision of the heart. For Abraham was counted righteous by faith before he was ever circumcised. The latter was a sign in the flesh of the former transaction of the heart. All those, then, who experience Abraham's kind of faith are true offspring of Abraham whether or not they are circumcised in the flesh.

In other words – to have a relationship with God by faith is an experience on offer by God to his human creation from the day he breathed life into the first being made in his own image and likeness. Is Abraham a believer? Well, yes, in that he experienced saving faith in God. Is Abraham a Christian? Well, no, not in the sense of signing up to an institutionalized religion that makes the earthly history of Jesus of Nazareth its pivotal story. But, yes, in the sense that it is only through being "in Christ" that anyone can come to a vital relationship with God.

Hearing one another?

Such a kind of thinking about "faith" as opposed to "Christianity" is somewhat parallel to the distinction I am making between "Islam" and "*islâm*". If we can grasp this significant point, we will be greatly helped in our journey of discovery concerning the relationship between Islam and Christianity. For one thing, it takes us away from the normal Western presupposition that Muḥammad was the "founder" of Islam. According to this "standard" view, what Muḥammad founded is quickly identified as a post-Christian religion, for it emerges, historically, after Christ. Islam is thereby open to the charge of being deliberately anti-Christian due to the Qur'ân's alleged critique and rejection of several key doctrines of Christian belief – such as the Trinity, the incarnation, the crucifixion, and humankind's need for redemption. Polemical exchanges almost inevitably follow such a view of the development of the religion of Islam. Christians find in the Islamic faith a step backwards from a revelation of the grace of God to a religion of law and prophecy. Why should they entertain positive views about a faith that deliberately caricatures the precious core beliefs of Christianity? Muslims, meanwhile, find in the Qur'ân definitive, alternative accounts of the central tenets of the Christian faith. So why listen to Christian apologetics concerning that faith? The Islamic doctrine of *taḥrîf* (scriptural alteration or corruption) allows the Muslim to judge where the former religionists have departed from what was originally given (to Moses or Jesus) as scripture. So why persist in reading a copy of the corrupted text today? The Christians have lost what was originally theirs, but Muslims have it, corrected and completed, in the Qur'ân. The result is impasse, non-understanding.

What if, as will be suggested in this book, that standard or normal Western understanding of Islam has no basis in the Qur'ân or in Muḥammad's self-awareness? What if the Qur'ân and Muḥammad's concern was more with *islâm* than Islam? In grasping that, we might well find ourselves better able to study Islam in dispassionate mode. Perhaps also, the polemical route, the defensive route, the argumentative route between the two faiths might more successfully be avoided. If that could be achieved, it might prove possible for Muslims and Christians to begin to listen to where each other say they are coming from.

My hope in this book is that our taking hold of such a shift in perspective will help us immensely in our journey of discovery concerning Islam and Christianity. In a negative sense, it may lead us away from simply trying to compare and contrast certain doctrines or formulations of the two formal faiths. Those formulations or doctrines are important, of course, but they may not be the most productive route for comparing the two faiths for they necessarily support different purposes or goals or understandings of what religion is about. In a positive sense, it hopefully helps us look beyond the systematizing processes of institutionalized religion to search for the intentions of faith. In what kind of ways is connection to be expected between God and humankind? What are people of faith – Muslim or Christian – buying into? Furthermore, a shift in perspective may also help us allow that each faith needs to be its own interpreter. Understanding must be pursued within each faith's own constructs. In that sense, comparisons or contrasts are almost incidental or accidental, by-products of humble listening. The most helpful insights often emerge when people of different faiths become attuned to each other's wavelengths of thought and manage to feel their way into the other's heart.

Exploration

In the immediately following chapters, we shall investigate in some depth the three fundamental matters of prophethood, scripture and doctrine of God. I have entitled this section of the book "Comparable Cousins?" The question mark applies as much to those of us who think that there is considerable comparison between Islam and Christianity on these basic subjects as to those of us who think the opposite.

We begin where Islam – at an earthly level – begins, with the life and ministry of the man Muḥammad. What was his experience of speaking for God? We note the cost to him of proclaiming a counter-cultural message and observe how the difficulties undergone in Mecca were followed by a liberation of message and method in Medina. We examine Muḥammad's own assessment of what "inspiration" involved. How does a human being grasp God's word? Comparisons are made with the equivalent processes in the experience of some of the Old Testament prophets. What constitutes being a "successful" prophet or spokesperson for God? When a prophet's words are heeded – in the Sinai desert or Medinan metropolis – how does living by God's law get worked through? We also broach the difficult issue of evaluating Muḥammad: can Christians consider him truly a prophet?

Scripture is dangerous stuff. Assessments of the Qur'ân by Christians stretch far across a continuum, with people at one extreme viewing it as from the devil and with folk at the other extreme accepting it as validly God's word. The Qur'ân is not easy to read, so some details are given concerning its make-up and historical formation. The compilation of the Qur'ân is described as Muslims record it. Our main focus, however, is not on the earthly bringing together of text but on what it means, in Islam, for scripture to be given by God. What are the implications – for God and man's relating – of "recitation", for example? Our study leads us to ask whether it is appropriate to simply compare Qur'ân and Bible as "scripture". Perhaps the two texts constitute non-comparable phenomena. Might it prove more appropriate to compare Qur'ân as "Word of God" in Islam with Jesus Christ as "Word of God" in Christianity? We consider some of the difficult questions arising from the Islamic concept of revelation, and investigate the claims of some Christians that elements of the qur'ânic text can be traced to Jewish and Christian apocryphal materials. There arise questions for both Muslims and Christians concerning the kind of certainty that might be derived from scripted texts and the claim of such texts to constitute revelation from God.

Any kind of engagement by Christians in the study or lived practice of another world faith leads to questions – uncomfortable or difficult questions – about God. That is especially true of related, monotheistic faiths. We face up to some of those questions in a chapter focused upon "God". The underlying issue is the identity of the God of the Qur'ân; is that God the same as the God of the Bible? We investigate the origins of the word *Allâh*, and consider some of the associations of that word – and the concept of God that it connotes – with similar words in other

Middle Eastern languages. Theological enquiry constitutes the major means for drawing some conclusions concerning who God is conceived to be in both Islam and Christianity. We conclude this chapter with an exposé of missiological intent. Some Christians are philosophically inclined towards a pluralist conception of religious phenomena, so for them the matter of the identity of Christian and Muslim "God" is simple: he is the same God. Other Christians are just as assuredly exclusivist in their view of religious truth, and for them also the issue of identity is uncomplicated: the God of Islam is different from the God of Christianity. In between such definite perceptions lies a variety of inclusivist perspectives where Christians want to say that the issue of identity is complex and messy with as many questions being asked of themselves and the Bible as of Muslims and the Qur'ân.

The next section of this book – "Uncomfortable Cousins?" – deals with some subjects that offer insight into how both Islam and Christianity developed. Interesting comparisons arise out of such a study. Christianity grew out of a Jewish background, wrestling increasingly with what it might mean to be a truly inclusive faith – inclusive, for example, of non-Jews, women and slaves. How was the Christian faith to be made directly accessible to the Greek mind? As Gentiles became followers of Jesus, what sense of continuity with their previous worldview was to be allowed? Where was that worldview to be challenged? The definition of what is meant by "Trinity" illustrates this continuity/discontinuity issue; Christian Greek and Roman minds communicated and miscommunicated with one another over the "Trinity" in the period prior to Islam's appearance. For Prophet Muḥammad also, in the inception of his message, what sense of continuity was to be allowed to Arabs of the seventh century as they became Muslims? At what point did the religio-cultural revolution that he was promoting impinge on the norms, customs and mores of his contemporaries? Questions about continuity and discontinuity remain at the forefront of current missiological methodology. In the sharing of the gospel with Muslims, how much of Muslims' own religious and cultural inheritance is validly to be retained as they find faith in

Jesus Christ? What is to be challenged and discarded? And who decides?

Such questions lead to our next consideration, that of the complex relationship between truth and power. This chapter takes up the issue of "success" in religion and asks what constitutes real success. Is truth its own vindicator or does it need to be enforced in some way? The Old Testament provides a strong example of intended theocracy, mediated through the prophet Moses. That theocracy functioned with some pretty strong sanctions! Jesus found himself challenging two huge power machines and their monopoly on "truth" in his day – the Jewish leadership and the Roman occupying force. The history of the growth of Christianity changed dramatically when Emperor Constantine made that "outsider" faith the official religion of the world he ruled. Theological questions about the nature of Christ now came to be debated in front of the emperor or his representative. In consequence, solutions to controversies often spoke as much about power politics as about conviction of spirit. Such processes, incidentally, muddied the theological water for when Muḥammad came to reflect on the Christians' description of the person of Jesus Christ. For Muḥammad, also, the shift from Mecca to Medina marked a difference in style and leadership – a difference often noted by Muslim and Christian commentators. As preacher turned into statesman, Islam took on a radically different feel.

The third chapter in this section investigates the twin concepts of the sacred and the secular. A debate has continued within both Islam and Christianity about how integrated or separate these facets of human living are or should be. They especially provoke difficult questions in contemporary societies where people of different faiths and worldviews live in such proximity to one another. The chapters in this section deal with delicate but powerful issues and provide many comparisons between the two religions. They show that no faith expression on earth is really free from controversy or complex human relating. The processes of defining orthodoxy (proper belief) or orthopraxy (proper practice) can sometimes be sadly ungodly or inhumane!

The history of relationships between Christians and Muslims – "Competing Cousins?" – does not really help to provoke a dispassionate, humble listening to one another. From the rapid early expansion of Islam and the infamous Crusades of the medieval world to the perceived equivalents today, Muslim–Christian clashes prejudice the possibility of seeing things from the other community's perspective.

At the same time, both Christianity and Islam are avowedly missionary faiths. There is a world to be won for God and members of each faith community sense a calling to win that world. Highly motivated, articulate representatives of both religions live in each other's domain, and beyond, calling all who will to believe. How can two missionary faiths "live and let live" with integrity in today's interconnected world?

"All who will" focuses us on the "fodder" for faith – humankind. Human beings are the focus of mission or *daʿwa* (inviting to faith). So who or what is "man" and how is he being invited to fullness? We interrogate in this section of the book some of the Islamic and Christian concepts of humanity, perhaps discovering ourselves to be "Cousins in Hope?" At surface level, it would appear that different concepts of what humankind is lead to alternative approaches to the question of how human beings might connect or reconnect with God. Under the surface, however, we might be perceived to hold more in common than meets the superficial eye.

We look finally at the person of Christ, critical in whom he is to Christians, and critical in whom he is not to Muslims. Are there ways of communicating across the different perceptions and in the face of the reasons for them? Can we Christians restate the meaning of Christ in ways more attuned to the Muslims' mind-set? How does the Jesus who knows that he has "other sheep, not of this fold" expect those others to be gathered in? Or are the categories of conceiving religious thoughts in members of each faith community too far apart to make any true communication possible or meaningful?

Such is the task of exploration before us. It is a task asking as much of us as of any Muslim believer. Can we really begin to see how radically different a conception is Islam from

Christianity? Can we comprehend how it makes sense in itself? Can we then perceive how many of the elements of its make-up and history have parallels in our own faith? Does such understanding help us restate our faith in ways that might be heard by Muslims? These are the questions by which the following chapters should appropriately be judged.

Interlude

If you were God, how would you convince Muslims that – all along – they had a special place in your divine heart?

Step-brothers in God

Genesis 10 describes the nations of the world as they derived from the sons of Noah, after the end of the great flood. Appearing – or not appearing! – in the loins of Arphaxad, son of Shem, is Abram. Many generations after Arphaxad, some time around 1800 BC, God calls Abram to leave his land and his people and instead to follow him. In Abram, God has picked on an Aramean, an idol-worshipper living in Ur, a man typical of humankind in its neglect of the creator-God.

To Abram in Ur, God promises:

> "I will make you into a great nation
> and I will bless you;
> I will make your name great,
> and you will be a blessing.
> I will bless those who bless you,
> and whoever curses you I will curse;
> and all peoples on earth
> will be blessed through you." (Genesis 12:2–3)

In contrast to the arrogant men who lived in Babylonia or Shinar, and who thought to make a name for themselves by consolidating themselves into a city (Genesis 11:4), Abram is here promised a "great name" if he will turn his back on that kind of human security and follow the Lord – Yahweh – in his ways. Through a two-step process Abram extricates himself from Ur, and then from Haran after his father's death there, and travels to the land of Canaan.

Over the years, Abram marries several women and has children by them. He also produces unnamed sons by unmarried concubines. It is the interrelationship of these different sons of Abram that interests us in this "interlude" (see Figure 3).

Figure 3
Abram's male progeny

Age	Progeny	Reference
75 years	Abram sets out from Haran, already married to Sarai	Genesis 12:4
86 years	Abram's first son, Ishmael, is born by Hagar, his second wife	Genesis 16:15
100 years	Abraham's second son, Isaac, is born by Sarah, his first wife	Genesis 17:1; 21:2
? years	Abraham's sons, Zimran, Jokshan, Medan, Midian, Ishbak, Shuah, are born by Keturah, his third wife	Genesis 25:1–2
? years	Abraham's sons by unnamed "concubines" are sent away to the land of the east	Genesis 25:6

Isaac and Ishmael

A strong distinction is made between Isaac and Ishmael in Genesis. It is clear that Isaac is presented as the son of promise, born by God's help to Abraham and Sarah. Abraham's wistful prayer that Ishmael would live under God's blessing (Genesis 17:18) is answered by God's "Yes, *but*" (Genesis 17:19). It is going to be with Isaac, Abraham's son by Sarah, that God will establish his covenant. Not Ishmael, but Isaac! God has earlier promised the patriarch that Canaan, where Abraham is living as an alien, will be given to him as an everlasting possession – "to you and your descendants after you" (Genesis 17:8). That same promise, God affirms, he will establish with Isaac as an everlasting covenant for his descendants after him.

The distinction between Isaac and Ishmael, however, comes across also as a somewhat blurred one. As we have noticed, God's reply to Abraham's request for Ishmael to live under his blessing is a "Yes, *but*". It is also a "*Yes*, but"! There is a "yes" in the response as well as a "but". Ishmael will be fruitful, father of twelve rulers, patriarch of a great nation. In some manner also, Ishmael is included in what God covenants with Abraham. The sign of that covenant is for all Abraham's males to be circumcised. "This is my covenant with you and your descendants after you, the covenant you are to keep: Every male among you shall be circumcised" (Genesis 17:10). At the respective ages of 99 and thirteen years, Abraham and Ishmael are circumcised, along with all the males serving in Abraham's household or bought with his money.

Later in Genesis we learn that Abraham at some point takes another wife, Keturah. By her, he sires seven more sons. Then, apparently, he also indulges in some concubines, for we are told that prior to his death he gives gifts to the "sons of his concubines" (Genesis 25:6) and sends them away from his son Isaac to the land of the east. Ishmael, and Abraham's sons by Keturah, cannot be in mind here as their mothers were wives, not concubines, of Abraham. At Abraham's death, a distinction is made between the sons of Abraham by Keturah and his sons by Hagar and Sarah. We are told that "his sons Isaac and Ishmael buried him in the cave of Machpelah near Mamre ... " (Genesis 25:9). So there is a special sense in which Isaac and Ishmael are together involved in the life of faith of their father (see Figure 4).

Yahweh and Ishmael

Hagar's experience of being manipulated and then ousted by her employer calls down God's great compassion. Sarah's aim in getting her maidservant Hagar to become Abram's second wife is a hope that "perhaps I can build a family through her" (Genesis 16:2). Incidentally, a Jewish tradition suggests that Hagar was a daughter of Pharaoh by one of his concubines. That tradition, reproduced in the Islamic prophetic tradition (the *hadîth*), declares that Pharaoh gave Hagar to Sarah as a maidservant when he discovered – during Abraham and Sarah's stay in Egypt – that Sarah was in fact wife, not sister, to Abraham. Today, we would call Hagar a surrogate. In a culture in which the ability to produce progeny (especially sons) is the most important role for a woman, tension soon flares up between

Figure 4
Different sons of Abraham

Name	Mother	Status
Isaac	Sarah	God's covenant with Abraham proceeds through him and his descendants
Ishmael	Hagar	is included in the covenant sign (circumcision); receives his own blessing from God; is present to bury Abraham
Zimran, Jokshan, Medan, Midian, Ishbak, Shuah	Keturah	are included in Abraham's family as sons; are not present to bury Abraham; are not specially blessed
unnamed "sons"	concubines	are sent away to land of the east

barren mistress and pregnant maidservant. The mistreatment of the latter by the former becomes so great that Hagar flees.

Considering that the whole episode with Hagar is an attempt by Sarah and Abraham to force God's hand – to get the hoped-for progeny by the only seemingly possible route – it is amazing that God involves himself at all in the ensuing mess. After all, Hagar and Ishmael comprise mirror images of Sarah and Isaac. They represent the human, non-divine way of sorting out salvation. They are counterfeit, if you like – so close in idea to what God wants to do and yet so far from God's way of accomplishing that end. Despite the humanness of what has been attempted, the Bible declares that God goes searching for Hagar. The person at the centre of the "alternative family" is sought after and found by the angel of the Lord (Genesis 16:7). Hagar is not castigated nor cursed. Submission to her human mistress is required of her. Ishmael's mother is asked of God to offer obedience to him by learning submission. Interestingly, Ishmael's children (Muslims) will later insist that this is their calling also! Such submission by Hagar will lead to real blessing. Descendants beyond number will honour her as their progenitor. Hagar will have a son whose name is to indicate that God hears what is going on. God, we learn through this naming, is a God who attends the cries of those who find themselves the playthings of the strong. God will make Ishmael provocatively strong within the extended family of Abraham, upsetting his brothers, reminding his parents that human attempts to force God's hand are not acceptable. Hagar confesses that not only does God hear but he sees also. He has seen into her heart, into her situation, into her future.

Something must have marked Hagar deeply as a result of this encounter with the God who hears and sees. She returns from the desert and from despair to live in willed (probably difficult) submission to her mistress. Some time later her son is born. Abram, 86 years old, gives the name "Ishmael" to the boy born by Hagar (Genesis 16:15). What made him agree with his second wife on that name? What dynamics of relationship between Abraham, Sarah and Hagar marked the last months of the maidservant's pregnancy? The patriarch certainly decided to call his progeny by the choice of name of his second wife. Did Hagar's submission to Sarah warm Abraham's heart towards her? After the birth of Ishmael, and for thirteen years, the patriarch evidently lavished his love upon this boy whose sex, character and name an angel had predicted. That there developed a strong bond between father and son is witnessed by Abram's plea to the Lord – "Can't Ishmael be the one?" When the detailed terms of the covenant are revealed by God, there is no question in Abram's mind that Ishmael is included with himself – "that very day" he circumcises both of them.

Ishmael, then, is "out". Ishmael is also "in". He is excluded from God's purposes via Abraham and Sarah, yet he is also to some degree included in those purposes.

This son of Abraham, who is partially included in the covenant God makes with his father, marries an Egyptian woman procured for him by his mother from among her own people. Ishmael's descendants subsequently peopled Arabia (Genesis 25:12–18). Through his daughter Basemath, moreover, Ishmael contributed to the formation of the Edomites. Basemath became one of Esau's wives – Reuel was born to them

(Genesis 36:3, 10). The land where the Edomites settled – "the mountain of Seir" – extended from the head of the Gulf of Aqaba to the foot of the Dead Sea (1 Kings 9:26). That land was apportioned to the descendants of Esau by Yahweh himself (Deuteronomy 2:5, 12). It contained, among other cities, the rock-hewn Sela, generally known by its Greek name of Petra. The Edomites were conquered by David and eventually intermarried with the people of Israel. From far earlier, however, the Israelites were strictly ordered not to abhor the Edomite, "for he is your brother" (Deuteronomy 23:7). We shall consider other representatives of the Ishmaelites in further interludes.

Many centuries after these "beginnings", the large-hearted prophet Isaiah recounted a striking vision of nations and kings of the whole earth being drawn to a renewed people of God (Isaiah 60). He expresses that movement in terms of myriads of camels from Midian and Ephah coming to cover the land. Gold and incense and praising lips will arrive from Sheba. Kedar's flocks and Nebaioth's (Basemath's brother) rams will provide the offerings to lay on the altar, dedicated to the Lord God of Israel. Isaiah is describing in vision the inclusion of Ishmael's children with Isaac's in true worship of the living God.

Perhaps such prophetic images flicker through Jesus' mind when he announces himself as good shepherd of the sheep (John 10:11). As such a good shepherd he will lay down his life for the sheep. For what sheep? Well, the lost sheep of the house of Israel, certainly. But Jesus also has in his heart "other sheep that are not of this sheep pen". They need to be rescued, rehabilitated also, so that "there shall be one flock and one shepherd". Perhaps, here, the "flocks of Kedar" are specifically included in Jesus' all-embracing vision.

Comparable Cousins?

Chapter 2 Voicing God's Concerns

It is AD 610 and Gabriel is on a mission. The archangel has been sent from above to accost a businessman – a businessman who has taken to meditating on the top of a rocky, arid mountain three miles north-east of Mecca. Gabriel's mission is to impart to this 40-year-old a word that God wants all humankind to hear and receive. The angel is to make a prophet of the man.

To be a prophet

In this chapter we focus on the theme of prophethood. Speaking out for God, often against the norms of culture or contemporary political and economic correctness, can be a costly affair. Prophets tend to be people whose perseverance in an unrewarding task is sustained out of a strong sense of divine commission. God has called them; how can they not obey? Both Christianity and Islam endorse the role of prophets. This chapter considers some of the similarities and differences of their roles.

In the case of Gabriel's client in AD 610, the businessman was Muḥammad, son of Abdullah and Amina. Muḥammad's father had died before he was born in AD 570 and his mother passed away when he was less than six years old. Muḥammad was looked after for a while by his grandfather ʿAbd al-Muṭṭalib. When his grandfather also died not long afterwards, his paternal uncle Abû Ṭâlib took care of him. Muḥammad was born into the leading tribe of Banû Hâshim, part of the Quraysh tribal federation. Mecca was his home. This city was well established as the centre of commercial, political and religious life in western Arabia. Power in the city was monopolized by the leading families of the Quraysh.

At the age of 25, Muḥammad married a relative of Abû Ṭâlib, a wealthy widow named Khadîja. He had worked successfully for this businesswoman and had earned her respect as a business manager, so much so that she invited him to become her husband. After his call to prophethood, Khadîja became Muḥammad's first convert. Seven children were born to Khadîja and Muḥammad, though the three boys died in infancy. In fact, only one daughter, Fâṭima, survived Muḥammad, and she by just six months. While Khadîja remained alive, Muḥammad did not take another wife. Her death, and that of his uncle Abû Ṭâlib – both in AD 620 – would leave Muḥammad emotionally and politically isolated, encouraging his quest beyond Mecca for a more stable environment for his family and followers (see Figure 5).

Figure 5
Significant dates in Muḥammad's life

Date AD	Event
570	birth
595	marriage to Khadîja, a wealthy widow. Fâṭima, who became the wife of ʿAlî (the fourth caliph) came from this marriage
610	first revelation at Mount Ḥirâ, recorded in Sura 96:1–5
620	deaths of Khadîja and Abû Ṭâlib
622	*hijra*; flight to Yathrib/Medina
630	conquest of Mecca
632	death on same day of the year as his birth

Costly calling

On Mount Ḥirâ were caves to which men dissatisfied with Meccan idolatry used to retreat for solitary meditation.[9]

Muḥammad took to making such retreats, sometimes for several days at a time. Islamic tradition identifies Muḥammad at this stage as a man with ascetic leanings. One evening, Muḥammad failed to return from his time of meditation and Khadîja grew anxious. She sent someone to look for him, but soon Muḥammad himself appeared on the doorstep. He was trembling and looking pale, evidently badly shaken by something. He asked to be wrapped up and consoled. When the trembling eventually died down, he gave his account to Khadîja of what had happened that day on the mountainside. His account has survived in testimony passed down by his later wife ʿÂ'isha. That testimony constitutes the only record of Muḥammad's personal description of his initial call to prophethood:

> Narrated Aisha the mother of the faithful believers: The commencement of the Divine Inspiration to Allah's Apostle was in the form of good dreams which came true like bright day light, and then the love of seclusion was bestowed upon him. He used to go in seclusion in the cave of Hira where he used to worship (Allah alone) continuously for many days before his desire to see his family. He used to take with him the journey food for the stay and then come back to (his wife) Khadija to take his food likewise again till suddenly the Truth descended upon him while he was in the cave of Hira. The angel came to him and asked him to read. The Prophet replied, "I do not know how to read."
>
> The Prophet added, "The angel caught me (forcefully) and pressed me so hard that I could not bear it any more. He then released me and again asked me to read and I replied, 'I do not know how to read.' Thereupon he caught me again and pressed me a second time till I could not bear it any more. He then released me and again asked me to read but again I replied, 'I do not know how to read (or what shall I read?).' Thereupon he caught me for the third time and pressed me, and then released me and said, 'Read in the name of your Lord, who has created (all that exists) has created man from a clot. Read! And your Lord is the Most Generous'." (96:1, 2, 3) Then Allah's Apostle returned with the Inspiration and with his heart beating severely. Then he went to Khadija bint Khuwailid and said, "Cover me! Cover me!" They covered him till his fear was over and after that he told her everything that had happened and said, "I fear that something

> may happen to me." Khadija replied, "Never! By Allah, Allah will never disgrace you. You keep good relations with your kith and kin, help the poor and the destitute, serve your guests generously and assist the deserving calamity-afflicted ones."[10]

Muḥammad's confession to Khadîja that this encounter made him fear for his life sent her running with him to consult her Christian cousin Waraqa ibn Nawfal. Waraqa had long been urging Muḥammad to distance himself from the idolatry of the Quraysh and instead to meditate. Waraqa now gave his encouragement to Muḥammad, though he himself died not long after. The words revealed in this first encounter between Gabriel and Muḥammad on Mount Ḥirâ comprise Sura 96:1–5 (see Figure 6).[11]

Following this incident, Muhammad went twice more up Mount Ḥirâ to meditate, but nothing startling happened. He came to doubt the earlier experience and even contemplated suicide. For some while no further message came – different accounts state that the gap was three days or three months or three years. The silence lasted until Sura 74 was revealed:

> Narrated Jabir bin Abdullah Al-Ansari while talking about the period of pause in revelation reporting the speech of the Prophet, "While I was walking, all of a sudden I heard a voice from the sky. I looked up and saw the same angel who had visited me at the cave of Hira sitting on a chair between the sky and the earth. I got afraid of him and came back home and said, 'Wrap me (in blankets).' And then Allah revealed the following Holy Verses (of Qur'ân): 'O you (i.e. Muhammad)! Wrapped up in garments!! Arise and warn (the people against Allah's Punishment),' ... up to 'and desert the idols' (74:1–5). After this the revelation started coming strongly, frequently and regularly."[12]

As the revelations restarted, Muhammad shared them secretly and within a limited circle of friends. The ten or so suras that followed the opening passages would seem to imply that Muhammad quickly began to encounter derision and rejection of his message by his audience, even though it was selected. Such opposition he took personally, enduring periods of hesi-

Figure 6
Earliest revelations

Reference	Content
First revelation: Sura 96:1–5 entitled *Iqraa*: "Proclaim!" or "Read!" or "Recite!"	Proclaim! (or Read!) In the name Of thy Lord and Cherisher, Who created – Created man, out of A (mere) clot Of congealed blood: Proclaim! And thy Lord Is Most bountiful, – He Who taught (The use of) the Pen, – Taught man that Which he knew not.
Silence	Silence
Second revelation: Sura 74:1–5 entitled *Muddaththir*: "One Wrapped Up"	O thou wrapped up (In a mantle)! Arise and deliver thy warning! And thy Lord Do thou magnify! And thy garments Keep free from stain! And all abominations shun!

tancy throughout which verses came down to encourage him. Sura 93, for example, proclaimed: "Thy Guardian-Lord hath not forsaken thee, nor is He displeased. And verily the hereafter will be better for thee than the present" (verses 3, 4). Sura 94 questioned: "Have We not expanded thee thy breast? – and removed from thee thy burden the which did gall thy back? – and raised high the esteem (in which) thou (art held)?" (verses 1–4).

Soon came the call to go public. Sura 26:214 instructed him to "admonish thy nearest kinsmen", and so Muḥammad summoned the chiefs of the Quraysh to a meeting on the hill of Safa. When they were all present, he urged them to embrace Islam.

One of his influential uncles, nicknamed Abû Lahab (meaning "Father of Flame") cursed him, asking him what he thought he was doing bringing the tribal eldership together to listen to such insulting demands. Sura 111 addressed Abû Lahab's stinging criticism with a promise of judgement on those who opposed the prophet: "Perish the hands of the Father of Flame! Perish he!" (verse 1). Abû Lahab's wife also came in for castigation – she had strewn thorns in Muḥammad's path: "His wife shall carry the (crackling) wood – as fuel! – a twisted rope of palm-leaf fibre round her (own) neck!" (verses 4–5).

For a total of thirteen years in Mecca, Muḥammad preached his uncompromising message in an atmosphere of ridicule and hostility. At one point he became so desperate that he sent some of his followers to Abyssinia (modern Ethiopia) to try and recruit the assistance of the *negus* or king, the Christian ruler of that country.[13] Muḥammad was derided as heirless when his young son Qâsim tragically died. His uncle Abû Lahab took it upon himself to warn visiting tribal chiefs of his nephew's madness, steering them away from him. Muḥammad was accused of being a madman possessed by jinn (malevolent spirits), or a sorcerer allied with the devil. He was dismissed as a visionary obsessed with delusions, or a poet peddling the colourful imaginations of his mind as reality. Muḥammad evidently retained a hope for reconciliation with his opponents. Sura 17 (verses 73–75) speaks of Muḥammad's being tempted to fabricate verses that would have made his enemies his friends but that would have turned God into his opponent. Salman Rushdie constructed a whole novel around the delicate reference in Sura 53 to the famous female idols in the *ka*ᶜ*ba* at Mecca – al-Lât, al-Manât and al-ᶜUzzâ.[14] Muḥammad initially referred to these goddesses as potential intercessors with God, maybe out of a desire to make conversion to Islam easier for his fellow citizens. His Meccan hearers reputedly acquiesced to his invitation to become Muslims as a result of his gesture of respect towards three of their idols. Soon came a strong rebuke from God and the prophet's realization that these revelatory lines concerning the three goddesses had been interposed by Satan – they were "the Satanic verses". A restating of this Sura led to opposition being increased from the Meccans. Very soon, Prophet Muḥammad and his followers would need to seek refuge elsewhere. A prophet's lot can be a very lonely one.

Moses knew as much. His initial engagement with the divine was an uneasy affair and seemed only to lead him from one difficult situation to another. He was working, rather than meditating, on a mountain when God called him. The commission from above was expressed in terms of Moses becoming a messenger to Pharaoh. Moses struggled greatly with what he was being asked to do (see Figure 7).

Figure 7
Moses' calling to prophethood

Exodus	Moses	God
3:11	I am not up to the job.	I will be with you.
3:13	How am I to explain to people who you are?	"I am" is God of their ancestors and God of the present.
4:1	The people will not believe me.	Here are three signs to convince them.
4:10	I am no speaker.	I made you; I will enable you to speak.
4:13	Please send someone else.	I am sending *you*, but Aaron may be your spokesman.

Down in Egypt as spokesperson for Yahweh, Moses found himself almost immediately thrown out of Pharaoh's presence. Soon the slave population whom he was supposed to be rescuing discovered that it was being punished for his insubordination. His own people naturally turned against him and the whole adventure began to deteriorate into what seemed like a cruel divine joke!

Other prophets in the biblical tradition found their experience of encountering God a frightening affair. Isaiah was "undone" by his vision of the Lord and accompanying seraphs (Isaiah 6:5). Jeremiah squealed that he was but a child, not knowing how to speak (Jeremiah 1:6). Ezekiel found himself prostrate, lifeless, as an "immense cloud with flashing lightning and surrounded by brilliant light" overwhelmed him (Ezekiel 1:4). The processes involved in encountering the living God and being commissioned to represent him constituted no easy thing, even for these spiritual giants.

Grasping God's word

Our earlier mention of the "Satanic verses" incident raises the issue of "inspiration". We shall look at this matter in more philosophical detail in the following chapter, but here we are concerned with the processes involved when God commissions a prophet to speak for him. What went on at the cave's entrance on the mountain as Gabriel interrupted Muḥammad's meditation? What did Muḥammad describe as happening while he received the revelation? Several reliable traditions relay his recollections of what transpired (see Figure 8).

God, the angel Gabriel, Gabriel-as-a-man and Muḥammad – somehow in that mix of persons the revelation is conveyed, grasped, recited. It is not so dissimilar from Moses' experience. Back on the same mountain where he had been commissioned, many years and many miracles later, Moses receives the Law – the *Torah* – from God. This Sinaitic moment is probably the crowning point of Moses' relationship with God. Through the exodus event, Yahweh powerfully vindicated his prophet, rescued his people and humbled Pharaoh. In the giving of the Law, however, Yahweh offers his guidance for the proper relating of the people of Israel to himself. Indeed, the Decalogue is uttered directly from the mouth of Yahweh in Exodus 20:1–18 – it is that important! This is a formative moment in the unveiling of God's desire for humankind. How does the Bible describe the giving/grasping of the Law? The main protagonists are identified as God, angels and Moses (Figure 9). The different ways of

Figure 8
Processes of inspiration

Process	Reference in al-Bukhârî, *al-Ṣaḥîḥ*, vol. 1
Ringing of a bell	ᶜÂ'isha narrating: "Allah's Apostle replied, 'Sometimes it is (revealed) like the ringing of a bell, this form of Inspiration is the hardest of all and then this state passes off after I have grasped what is inspired ... ' "(no. 2, p. 2)
Angel presses on Muḥammad until he recites	ᶜÂ'isha narrating: "The Prophet added, 'The angel caught me (forcefully) and pressed me so hard that I could not bear it any more. He then released me and again asked me to read ... ' " (no. 3, p. 3)
Angel in the form of a man recites	ᶜÂ'isha narrating: " '... Sometimes the Angel comes in the form of a man and talks to me and I grasp whatever he says'." (no. 2, p. 2)
Gabriel teaches Muḥammad the Qur'ân	Ibn ᶜAbbâs narrating: "... Gabriel used to meet him every night of Ramadân to teach him the Qur'ân." (no. 5, p. 6) Ibn ᶜAbbâs narrating: "Allah's apostle used to listen to Gabriel whenever he came and after his departure he used to recite it as Gabriel had recited it." (no. 4, p. 6)
Prophet under stress and moving his lips quickly	Ibn ᶜAbbâs explaining Sura 75:16 ("Move not thy tongue concerning the [Qur'ân] to make haste therewith"), related: "Allah's Apostle used to bear the revelation with great trouble and used to move his lips (quickly) with the Inspiration." (no. 4, p. 5)
God makes Muḥammad recite the words	Ibn ᶜAbbâs explaining Sura 75:18 ("But when We have promulgated it, follow thou its recital [as promulgated]"), related: this "means 'listen to it and be silent'." Sura 75:19 ("Nay more, it is for us to explain it [and make it clear]"), related: this "means 'Then it is (for Allah) to make you recite it (and its meaning will be clear by itself through your tongue)'." (no. 4, p. 5)

Figure 9
Revelation at Mount Sinai

Process	Reference
By direct divine speech in the hearing of all	"And God spoke all these words: ... " (Exodus 20:1–18)
By direct divine speech to Moses	"Then the Lord said to Moses, ... " (Exodus 20:22 onwards)
By direct divine writing on the two tablets	First time: the Lord "gave [Moses] the two tablets of the Testimony, the tablets of stone inscribed by the finger of God." (Exodus 31:18). The tablets "were inscribed on both sides, front and back. The tablets were the work of God; the writing was the writing of God, engraved on the tablets." (Exodus 32:15–16; see also Deuteronomy 9:10 where Moses describes the tablets). Second time: the Lord promises to Moses "I will write on them the words that were on the first tablets" after Moses has chiselled out new tablets. (Exodus 34:1; recollected by Moses in Deuteronomy 10:4, where God orders him to bring a wooden chest in which to put the replacement tablets).
By Moses writing on the two tablets	Second time: The Lord told Moses, "Write down these words ... And [Moses] wrote on the tablets the words of the covenant – the Ten Commandments." (Exodus 34:27–28)
By angelic mediation	As part of his blessing of the Israelites before his death, Moses recalls that the Lord came from Sinai "with myriads of holy ones; on his right hand were his angels with him". (Deuteronomy 33:2 in the Septuagint[15] version) The part played by angels in the communication of the Law was often discussed by Jewish leaders in the pre-Christian era. The message on Mount Sinai was "spoken" and "put into effect" by angel(s) (Hebrews 2:2 and Acts 7:38; Galatians 3:19 and Acts 7:53 respectively).

expressing what happens in Moses' case find strong reminiscences in Muḥammad's later experience.

No thank you!

Despite the message being sourced from God, mediated via an angel and uttered at considerable personal cost by Muḥammad, very little impact was made upon the people of Mecca over the thirteen years that the new prophet prophesied there. A few men of substance, such as Abû Bakr, ʿUmar and ʿUthmân were converted, but most of the several hundred followers whom Muḥammad managed to convince were younger men or people with no clan to protect them.[16] The most powerful members of the Quraysh remained opposed to Muḥammad and his new teaching. A plot to kill the prophet was eventually conceived in an effort to silence him once and for all. The plan required representatives of all the Quraysh clans to be involved so that no particular clan should be exposed to Hashimite acts of vengeance. The murder plan led to Muḥammad's decision to withdraw from Mecca.

Opposition from kith and kin was a common experience of the biblical prophets. Jesus commented on the common experience that prophets tend to be people especially dishonoured within their own communities. Amos was typical in this respect. He managed to upset everyone – both his own people and his neighbours! Amos was a country shepherd and dresser of fig trees who lived in Tekoa, about twelve miles south of Jerusalem, on the edge of the Judaean desert. God chose to send this southerner as his spokesman to the northern kingdom of Israel, to the religious centre at Bethel where Jeroboam had cunningly set up a calf image when the nation first split into two rival kingdoms (see Figure 10).

Amos lived in the time of Jeroboam II (793–753 BC), during years of considerable prosperity for the northern kingdom. Beneath the affluence, however, the nation was deemed rotten by God. Amos was sent to denounce the social and religious corruption of his northern neighbours and to warn them of impending judgement from above. At first, Amos railed against the short-

Figure 10
The northern kingdom of Israel and the southern kingdom of Judah

Northern kingdom	
King	**Prophet**
930 BC Jeroboam I	
782 BC Jeroboam II	Amos
753 BC Zechariah	Hosea
752 BC Shallum	
752 BC Menahem	
742 BC Pekahiah	
740 BC Pekah	
732 BC Hoshea	
722 BC destruction of Samaria	

Southern kingdom	
King	**Prophet**
930 BC Rehoboam	
767 BC Uzziah	
740 BC Jotham	Isaiah
732 BC Ahaz	Micah
715 BC Hezekiah	

comings of the non-Jewish nations surrounding Israel and Judah, a message welcomed by all sectors of the Jewish community. Then Amos turned his attention to his own people, the southerners. This was shocking to the northern audience, but acceptable – after all, they had had plenty of conflicts with their southern neighbours. Amos highlights the great sins of his own people, the people of Judah. They have rejected God's Law, despised his truth and followed false gods (Amos 2:4). Abandoning God's word, refusing to heed him and indulging in idol worship will result, announces Amos, in a judgement of fire upon Judah.

After this strong condemnation of the people of the south, Amos proceeds to attack his northern hosts. He dares to suggest that the prosperous, politically successful kingdom of Israel –

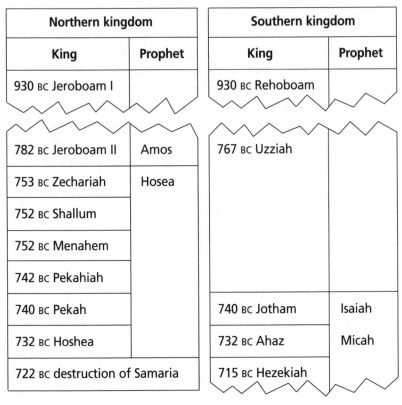

the northern kingdom – is also in for judgement. Injustice and hypocrisy mark the whole society from top to bottom. Judgement from Yahweh is consequently coming for the northern kingdom and, indeed, is well on its way. Well, who wants to hear those words? The king's chaplain tells Amos in no uncertain terms to go back to Judah (Amos 7:10–13) and the northern nation stubbornly ignores the southern prophet – to its cost. Thirty years after King Jeroboam's death, the Assyrian empire's forces swooped southwards from Nineveh and destroyed the northern kingdom's capital city of Samaria, taking many people into exile.

In a way, Amos was an "unsuccessful" prophet – after all, the opposition won. In another sense, he was "successful" in that his warnings came true – God evidently had the last word. Many of the biblical prophets, besides Amos, experienced this "catch-22" situation. No one heeded their representations on behalf of God. They were personally mocked, cursed, exiled, imprisoned and tortured. In that sense their missions were failures. Yet their warnings came true as God acted to vindicate his word through them. So Samaria fell to the Assyrians in the eighth century BC, and Jerusalem would similarly fall to the Babylonians a century or so later.

There are many parallels in the experience of the biblical prophets to the opposition Muḥammad endured at Mecca during the first thirteen years of his calling. Indeed, the messages being proclaimed were strikingly similar in their attacks upon idolatry and injustice, and in their upholding of God's authority and will for ethical societal interaction.

From thorn to theocrat

The number of believers in Mecca gradually increased over the years. Muhammad's preaching, meanwhile, grew in confidence as more messages were received from God by him with only short intervals between them. The opposition, nevertheless, remained widespread and entrenched and, as we have noted, resorted to a plot to kill Muḥammad. Muḥammad eventually began to look for a place other than Mecca in which to continue his work of transformation. Ṭa'if was the summer resort for

Meccans, and its people made significant profits from Meccan visitors and business connections (see Figure 11). Muḥammad journeyed to Ṭa'if in AD 620 after the deaths of his protector-uncle Abû Tâlib and his wife Khadîja. He hoped to find refuge and support in Ṭa'if from the Banû Thaqif tribe to whom he was related through his mother. However, the potential loss in trade revenue from Meccan sources implicit in any harbouring of the young prophet dissuaded the Thaqif chiefs from accommodating Muḥammad. Indeed, their hostile dealing of him made worse the reception given to Muḥammad on his return to Mecca.

Alongside Ṭa'if, one other town in the region rivalled Mecca in economic and social importance. The oasis town of Yathrib, known to us now as Medina,[17] had a flourishing agricultural sector as well as a substantial commercial base. The population of

Figure 11
Arabia

the town was relatively literate, religiously mixed and in competition with their rivals in Mecca (see Figure 12). The two major tribal federations – the Aws and the Khazraj – had recently engaged in civil war, leaving both groups exhausted and vulnerable. At the same time, each federation enjoyed strained relations with the economically powerful Jewish tribes of the town and region. A group of Muslims also lived in Medina ever since Muḥammad had earlier visited and preached in the town.

Various delegations of people from Medina met with

Figure 12
Tribes in Medina

Tribe	Comment
Aws	Qahtâni Arabs of Yemeni origin, hostile therefore to Quraysh who were north Arabian feuded with Khazraj, culminating in the Battle of Buʿâth in AD 617
Khazraj	Qahtâni Arabs of Yemeni origin, hostile therefore to Quraysh who were north Arabian feuded with Aws, culminating in the Battle of Buʿâth in AD 617
Banû Qayla	related stems of the Aws and the Khazraj; formed the *Ansâr* who welcomed the Meccan, Muslim emigrants
Banû Qurayza	Jewish tribe
Banû al-Nadîr	Jewish tribe
Banû Qaynuqâʿ	smaller Jewish tribe
Other groups of Arabs	

Muḥammad in AD 620 and 621. A migration of Muḥammad, his family and followers to Medina was agreed. It occurred in AD 622 with small groups slipping out of Mecca and making their way north. Muḥammad, ᶜAlî and Abû Bakr were the last to leave. The Muslims from Mecca became known as the *Muhâjirûn* or "Emigrants"; their welcomers in Medina were celebrated as the *Anṣâr* or "Helpers". The event was referred to as *al-hijra* or "emigration".[18] The *hijra* carries equivalent weight in the narrative of Islam to the exodus in the Judaeo-Christian tradition. Just as the latter marked the liberation of the children of Israel from the tyranny of pagan Egypt – stage-managed, we note, by "the angel of the Lord" (Judges 2:1) – so the former marked the inauguration of the Muslim community as a historical reality. Muḥammad was in his early 50s. Who would have guessed what this migration of a few hundred people under the leadership of an ageing man would have meant for Medina, for Mecca, for the world?

Laying down the law

Muḥammad in Medina proved to be a very different man from Muḥammad in Mecca.[19] During those earlier years of preaching, no laws had been enacted. Most of the Meccan verses of the Qur'ân constitute exhortations to piety, to worship and praise of the one God, to charitable concern for others and to self-discipline in eating and drinking. A few principles had been ordained on such subjects (see Figure 13).

ᶜÂ'isha is reported to have said, "In the Meccan Qur'ân, heaven and hell are the only subjects."[20] Badru Kateregga summarizes the shift in revelatory content as verses began to emerge via Muḥammad in Medina:

> While the Makkan revelations centered mainly on faith, the revelations he received while in Madinah covered a broader range. They dealt with human conduct, including food and drink, marriage and family life, morals and manners, peace and war, trade and commerce, contracts, jihad (striving in the way of Allah) and crime and punishment.[21]

Figure 13
Principles ordained in Meccan suras

Principle	
1	belief in one God and the appointment of prophets
2	prayer
3	almsgiving, by voluntary donation
4	fasting, in the manner of the Jews
5	pilgrimage, visiting the *kaʿba*

In Medina, Muḥammad emerged as a statesman, ruler and legislator. As the Muslim community increased in size, Muḥammad concretized its norms in a constitution known as "The Charter of Medina". In this charter, the leader of the community was formally identified as "Muḥammad the Prophet". The charter insisted that kinship in faith should transcend the blood kinship of tribe. Fighting within the community was forbidden. Jewish tribes were to share in the life of the community so long as they helped to defend it. Economic affairs were to be regulated by qur'ânic norms and Muḥammad was to be arbiter in all community disputes. Three or four years after the *hijra*, and especially after the neutralization of the Medinan Jews and the defeat of a Bedouin tribe (Banû Mustaliq) occupying land to the west of the town, signs of strong rulership began to emerge in Muḥammad's actions and decrees. One of his earliest actions was to change the direction of prayer from Jerusalem to Mecca. He also changed the practice of annual fasting from the Jewish norm to a number of days during the month of Ramaḍân, and later to the whole of that month.

Over a ten-year period, Muḥammad took steps to establish, in effect, a religion-based state, a theocracy. The Medinan suras 2 (*al-Baqara* or "The Heifer"), 4 (*al-Nisâa* or "The Women"), 47 (*Muḥammad*) and especially 9 (*al-Tauba* or "Repentance") convey the urgency with which Muḥammad pursued his goal (see Figure 14).

Figure 14
Rules emanating from the Medinan period

General subject	Details
Family matters	marriage, kindred, affinity, polygamy, divorce, menstruation, inheritance, etc.
Civil and penal matters	punishment for adultery and theft, retaliation and compensation for murder and injury, rules concerning defilement, circumcision, food and drink bans, etc.
Ritual matters	pilgrimage rites, liturgies, etc.
Financial matters	loans, contracts, income and property taxation as *zakât*, etc.
Military matters	obligation of holy war or *jihâd*, treatment of enemies, prisoners, etc.
Community matters	solutions to community difficulties and questions concerning the Prophet's marriages, lifestyle, etc.

Laws and regulations enacted during Muḥammad's residency in Medina gave Islam a new legal feel and, in effect, paved the way for the formation of an Arab state. The establishment of the obligation of holy war or *jihâd* illustrates the kind of changes arising from the powerful process of law-making. In the Meccan suras, there is no mention of holy war, nor of fighting polytheists. In Medina, at first, war was only conceded as permissible for defensive reasons. Sura 22:40 declares: "To those against whom war is made, permission is given (to fight), because they are wronged; – and verily, God is Most Powerful for their aid." Later, *jihâd* was made obligatory, with many passages in the Medinan suras (especially within suras 2, 8 and 9) enjoining the use of force. Polytheists were to be fought until they converted to Islam (Sura 9:5) while Jews and Christians were to be tackled until they submitted to Islamic rule and paid the *jizya* tax (Sura 9:29). The theme of holy war occurs so frequently that it might appear that this requirement is stressed over all others. In Medina, Muslims were to live by the laws of God, and those laws touched every aspect of life.

Soon after arriving in Medina, the Muslims with Muḥammad at their head built what became the mosque of Medina. Muḥammad and his wives would live in this complex, and the Prophet would eventually be buried there in AD 632. Muḥammad wanted the Jewish tribes to convert and join him, a desire that they resisted – hence the change in the direction of prayer and the timing of the annual fast. The greatest external threat to the nascent Muslim community came from the Meccans, a threat that escalated after the Muslims under Muḥammad's authority raided caravans travelling to and from Mecca. March AD 624 saw a significant Muslim victory at Badr, a valley between Medina and the Red Sea. In the still-celebrated battle, some 300 Muslims defeated 1,000 Meccans who had massed to protect one of their large trading caravans from marauders. Sura 8 (*Anfâl* or "Spoils of War") was received after this battle. In it, lessons from Badr are driven home and the concept of *jihâd* begins to find expression. Two other major battles brought the Medinan Muslims and the Meccan pagans face to face: the Battle of Uhud (a Muslim defeat), and the Battle of the Trench (a Muslim victory). One of the by-products of these battles was the neutralizing of the three Jewish tribes of Medina who proved to be more inclined to connive with the distant Meccans than to support the local Muslims. The last 600 to 900 Jewish men to resist were massacred and their wives and children sold as slaves. The rift that developed between Muḥammad and the Jews is reflected in the Qur'ân:

> It is a wish of a section
> Of the People of the Book
> To lead you astray.
> But they shall lead astray

(Not you), but themselves,
And they do not perceive!
Ye People of the Book!
Why reject ye
The Signs of God,
Of which ye are
(Yourselves) witnesses?
Ye People of the Book!
Why do ye clothe
Truth with falsehood,
And conceal the Truth,
While ye have knowledge? (Sura 3:69–71)

By AD 627, the Jews were banished from all of the Arabian peninsula. Many other campaigns, raids and significant battles punctuated the ten years from AD 622–632 (see Figure 15).[22]

In AD 628, after the Battle of the Trench, the Muslims sought to go to Mecca on pilgrimage. Negotiations resulted in a treaty and a truce, agreed at Ḥudaibiya. For the first time, the Muslims gained official recognition by the Meccans, an event celebrated as a "manifest victory" in the Qur'ân (Sura 48:1). The following year the Muslims returned to Mecca for several days to perform the lesser pilgrimage. In AD 630, allies of the Meccans attacked allies of the Muslims, effectively breaking the Ḥudaibiya treaty. The Muslims marched on Mecca in overwhelming numbers and took the city without a fight. Muḥammad granted a general amnesty, the *kaᶜba* was purged of idols and Mecca immediately became the holy city of Islam. The conquest of Mecca, plus numerous raids in various directions of Arabia, led to mass conversions to Islam. Delegations came throughout AD 631 to submit and embrace Islam. That year it was also announced that from the following year onwards, the territory of Mecca would be closed to non-Muslims for pilgrimages. The pilgrimage of AD 632, known as the "farewell pilgrimage" (because it was led by Prophet Muḥammad himself a few months before his death), consisted only of Muslims. Later that year, Muḥammad died at Medina on the same day of the year on which he had been born.

Figure 15
Major battles during the Medinan period

Date AD	Known as	Details
624	Battle of Badr	victory for Muslims
	Siege of Banû Qainuqâᶜ	unconditional surrender by the Jewish tribe
625	Battle of Mount Uḥud	defeat of Muslims in revenge for Badr
626	Battle of al-Muraysîᶜ	versus Banû al-Mustaliq
627	Battle of Ahzâb (Trench)	defeat of Meccans plus Jewish and other allies
628	Treaty of Ḥudaibiya	Muslims gained official recognition
	Battle of Khaibar	Jews of Banû Nadîr conquered in their fortress
629	Battle of Mu'ta	against overwhelming Greek and Arab forces
630	Conquest of Mecca	Muslim army entered Mecca without incident
	Battle of Ḥunayn	defeat of the polytheists
	Siege of Ṭâ'if	siege by Muslims failed
	Battle of Tabûk	raid on Byzantines

A Jewish theocracy?

How are a people to live in agreement with the desires of God? This was a fundamental concern for both Yahweh and his people in Old Testament times. As long as Moses was still present, the people of Israel were guaranteed up-to-date communication concerning God's guidance. After Sinai, a blueprint for life in Canaan was handed down by the prophet through the details delineated in Deuteronomy and the books preceding it. *Torah* was given and recorded. Willing application of the Law would lead to security and blessing in the promised land. Authority to accomplish that application was vested in the leaders of Israel, in the Levites, in the prophets and in the parents of Jewish families. Included alongside the many details of family, civil, ritual, liturgical and financial matters covered in the *Torah*, military affairs were also addressed. Holy war legislation and conquest narratives came to form part of Jewish and Christian holy writ. In consequence, the Old Testament, for example, records the divine command to kill the Canaanites and occupy their land (Deuteronomy 7:16–26). The language used indicates a complete "eating up" of the inhabitants – in modern parlance, an ethnic cleansing. The conquest of Canaan is presented as a deliberately religious affair, instigated and led by the "captain of the host of the Lord" who gives Joshua his instructions as battle commences (Joshua 5:3–15). The detailed working out of living or fighting according to God's will is addressed in much of the Pentateuch and in the historical books of the Old Testament. Sorting out how to deal with a wife suspected of infidelity or a people obstructing the conquest of their land are part and parcel of learning to live with Yahweh at the centre of all life.

For many modern Christian readers of the Old Testament, myself included, passages about military conquest and certain aspects of the ordering of Israelite society constitute difficult material both to read and to accept. The former passages reflect on the nature of God's governance. The explicit endorsement of violence seems only partly to be ameliorated by the recognition that Yahweh had patiently striven with these other nations in Canaan for many generations, without any reciprocal response towards him on their part (Deuteronomy 9:5). I find it very hard to appreciate the notion of *ḥerem* in ancient Israel. The authorization for Israelite leaders to destroy the nations as "devotion" to Yahweh seems excessive in the extreme. The destruction of "seven nations" in order to make room for Israel in the "land of promise" suggests that, indeed, God does has favourites. I do acknowledge, however, that Yahweh is just as robust about evicting the Israelites from the same land when they prove unfaithful to him. Evidently, God takes seriously any human tenancy of the world he has created. Equally, the fixing of norms for living as the people of God seems strongly biased towards the priorities of a patriarchal world. The "tests" about sexual fidelity, for example, tend to be focused on women, rather than men and women. I do again accept, however, that there is a strong counter-cultural element to Yahweh's insistence, within a patriarchal society, on caring for widows and other females who find themselves at the fringes of a male-oriented society.

Whatever my, and others', hesitations over these difficult passages of the Old Testament, the point for our consideration of the role of prophetic leadership in ancient Israel is this: exodus and wilderness episodes under Moses acted as preparation for theocratic, or at least theocentric, living – also under Moses or his successors – within the land that God gave the Israelites. That "giving" of the land just as much constituted a "taking", for the Israelites had to fight for it. God was involved for sure, but so were the Israelites' swords. The warriors for Yahweh had to learn that there is a proper way to conquer – not Achan's way, for example. They and their clans had also to appreciate that there is a proper way to live in the "conquered" land. Moses became instructor and judge about God's will in so many aspects of Israelite living.

"In it for the women"

After twenty years of conjugal life with Khadîja, during which Zaynab, Ruqayya, Umm Kulthum and Fâṭima were born, Muḥammad was widowed whilst still surviving in Mecca. He asked for the hand of ᶜÂ'isha, daughter of Abû Bakr who was one of his earliest converts. As she was only seven, he also married Sawda, widow of a Meccan emigrant who had died in Abyssinia. After his move to Medina, Muḥammad contracted many marriages, several of them explicitly approved of in the Qur'ân:

> O Prophet! We have
> Made lawful to thee
> Thy wives to whom thou
> Hast paid their dowers;
> And those whom thy
> Right hand possesses out of
> The prisoners of war whom
> God has assigned to thee;
> And daughters of thy paternal
> Uncles and aunts, who migrated
> (From Mecca) with thee;
> And any believing woman
> Who dedicates her soul
> To the Prophet if the Prophet
> Wishes to wed her; – this
> Only for thee, and not
> For the Believers (at large);
> We know that We have
> Appointed for them as to
> Their wives and the captives
> Whom their right hands
> Possess; – in order that
> There should be no difficulty
> For thee. And God is
> Oft-Forgiving, Most Merciful. (Sura 33:50)

'Ali Dashti summarizes the Prophet's marital privileges as specified in many verses of Sura 33. He could take more than four wives. He was permitted to marry first cousins who had migrated to Medina with him. He could take as a wife, without paying a dowry or needing witnesses, any female Muslim who gave herself to him. If he sought a woman's hand, other suitors must give way. After his death, no other men might marry his widows.

The actual number of women with whom Muḥammad contracted marriage differs according to various sources.[23] As we have noted, throughout Khadîja's lifetime, Muḥammad remained married only to her. One of his later wives predeceased him as did a slave-concubine. Two of his marriages he did not consummate. At the time of his death he had fewer than nine or ten contractual wives. He also paid a price for his large retinue. Two rival factions arose among his women, with ᶜÂ'isha, Ḥafṣa, Sawda and Ṣafiya on the one side and Zaynab, Umm Salama and three more on the other. Some of the Prophet's marriages were doubtless contracted in order to establish bonds of kinship and strengthen his fledgling community (Figure 16).

Muḥammad is not the only religious leader to have had multiple wives and concubines. The twelve tribes of Israel came from the loins of Jacob via Leah, Bilhah, Zilpah and Rachel – co-wives and co-wives' maidservants. David was a handsome, strong, brave, musical and deeply religious king. He is honoured in the Bible, not only for his role in establishing the united kingdom of Israel, but also for the quality of his relationship with God. In David, we are informed, God finds a man after his own heart (1 Samuel 13:14). Yet David establishes and directs a household of multiple and sometimes conniving wives. And what about David's son, Solomon? There is not enough space in this book to list the 700 wives and 300 concubines of this "wisest" man in the world. How Solomon found time to produce 3,000 proverbs and 1,005 songs, write scientific works on botany and zoology (1 Kings 4:32–33), let alone run a vast, successful kingdom while keeping his gigantic household in order – has to be a mystery!

The Bible is no stranger to prophet-kings or religious leaders maintaining domestic arrangements that we would view as suspect today. Many of those biblical characters, surely, were "in it for the women". Or were they? The overriding goal of Jewish law and custom, as far as human sexuality is concerned, appears to have been the promotion of procreation.[24] Polygamy, concubinage and divorce increased opportunities for reproduction and the continuation of the patriarchal line. One might argue that the sexual acts specifically banned by Jewish law as "abominations" were those that could not lead to procreation. Impurity laws, similarly, prohibited marital intercourse except at times when conception might result. The perceived necessity of establishing and maintaining a strong clan, tribe or dynasty is not so far removed from some of Prophet Muḥammad's polit-

Figure 16
Prophet Muḥammad's wives/concubines

	Name	Details
1	Khadîja bint Khuwaylid	about 595; aged 40 years
2	Sawda bint Zamᶜa	about 620; aged 30 and widow of an early Muslim
3	ᶜÂ'isha bint Abû Bakr	623; daughter of Abû Bakr
4	Hafsa bint ᶜUmar	625; aged 18 and widow of a Muslim killed at Badr
5	Umm Salama (Hind)	626; aged 29 and widow of a Muslim who died from his wounds received at Uhud
6	Zaynab bint Khuzayma	626; aged 30 and widow of a Muslim killed at Badr
7	Juwairiya	627; aged 20 and captured; married on her profession of Islam and set free
8	Zaynab bint Jahsh	627; aged 38 and married after her divorce from Zaid
9	Mariya the Copt	628; slave concubine presented by ruler of Egypt, bore a son named Ibrâhîm
10	Umm Habîba (Ramla)	628; aged 38 and a widow; had emigrated to Abyssinia
11	Safîya bint Huyayy	628; aged 17 and a Jewess captured at Khaibar
12	Maimûna bint al-Hârith	629; aged 27 and married as Muḥammad returned from *hajj*
13	Raihâna bint Zayd	627; Jewess and concubine

ically motivated marriages. It is important that we acknowledge that questions of Muḥammad on this subject are equally valid for Old Testament patriarchs and kings.

What makes a prophet?

In the circumstances of Muḥammad's "call", in the manner in which the word of God was revealed, in the moves towards the establishment of a theocracy, in the obligation for war in the name of God – even in the prophet's personal attachment to women – we find parallels with the experience of Moses and other Old Testament leaders. So, what makes a prophet?

The Hebrew word for "prophet" that is used in the Bible is *nâbî*, a word close in derivation to the Arabic word *nabî*. Its essential root meaning can best be expressed as "the called". In the Old Testament, individual prophets were people who came with a word from Yahweh. Groups or "schools" of prophets were known for encouraging ecstatic utterances – Saul got caught up with such a body (1 Samuel 10:5–6). Books later produced by individuals commissioned by Yahweh are referred to as prophetic writings – Hosea, for example, refers to himself as a "prophet" (Hosea 9:7–8). Significant figures in Israel's earlier life of relationship with Yahweh came to be referred to as prophets – people like Abraham (Genesis 20:7), Miriam (Exodus 15:20) and supremely Moses (Numbers 12:6–8; Deuteronomy 34:10). The promise of Yahweh through Moses (Deuteronomy 18:15–19) is that he will continually send a prophet like Moses who will declare his will to the people. In that sense, the office is strongly related to the Law, whose protector, mediator and interpreter the *nâbî* is to be. Through word, visions and symbolic acts the prophet is to help keep God's people "on track", faithful to their covenant with Yahweh.

In the New Testament, a *prophêtês* is a person who stands in the biblical tradition and proclaims the divinely inspired message. In this sense, Jesus includes himself among the prophets (Luke 13:33). He, like those before him, will pay the price for such proclamation and, again like them, will die in Jerusalem. One valid way of reading Matthew's Gospel is through the presentation this writer makes of Jesus as a new Moses (see Figure 17).

Figure 17
Jesus as a second Moses in Matthew's Gospel

Jesus	Moses
Matthew 2:2–16 Intimation of birth by astrologers Slaughter of the innocents by Herod Saving of the child through a warning given to his father in a dream	Moses legend of rabbinic tradition Prophecy of the birth of the liberator of Israel by an Egyptian scribe or by astrologers Slaughter of children of Israelites by Pharaoh Father of Moses told in a dream that his son would be saved
Matthew 2:20 Jesus returns to Palestine	Exodus 4:19 Moses returns to Egypt
Matthew 4:2 Jesus stays 40 days in wilderness	Exodus 24:18 Moses stays 40 days on mountain
Matthew 5:1 – 7:29 Jesus proclaims God's will from the mount	Exodus 19:17 Moses reveals God's commandments from the slopes of Sinai
Matthew 8 and 9 Ten miracles follow after Sermon on the Mount	Exodus 7:6 – 12:30 Ten miracles in Egypt before the Exodus
Matthew 11:5 Jesus replies to John the Baptist that the blind receive sight, the lame walk, those with leprosy are cured, the deaf hear, the dead are raised and the good news is preached to the poor.	Rabbinic tradition Prior to the incident of the golden calf, there were no Israelites with fluxes, no lepers, no dumb, blind or deaf, no imbeciles and no death

There are many parallels between Jesus and Moses, especially as brought out by Matthew. Stronger, though, are the deliberate contrasts – statements and actions that show Jesus fulfilling the ideals that Moses hinted at. Moses managed to procure bread by God's help in the wilderness but Jesus is the Bread that has come down from heaven. Moses delivered the "thou shalt nots" but Jesus is the Messianic prophet who lives out the spirit of the Law. Moses' miracles were penal acts, bringing sickness and death to the Egyptians but Jesus' miracles are healings that banish sickness and societal discrimination.

The New Testament also offers comment on how prophets are inspired. The origin of prophecy is not to be found in the will of man, but in God. According to Peter, "prophecy never had its origin in the will of man, but men spoke from God as they were carried along by the Holy Spirit" (2 Peter 1:21). In the sense, then, of "prophecy" being instigated, human beings are clearly subject to the inspiration of the Holy Spirit. In the delivery of such prophecy, however, a more nuanced balance of wills (divine and human) is suggested. The New English Bible rendition of the verse from 2 Peter seeks to reflect the significance of the word order in the Greek: "men they were, but they spoke from God". According to Gerhard Friedrich, Peter's assertion indicates that "the Spirit gives them words which they pronounce, but without fully knowing what they are saying".[25] Yet, it is human beings who are doing the pronouncing, cooperating voluntarily with God, even if the import of what they are delivering is not completely clear to them.

The author of the letter to the Hebrews illustrates this process at work in Old Testament times when God spoke "through the prophets" (Hebrews 1:1). The prophets spoke plainly, selecting their prose or poetry, delivering their sentences. At the same time their every prophecy clearly needs interpretation to make the import of what was spoken plain. Peter declares – of the Old Testament prophets – that it was the Spirit of Christ in them who was speaking through them (1 Peter 1:10–11). It is only in Jesus of Nazareth – that is, post-incarnation – that the intimations of the prophets can be fully understood. The Gospel-writer John, for example, says that

Isaiah saw Jesus' glory and spoke about him (John 12:41). John is referring to the time when Isaiah was at the temple in the year during which King Uzziah died. In Isaiah's own prophesying – and personal understanding? – at the time, however, there appears no hint that he knows it is Christ that he is seeing on the throne. Such an interpretation of the vision-experience only finds expression after Jesus' incarnation, death and resurrection.

Peter's view of prophecy lays a lot of emphasis on the initiative and role played by God. Nevertheless, in his view it was still "men" who spoke and such speaking was subject to their control. Paul emphasizes this strong element of human cooperation in the processes of prophesying in his instructions to the charismatic believers at Corinth. Church services that are full of the use of the gifts of the Spirit can nevertheless be ordered affairs because "the spirits of prophets are subject to the control of prophets" (1 Corinthians 15:32). Scripture emphasizes both the divine and the human elements in the processes of inspiration.

In Islam, there are two important words descriptive of a prophet. Between them, they carry many of the nuances of the biblical concept. The Arabic word *rasûl* refers to a messenger from God who receives a Book and is sent on a mission. In the Qur'ân, God instructs Muḥammad:

> Say: "O men! I am sent
> Unto you all, as the Apostle [*rasûl*]
> Of God, to Whom belongeth
> The dominion of the heavens
> And the earth: there is no god
> But He: it is He that giveth
> Both life and death. So believe
> In God and His Apostle [*rasûl*] ... (Sura 7:158)

The Traditions speak about a total of 315 *rusul* (plural of *rasûl*) but the most important of them are Moses, David, Jesus and Muḥammad. The second Arabic word used to describe a prophet is *nabî*. A *nabî* is someone who also receives direct inspiration (*waḥy*) from God but is not given a Book. Again, the

Traditions speak of 124,000 *anbîyâ'* (plural of *nabî*). The Qur'ân names some 25 of them, stretching from Adam to Muḥammad. Apart from the difficult-to-identify prophet Idrîs – perhaps referring to Enoch or Elijah – Muḥammad is the only non-Jewish person to be given the title of *nabî* in the Qur'ân. Many of the 25 *anbîyâ'*, while appearing in the Old Testament, are not categorized as "prophets" in the Old Testament. They are, however, named as prophets in the later Jewish *Aggada* or folklore. It can be seen, then, that in the Qur'ân all messengers are prophets, but not all prophets are messengers. Prophet Muḥammad is acknowledged as both *rasûl* and *nabî*:

> Muhammad is not
> The father of any
> Of your men, but (he is)
> The Apostle [*rasûl*] of God,
> And the Seal of the Prophets [*nabiyîn*]:
> And God has full knowledge
> Of all things. (Sura 33:40)

Prophets are people with a special calling upon their lives. They are not necessarily any better than other human beings, but they are protected by God from serious sins. They consequently set excellent examples in their lives and conduct – though (with one exception) they are not sinless. They are selected to convey God's word for the guidance of a group or a nation. That word is transmitted to them and through them by a process of inspiration. There is a variety of emphasis on the relative involvement of God and a human being in the processes of prophesying. The Islamic view places the onus strongly on God. Although God certainly makes use of the human instrument concerned, the initiative and content is conveyed without the willed involvement – let alone the understanding – of the human agent. Angels may well be engaged as intermediaries on behalf of God, as with Gabriel and the businessman. Some verses of the Qur'ân, nevertheless, would seem to presuppose a detailed comprehension of the human context and Muḥammad's decisions or desires in order for the later listener to make sense of them.

In both the biblical and qur'ânic contexts, the mechanism of "inspiration" is not simply described.

So is he – isn't he?

Is/was Muḥammad a prophet? The question comes quickly from our Muslim friends, if not from ourselves. Early in many an encounter with a Muslim, we Christians are put onto the defensive. Our Muslim acquaintance says to us: "We believe in Jesus. Why do you not believe in Prophet Muḥammad?" Of course, such an affirmation of belief in Jesus does not cost a Muslim anything, for in Islam Jesus speaks from within the qur'ânic perspective on prophethood. Jesus is a prophet like Adam and Noah and the rest. That kind of prophet is a man who brings a message from God and who must therefore be unreservedly acknowledged and obeyed. The qur'ânic Jesus, moreover, supports the Islamic view of Muḥammad. Some Muslims perhaps justifiably feel, from their perspective, that Christians have been able freely to insult Muḥammad whilst they have been prevented from retaliating in like manner because for them Jesus is a revered prophet. Whether or not a positive view of Jesus is painlessly declared by Muslims, the question of the status of Muḥammad tends to be seen by them as a central issue of interaction with Christians. Will Christians acknowledge Muḥammad as a prophet, reciprocating their acknowledgement of Jesus?

A Christian hearing such a question is most likely hearing the words, "Is/was Muḥammad a prophet *in the biblical sense*?" and that is a difficult issue with which to wrestle. The response of Christians to such a question falls somewhere on a long continuum between two extremes. At one end of the continuum is the conviction that Muḥammad is validly a prophet in the biblical tradition. Patriarch Timothy (AD 727–823) of the Nestorian Church in Assyria assessed Muḥammad's prophethood in such terms in the late eighth century:

> Muhammad is worthy of all praise, by all reasonable people, O my Sovereign. He walked in the path of the prophets and trod in the

track of the lovers of God. All the prophets taught the doctrine of one God, he walked, therefore, in the path of the prophets. Further, all the prophets drove men away from bad works, and brought them nearer to good works, and since Muhammad drove his people away from bad works and brought them nearer to the good ones, he walked, therefore, in the path of the prophets. Again, all the prophets separated men from idolatry and polytheism, and attached them to God and to His cult, and since Muhammad separated his people from idolatry and polytheism, and attached them to the cult and the knowledge of one God, beside whom there is no other God, it is obvious that he walked in the path of the prophets. Finally Muhammad taught about God, His Word and His Spirit, and since all prophets had prophesied about God, His Word and His Spirit, Muhammad walked, therefore, in the path of all the prophets.[26]

At the other end of the spectrum is the conviction that Muḥammad is definitely not a prophet of God. Mark Gabriel, former professor of Islamic history at al-Azhar University in Cairo, insists on this evaluation of the prophet of Islam: "When a Muslim is interested in praying to accept Jesus as Lord and Saviour ... I make sure he denies Muhammad as the prophet of God ... "[27] At this end of the spectrum, also, we find the language about false prophet "Mahound" – the pejorative medieval term for Muḥammad, taken up by Salman Rushdie in his *The Satanic Verses* – deceived and deceiver. Somewhere between these extremes is the kind of reflecting that this chapter represents.

A purely pragmatic view would respect the evident relationship between Muslims and God and acknowledge the decisive role that Muḥammad played in the development of such a relationship. A maximalist view would allow that Muḥammad is a prophet sent by God to the sons of Ishmael, through whom revelation is offered in terms of where seventh-century Arabian society cohered. A minimalist view would aver that Muḥammad could not be counted a full prophet in the biblical tradition because his message disagreed with that tradition in terms of continuity and essential conviction.[28] Even then, perhaps Muḥammad could be conceived as a prophet to some degree, for there are elements of continuity with the biblical tradition and there are some shared convictions.[29] At the 1984 Conference of European Churches, meeting to reflect on Christian–Muslim dialogue in Europe, the final statement made the following suggestion:

> Christians respect the prophetic tradition of the Old Testament. It calls people to repentance in the service of the one God. It is unjust to dismiss Muhammad out of hand as a false prophet. Christians may recognise Muhammad as part of the same prophetic tradition, and in the past some have done so. We must nevertheless ensure that our Muslim friends understand the subtle differences between the two perspectives, for Christians confess that the Word became flesh and dwelled among us.[30]

Even for the least positive assessors of Muḥammad perhaps he might be acknowledged as prophet in the same sense that both Muslims and Christians might respect the prophetic role and life of a Hindu such as Mahatma Gandhi.

Questions asked of Muḥammad's prophethood must also be asked of the prophets in the Bible. Hesitations about the difference between Muḥammad in Mecca and Muḥammad in Medina have to be tempered by the unfolding in the Old Testament of a community strongly regulated by revealed Law. Concerns over Muḥammad's personal circumstances need to be read alongside parallel human failings in leaders like David and Solomon.[31] Who knows, ultimately, what was involved in the process of revelation/inspiration for either Muḥammad or Moses? Who is to say who were the main players?

Is it possible, from a biblical perspective, that there might exist a "prophet" who speaks the truth, yet from outside the biblical corpus? Crete was home to a special poet in the sixth century BC. The poet's name was Epimenides and he lived in Knossos. In Greek religious tradition, Crete was of special importance because it was the birthplace of Zeus, highest of the gods in the pantheon. Many legends survive concerning Epimenides' life and teachings. Stories of his advanced age (157 or 299 years), of his miraculous sleep of 57 years and of his wanderings outside his body have led some scholars to regard him as a legendary shamanistic figure. He is commemorated as one of the Seven Wise Men of Greece. His speciality was exorcism but he was also reputed to be able to predict future events. He conducted purificatory rites at Athens in 500 BC (according to Plato; 600 BC according to Aristotle). It has to be said that all surviving fragments of Epimenides' poetry are potentially attributable to other sources, including the fragment quoted by the Apostle Paul (Titus 1:12). Nevertheless, the weight of tradition affirms that the fragments all come from Epimenides.

What about the fragment quoted by the Apostle Paul? Significantly, Paul only uses the word "prophet" (*prophêtês*) ten times in his contribution to the New Testament. On one of those ten occasions he applies the term to a Gentile – our Wise Man of Greece from six centuries prior to Paul's time. Paul quotes part of a hymn, reputedly by Epimenides, in which the Cretan poet exclaimed about the propensity of his fellow islanders to be less than perfect: "'Cretans are always liars, evil brutes, lazy gluttons'" (Titus 1:12). Bearing in mind the significance of Crete within the Greek religious tradition, it is remarkable that Paul should call the author of this exclamation a prophet: "one of their own prophets". Epimenides, exorcist and poet at the birthplace of Zeus, a "prophet"! Even if Paul is being ironic here, suggesting that Epimenides is a prophet in the Cretans' estimation and not necessarily in his, the point that Epimenides made in his day is now being endorsed by Paul. In this instance at least, in the argument of Paul, Epimenides proves to be an accurate prophet.

Can Muḥammad not then be validly considered "prophet" in some senses, parallel to the case of Epimenides? At the very least, "their" prophet? And – wherever he speaks truth – an accurate prophet. Far from "founding" Islam as a new religion, Muḥammad believed that he was called by God to preach the religion of Abraham, a *muslim*, and to fulfil Abraham's prayer that his offspring should form a Muslim community:

> "Our Lord! Make of us
> Muslims, bowing to Thy (Will)
> And of our progeny a people
> Muslim, bowing to Thy (Will);

And show us our places for
The celebration of (due) rites;
And turn unto us (in Mercy);
For Thou art the Oft-Returning,
Most Merciful.
Our Lord! Send amongst them
An Apostle of their own,
Who shall rehearse Thy Signs
To them and instruct them
In Scripture and Wisdom,
And sanctify them:
For Thou art the Exalted in Might,
The Wise." (Sura 2:128–129)

In what sense and to what degree might Muḥammad be acknowledged as prophetic in calling his people – polytheists – back to the monotheism of their forefather Abraham and in allowing that faith in the one God to mould the new community of submitters? Or was he rather just trying to sidestep a concept of godhead as "Trinity" – a concept about which he knew and which he strongly rejected?

If "truth" as conveyed by the Bible is primarily about relationship between God and humanity, rather than a collection of propositions to be acknowledged, then surely all statements from Muḥammad that reflect the reality of God's self-revelation are prophetic. I do not want to undermine the importance of propositional statements derived from the biblical text. But I do want to suggest that those are secondary. After all, as we shall explore in the next chapter, the Bible is not an end in itself; it bears witness to Another. Nor did God simply bellow into humans' ears a handful of propositions. "Truth", in its Christian sense, is more subtle, more nuanced, than that. It finds its essence in a Person. Where Prophet Muḥammad gained insight into who that Person is – for example in his conviction, against a polytheistic background, of the oneness of God – his utterances to that effect are truly in the lineage of the biblical prophets. Whether and to what extent Muḥammad himself lived by such insights will be evaluated by the One who will evaluate all of us.

I conclude this chapter with two questions – one for the detractors, and one for the supporters, of Muḥammad as "prophet" in the biblical sense. For those who see Muḥammad only as false, inspired by the devil and an impostor – could there not be the possibility that, in some respects, that part of the messenger's perspective that matches God's perspective was or is prophetic? Truth, after all, is truth, wherever it is found. For those who see Muḥammad as prophet in the sense of inspired always and only by God – could there not be the possibility that, in some respects, the "word passed on" by him was muddied by the human vehicle or other spiritual powers involved, unfaithful to the truth that is in Christ, for it is evident that Muḥammad didn't really "know" Jesus? It seems to me that Paul's quoting of Epimenides' poetic comment, and his referring to that poet as in some sense a "prophet", must allow both possibilities. Remember, also, that we have established the "far from perfect" nature of many of the biblical prophets. They, we all agree, were definitely recruited by God himself for his purposes. Muḥammad may have had some failings, but he was by no means unique in that. I find myself, in my estimation of Prophet Muḥammad, somewhere in that uncomfortable, in-between area as defined by such questions.

Whatever the mechanics and measurement of "prophethood" in Muḥammad's case, "Gabriel" certainly did his job well – at least from an Islamic perspective. Deriving from the selected human instrument, a new religious community emerged and grew in the desert of Arabia. That community was strongly informed and guided by the material passed on by the angel to and through Muḥammad. The businessman emerged as a messenger or apostle, a man with a Book. To a consideration of that book we now turn.

Chapter 3 Words Perfectly Spoken

Devilish, divine or human?

The visiting preacher held aloft a copy of the Qur'ân, shaking it above his head as he shouted from the pulpit: "This is Islam's holy book, the Qur'ân. It is false, a counterfeit! It originates from the devil!" I cringed and sank lower in my pew at the back of the church, wondering what kind of relationship this Christian missionary had managed to build with Muslims in the part of the world where he worked for God. Even if he were absolutely right, should not such a pronouncement be made with weeping and with acknowledgement that our historic Christian failure in mission had probably left the field open for the development of alternative, indigenous, religious allegiances such as Islam?

The Egyptian who inspired the militant extremists of Egypt and elsewhere during the 1980s and 1990s was a quiet little man. He spent most of his best years in prison under Nasser. He ended up being executed in 1966, a year before the Six Days War that was to shake the Arab world to its foundations. Whilst in prison, Sayyid Qutb made a detailed study of the Qur'ân, coming to the conclusion that its text was taken neither literally nor seriously enough by contemporary Muslims. If God's word is *God's* word, then a much more fundamental and obedient approach must be taken to it. And nowhere is this more important than with regard to *jihâd*, or striving on behalf of God. Thus, concluded Qutb's disciples, when God's word tells Muslims to fight the non-believers, it means precisely that: "Get the guns and murder the tourists!" or "Kill Americans everywhere!" or "Hijack the planes and punish the Great Satan!" The reward for obedience is the possibility of martyrdom and immediate entry into paradise. The highest calling is that of fighting with faith and bombs to uphold God's word.

How many people died in the 1980s during the explosive scenes around the world after the publishing of Salman Rushdie's *The Satanic Verses*? And how many of the folk who died in the various riots had actually read the book? As the title implies, the burning issue explored in its pages is the nature of certain "verses" of the Qur'ân. Salman Rushdie dared to suggest – as an insider, one born a Muslim – that the verses attributed to Satan's intervening in the revelatory process were actually no different in form from the rest of the text. All of it, claimed Rushdie, came – neither from God nor from Satan – but from Muḥammad's own mouth. The Qur'ân is, in Rushdie's provocative view, a projection of the thoughts and aspirations and shortcomings of "Mahound", his disparaging nickname for Muḥammad.

From the devil and to be castigated? From God and to be literally obeyed? From Prophet Muḥammad's mind and to be sneered at? In this chapter, we focus our thinking on the Qur'ân. A consideration of Islam's holy text leads us to a pondering of the nature of scripture. How can it be said that scripture mediates revelation? How does text – Islamic, Jewish or Christian – speak of or bear witness to the divine?

Vaguely connected

> ... the righteous will inherit the land and dwell in it forever. (Psalm 37:29)

> Before this We wrote
> In the Psalms, after the Message
> (Given to Moses): "My servants,
> The righteous, shall inherit
> The earth". (Sura 21:105)

In this half-verse from a psalm of David, the Qur'ân and the Bible meet. These few words constitute the only direct quotation from the Bible to be found in the Qur'ân. There are plenty of reminiscences from other canonical and apocryphal books of both Old and New Testament eras and we shall have a look at them later in this chapter. The quotation from Psalm 37 appears in a sura dating from the period when Muḥammad was facing early opposition to his preaching in Mecca. Just as the biblical David had had to endure years of humiliation and frustration between his anointing as king and his actual enthronement in Saul's place, so Muḥammad the prophet faced increasing hostility after his call to proclaim God's word to his contemporaries. Psalm 37 is a poem of encouragement in the midst of trouble. The half-verse comprised a very apt quotation for the Meccan moment.

The Qur'ân is not an easy book to read. All of its suras or chapters are assigned, in their heading, to Mecca or Medina according to where Muḥammad was living when they were revealed. Otherwise, chronology is ignored and the Qur'ân is arranged, more or less, from longest to shortest sura. Even within specific Meccan or Medinan suras, subject-matters sometimes derive from different times and circumstances. It has become common to identify three separate "Meccan" periods (first/early, second/middle, third/late) and then, after the *hijra*, the Medinan period (see Figure 18).

A rough chronological order of the suras given in each period is also suggested in Figure 18.[32] Of the 114 suras in total, about 75 per cent date from Muḥammad's residency in Mecca and 25 per cent from his stay in Medina. The Medinan suras, however, tend to be considerably longer than the Meccan suras, accounting for nearly one-third of the whole content of the Qur'ân. Different themes in Prophet Muḥammad's preaching are associated with the various periods of revelation. Figure 19 reflects G. Margoliouth's rationale – by theme – for dividing the suras according to the development of Muḥammad's prophetic ministry.[33]

Most of the short suras found at the end of the Qur'ân (numbers 90 to 114) date from the early Meccan period. The terse, dramatic, poetic language of these proclamations gradually gives way to more narrative form and to controversy. Sura

Figure 18
Suras given in Mecca and Medina

Period	Suras
Early Meccan AD 610–615	96, 74, 111, 106, 108, 104, 107, 102, 105, 92, 90, 94, 93, 97, 86, 91, 80, 68, 87, 95, 103, 85, 73, 101, 99, 82, 81, 53, 84, 100, 79, 77, 78, 88, 89, 75, 83, 69, 51, 52, 56, 70, 55, 112, 109, 113, 114, 1
Middle Meccan AD 615–619	54, 37, 71, 76, 44, 50, 20, 26, 15, 19, 38, 36, 43, 72, 67, 23, 21, 25, 17, 27, 18
Late Meccan AD 619–622	32, 41, 45, 16, 30, 11, 14, 12, 40, 28, 39, 29, 31, 42, 10, 34, 35, 7, 46, 6, 13
Medinan AD 622–632	2, 98, 64, 62, 8, 47, 3, 61, 57, 4, 65, 59, 33, 63, 24, 58, 22, 48, 66, 60, 110, 49, 9, 5

23 from the middle Meccan period, for example, embodies this changing emphasis. The chapter is entitled "The Believers" and its 118 verses set forth the contention that faith, coupled with piety, will lead ultimately to success even though people mock and accuse the righteous of false motives. Often, in suras from this period of Prophet Muḥammad's preaching, the refrain recurs: "They say ... Say thou ... " ("they" being the hostile listeners and "thou" being the prophet; see, for example, Sura 20: 133, 135). It is in this period that the Bible and the Qur'ân find considerable connection. The patriarchs and prophets of biblical times are selectively portrayed in the Qur'ân in order to make two major points. The first is that such former spokesmen for God, like Muḥammad now, had to suffer rejection and threats; yet in the end they were vindicated – Sura 23 refers to Noah, Moses and Jesus in this way. Secondly, the precedents quoted give a strong warning to Muḥammad's contemporaries. The Meccans would be wise to take notice of what happened to the scornful populace of Noah's time or to the Pharaoh who dared oppose Moses. The most detailed story of any offered in the Qur'ân is that of Joseph, told in Sura 12 (probably late

Figure 19
Margoliouth's description of "Meccan" and "Medinan" suras

Period	Muḥammad	Style/Content
Early Meccan	Muḥammad as hesitant prophet	strongly poetic, brief, impassioned utterances expressing appreciation of nature, denunciations of idolatry
Middle Meccan	Muḥammad as public warner	more prosaic teaching style expressing arguments and persuasion, countering charges of jinn-possession, madness or pretension
Late Meccan	Muḥammad as caller to conversion	assertion of dogmatic truths, with many allusions to Jewish and Christian histories
Medinan	Muḥammad as legislator and warrior	disputations with opponents to faith, calls to military action and the development of legislative material for the Muslim community

Meccan). In no other sura besides this, moreover, is only one subject treated throughout. The sura was reputedly recited to the first eight of the *Anṣârs* (the Medinan "Helpers") who converted. It follows broadly the biblical account, but includes details found only in rabbinical *midrashîm*[34] on Genesis. The point of the qur'ânic recounting is that Joseph suffered severely but ended up triumphing victoriously; his brothers hated and plotted but ended up bowing before Joseph. Prophet Muḥammad may find inspiration and hope, and his detractors warning of judgement, in the precedents deriving from the Bible.

The *hijra* constitutes a watershed, both for Muḥammad's

own life and for the Qur'ân. During the Prophet's residency in Medina, the suras become longer and within them argument or dialogue gives place to authoritative announcements. Public affairs in the city and the activities of the army beyond its walls are addressed as the legislative aspects of the revelation come into their own. Personal events in the life of Muḥammad and those around him become far more pronounced. Quite often in the Medinan suras we meet a deliberate linking of heavenly and earthly authority as expressed in the phrase "God and his Apostle".[35]

From speech to book

During Prophet Muḥammad's life, no complete, written copy of the Qur'ân existed. According to a well-known tradition or *ḥadîth*, the angel Gabriel used to check the recitation – from memory – with the Prophet every Ramaḍân, and in the final year of Muḥammad's life he rehearsed it with him twice:

> Fâtima said, "The Prophet told me secretly, 'Gabriel used to recite the Qur'ân to me and I to him once a year, but this year he recited the whole Qur'ân with me twice. I don't think but that my death is approaching'."[36]

The recitations gradually came to be jotted down on tablets, parchment, bones, leaves and skins though mostly they continued to be retained within the memories of men and women. Some of Muḥammad's closest companions devoted themselves to learning the text of the Qur'ân by heart. It needs to be acknowledged by those of us who live in a culture where written material alone is taken seriously that in an oral culture the reliability of human memory is equivalent to the trustworthiness of a hard disk within a modern computer. There is nothing inherently suspect about memorized material. Quite the opposite is true! The trouble for the early Muslim community after Prophet Muḥammad's demise was that people who had committed the Qur'ân to memory were dying or being martyred. According to the *ḥadîth*, the earliest written compilation of the whole Qur'ân was made by Zaid ibn Thâbit at the instruction of Abû Bakr, first caliph or leader of the Muslim community after Prophet Muḥammad's death in AD 632 (see Figure 20).[37]

Figure 20
The first caliphs

Dates	Caliph
AD 632–634	Abû Bakr al-Siddîq
AD 634–644	ᶜUmar al-Fârûq
AD 644–656	ᶜUthmân al-Ghanî
AD 656–659	ᶜAlî al-Murtadâ

Zaid's compilation was kept with Abû Bakr and then with Ḥafṣa, daughter of the next caliph, ᶜUmar. The compilation came to be referred to as "Ḥafṣa's copy". Meanwhile, different reciters (*qurrâ'*) of the Qur'ân continued to offer different renderings of the revelation according to what they had heard from the Prophet or learned from those who had:

> During the reign of ᶜUthmân, teachers were teaching this or that reading to their students. When the students met and disagreed about the reading, they reported the differences to their teachers. They would defend their readings, condemning the others as heretical. News of this came to ᶜUthmân's ears and he addressed the people, "You who are here around me are disputing as to the Qur'ân, and pronouncing it differently. It follows that those who are distant in the various regional centres of Islam are even more widely divided. Companions of Muhammad! Act in unison; come together and write out an *imam* for the Muslims."[38]

According to this account, there appear to have been disputes concerning the true content of the revelation not only between Muslims in Medina and those in the provinces, but even between Muslims in Medina themselves. ᶜUthmân's solution to the growing problem was to aim at uniting all Muslims on the basis of a single text of the Qur'ân. He therefore ordered Zaid ibn Thâbit (with several other men) to examine independent sources of the Qur'ân and compare them with Ḥafṣa's copy.[39] The independent sources consulted comprised various codices emanating from different places such as Basra, Kufa and Syria. Figure 21 lists the major source texts involved in this process.

Figure 21
Significant codices of the Qur'ân consulted by Zaid ibn Thâbit

Source text from ...	Place of origin
Zaid ibn Thâbit, a native of Medina; one of the *Anṣârs* and Muḥammad's amanuensis	Medina
ᶜAbdullah ibn Masᶜud, a Companion; one of the "illustrious ten" to whom Muḥammad gave an assurance of paradise	Kufa
Muᶜadh ibn Jabal (sometimes referred to as Miqdad ibn al-Aswad), one of the most famous of the Companions	Damascus and Homs
Ubai ibn Kaᶜb, a secretary of Muḥammad about whom the *Ṣaḥîḥ* of al-Bukhârî states that of all the Muslims he was acknowledged to be one of the best Qur'ân reciters[40]	elsewhere in Syria
Abû Mûsâ Ashᶜari, one of the early authorities on the Qur'ân	Basra

From the researches made by Zaid and his companions, a definitive text was produced. Within that production, the suras were finally ordered and the text was restricted to a single (Quraysh) dialect. As John Burton, senior lecturer in Arabic at the University of St Andrews, summarizes, "a divine Book revealed to a man of Mecca came to be preserved in the recension prepared by a man of Medina".[41] In effect, then, a Medinan text was established as standard – and Medina was, of course, the seat of ᶜUthmân's government! A single copy of that definitive text was sent to each Muslim province with instructions that all other qur'ânic materials – fragments or whole copies – were to be burnt.[42] Details about the major codices consulted in this process, plus many others extant at the time but not consulted by Zaid ibn Thâbit, may easily be garnered from various later Islamic theological writings in which alternative renderings of words or verses of the Qur'ân were drawn from those different codices.[43]

The *ḥadîth* also indicate that different "forms" or "modes" (*qirâ'ât*) of reading the Qur'ân were customary, even during the life of Prophet Muḥammad. Recitations could sound quite different:

> Narrated ᶜUmar bin Al-Khattab: I heard Hisham bin Hakim reciting Surat Al-Furqan during the lifetime of Allah's Apostle and I listened to his recitation and noticed that he recited in several different ways which Allah's Apostle had not taught me. I was about to jump over him during his prayer, but I controlled my temper, and when he had completed his prayer, I put his upper garment around his neck and seized him by it and said, "Who taught you this Sura which I heard you reciting?" He replied, "Allah's Apostle taught it to me." I said, "You have told a lie, for Allah's Apostle has taught it to me in a different way from yours." So I dragged him to Allah's Apostle and said (to Allah's Apostle), "I heard this person reciting Surat al-Furqan in a way which you haven't taught me!" On that Allah's Apostle said, "Release him, (O ᶜUmar!) Recite, O Hisham!" Then he recited in the same way as I heard him reciting. Then Allah's Apostle said, "It was revealed in this way," and added, "Recite, O ᶜUmar!" I recited it as he had taught me. Allah's Apostle then said, "It was revealed in this way. This Qur'an has been revealed to be recited in seven different ways, so recite it whichever (way) is easier for you ... "[44]

The same tradition is repeated within another famous collection of *ḥadîth* in a chapter headed "'The Qur'an has been revealed in seven modes of reading' and its meaning".[45] Other traditions along similar lines are added:

> Ibn ᶜAbbâs reported Allah's Messenger (may peace be upon him) as saying: Gabriel taught me to recite in one style. I replied to him and kept asking him to give more (styles), till he reached seven modes (of recitation). Ibn Shihâb said: It has reached me that these seven styles are essentially one, not differing about what is permitted and what is forbidden.[46]

These seven "styles" or "modes" of reading (*al-ahruf al-sabᶜa*) are identified in this collection of *ḥadîth* as different "dialects".[47] The different "modes" or "dialects" historically became associated with the names of specific "readers" through whom they are traced (see Figure 22). In each case, at least one recognized "transmitter" was at some stage responsible for handing on his own recension of the "reading" concerned. These transmitters lived in the fourth Islamic century. Of their transmissions, most gradually fell into disuse. Just two – those of Warsh (who revised the reading of Nafi) and Hafs (who revised the reading of ᶜAsim) – became generally known and were rigorously preserved.[48] Warsh's recension for a long while tended to be used in North Africa, mainly because of its association with the Mâliki

Figure 22
Seven "Readers" of the Qur'ân and their "Transmitters"

Centre	Name of "Reader"	Name of "Transmitter"
Medina	Nafi (d. AD 785)	Warsh & Qalun
Mecca	Ismâᶜîl ibn ᶜUmar ibn Kathîr (d. AD 737)	Al-Bazzi & Qunbul
Damascus	Ibn ᶜAmir (d. AD 770)	Hisham & Ibn Dhakwan
Basra	Abu ᶜAmr al-ᶜAla' (d. AD 736)	Al-Duri & al-Suri
Kufa	Abu Bakr ᶜAsim (d. AD 778)	Hafs & Ibn ᶜAyyash
	Hamza (d. AD 772)	Khalaf & Khallad
	Ya'qûb or al-Kisai (d. AD 804)	Al-Duri & Abu'l-Harith

school of law that became the main source for jurisprudence in that region. However, it is the recension of Hafs that eventually gained almost universal currency in the Muslim world, especially after the mass printing of Qur'âns began to be undertaken. It is the Hafs version that is currently printed throughout the Muslim world, with all the vowel signs and other diacritical details included.

Perhaps the different "readings" merely reflect the fact that various dialects of Arabic influenced how the suras came to be remembered. Equally, it is possible that different "readings" reflect the fact that for a long while the Qur'ân was written consonantly (quite normal in Arabic) with the diacritical marks (indicating different consonants, vowels and other grammatical matters) only being added much later. The writing of consonant-only texts can produce different words or tenses, according to context or interpretation.[49] ᶜUthmân's standardized text, it must be remembered, was also a consonant-only version of the Qur'ân. For many centuries, it was read in a variety of ways, reduced eventually by Ibn Mujahid to the seven mentioned here.

The intention of the Muslims involved in seeking to deduce one authoritative copy of the Qur'ân with one distinct pronunciation was consistently to reclaim the authentic Word amidst the various written and oral versions or "readings" that had come into being. Exactly what was it that Prophet Muḥammad recited when God's revelation came to him? The kind of detailed research and sifting of sources that the Muslims undertook, especially under Caliph ᶜUthmân, mirrors the equivalent activity of Christian scholars in their search for as-original-as-possible text for the documents of the Old and New Testaments.

From heaven to earth

So far, we have been describing the human story of the Qur'ân's formation. For Muslims, that human story may be interesting, even argued about, but it pales into insignificance when placed alongside the divine story. It is God's action with regard to the "giving" of the Qur'ân that occupies their minds and elicits praise from their hearts. A key Arabic word, describing the "givenness" of the Qur'ân, is *tanzîl*. It carries the sense of a divine "sending down". God conveys meaning and words to and through his Prophet who finds himself at the time in a state of inspiration (see Figure 23).

Figure 23
Examples of reference to *tanzîl* or "sending down" in the Qur'ân

We sent down the (Qur-ân) in Truth, and in Truth has it descended: and We sent thee but to give Glad Tidings and to warn (sinners). Sura 17:105	We have sent it down as an Arabic Qur-ân, in order that ye may learn wisdom. Sura 12:2	And this is a Book which We have sent down, bringing blessings, and confirming (the revelations) which came before it ... Sura 6:92

During thirteen years at Mecca and ten years at Medina, the text is gradually given via Prophet Muḥammad. That text is preserved on an eternal tablet in heaven (Sura 85:22), a tablet-text sometimes referred to as "the Mother of the Book" (as in Sura 13:39). Its message has been consistently "sent down" by God to different audiences via inspired prophets (see Figure 24).

So, Moses was given "the Book" of the Law to educate his people. This scripture is designated in the Qur'ân as "the criterion" or *al-furqân* (Sura 21:48), a designation used also of the Qur'ân itself (Sura 25:1). David was entrusted with the Psalms and Jesus with the *Injîl* or Gospel. The Gospel is spoken of as having universal significance, constituting a "guide to mankind" (Sura 3:3). Unfortunately, we gradually discern from the Qur'ân, the Jews altered a lot of what had been revealed to them, while the Christians "lost" significant portions of their Gospel inheritance. Now, the definitive, correcting, final edition of God's communication to humankind is offered via Prophet Muḥammad – in Arabic. The very words of the eternal original are conveyed, so there can be no room for error. Only these words will do.

Figure 24
Books "sent down" by God to humankind

Book	Prophet	Reference
Unnamed and lost *Suhuf* (Scrolls)	Abraham	The Books of Abraham … Sura 87:19
Taurât (Torah)	Moses	It was We who revealed the Law (to Moses) … Sura 5:47 And We gave Moses the Book, in order that they might receive guidance. Sura 23:49
Zabûr (Psalms)	David	… and We gave to David (the gift of) the Psalms. Sura 17:55
Injîl (Gospel)	Jesus	We sent him [Jesus] the Gospel … Sura 5:49
Qur'ân	Muḥammad	We sent down the (Qur-ân) in Truth, and in Truth has it descended: and We sent thee [Muḥammad] but to give Glad Tidings and to warn (sinners). Sura 17:105

The concept of *tanzîl* says something very distinctive about the nature of Muslims' scripture. At the same time, it raises some tough questions.

The Islamic insistence on *tanzîl* places the whole onus of the revelatory process on God – indeed, on God alone. He is the one who sends down – whether to Adam, Abraham or Aḥmad.[50] No human being can be conceived as initiating a dialogue with God, calling him to account (like Moses after the rejection of his demands by Pharaoh) or crying out to him (like Jeremiah ruing the day he was born) or complaining to him (like Job). Human agency of any kind is outmanoeuvred by this concept of "sending down". The motion of *tanzîl* is in one direction only. No human error can be risked in the process, so no risk is taken. Prophet Muḥammad provides the mouthpiece for the revelation but he in no way cognitively participates in the process:

> And thus (it is) that We
> Have sent down the Book
> To Thee ...
> And thou wast not (able)
> To recite a Book before
> This (Book came), nor art thou
> (Able) to transcribe it
> With thy right hand ... (Sura 29:47–48)

It is thus emphasized that Muḥammad has no human qualifications that would enable him to come up with something like the Qur'ân. He is not learned, nor in the habit of preaching eloquently. He is not even able to write with his own hand – he is the quintessential "illiterate" prophet.[51] As Wilfred Cantwell Smith rightly points out:

> the Muslims' affirmation about their prophet is not a statement about Muḥammad's person at all, but about the Qur'an and "what Muḥammad brought" ... it is to assert ... that the message purveyed by Muḥammad is authentic.[52]

The very circumstances in which the Qur'ân arrives with humankind thus bear testimony to its truth as originating only from God. The ensuing word on earth is consequently to be received and obeyed confidently for it is clearly "*God's* word." There is no question, then, of its being interrogated, evaluated or criticized. The idea that a contemporary Muslim theologian might investigate the text of the Qur'ân for whispers of "the historical Muḥammad" in a way parallel to the quest within the New Testament for "the historical Jesus" is laughable and risky.[53] Those few who have published thoughtful speculation about the (human) sources of the Qur'ân have found themselves condemned in decrees declaring them to be apostates and beyond the pale of Islam.[54] God's word in the Qur'ân is simply a rendering on earth of the eternal text. It is in essence a "recitation" – the Arabic word "Qur'ân" comes from *qara'*, meaning "to recite". That, after all, is how it began for Prophet Muḥammad, as recorded in the first (chronological) sura:

> Proclaim! (or Read!)
> In the name
> Of thy Lord and Cherisher ... (Sura 96:1)[55]

The concept of recitation is not strange to the Bible – indeed the same root word *qara'* is used in Nehemiah 8:8 when Ezra reads the Book of the Law of Moses to the Jewish returnees in Jerusalem. At this point in the biblical story, however, the recitation is a proclamation or reading from an existing text. An idea of recitation, closer to the Islamic concept, does occur elsewhere in the Old Testament. It comes from the dangerous years when the people of Judah were risking exile by their unfaithfulness. At that time, Jeremiah was preaching in Jerusalem. At one point, we are told, he dictated to his scribe Baruch "all the words the Lord had spoken to him" (Jeremiah 36:4). Baruch subsequently went and publicly declared those words at the Lord's temple. Soon, officials from the royal palace get to hear about the incident and call in Baruch to account for his actions. Baruch is made to read to the officials the words on his scroll. The officials then ask him how he had come to write down these words of Jeremiah; was it "from his mouth?" they enquire. Baruch answers in the affirmative: "From his mouth he read [*yiqrâ* in Hebrew] to me all these words" (Jeremiah 36:17–18). *Qara'* amounts to "reading from the mouth", a concept closely akin to what happened with Prophet Muḥammad.

Long before Jeremiah, Moses had used Aaron as his "mouthpiece". The Lord proposed this arrangement in response to Moses' continuing attempts to shirk his calling: "He will speak to the people for you, and it will be as if he were your mouth and as if you were God to him" (Exodus 4:16). The important difference is that Jeremiah and Aaron are each identified as the subject of the reading or speaking. As the Lord inspires Jeremiah, so he "recites" or "reads from his mouth". As Moses comes up with the words, so Aaron speaks them out to the people. For Prophet Muḥammad, the subject of the action is not the human agent but "Gabriel" or "the Holy Spirit". Muḥammad is merely the passive agent or site of revelation. As a result, in Islam, inspired recitation *is* revelation. Through that medium, unimpeded in the process by any conscious human participation, the divine word is mediated to human listeners. Those listeners may be confident in the origin of the revelation for the very process itself stands guarantee to its freedom from human contamination.

The concept of inspiration in Christianity, by contrast, included from the very first a strong human element to the process of revelation. Various human speakers, writers, collators and communities of believers collaborated with God over many centuries to produce and formalize the text of the Bible. Such human agents were active, not passive, participants in the process. They cooperated with the Spirit, acting out and speaking out his in-breathed burden: "men spoke from God as they were carried along by the Holy Spirit" (2 Peter 1:21). The resultant text bears witness, not to a heavenly Book but to a divine Person. The "Word" in a Christian sense is not a text but Jesus Christ himself. At incarnation, the divine Son – the "Word" or *logos* in Greek – comes down. The divine–human relational element is thus fundamental to both inspiration and incarnation in the Christian perspective. Figure 25 contrasts this Christian view of revelation with the Islamic one.

In Islam, text is paramount, with Prophet Muḥammad simply the conveyor of it. In Christianity, Christ is paramount, with text bearing witness to him. We need, therefore, to note the underlying barrenness of trying to compare Qur'ân with Bible or Gospels. That activity does not constitute a comparing of like with like. The more appropriate comparison would be between "sent down" Word (Qur'ân) and "come down" Word (Jesus Christ). Indeed, in Arabic the Qur'ân is known as *kalâm Allâh*, while Jesus is given the title *kalimât Allâh* – in Tobias Mayer's succinct summary: the Qur'ân is "Divine Word inlibrate" while

Figure 25
Revelation as portrayed in Islam and Christianity

Islam	Christianity
eternal speech ("**Word**") in heaven ↓ sent down via dictation (*tanzîl*) ↓ recited Word on earth as **Qur'ân** + witness of Muḥammad ↓ recorded in **Traditions** (*ḥadîth*) + exegesis of Qur'ân ↓ explained in **Commentaries** (*tafsîr*)	eternal person ("**Word**") in heaven ↓ comes down via incarnation ↓ Word as flesh on earth as **Jesus Christ** + witness of disciples ↓ recorded in **Gospels** + implications of Gospels ↓ explained in **Epistles**

Jesus is "Divine Word incarnate".[56] Cantwell Smith underlines the significance of such a recognition:

> Muslims and Christians have been alienated partly by the fact that both have misunderstood each other's faith by trying to fit it into their own pattern. The most usual error is to suppose (on both sides) that the roles of Jesus Christ in Christianity and of Muḥammad in Islâm are comparable ... If one is drawing parallels in terms of the structure of the two religions, what corresponds in the Christian scheme to the Qur'ân is not the Bible but the person of Christ – it is Christ who is for Christians the revelation of (from) God.[57]

In the Islamic tradition, God speaks to humankind via text. Whatever we make of the details of that text, doesn't the very will to communicate carefully with humanity say something significant about the God of Islam – something quite different from the usual stereotype of a transcendent, faraway, aloof, even despotic God? The God of *tanzîl*, rather, wants a relationship with his creation; he sends the Book down to Moses' generation "that haply they would be guided". Grace is mixed with transcendence in this will (even need?) of God to be in relationship with humankind. God tries many times to bridge the gap: many prophets to many peoples. In Islam, "faith" is not where human beings end in conclusion, but where people begin their response in submission to God's prior approach. In Sura 7:172, God takes the initiative in addressing the whole of humanity, including the unborn, with the question: "Am I not your Lord?" The response, unanimously given in this vision-picture of everyone in their right mind being true to what they really know in their hearts, is a resounding: "Yea! We do testify!" That is what God longs for – everyone to live in willed submission to him. Interestingly, the Qur'ân refers to the specific site of its reception in Prophet Muḥammad. The revelation is brought down to Muḥammad's "heart" by God's will (Sura 2:97). Fazlur Rahman makes a lot of this reference. For him, it suggests that Muḥammad is necessarily "involved" in the process of the revelation's transmission:

> The Qur'ân is thus pure Divine Word, but, of course, it is equally intimately related to the inmost personality of the Prophet Muḥammad whose relationship to it cannot be mechanically conceived like that of a record. The Divine Word flowed through the Prophet's heart.[58]

Rahman's view remains, of course, a minority Muslim interpretation of the intricacies of inspiration, unacceptable to the majority of orthodox theologians. Nevertheless, "heart" does convey something much more than mere "tongue" or "mouth" or "mind". The very concept of *tanzîl* speaks some gracious things about its divine author.

Not so easy to swallow

The Islamic concept of *tanzîl* also speaks some difficult things. The book has an eternal existence, on a "tablet preserved". It is in essence, then, the speech of God – something existing for ever. Yet when it is revealed, it engages with unfolding human events, such as that described in Sura 33:37:

Behold! Thou didst say
To one who had received
The grace of God
And thy favour: "Retain thou
(In wedlock) thy wife,
And fear God." But thou
Didst hide in thy heart
That which God was about
To make manifest: thou didst
Fear the people, but it is
More fitting that thou shouldst
Fear God. Then when Zaid
Had dissolved (his marriage)
With her, with the necessary
(Formality), We joined her
In marriage to thee:
In order that (in future)
There may be no difficulty
To the Believers in (the matter
Of) marriage with the wives
Of their adopted sons, when
The latter have dissolved
With the necessary (formality)
(Their marriage) with them.
And God's command must
Be fulfilled.

This verse deals with the *ménage à trois* between Prophet Muḥammad, his freed slave Zaid, and Zaynab, highborn daughter of Muḥammad's paternal aunt and wife to Zaid. Abdullah Yusuf Ali glosses this verse with the following explanation. The former slave (Zaid) and his highborn wife (Zaynab) discovered in marriage that they were not well matched. Zaid wanted to divorce Zaynab but Prophet Muḥammad dissuaded him, fearing for Zaynab's reputation. Zaid obeyed and the couple struggled on as married partners until the inevitable happened and they did divorce. After that, God gave Zaynab to Muḥammad in marriage.[59] Yusuf Ali is a Pakistani conveyor of the Qur'ân in modern English to a Western audience – the quotations from the Qur'ân in this book are taken from his translation. Ali's gloss on this verse is as concealing as it is explanatory. We have to turn to some of the traditional offerers of qur'ânic commentary to gain meaningful insight. "The two Jalâls" (*al-Jalâlân*) is the nickname given to two famous commentators of the name Jalâlu'l-Dîn, whose joint work is called *Tafsîru'l-Jalâlayn*. In their commentary it is reported, concerning this incident, that Prophet Muḥammad fell in love with Zaynab after her marriage to Zaid: "After a time his eye fell on her, and love for Zaynab budded in his heart."[60] According to this interpretation, the verse in Sura 33 reads differently. Dashti explains:

> The Prophet had taken a liking to Zaynab, but when Zayd had come to ask him permission to divorce her, he had advised Zayd not to do so but to keep her. In giving this advice to Zayd, he had concealed his inner wish. But God told him that he had suppressed his inner wish for Zaynab's divorce because he feared that the people would speak ill of him, whereas he ought to fear God alone. When in spite of his advice, Zayd finalized the divorce, God authorized him to marry Zaynab so that the Moslems should no longer be debarred from marrying former wives of their adopted sons.[61]

Whichever explanation of the context most faithfully reflects the true situation, the point is that events like this "come about" through the vagaries of human interaction set within time, yet the text relating to them is "from eternity". Does that make an eternal word responsible for the unethical yearnings of the human Prophet? In what way can the eternal in Islam be seen to be associated with the temporal? The issue becomes more complicated when the doctrine of "abrogation" is taken into account.

Potentially contradictory passages of the Qur'ân are often reconciled by means of abrogation or cancellation – the later verse (usually) replacing the former. Verses that are abrogated are known as *mansûkh*; those doing the abrogating are referred to as *nâsikh*. This process is applied with qur'ânic approval:

> None of Our revelations
> Do We abrogate
> Or cause to be forgotten
> But We substitute
> Something better or similar:
> Knowest thou not that God
> Hath power over all things? (Sura 2:106)

Jalâlu'l-Dîn produced a list of 20 verses acknowledged by all commentaries at his disposal to be abrogated during the lifetime of Prophet Muḥammad. In other words, while the process of "sending down" was still going on, it was made clear which verses were being replaced by new revelation. Jalâlu'l-Dîn's list is produced as Figure 26.[62]

The "problem" of abrogation lies in two areas. Firstly, the Qur'ân specifically says on the one hand that "No change can there be in the Words of God" (Sura 10:64) and on the other hand that "We substitute one revelation for another" (Sura 16:101). Secondly, if the Qur'ân is an earthly copy of an eternally preserved Word, why does it need to contain changes that only apply to its manifestation on earth? Could not the "correcting" verses have been substituted before sending down the ones that would need abrogating? This philosophical conundrum is not just a delicacy reserved for theologians to squabble about – it is highly relevant to some of the extremist movements gathering pace today within the Islamic world. The Islamists (the "fundamentalists") make detailed appeal to verses (about killing nonbelievers for example) that are said to abrogate other verses (about respecting non-Muslims). Why does an eternally existing word need recourse to a doctrine of abrogation? Could it not make up its eternal mind?

God – in Islam – is very precise about what is sent down; it is his speech, an eternal, uncreated word. That word God sent down via the verses of the "clear Book" as "an Arabic Qur'ân" (Sura 12:1–2) – a created word. The Qur'ân is thus perceived as both eternal and created. This dual status of the Qur'ân constitutes another philosophical conundrum. The rationalistic Muᶜtazilî reacted strongly to such a conundrum during the

Figure 26
Abrogated verses in the Qur'ân

Subject of abrogation	Abrogated verse	Abrogating verse
facing the *qibla* (Mecca for Jerusalem)	2:115	2:144
retaliation (against person of equal rank to the one murdered, or against murderer only)	2:178	5:48
fast of Ramaḍân	2:183	2:187
expiation	2:184	2:185
the fear of God	3:102	64:16
jihâd	4:89	4:90
jihâd in sacred months (forbidden or allowed)	2:217	9:36
provision for widows	2:240	2:234
slaying enemies in sacred mosque	2:191	9:5
imprisonment of the adulteress	4:15	24:2
witnesses	5:109	65:2
jihâd with infidels	8:65	8:66
marriage of adulterers	24:3	24:32
the Prophet's wives	33:52	33:50
giving alms before assembling a council	58:13a	58:13b
giving money to infidels for women taken in marriage	60:11	9:1
jihâd with infidels	9:39	9:91
the night prayer (how long)	73:2	73:20
permission to young children to enter a house	24:58	24:59

early years of the Islamic faith.[63] The Muᶜtazilî (their name means "separatists") comprised a sect founded by Wâsil ibn ᶜAtâ, who "separated" from the theological school of Ḥasan al-Basrî about 100 years after Prophet Muḥammad's death. These "separatist" theologians argued from the perspective of *tawḥîd*, or the unity of God, that nothing could be set alongside God's essence as eternal being. Not even the attributes of God could be equated with him. To assert that an attribute of God was eternal, declared Wâsil, amounted to declaring that there were two gods. The same, they said, applies to God's speech. The Word of God can only be created, not eternal. Argument arose, for example, over the interpretation of Sura 36:82:

> Verily, when He intends
> A thing, His Command is,
> "Be", and it is!

The assertion of the orthodox theologians was that God created all things by means of the word "Be". Since one created thing cannot create another, the word "Be" must be uncreated and eternal. The Muᶜtazilî responded that if this is so, there are two Eternals. And to say that, of course, constitutes the unforgivable sin of "associating" something with God. This argument over whether the Qur'ân is eternal or created or somehow both became the most important issue in the religious politics of the ᶜAbbasid caliphate.

Wâsil's motive in declaring the "createdness-only" of the Qur'ân was a desire to defend the unity of God against the possibility that God could be perceived as accommodating any other eternally existing attributes or – as per Christians – persons. No "Trinity" was allowable, but neither, then, was an "uncreated" or eternal Qur'ân. The concerns of the Muᶜtazilî raise the following awkward question for Muslim theologians of other (Sunnî and Kharijî) persuasions: how can there be an eternally existing phenomenon (the Word of God) besides God? Moreover, if the Qur'ân is conceded to be both eternal (as God's Word) and created (as "sent down", Arabic recitation) how can such an assertion be any less difficult to hold together than the

Christian insistence that God is both "One" and "Three"? Isn't there delicate mystery in both ideas?

Cantwell Smith perceives some contemporary Muslim hesitation or wistfulness over the manner in which the Qur'ân can be conceived to be "the word of God". The noisy, modern world asks questions, if only from a distance, about the nature of religious "words". Muslims, it seems, cannot remain totally immune from such asking:

> The Muslim world, also, is moving into what may possibly become a profound crisis, too; in that it also is just beginning to ask this question, instead of being content only with answering it. Young people in Lahore and Cairo, labour leaders in Jakarta and Istanbul, are beginning to ask their religious thinkers, and beginning to ask themselves, "Is the Qur'an the word of God?" Answering this question has been the business of the Muslim world for over thirteen centuries. Asking it is a different matter altogether, haunting and ominous.[64]

Sourced from below?

While, as we have seen, the Qur'ân contains only one direct quotation from the Bible, it nevertheless offers many paragraphs that reflect strongly an acquaintance with Old and New Testament apocryphal material (see Figure 27).

At a human level, we might ask how Prophet Muḥammad came to know these stories? A number of Jewish communities ended up living in the Arabian peninsula after their dispersion following the Roman destruction of Jerusalem in AD 70. For many of these communities Aramaic rather than Hebrew was their heart language. The targums[65] (paraphrased translations into Aramaic of the Hebrew Bible), plus other Talmudic writings, became their common spiritual fare. Through the targums, the Talmud and the *midrashîm* as rehearsed within these Jewish communities, Prophet Muḥammad may well have become acquainted with the non-biblical traditions reflected in many suras of the Qur'ân. With regard to Muḥammad's contacts with Christians there are a few potential hints. Muḥammad's biographer Ibn Isḥâq mentions people like the Christian monk

Figure 27
Stories in the Qur'ân reflective of Jewish and Christian apocryphal material

Qur'ân	Apocryphal material
Cain and Abel (Qâbîl and Hâbîl) whose parents weep while the raven shows them how to bury the dead Sura 5:30–35	*Targum of Jonathan ben Uzziel and Targum Yerushalmi I* give a similar dialogue between Cain and Abel. In Jewish tradition the raven shows the mode of burial to Adam, not Cain (*Midrash Pirkei Rabbi Eleazar*, chapter 21)[66]
Abraham saved unhurt from Nimrod's fire Sura 2:258; 6:74–83; etc.	*Midrash Rabba* on Genesis 11:28, explaining how Haran came to die in the presence of his father Terah in Ur[67]
Visit of the Queen of Sheba to Solomon when she uncovers her legs by walking towards Solomon over the glass floor Sura 27:17–44	*Targum Sheni of the Book of Esther* 1:2[68]
Hârût and Mârût and other spirits descend from above to tempt humankind Sura 2:102	*Midrash Yalkut Shimeoni* on Genesis section 44; *Targum Yerushalmi I* on Genesis 6:4[69]
The Seven Sleepers who slumber for 309 years in the cave, fearing persecution Sura 18:9–26	The Seven Sleepers of Ephesus form the subject of a Syriac homily in verse by Mar Jacob of Saruq, bishop of Batnan (died AD 521)[70]
The biography of Mary: being fed by angels in the temple; giving birth under a palm tree Sura 19:16–33	The *Gospel of Pseudo-Matthew* chapter 20 describes a "palm-tree" incident during the holy family's flight to Egypt[71]
The childhood of Jesus: speaking from his cradle, breathing life into birds of clay Sura 3:46, 49; 5:113	The *Gospel of Thomas* chapter 2 and the *Arabic Gospel of the Infancy of the Saviour*, chapters 36 and 46, describe an incident of the child Jesus and clay birds[72]

Baḥîrâ, Khadîja's cousin Waraqa ibn Nawfal and the Christian slave Jabr (said by the Meccans to have influenced the Prophet). Mary, Christian Coptic co-wife of Muḥammad, was brought to him as a slave from Alexandria with her brother and sister. Perhaps the diplomatic encounters of Muḥammad with African Christians from Abyssinia and Arab Christians from Najrân (an area of the Arabian peninsula north of Yemen) gave some sources for Muḥammad's view of Christians' belief about Christ. The *Arabic Gospel of the Infancy of the Saviour* would seem to be a significant potential source for some of Muḥammad's understanding of Christian convictions:

> This Gospel, which was translated into Arabic early on, and which has only survived in this language, had acquired a considerable reputation among Christians of the remote parts of the East, and had almost eclipsed the canonical texts.[73]

Before we quickly conclude that potential non-scriptural sources for part of the qur'ânic corpus makes the whole "revelatory" process invalid, we need to acknowledge that the Bible also contains quotations or allusions to material deriving from other-than-biblical sources. Did not the author of Psalm 104, for example, pick up some of his themes from the famous Egyptian hymn of Amenhotep IV? That hymn of praise to the deity that is manifested in Aten the sun disk, constitutes a remarkable statement of monotheism, standing out like a beacon in the history of ancient Egyptian polytheisms. Amenhotep IV even changed his pharaonic name to Akhenaten – one who serves Aten – and built a new capital city dedicated to the god represented by the sun. Figure 28 offers a few extracts from his *Hymn to Aten* and suggests some reminiscences of it to be found in Psalm 104.

Perhaps there was a direct borrowing from the former Egyptian hymn. Perhaps the ideas expressed in the Egyptian hymn reflect a common way at that time of acknowledging God's providence, and the psalmist later simply adapted them to express his own praise. C.S. Lewis certainly had no problem

Figure 28
***Hymn to Aten* and Psalm 104**

Extracts from *Hymn to Aten*	Verses from Psalm 104
At daybreak, when thou arisest on the horizon, When thou shinest as the Aten by day, Thou drivest away the darkness and givest thy rays. The Two Lands are in festivity every day, Awake and standing upon (their) feet, For thou hast raised them up. Washing their bodies, taking (their) clothing, Their arms are (raised) in praise at thy appearance. All the world, they do their work.	The sun rises, and they steal away; They return and lie down in their dens. Then man goes out to his to his work, To his labour until evening.
All beasts are content with their pasturage; Trees and plants are flourishing. The birds which fly from their nests, Their wings are (stretched) out in praise to thy Ka. All beasts spring upon (their) feet … Whatever flies and alights, They live when thou hast risen (for) them. The ships are sailing north and south as well, For every way is open at thy appearance. The fish in the river dart before thy face; Thy rays are in the midst of the great green sea.	You bring darkness, it becomes night, And all the beasts of the forest prowl. The lions roar for their prey And seek their food from God.
How manifold it is, what thou hast made! They are hidden from the face (of man). O sole god, like whom there is no other! Thou didst create the world according to thy desire, Whilst thou wert alone; All men, cattle and wild beasts, Whatever is on earth, going upon (its) feet, And what is on high, flying with its wings.	How many are your works, O Lord! In wisdom you made them all; The earth is full of your creatures.
For thou hast set a Nile in heaven, That it may descend for them and make waves upon the mountains, Like the great green sea, To water their fields in their towns.	He makes springs pour water into the ravines; It flows between the mountains. They give water to all the beasts of the field …

with such an Egyptian offering becoming part of the heritage, via Moses, of the Hebrew people:

> It is conceivable that ideas derived from Akhenaten's system formed part of that Egyptian "Wisdom" in which Moses was bred. Whatever was true in Akhenaten's creed came to him, in some mode or other, as all truth comes to all men, from God. There is no reason why traditions descending from Akhenaten should not have been among the instruments which God used in making Himself known to Moses.[74]

Similarly, many scholars of the Old Testament are convinced that Proverbs 22:17 – 24:22 was strongly influenced by the author's acquaintance with an earlier Egyptian wisdom tradition called *The Book of Wisdom of Amenemope*. The "thirty chapters" of Amenemope's well-known book start with a call to heed:

> Give your ears and hear what is said,
> Give your mind over to their interpretation:
> It is profitable to put them in your heart ...

The "thirty sayings" (Proverbs 22:20) of the "Wise" begin similarly:

> Pay attention and listen to the sayings of the wise;
> Apply your heart to what I teach,
> For it is pleasing when you keep them in your heart ...

In both structure and content, the two texts resemble each other. If the profession of scribe was common in various cultures at that time and if scribes were trained in a wide range of wisdom sayings, there is every reason to believe that the Hebrew composer was here likely drawing on a shared wisdom tradition even if he wasn't directly consulting the Egyptian text itself.

In the case of the Bible, there is no real problem if sources for certain passages can be traced directly or indirectly to earlier, non-Hebrew material. *Truth is truth and revelation is revelation, wherever it is found.* The Bible constitutes the material brought together by the Holy Spirit as bearing witness to what God says and does in the human story. For the Qur'ân, it is a little more difficult to reconcile the presence in it of material that can be identified as deriving from non-biblical sources. The difficulty is twofold. Firstly, the non-biblical material undermines the Qur'ân's insistence that the former scriptures were "protected" by God through prophets, Jewish rabbis and doctors of the law:

> It was We who revealed
> The Law (to Moses): therein
> Was guidance and light.
> By its standard have been judged
> The Jews, by the Prophets
> Who bowed (as in Islam)
> To God's will, by the Rabbis
> And the Doctors of the Law:
> For to them was entrusted
> The protection of God's Book,
> And they were witnesses thereto ... (Sura 5:47)

Secondly, it raises the philosophical question of how such material could be part of the eternal speech of God when its sources on earth are outside the canonical Old or New Testament. Did God "send down" such revelation to Egyptian authors or does such material form part of the revelation "lost" or "forgotten" by former recipients of God's word?

Qur'ân and Bible

We have already suggested that a comparison of Qur'ân and Bible is not the most helpful task in terms of trying to elucidate similarities or differences. Each book serves a different purpose within its faith's context and should really be evaluated for its unique part in the larger revelatory process within those contexts.

Sometimes, at the more polemical extreme of Christian–Muslim relating, attempts to compare and contrast Qur'ân and Bible have simply yielded ammunition for predetermined conclusions. From the Islamic side, Ahmed Deedat – a South African of Gujarati origin – and others have "jumped on the bandwagon" of liberal Christian theologians, employing the latters' doubts about the authenticity of certain texts or doctrines to "prove" that the Bible is false and full of contradictions. Maurice Bucaille, for example, ends his book on *The Bible, the Qur'ân and Science* with a summary comparing the multiplicity of sources accumulated over many centuries for the Bible as compared with the single, memorized source of the Qur'ân:

> Contradictions, improbabilities and incompatibilities with modern scientific data may be easily explained in terms of [such multiplicity of sources over many centuries]. Christians are nevertheless very surprised when they realize this, so great have been the continuous and far-reaching efforts made until now by many official commentators to camouflage the very obvious results of modern studies, under cunning dialectical acrobatics orchestrated by apologetic lyricism.[75]

The integrity of the Christian scriptures is thus brought into question.[76] At the same time, those same ("compromised") scriptures are utilized to show that Prophet Muḥammad was predicted in both Old and New Testaments. The Qur'ân says quite clearly that God refers to:

> "Those who follow the apostle,
> The unlettered Prophet,
> Whom they find mentioned
> In their own (Scriptures), –
> In the Law and the Gospel ..." (Sura 7:157)

Jesus, moreover, predicts the coming Prophet's name:

> And remember, Jesus,
> The son of Mary, said:
> "O Children of Israel!
> I am the apostle of God
> (Sent) to you, confirming
> The Law (which came)
> Before me, and giving

> Glad Tidings of an Apostle
> To come after me,
> Whose name shall be Ahmad." (Sura 61:6)

The Old Testament yields, for Muslims choosing this approach, the promise of Deuteronomy 18: "The Lord your God will raise up for you a prophet like me from among your own brothers. You must listen to him" (verse 15; see verse 18 also).[77] Muḥammad is posited as a prophet like Moses, who is speaking in this passage. The New Testament provides Jesus' promise of the "Comforter" in John 14:16: "And I will ask the Father, and he will give you another Counsellor to be with you for ever ... " The Muslims' argument here is that Aḥmad (another form of the name Muḥammad) means "the praised one" in Arabic. It is alleged that Christians changed the Greek text of John 14:16 from *periclêtos* (meaning "praised one" in that language) to *paraklêtos* (meaning "comforter" or "counsellor").[78]

Some Christians, similarly, have felt that if they could but identify various earthly sources for the qur'ânic text, then the whole Islamic faith would implode. William St Clair-Tisdall, for example, wrote a treatise in Persian on the sources of Islam at the turn of the nineteenth and twentieth centuries. His thesis was simple. Muslims hold that their faith came directly from heaven, the Qur'ân being sent down by Gabriel from God himself to Muḥammad. The Qur'ân is of eternal origin, recorded in heaven and remaining there on the "tablet preserved". All human effort to find a human origin for any part of the Qur'ân must therefore be in vain:

> Now, if we can trace the teaching of any part of it, to an earthly Source, or to human systems existing previous to the Prophet's age, then Islam at once falls to the ground.[79]

In contemporary days, "Brother Mark" concludes his investigation into the history of the textual development of the Qur'ân with the following statement:

> The Qur'an is asserted to be the "Words of God", "His Eternal Witness" against mankind – yet because of the fact that the "7

> readings" are not the "7 Ahruf", "readings" based on admitted scribal errors, and other corruptions, its followers acknowledge openly that they do not know what the "Words of God" are supposed to be![80]

If a human history for the qur'ânic text can be unravelled, then it is assumed that the faith of millions of Muslims will collapse. That assumption has proved true in neither the generation of Clair-Tisdall nor of Brother Mark.

Steven Masood, himself a Christian from an Ahmadîya Muslim background, has sought to retrieve both Muslims and Christians from such non-profitable approaches to each other's source text. His rule of thumb is evidently that questions of the goose are as valid as questions of the gander. In a careful and considered way, Masood addresses seeming contradictions, weaknesses, inaccuracies, questions of transmission and so on with regard to both Qur'ân and Bible. He concludes his book *The Bible and the Qur'an* with the following comment:

> The messages of both the Bible and the Qur'an are well preserved. Instead of arguing about their integrity, we should be listening, comparing and analysing, what these books have to say. Why talk about God, prophethood and the hereafter. Why is God so interested in us? Why has he been sending his guidance to us? What do these books say about what we are as humans and where we are heading? What is life, death, God, mercy and salvation, now and in the hereafter?[81]

Kenneth Cragg stands back from the details of enquiry into the variety of material in the Qur'ân that is reminiscent of extra-canonical Jewish and Christian writings, concluding:

> The debate then about the How? of the Qur'ân is proper and fascinating. It is a significant, objective, historical and scholarly pursuit. But whether allowed or disallowed, alien or congenial, it will leave intact the Quranic allegiance to Islam, the conviction, that is, of a revelatory directive as to the meaning of man. The orthodox theory of the Qur'ân, as heavenly dictation, is no more, no less, than the form of its definitive authority to faith.[82]

In other words, the conviction about the integrity of the Qur'ân as deriving from God swallows up the not-so-understandable details of how that text on earth bears resemblance to other religious writing or came to be concretized in the form that it is known today. In a similar way, the Christian conviction about the integrity of the Bible allows for considerable mystery in the details of how the human putting-together of the text occurred.

Certainty

We come finally, in this chapter, to a consideration in common, for both Islam and Christianity. The issue of "certainty", or perhaps more accurately "confidence", in scripted texts as conveyors of revelation lies behind much that has been considered in this chapter concerning Qur'ân and Bible. Such confidence, it seems to me, has to come to terms with the fact of historicity. For Islam, knowledge of the human context is often required in order adequately to explain the "sent down" text. For Christianity, the historicity of Christ-event and eyewitness recollection of that event somehow constitutes the "revelation". At the same time, such confidence has also to deal with the primacy of the non-historical. For Islam, a call to submission before the author of recitation is what is above all else conveyed through the text. For Christianity, the text offers not just time-referenced information but saving knowledge of its primary Subject. Confidence, finally, needs to be resourced out of the dynamics involved in contemporary wrestling with the historical and non-historical aspects of heeding ancient texts. For Islam, what has been said has been said, but how is such recitation to be heard with submissiveness today? For Christianity, what has happened has happened, but how does the recording of that engender a saving response today?

Austin Farrer (1904–1968), philosopher of religion, wrestled from a Christian perspective with this elusive question over many years:

> If God inspires St Paul to speak, how are we to strain out St Paul, so as to be left with the pure word of God? ... How are we to draw the line between the Apostle's oddities and the word of God?[83]

Farrer develops the idea of having "an ear that can hear". Beyond mere scholarship or readership skills, Farrer suggests that an ear attuned to the voice of God is the only dynamic that will unlock God's word to us. So a spiritual transaction between a human being and God is just as much a requirement for the receiver/hearer of God's word as it is of its first channel. A Christocentric reading of scripture alone does justice to it original inspiration. In that sense of subjective involvement in a faithful reading of scripture, "certainty" in revelation is dependent upon human openness to God and hence conditional – after all, who of us can claim to have the mind of Christ? Even the great Apostle Paul could only suggest that he might have such a mind. All of us bring to the reading/receiving of scripture a human dynamic in which none of us can accurately disentangle the human from the spiritual.

God's word as received or heard by *human* faith somehow makes it truly *God's* word to us mortals. So what God lies behind such "words received" within Islam and Christianity?

Chapter 4 And Who Exactly is God?

In this chapter we face up to the "big" question for any comparison of Islam with Christianity: "Is the God of the Qur'ân the same as the God of the Bible?" Or, expressed another way, is the Muslim's *Allâh* the same as the Old Testament's Yahweh or the New Testament's *theos*?

Perhaps the humorous Mulla Nasrudin story, "How Nasrudin created Truth",[84] can serve as a health warning as we begin to look at this subject.

> "Laws as such do not make people better," said Nasrudin to the King; "they must practise certain things, in order to become attuned to inner truth. This form of truth resembles apparent truth only slightly."
>
> The King decided that he could, and would, make people observe the truth. He could make them practise truthfulness. His city was entered by a bridge. On this bridge he built a gallows. The following day, when the gates were opened at dawn, the Captain of the guard was stationed with a squad of troops to examine all who entered. An announcement was made: "Everyone will be questioned. If he tells the truth, he will be allowed to enter. If he lies, he will be hanged."
>
> Nasrudin stepped forward.
>
> "Where are you going?"
>
> "I am on my way", said Nasrudin slowly, "to be hanged."
>
> "We don't believe you!"
>
> "Very well, if I have told you a lie, hang me!"
>
> "But if we hang you for lying, we will have made what you said come true!"
>
> "That's right: now you know what truth is – YOUR truth!"

It is very hard to address the question about the relationship of the God of the Qur'ân to the God of the Bible without bringing one's own prejudged "answer" into the asking of it. Think for a moment of the difficulties entailed in just asking whether the God of the Old Testament is the same as the God of the New Testament. Many people, including Christians, speak as if they are completely different: the former is heralded, for instance, as a God of judgement, the latter as a God of love. Such a view, however, cannot be true, for God is only one God! At the same time, it is fair to make a distinction between the ways in which Old and New Testaments tend to portray that one God, for there are qualitative differences of enlightenment and emphasis.[85]

Similarly, how you ask the "big" question about the God of Qur'ân and Bible, or what you mean by that question, determines the kind of answer for which you are looking.

I propose in this chapter to come to some understanding of the *Allâh* of the Qur'ân and his relationship to the God of the Bible via four routes: the history route, the philology (language) route, the theology route and the missiology (missions) route.

A brief history of *Allâh*

Imagine yourself transported back in time to AD 610. Something dramatic is unfolding on a mountain outside Mecca. A man who has been in the habit of meditating on its slopes is "squeezed" into reciting a holy message. The "sending down" has begun. Muḥammad, the mountain-top meditator, awakens to a realization that God is speaking through him.

When the new prophet comes to speak of the God with whom he has begun to have such dynamic and somewhat frightening encounters, what word should he use to refer to him? Should he make up a completely new word for the giver of this startling, new revelation? Or should he borrow a word from another people or language – a loan-word describing the kind of God who sends down the sort of message that he is now receiving? Or could he invest a locally known word for God with vibrant, new meaning? What would be your strategy if you were him?

Arab clans in the sixth and seventh centuries AD recognized their own tribal gods and goddesses. Some of such deities were astral – like the moon, sun or stars. Some were nature gods, discerned in the "life" of rivers, trees and animals. Others took the form of stone idols found ready-made on the ground – probably volcanic or meteoric in origin. The best known among the gods of the Arabs who lived in and around Mecca were those represented by four stone idols: the male god Hubal and the three sister goddesses al-Lât, al-Manât and al-ᶜUzzâ (see Figure 29).

Figure 29
Arab gods and goddesses

Allâh	principal god of Quraysh tribe "Lord of the *kaᶜba*" invisible deity, not represented by an idol
Hubal	chief idol of the *kaᶜba* man-like stone statue arrows laid at his side were used in divination
al-ᶜUzzâ	goddess of east Mecca most venerated idol of Quraysh Muḥammad's grandfather almost sacrificed Muḥammad's father to al-ᶜUzzâ
al-Lât	feminine form of *Allâh* sanctuary in the city of Ṭa'if
al-Manât	goddess of fate sanctuary in town of Qudayd

Mecca was, as we have seen, a major trading and religious centre. It was home to the Quraysh tribe, the clan-group into which Muḥammad was born. The Quraysh gained a prominent position among the Arabs, not least because of their protection and control of the wealthy and strategically placed town of Mecca. In Mecca stood the *kaᶜba*,[86] a shrine reputedly housing some 360 idols that were honoured by different tribal groups. Prominent among the idols housed in the *kaᶜba* was Hubal, favourite god image of the Quraysh. The most important of the deities honoured by the Quraysh, however, was not represented in the idol-house at all. We will consider this deity in a moment.

Besides the tribal gods acknowledged as powerful by different clan groups, there also seems to have emerged among the Arabs a concept of "high god" or "supreme god". Some commentators think that this "supreme god" idea arose through the universalization of a tribal god – an "our god goes cosmic" perception. The exalted god concerned came to be referred to as "*the* god" (*al-ilâh* in Arabic). Other commentators think that when one tribe with a "*the* god" idea met another tribe with a similar thought about their god, then the two tribes must have concluded that they were talking about the same "*the* god" – so the idea of a universal god took root. Still other commentators think that such premonitions of monotheism among the Arabs must have been due to their exposure to Christian and Jewish conceptions of God.

In both types of thinking about god – tribal gods and high god – the word *Allâh* was to be found. In fact the word had been around for a long time. It referred to the most important god of the Quraysh tribe. *Allâh* was considered the owner of the *kaᶜba*; indeed, the temple-cube was referred to as *bayt-Allâh* or "house of *Allâh*". Although *Allâh* was lord of the *kaᶜba*, he was not in any way represented among the 360 idols honoured within its walls (see Figure 29 again). So *Allâh* was an important tribal god, but he was in a different league from the idols of stone worshipped within Mecca. At the same time, as we have seen, the high god concept (the "*the* god" idea or in Arabic, *al-ilâh*) had also developed by the time of Muḥammad. The Arabic word for "God" (*Allâh*) is a contraction of *al-ilâh*. It would seem fair to conclude that some Meccans saw themselves as worshipping the high god – *al-ilâh*, "*the* god", *Allâh* – in worshipping *Allâh* the lord of the *kaᶜba*. The impression given in the earliest passages of the Qur'ân is that the verses are addressed to people who already believe in God, in a sense at least of "*the* god":

For the covenants
(Of security and safeguard
Enjoyed) by the Quraysh,
Their covenants (covering) journeys
By winter and summer, –
Let them adore the Lord
Of this House,
Who provides them
With food against hunger,
And with security
Against fear (of danger).
(Sura 106:1–4; this sura is entitled "The Quraysh")

In this early sura, the Meccans are appealed to on the ground of their special privileges. The "Lord of this House" has supplied them with incredible bounty and the Quraysh should be grateful to him. The phrase "Lord of this House" (that is, of the *ka*ᶜ*ba*) refers of course to *Allâh* – the *ka*ᶜ*ba* is his house (*bayt-Allâh*).

Just to add weight to the emerging conclusion that *Allâh* was increasingly being thought of as a supreme or high rather than a local or tribal god, we should note that the Christian Syriac word for "God" is *Alâhâ*. The Arabic word *Allâh* may possibly constitute an Arabized form of this Syriac word. Some commentators believe this to reflect the truth, in which case the word *Allâh* would have amounted originally to a borrowed term.

Whether *Allâh* is in origin a borrowed term from Syriac or simply a contraction from the Arabic *al-ilâh*, the point is the same – the word *Allâh* came to carry connotations of cosmic god, high god, only god. Those connotations constituted strong grounds for appeal in the early preaching of Prophet Muḥammad.

Figure 30 depicts the most significant suggestions concerning the origin of the term *Allâh* for "God" in Islam. The familiarity of the name as a (special) tribal deity is indicated. *Allâh* was lord of the *ka*ᶜ*ba*. Three sister goddesses worshipped at the *ka*ᶜ*ba* were known as "the daughters of *Allâh*". These three goddesses, significant to the Quraysh tribe, came to prominence in the transmitting of Sura 53 – another fairly early Meccan sura – where Prophet Muḥammad "lost the plot" with regard to lis-

Figure 30
***Allâh*: local and cosmic**

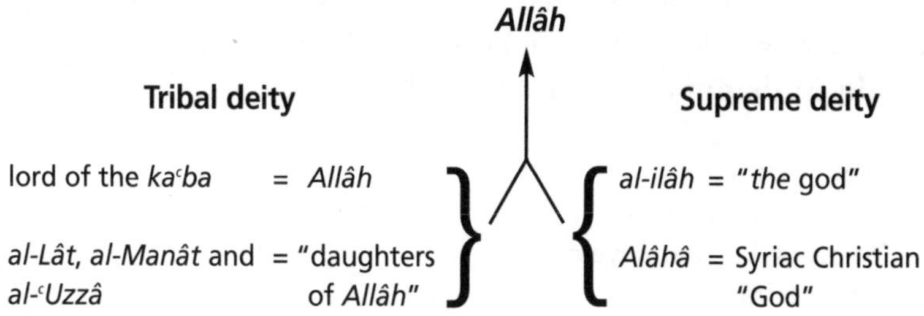

tening to God. He listened to the devil by mistake and the first delivery of certain verses of that sura was said to have been inspired by Satan, not God. Those verses, as we have seen, came to be nicknamed "the Satanic verses". In those verses it was (wrongly) conceded that intercession (or mediation) by these three popular goddesses was acceptable to God. Yet, even as a tribal deity, *Allâh* was conceived of in a special sense – there was no idol depicting him within the *ka^{c}ba*. The use of the term *Allâh* to represent *al-ilâh*, the supreme "*the* god" concept, is also indicated, as is the possibility that *Allâh* constitutes an adaptation of a Syriac word. The notion of *Allâh* as supreme or high god, it would seem, may or may not have been an import. Somewhere in this mix of possibilities lies the likely origin of the term *Allâh*.

The word *Allâh* was thus around before Muḥammad was born and in currency while he was receiving his revelations. There was a strong likelihood, therefore, that he might use it when referring to the God whom, he was convinced, was speaking through him. The question arises, "Did he use the name *Allâh* for God?"

The answer is "Yes, he did." Prophet Muḥammad used the name *Allâh* for God right from the beginning of his involvement in receiving the qur'ânic revelation. However, he did not use it very often at first. In suras dating from the early Meccan period the name *Allâh* is used less than 40 times (maybe less than 26 times) as against more than 2,660 times in the rest of the Qur'ân. Does such a conservative use of the word reflect a desire on Muḥammad's part to distance his own worship of God from the *Allâh*-worship historically entered into at Mecca, with its partial connotation of honouring only a tribal deity?

During the middle Meccan period, at least, there is some fairly strong evidence to suggest that the name *al-Raḥmân* was used by Muḥammad to refer to God:

> Say: "Call upon Allah, or
> Call upon Rahman:
> By whatever name ye call
> Upon Him, (it is well):
> For to Him belong
> The Most Beautiful Names ..." (from Sura 17:110)

This name – *al-Raḥmân* – seems always to have carried a sense of uniqueness, depicting a God besides whom there is no other god. Way back in the early days of biblical history (Exodus 34:6), Yahweh revealed himself to Moses at Sinai as "merciful" (Hebrew *raḥôm*, from *raḥam*; see Psalm 78:38 also). Reference to God by this title has been discovered in inscriptions of Jewish, Christian and Sabaean origin. Moreover, *al-Raḥmân* was evidently used by the *ḥanîf* (ascetic), Zaid ibn ᶜAmr ibn Nufail. Interestingly, the appearance of this name for God during the middle Meccan period coincides with the time when the prophet was most sympathetic towards the Jews. Some researchers think that this is the name by which Muḥammad would have preferred to refer to God. Did he drop it because he feared that his hearers might conclude that *Allâh* and *al-Raḥmân* described two gods?

Another name or title that appears frequently in the suras of the early Meccan period is *Rabb*, meaning "Lord". This word, however, is never used as a proper name ("the Lord"), but rather to give the sense of "your Lord" or "Lord of the East and the West" and so on. Figure 31 illustrates the number of times the names *Allâh*, *Rabb* and *al-Raḥmân* appear in the different periods of the Qur'ân's being sent down.[87]

So what happened in AD 610? How did Muḥammad refer to God? Well, he did not make up a completely new word. The prophet, rather, used known names, accepting that the content

Figure 31
Names for God

Period	*Allâh*	*Rabb*	*al-Raḥmân*
Early Meccan	40	155	4
Middle Meccan	143	260	57
Late Meccan	794	412	2
Medinan	1,644	138	2
Total	2,621	965	65

of those names needed considerable reconstruction. After a possible consideration of using *al-Raḥmân*, the prophet settled on *Allâh* as his major referent for God. Thus the name *Allâh* came to take on a new lease of life, and a whole new meaning, in Islam.

Talking the same language: philology

Arabic is a Semitic language, akin to Hebrew, Aramaic, Syriac and other ancient Middle Eastern languages. The Arabic word *Allâh* (a contraction of *al-ilâh* as we have seen) is related to similar words in other Semitic languages (see Figure 32). Was there, we now ask, a widespread concept of a supreme God, reflected in the languages of Semitic peoples in the period leading up to the revealing of the Qur'ân?

The discovery of the Ugaritic texts beginning in AD 1929 removed any doubt that in the Canaanite pantheon *Il* (El) was the proper name of the supreme god, the head of the pantheon.

> One cannot describe El as a sky-god like Anu, a storm-god like Enlil or Zeus, a chthonic-god like Nergal, or a grain-god like Dagon. The one image of El that seems to tie all his myths together is that of the patriarch. He is the primordial father of gods and men, sometimes stern, often compassionate, always wise in judgment.[88]

Figure 32
Related Semitic words for "God"

Old Akkadian	= *ilu* (masculine), *iltu* (feminine)
Ugaritic	= *il* (masculine), *ilt* (feminine)
Hebrew	= *'êl*, mainly in poetic and archaic texts of Old Testament *'elôah*, 57 times in Old Testament (41 of them in Job) *'elôhîm*, 2,570 times in Old Testament with both plural and singular meaning
Aramaic	= *elah*
Arabic	= *ilâh*

El was a "*the* god", a supreme or high god, concept. At the same time, in Akkadian and Amorite religion, as in Canaanite, El also played the role of god of the tribe. He led the people in its migrations, he directed its wars, he established its justice and often became bound to the people or their leader with covenant ties. So, El was a tribal deity as well as a supreme god. This double conception of local and cosmic deity is similar to that found in our reflections on the history of *Allâh*.

The Hebrew Old Testament uses three different words for "God": *'êl* (El), *'elôah*, and *'elôhîm*. For the most part, these words are interchangeable. El, however, is hardly ever used in the Bible as a proper name for a non-Israelite, Canaanite deity. It refers rather to the supreme God who comes to be known as Yahweh, the self-revealing God of Israel. In the patriarchal narratives of Genesis, there occurs a series of names in which *'êl* is combined with another word to depict a characteristic of God in relation to man. These *'êl*-combinations are unveiled at specific places (see Figure 33).

In the Bible, El is often used simply as an alternative name for Yahweh. Frank Cross proposes that "the wide overlap in attributes, epithets, and names of Yahweh with El suggests that Yahweh originated as an El figure, splitting apart from the old

Figure 33
El in Genesis

Hebrew	English	Reference	Place
'êl ᶜolam	"the Everlasting God"	Genesis 21:33	Beersheba
'êl ᶜelyôn	"God Most High"	Genesis 14:18–22	Jerusalem
'êl shaddai	"God Almighty"	Genesis 48:3	Bethel
'êl 'elôhe yisrael	"God, the God of Israel"	Genesis 33:20	Shechem
'êl roi	"a God of seeing"	Genesis 16:13	Beer-lahai-roi

god as the cult of Israel separated and diverged from its polytheistic context".[89] If Cross's conclusion is accurate, the kind of process he describes with regard to El and Yahweh is similar to that suggested in earlier paragraphs concerning the Qur'ân's adaptation and redefinition of the term *Allâh*. In the Old Testament, Yahweh came to be the name of the supreme, unique God (El) as revealed to humankind. According to Exodus 3 and 6, the name Yahweh was first revealed to Moses when God met him in the desert: "I am the Lord [Yahweh]. I appeared to Abraham, to Isaac and to Jacob as God Almighty [*'êl shaddai*], but by my name the Lord [*Yahweh*] I did not make myself known to them" (Exodus 6:2–3). Yet, earlier people *had* called on Yahweh: "At that time men began to call on the name of the Lord [Yahweh]" (Genesis 4:26). How could that be the case? The composer of Genesis evidently makes the assumption that the God who revealed himself in a special way to Moses was the same God whom men had worshipped from the very beginning. Job is introduced as a man outside the Abrahamic covenant who "'fears God [*'elôhîm*] and shuns evil'", yet finds himself in dialogue with Yahweh: "the Lord [Yahweh] answered Job out of the storm" (Job 38:1). The message of the Old Testament is that the one, supreme, cosmic deity has at different times revealed himself to humankind. In an awesome step, he condescended to enter into covenant relationship with a specific people, allowing them to know him more fully. In a somewhat parallel way in the Qur'ân, the supreme God (*Allâh*) reveals himself to be the only God, yet the God who will embrace those who submit to him.

It would appear to be highly unlikely that there existed a translation of the Bible into Arabic prior to Prophet Muḥammad. The earliest known Arabic version of the Old Testament dates from AD 900, while the oldest Arabic version of the New Testament most likely appeared around the ninth century. These translations seem to have been made with reference to the Vulgate and the Septuagint, plus Syriac and Coptic manuscripts and (New Testament) Greek sources. Similarly, it does not seem probable that Prophet Muḥammad had direct access to the Old or New Testament themselves. As we have seen, there is only one direct quotation from the former scriptures in the Qur'ân (Sura 21:105 quoting Psalm 37:29). It is possible that fragments of Old or New Testaments reached Muḥammad through Khadîja or Waraqa or various Meccan Christians. A tradition from ᶜÂ'isha, conveyed by al-Bukhârî, refers to Waraqa bin Nawfal as a convert to Christianity who "used to read the Gospels in Arabic".[90] There is, however, no independent corroboration of this assertion, and it needs to be recognized that the point of the reference is to amass support for the candidacy of Muḥammad as a true "prophet". According to this tradition, a Christian who knows his scriptures – Waraqa – acknowledges his cousin's husband as a prophet. It certainly does appear to be the case that Prophet Muḥammad deliberately avoided the expression "the Lord" in reference to God (except in the phrase "the Lord of the Worlds" and in the circumstances discussed earlier). Was this done deliberately in order to distinguish his view of God from that of Christians of his acquaintance for whom the term "the Lord" referred uniquely to Christ?

It is a fact that Arabic-speaking Christians have historically used the word *Allâh* to speak of God. It is not clear, however, how Arab Christians came to use *Allâh* for "God". The earliest complete translation of the New Testament into Arabic dating from the ninth century used *Allâh*; this was, of course, well after the establishment of Islam. So did the Christians accept the Muslim word for God in their translation of the scriptures? It is impossible to say, for this earliest translation of the New Testament into Arabic appears to have been completed without any reference at all to the Qur'ân. What is sure is that 14 million or so Arabic-speaking Christians in the Middle East today refer to God as *Allâh*, and would never think of using a different word.

By the time of Prophet Muḥammad, there was certainly in existence a general Semitic concept of a supreme or high God, El. That concept was strongly defined in the Hebrew of the Old Testament. Perhaps it was through Jewish or Christian influence that Muḥammad came to equate the "cosmic god" sense of *Allâh* with the biblical El. Perhaps it was through his acquaintance with Syriac-speaking Christians that he learned that their term *Alâhâ* referred to the God of the Bible.[91] It is impossible to say with confidence. The philological argument is by no means unequivocal.

"Nailing God down": theology

In terms of the history of the development of the Islamic faith, one cannot draw very strong conclusions about where the term *Allâh* came from or how it came to be used to refer to the God who "sent down" the revelation contained in the Qur'ân. Similarly, it is difficult to argue conclusively on philological grounds that the *Allâh* of the Qur'ân is the linguistic equivalent of the Hebrew *hâ'êl* (*'êl* plus definite article).

Our original question about the comparison between the God of the Qur'ân and the God of the Bible really boils down to an interrogation of "meaning". With what content is the word *Allâh* invested, and is that content equivalent to the meaning offered in the biblical revelation with regard to *'êl*?

Prophet Muḥammad certainly thought that the *Allâh* from whom his recitations were originating was the same person as the God of Abraham, Isaac and Jacob:

And dispute ye not
With the People of the Book,
Except with means better
(Than mere disputation), unless
It be with those of them
Who inflict wrong (and injury):
But say: "We believe
In the Revelation which has
Come down to us and in that
Which came down to you;
Our God and your God
Is one; and it is to Him
We bow (in Islam)." (Sura 29:46)

"Our God and your God is one": this was an amazing claim for Muḥammad to be making, and the verse was reputedly cancelled (abrogated) later, near the end of his life, by Sura 9:29:

Fight those who believe not
In God nor the Last Day,
Nor hold that forbidden
By God and His Apostle,
Nor acknowledge the Religion
Of Truth, (even if they are)
Of the People of the Book ...

At the time of its revealing, however, in the context of a belief in a plethora of tribal gods and goddesses and against the backdrop of a house full of idols in the *kaᶜba,* Muḥammad identified the *Allâh* of his encounters with the God of Jews and Christians. Islamic tradition subsequently attempted to fill in the historical basis for the strong claim of this verse. It was suggested that Ishmael (first son of Abraham) and Hagar (Ishmael's mother) settled in Mecca – the well that God provided for the desperate Hagar is believed to be that of Zamzam in Mecca – where Abraham visited them frequently. In Mecca, after Hagar had died and Ishmael had married, Abraham built the *kaᶜba* with the help of his son and introduced the belief in one God to the Arabian tribes. Al-Bukhârî relates the following *ḥadîth* (tradition), emanating from Ibn ᶜAbbâs:

> "Then Abraham ... saw Ishmael under a tree near Zamzam, sharpening his arrows. When he saw Abraham, he rose up to welcome him (and they greeted each other as a father does with his son or a son does with his father). Abraham said, 'O Ishmael! Allah has given me an order.' Ishmael said, 'Do what your Lord has ordered you to do.' Abraham asked, 'Will you help me?' Ishmael said, 'I will help you.' Abraham said, 'Allah has ordered me to build a house here,' pointing to a hillock higher than the land surrounding it." The Prophet added, "Then they raised the foundations of the House (i.e. the *kaᶜba*). Ishmael brought the stones and Abraham was building, and when the walls became high, Ishmael was handing him the stones, and both of them were saying, 'O our Lord! Accept (this service) from us. Verily, You are the All-Hearing, the All-Knowing'." The Prophet added, "Then both of them went on building and going round the *kaᶜba* saying: 'O our Lord! Accept (this service) from us. Verily, You are the All-Hearing, the All-Knowing'."[92]

Perhaps it was because of Prophet Muḥammad's assumption that the *Allâh* of the qur'ânic revelation was the same God as the *'êl* or Yahweh of the Old Testament that there are no recorded *ḥadîth* bearing witness to Muḥammad's understanding of the attributes of *Allâh*. There was nothing, from his standpoint, to prove.

Whether Prophet Muḥammad conceived of his *Allâh* as identical with the God of previous Semitic revelation or not, the only meaningful way to make an evaluation of how much the Qur'ân and the Bible agree in their description of God is by analyzing the content of what they say concerning him. One of the earliest chapters of the Qur'ân declares:

> Say: He is God
> The One and Only;
> God, the Eternal, Absolute;
> He begetteth not,
> Nor is He begotten;
> And there is none
> Like unto Him. (Sura 112:1–4)

The words are reminiscent of the beginning of the *Shema* of Deuteronomy – where the imperative is not "Say" but "Hear": "Hear, O Israel: The Lord our God, the Lord is one" (Deuteronomy 6:4; recited centuries later by Jesus as recorded in Mark 12:29).

At the heart of the Islamic faith is a concept of *tawḥîd*, of the oneness or singularity of God. He is one. As one theologian expresses it, "*Tawḥîd* is the most important Islamic belief. It implies that everything on this earth is from the One and Only Creator, Allah, who is also the Sustainer of the universe and the Sole Source of its Guidance."[93] Contemporary Islamists especially emphasize this facet of God's essential oneness, for it has huge implications. Nothing in creation may be associated with the only God – that would amount to *shirk*, an unpardonable sin. No human being may lord it over another human being, for that would be usurping God's absolute right to absolute sovereignty. Abû'l-ᶜAlâ' Mawdûdî, for example, began a long section in his book *Towards Understanding Islam* with these words:

> The most basic and important teaching of prophet Muḥammad (peace be on him) is belief in the Oneness of God. This is expressed in the primary statement of Islam that "There is no other god but God." This beautiful phrase is the bedrock of Islam. It is its foundation and is the essential prerequisite for being a Muslim. It is this expression which differentiates a true Muslim from an unbeliever; one who associates others with God in His Authority, or an atheist.[94]

Intriguingly, the all-important word *tawḥîd* does not occur as such in the Qur'ân; it is derived from how God is spoken about through the pages of the revelation. This reminds us of the similar fact that the word "Trinity" does not occur in the Bible; it is discerned from how God is spoken about through the pages of the revelation.

God, in the Qur'ân, is transcendent. He has no needs. The famous "throne verse" expresses in beautiful Arabic this sense of God's otherness and self-sufficiency:

God! There is no god
But He, – the Living,
The Self-subsisting, Eternal.
No slumber can seize Him
Nor sleep. His are all things
In the heavens and on earth.
Who is there can intercede
In His presence except
As He permitteth? He knoweth
What (appeareth to His creatures
As) Before or After
Or Behind them.
Nor shall they compass
Aught of His knowledge
Except as He willeth.
His throne doth extend
Over the heavens
And the earth, and He feeleth
No fatigue in guarding
And preserving them
For He is the Most High,
The Supreme (in glory). (Sura 2:255)

But God is not just far off, not just remote. After all, *Allâh* is a personal God in distinction from the "gods" that he is not like: "There is no god but God." *Allâh* is a God who invites worship and obedience. He is a God who reveals his will; there is self-disclosure supremely via the Qur'ân, but also by all the acts of "sending down" to different peoples at different times. In the rendering of the word of God – eternally inscribed "in a Tablet preserved" (Sura 85:22) – into the language of Arabic-speakers of the seventh century, there can be discerned a movement somewhat parallel to the Christian concept of "incarnation". In the Christian case, the Word (as Person) comes down; in the Muslim case, the Word (as Recitation) is sent down. The two concepts are vitally different, of course, but both unveil a God who wills to include humankind in some kind of relationship with himself.

Kateregga, a Muslim who for many years was a university

lecturer in Islamic studies, concludes that it is the same God (in Islam and Christianity) who is perceived to be doing the revealing:

> When Christians and Muslims talk about God, they are talking about the same God, although their witnessing concerning God may be rather different. When they speak of God, Allah, *Yahweh*, or Elohim, they mean the God Who is the only one, the Creator, the loving, the just, the holy, the merciful, the living and eternal, the wise and knowing. Nevertheless, the Christian witness emphasizes the self-disclosure of God (hence the "Trinity"), while in Islam it is the will and guidance of God which is revealed.[95]

Cragg agrees. In his seminal volume *The Call of the Minaret*, he insists:

> Those who say that *Allâh* is not "the God and Father of our Lord Jesus Christ" are right if they mean that He is not so described by Muslims. They are wrong if they mean that He is other than the One Christians so understand.[96]

So for Cragg, God (in Islam and Christianity) is the same, even if he is described differently – for whatever reasons – by Muslims.

Every sura or chapter of the Qur'ân (except Sura 9, which may well have originally been part of Sura 8) begins with the *bismillâh*: "In the name of Allah, most Gracious, most Merciful" (*bismillâh al-Raḥmân al-Raḥîm*). It is possible that Muḥammad preferred the term *al-Raḥmân* to *Allâh*, at least for a while. As we have seen, the Qur'ân mentions *al-Raḥmân* as a different proper name for God. *Al-Raḥmân* appears to be an Aramaic loanword – not Arabic in derivation – and may have been used by Arabian Jews (as *Raḥmâna*) to refer to God. Christians in that area may also have used the name *Raḥmân* to refer to the first Person of the Trinity. An inscription found in Yemen and dating to AD 542 opens with the invocation: "In the power of al-Rahman and His Messiah and the Holy Spirit". Whilst in the Qur'ân, nothing is said of *al-Raḥmân* that is not said of *Allâh*, the attributes of mercy and compassion (*al-Raḥmân* and *al-Raḥîm*) are consistently highlighted as of great significance in God's act of revealing his word:

> And your God
> Is One God:
> There is no god
> But He,
> Most Gracious,
> Most Merciful. (Sura 2:163)

ᶜAṣmâ, daughter of Yazîd, reported that Muḥammad claimed, "The greatest name of Allah is in this verse". The fact that *Allâh* does not occur in this verse, but *al-Raḥmân* does, suggests that Muḥammad was indeed considering using *al-Raḥmân* as the name for God. Was there something about the God who in his very being extends mercy towards his human creation – akin, maybe, to Fatherhood – that attracted and overwhelmed the Prophet? That God, after all, had found him an orphan and given him a home, found him erring and guided him, found him needy and enriched him (Sura 93:6–8).

The attributes of God come to the fore in the "excellent titles" or Beautiful Names of God, *al-'ismâ al-ḥusnâ*. God is to be invoked by the use of these names:

> The most beautiful names
> Belong to God:
> So call on him by them ... (Sura 7:180)

Why "call on" God if there is no possibility of hearing or response from the divine listener? In Arabic, the word *ism* can mean either "name" or "attribute", so the Beautiful "Names" may be seen as nouns expressing who God is in essence ("titles" in effect) or as adjectives describing his "action-attributes". There has been some argument about this difference of meaning by Islamic theologians through the centuries.[97] The Beautiful Names – nouns or adjectives – number 99 according to a well-known *ḥadîth* (see Figure 34 for the names as given in that *ḥadîth*). Some of the Names are known as "glorious" (such as "the Noble", "the Forgiver"), others as "terrible" (such as "the

Figure 34
The "Beautiful Names" of God

Most Compassionate	Giver	All-aware	Perfectly Wise
Taker of Life	Hidden One	Creator of Distress	Most Merciful
Sustainer	Forbearing	Loving One	Ever-living One
Governor	Creator of Good	Absolute Ruler	Opener
Magnificent	Majestic One	Self-existing One	Supreme One
Light	Pure One	All-knowing	Forgiver and Hider of Faults
Resurrecter	Finder	Doer of Good	Guide
Source of Peace	Constrictor	Most Grateful	Witness
Noble	Guide to Repentance	Originator	Inspirer of Faith
Unfolder	Highest	Truth	Unique
Avenger	Everlasting One	Protector	Abaser
Greatest	Trustee	One	Forgiver
Inheritor of All	Mighty	Exalter	Preserver
Possessor of All Strength	Satisfier of All Needs	Clement	Righteous Teacher
Compeller	Bestower of Honours	Nourisher	Forceful One
All-powerful	Ruler of All	Patient One	Greatest
Humiliator	Reckoner	Protector	Creator of All Power
Lord of Majesty and Bounty	Creator	All-hearing	Sublime
Praiseworthy	Expeditor	Equitable One	Maker of Order
All-seeing	Generous	Appraiser	Delayer
Gatherer	Shaper	Judge	Watchful One
Originator	First	Rich One	Forgiver
Just	Responder to Prayer	Restorer	Last
Enricher	Subduer	Subtle	All-comprehending
Giver of Life	Manifest One	Preventer	

Taker of Life", "the Avenger"). The contrast is reminiscent of God revealing himself as "merciful" and "gracious" in Exodus 34:6 and "jealous" and "furious" in Ezekiel 16:38.

The austere, distant God of the Qur'ân is often contrasted with the loving, immanent God of the Bible. Yet on offer by *Allâh* is the possibility of love and forgiveness:

> Say: "If ye do love God,
> Follow me: God will love you
> And forgive you your sins:
> For God is Oft-Forgiving,
> Most Merciful." (Sura 3:31)

Relationship with God may be conditional, as it certainly also was between Yahweh and the people of Israel, but the possibility of an experience of divine love and forgiveness is plainly spoken. As Moucarry points out from his study of forgiveness in the Qur'ân, "to forgive is an essential characteristic of being divine".[98] Equally, an end to patience and forbearance is declared of God in both Old and New Testaments. After all, after death comes "the judgement"!

Too often, in giving a (negative) description of the God of the Qur'ân, Christian commentators gloss over the more difficult aspects of their own scripture. Instead of like being compared with like, the "worst" in the Qur'ân is exposed alongside the "best" in the Bible. The powerful, almost despotic divinity of the Muslim is contrasted with the self-emptying, self-sacrificing, divine Son of the Christian. Despotic-like qualities of an Old Testament God who seemingly condones ethnic cleansing are hushed up, as are references in the Qur'ân to a God who does draw near to his creation (Sura 2:186), at the very least in "sending down" his word if not in jugular-vein closeness of breath.[99] What is more, you cannot have your cake and eat it! You cannot claim that Muḥammad gained a lot of his understanding of who God is via his contacts with Jews and Christians and then claim that that there is no carry-over of conceptual meaning from Old or New Testament to Qur'ân. You cannot argue that the Qur'ân is not a "sending down" but a mish-mash of humanly acquired ideas from sources like the Bible and then argue that the God of the Qur'ân is totally different from that of Jews and Christians.[100] The picture, it seems to me, is much more complex than such half-claims allow.

Within Islam, moreover, there are different views about what the Qur'ân does in fact reveal about who God is. Moucarry has investigated some of the internal, Muslim debate on this important matter.[101] He concludes that orthodox, Sunnî Muslims have tended to emphasize that God is sovereign. In their view, God has the right, for example, to punish or forgive human beings. Muᶜtazilî theologians, on the other hand, says Moucarry, have tended to emphasize that God is just. For them, God's being just restricts what he might sovereignly do – he must reward faith or obedience and he must punish sin. The Islamic theological debate is reminiscent of Christian theologians coming to different views concerning how "sovereign" God might be. A strong Calvinist view goes so far as to predict "double predestination" – God assigns some people to heaven (like the "loved" Jacob) and some to hell (like the "hated" Esau). Other Christian theologies read "sovereignty" through a softer, more relational lens. "Process" theologians of the twentieth century went so far as to suggest that "God" himself in some respects changes essentially – becomes a different being – as he interacts with the created world. Within both the Islamic and Christian faiths, emphasis upon various aspects of God's nature or the presence of different lenses through which "God" is viewed, colour the manner in which he comes to be described theologically.

Colin Chapman offers a helpful model for comparing the concepts of God as expressed in Bible and Qur'ân. His motive in developing such a model is to provide a basis for dialogue, enabling Muslims and Christians to discuss reasonably their ideas of God. Chapman suggests some propositions about "God" to which both Muslims and Christians might assent (see Figure 35).[102] Beyond assent, the opportunity arises for discussion about what is meant, within each faith's construct, by those propositions. It is in the unpacking of the agreed propositions that commonality and distinction of detailed conviction arise.

Figure 35
Chapman's theological approach to Qur'ân and Bible

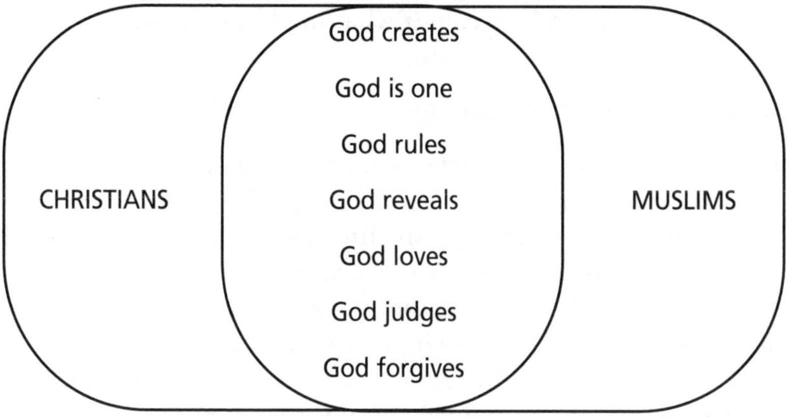

The implications of what is conveyed by the expression "God is one" within Islam, for example, need to be explained from within that faith's own constructs. Such explanation will doubtless include ideas strange to the Christian faith – for example, the specific exclusion of any concept of "three-in-one". Similarly, a biblical perspective on God as one who "loves" will involve ideas totally foreign to the Islamic faith – for example, that "love" expresses in an essential way who God is. However, a dispassionate and listening consideration of Qur'ân and Bible offers some points of convergence, some possibilities of "being on the same planet" with regard to a conviction about who God is. We can agree on much and we can agree to disagree on much, perhaps much more. Truth, however, is truth wherever it is found. To pretend otherwise is intellectually dishonest. Chapman concludes that there is *enough* in common between the two ideas of God for it to be valid to use the same word for "God". Moucarry goes further than this in the conclusion to his in-depth study of the theme of forgiveness and punishment within Islam. He suggests that "Christians and Muslims disagree not so much about who God is, but rather about the outworking of his attributes in history".[103] In that outworking, he maintains, there are reasons for the Muslim rejection of certain Christian emphases about God. We shall be considering some such reasons in the remaining chapters of this book.

Discovering who God is constitutes one of the overarching aims of theology. As we have seen, the kind of theological question asked tends to colour what might be discovered.

Of God and men: missiology

In November 1989, the Malaysian government issued a constitutional law banning the use of the word *Allâh* by Malaysian Christians or any other non-Muslim community. Only Muslims were to be allowed to use the word *Allâh*. Why? Because the assumption was being made that the Arabic word *Allâh* can only apply to the God referred to in the Qur'ân. Local people of other faiths needed to use different words to refer to God because their concepts of God fell far short of the Muslim understanding. Malaysian Muslims did not want *Allâh* to be tainted by association and so they took out a human sanction to protect his name.

A parallel argument has historically been constructed by many national Christians living in Muslim contexts and by Western missionaries working among them. That argument has applied to terms for both "God" and "Jesus". For some, it has been important to use a different word for "God" from the Muslims around them. In Bible translations in the Persian-speaking world, for example, the word consistently used by Christians for God has been *Khudâ*, a word derived from the Persian *khud* meaning "self" – so God is the self-existing one. He is thus referred to as *Khudâ*, not *Allâh*. Actually, some Iranian Muslims have also chosen to use the word *Khudâ* to refer to God, mainly because of the ancient rivalry between Persians (Shî^cas) and Arabs (Sunnîs). More commonly, it is the local word for "Jesus" that is strongly distinguished by Christians from the qur'ânic name. In Arabic, for example, Christians refer to Jesus as *Yasû^ca*, while Muslims use *^cÎsâ*. Theological, semantic and "spiritual" arguments are vigorously rehearsed in various attempts to distance the Christ of the New Testament from the *al-Masîh* of the Qur'ân. Figure 36 illustrates the use of language to distinguish Christian from Muslim content in words for "God" and "Jesus" in different parts of the Muslim world.

Figure 36
"God" and "Jesus" in Bible translations in languages spoken by Muslims

	Turkish	Arabic	Farsi	Malay in S. Thailand	Malay in Malaysia
"God"	*Allah/Tanrı**	*Allâh*	*Khudâ**	*Tuhan**	*Allah*
"Jesus"	*Isa*	*Yasuᶜa**	*ᶜÎsa*	*Isa Mesih*	*Jesus Kristus**

Asterisked items indicate that these are words chosen in distinction from the prevailing Muslim terms.

For the moment we are focusing on terms for "God". How do Christians go about relating their faith in God to Muslims? Do they accept that they and their Muslim friends are talking about the same being or do they think that there is a great gulf fixed between the two views of God? Much of the missiological discussion about "God" depends on where the missiologist is starting from – his or her theological viewpoint.

At one end of the missiological spectrum, pluralists think that behind the Arabic term *Allâh* and the Hebrew term Yahweh or the Christian concept of "Trinity" exists the same essential, divine being. In this view, all monotheists (and others) refer to the same God but relate to him out of their discrete religious traditions. Cantwell Smith, a distinguished scholar of Islam, argues for this view. His strong conviction is that God has revealed himself via Qur'ân to Muslims, via Yahweh to Jews and via Trinity to Christians. All of us, hence, need one another's revelatory input in order to attain the fullest possible understanding of God:

> It is an impoverishment of life, but an impoverishment also of theology, not to take seriously God's mission to us all through all traditions, all his servants everywhere. In a way, this constitutes the central point of my presentation here: that it is not only intellectually, and morally, wrong, to fail to recognize God's mission to other people through their traditions; and nowadays, through those traditions and those other people, to us. More than simply wrong, theologically one may say that it is blasphemous.[104]

My concern about pluralists like Cantwell Smith is that they do not take seriously enough the Bible's own claim, or the Qur'ân's for that matter, about the universality of the revelation it is conveying. It is certainly true that Islam and Christianity are both monotheistic faiths and that they are consequently related in many conceptual ideas, but each faith is also missionary, exclusive in its truth-claims. Nor does Cantwell Smith listen to those from a Muslim background who have come to faith in Christ. Such believers often describe their previous interacting with the God of Islam as constituting something completely different from their relating to the God of their new-found Christian faith. Many such brothers and sisters have been martyred as a result of their declarations of trust in Jesus Christ. This suggests that not only they but their persecutors also have been convinced that there is an irreconcilable difference between the "Gods" of the two faiths.

At the other end of the spectrum, some exclusivist missiologists think that behind the Arabic term *Allâh* lies Satan. Gerhard Nehls and Walter Eric conclude that the worship of the idol Hubal that went on at the *kaᶜba* was transferred (via Muḥammad's apostleship) to *Allâh*. They quote a long section of Ibn Isḥaq's *The Life of Muḥammad* (the oldest biography of the Prophet) concerning an incident in the life of Muḥammad's grandfather, Abdu'l-Muṭṭalib, when that gentleman nearly sacrificed his son – Muḥammad's father – to a god at the *kaᶜba*. Their line of reasoning is that Hubal was the focal idol for worship at the *kaᶜba* in Mecca. Hubal – suspiciously close, they notice, to *ha-baal* or "the Baal" in Hebrew – was allegedly brought by ᶜAmr ibn Luhayy from Moab to Arabia.[105] Hubal came to be referred to as "the Lord of this city" – that is Mecca – and, it is argued, was also called *Allâh*. I can find no evidence for this last claim; indeed in the passage from Ibn Isḥaq concerning Muḥammad's grandfather, it specifically says that "Abdu'l Muṭṭalib stood by Hubal praying to Allah".[106] The clearest import of this sentence must be that Hubal and *Allâh* are different, not the same. Although Nehls and Eric stop short of concluding that *Allâh* is Hubal, they nevertheless speculate on the "spiritual implications" of what happens when Muslims bow in worship towards the *kaᶜba* and submit to *Allâh*:

> If ... we look at Hubal and his role, one may well suspect that anyone bowing down to him to submit to him, could come under his influence, even if the worshipper has a totally different perception in his mind. The Ka'ba was, and I believe, could still operate as the house of Hubal. And even if this is unknown to Muslims, they may well submit to his influence and by that become resistant and blinded to the Gospel.[107]

This is like saying that Anglicans in England who today worship in places previously dedicated to pagan gods at the confluence of ley-lines are actually (unknown to themselves) submitting to the influence of the demons that used to hide behind those gods. Other missiologists at the "exclusive" end of the spectrum pursue a strongly polemical argument with Muslims about the origins of, and the content to be found in, the qur'ânic conception of *Allâh*. Samuel Zwemer, for example, accepted that in confessing there is only one deity Muslims confessed correctly, but their conception of that one God was in error:

> very much depends on the character of the God, who is affirmed to displace all other gods. If *Allah's* attributes are unworthy of deity then even the first clause of the briefest of all creeds, is false.[108]

Some 40 years later, however, Zwemer wrote in a very different vein. He cited the example of Ṣûfî saints as people of genuine religious experience, coming down on the "continuity" side of the debate as far as Muslims becoming Christians is concerned:

> No Jew since Paul's day, any more than Paul himself, was ever conscious of a change of "gods" when he accepted Christ as Saviour and Lord. The same is true of every Moslem convert today. Five times a day he prayed to Allah for guidance and then the miracle of grace took place. He bows to Allah as revealed in all his fullness of holiness and redemptive love in Jesus Christ.[109]

Georges Houssney, in his missiological article "What is Allah like?", represents a softer exclusivist approach. He adamantly concludes that "the concept of God in Islam is in clear opposition to the Christian concept of God".[110] He does not, however, blame that opposing Islamic conception specifically on Satan. What is more, he suggests that his exposure of its distance from the biblical view is for the Christian worker's own benefit rather than as fuel for some polemical attack on Islam: "Christians need to know the truth about what Muslims believe in order to share with them the truth of who God is, but they must always do it with love and gentleness."[111] Phil Parshall suggests that "Islam presents an inadequate and incomplete – but not totally misguided – view of God."[112] Parshall's view is informed by the experience of Christians from a Muslim background who have contended for some sense of continuity in their relationship with God before and after their conversion. Steve Bell, softer still, takes a slightly different tack, suggesting that it is "more helpful to see Allah as the God of the Bible, with the proviso that the Muslim understanding of Him is faulty".[113]

Between the strongly held extremes of insistent pluralism and convinced exclusivism lies a range of positions taken by missiologists concerning the identity of "God" in Islam and Judaism/Christianity. Cragg, for example, recognizes that descriptions of God vary between the two faiths but holds that the subject of the different perceptions is the one God:

> Since both Christian and Muslim faiths believe in One supreme sovereign Creator-God, they are obviously referring when they speak of Him, under whatever terms, to the same Being. To suppose otherwise would be confusing. It is important to keep in mind that though the apprehensions differ, their theme is the same.[114]

The perspectives of those who have come to know Christ from a Muslim background illustrate this range of positions. Such believers' experience of conversion and their reflection on such experience demonstrate the delicate dynamics of "continuity" and "discontinuity" (see Figure 37). Is there truth and accuracy in a Muslim's understanding and experience of God prior to

Figure 37
Continuity and discontinuity

Muslim

⇩

Believer in Christ

⇩

Continuity ⇦ ⇨ **Discontinuity**

Continuity	Discontinuity
Some aspects of previous belief acceptable: • who *Allâh* is • Qur'ân as containing truth	Some aspects of previous belief unacceptable: • who *Allâh* is • Qur'ân as false
Some aspects of previous lifestyle acceptable: • dreams as a way of discerning God's will • honouring of elders	Some aspects of previous lifestyle unacceptable: • magic, curses • shrine visitation

conversion? A new disciple who perceives a lot of continuity with his previous way of life in his new-found faith in Christ believes that there is. The question for such a person becomes: how much of that previous understanding and experience is to be brought into his life as a Christian believer, how much needs developing or transforming, how much needs dropping? A new disciple who mostly senses discontinuity between the different phases of his life will likely conclude that there is little or no proper relating to God for a person who grows up a Muslim. The question for this kind of person becomes: how much delivering does he need in order to be freed from his previous "relationship" with "God"? On the continuity side of the equation, there are those who feel that in Christ they have come to know fully the God they had formerly striven to submit to, the Qur'ân being an aid along the way.[115] On the discontinuity side of the balance, there are those from a Muslim background who say that their former faith is essentially false, that its God is the devil and that the Qur'ân is a deception.[116]

Missiologists are concerned with mission and their views on the continuity/discontinuity debate with regard to qur'ânic and biblical concepts of God reflect the theological commitments from which they start. Believers in Christ from a Muslim background line up differently from one another on this sensitive issue, according to their personal experiences of "God".

In the book of Acts, there are recorded two major speeches in which Paul addresses pagan audiences – the speech at Lystra, where the people were illiterate as well as pagan; and that at Athens where the listeners were literate in the extreme. Of course, from the perspective of the audience in both cases, *they* (with their trust in the Graeco-Roman gods) were the "believers" and the apostles were the "atheists"!

In the speech to the Lystrans (Acts 14:8–20), Paul speaks of the living God as creator God – as someone they knew about because he had gotten on their wavelength in terms of rain from heaven, crops on earth, food in their stomachs and joy in their hearts. In the context of a miraculous healing performed, presumably, in the name of Jesus Christ, the audience is told that the agents of the healing (Barnabas and Paul) are not gods, not part of their pantheon. Indeed, that whole way of thinking and worshipping is declared "worthless" (verse 15). Rather than looking to mythology and handed-down traditions (about previous divine visitations to the area of their town), the Lystrans should take notice of the providential facts of their everyday living and thank the God who thus sustains them. Paul appeals to a sense of the divine that stands outside the religious tradition of his listeners. Discontinuity is emphasized in this Lystran appeal.

In the speech to the "very religious" members of the famous Areopagus council (Acts 17:22–31), Paul does the opposite. Here, the Apostle makes clear that, in his view, "the intended referent of the Greeks, as they groped after him, was the true God".[117] He declares: "what you worship … I am going to proclaim to you" (verse 23). Paul uses the same word – *theos* – for both the "unknown God" and the "God" who raised Jesus from the dead. Paul does not deny that they "worship", nor does he detract from the "what" that they worship. It is simply that that "what" is "something unknown". Nor does Paul hesitate to quote philosophical hymns dedicated to Zeus and affirm that the messages those hymns convey of who God is are accurate and true: "'for in him we live and move and have our being'" and, yes, "'we are his offspring'". Thank you Epimenides and Aratus! The important issue in the Athens case is that God was still "unknown" to his hearers. God – the god after whom in a variety of ways the Athenians groped and about whom they knew a few things – is *known* only in Christ. A sense of continuity underlines Paul's approach to the Athenians.

Is there not justification in these two passages from Acts for each approach to the question of whether Muslim *Allâh* is to be identified with biblical God? Acts 14 warrants a "discontinuity approach", Acts 17 a "continuity approach". In the Islamic context, discontinuity and continuity of relationship may each constitute an appropriate response in differing situations. On the one hand, the Muslim conception of who *Allâh* is may be so far from the truth in Christ that it is better to leave behind all the trappings of that former submission as "worthless": forget *Allâh*! On the other hand, the Muslim conception of who *Allâh* is may approximate in many ways to the truth in Christ so that Muslims who become believers in Christ may be seen as getting to know in Christ the one whom they had previously sought after from a distance. My own inclination is to suggest that "forgetting *Allâh*" is for most circumstances not a reasonable option. A "continuity approach" seems to offer fewer cultural and psychological, as well as religious, hurdles for someone considering such a change of allegiance. Our role as Christians, it seems to me, needs to be one of accepting to use the term *Allâh* and seeking to fill that term with biblical meaning.

Either way, the insistence of scripture is on the "getting to know", on the process of becoming better acquainted with God. Jesus' problem with those contemporaries of his who had access to all the proper propositions (the Pharisees) about God was that they refused to "know him or his Father" (John 8:19). Paul suggests, in writing to the Romans (1:18–23), that having a sense of God without acknowledging him as he is – that is, "knowing him" – results in idolatry. So, in a sense, whether or not we say *Allâh* is not the issue. The issue is about knowing *Allâh* through Christ. Beyond the various propositions is the person of Christ as image or *ikon* of the creator: "*he* has made him known" (John 1:18).

In a Middle Eastern village situation, if you ask a member of the older generation the way to so-and-so's house, he responds: "I am the way" and gets up and takes you to your destination. When Jesus says, "I am the truth", he is not pointing in some direction, to some doctrines (important though they may be) and saying: "Hold them as true and you have the truth." He is saying: "Walk with me. Let me be the lodestar by which you evaluate whether verses in the Qur'ân or music by Bach or poems by Schiller or proclamations by televangelists help you to know me better or not. In me lives truth."

From within a different context, Vincent O'Donovan represents a (Roman Catholic) traditional missiologist who was led by the Holy Spirit and his Masai friends to revise his view of mission and the theological construct that lay behind it. He had assumed that he was bringing "the truth" – "the gospel" – to unbelievers in Africa. Gradually he discovered that God (the God indeed of the Bible) had been among the Masai a long time before he had arrived – revealing himself in a variety of strong, enculturated ways:

> The lion is God. Of course. Goodness and kindness and holiness and grace and divine presence and creating power and salvation were here before I got here. Even the fuller understanding of God's revelation to man, of the gospel, of the salvific act that had been accomplished once and for all for the human race was here before I got here. My role as a herald of that gospel, as a messenger of the news of what had already happened in the world, as the person whose task it was to point to "the one who had stood in their midst whom they did not recognise" was only a small part of the mission of God to the world. It was a mysterious part, a part barely understood. It was a necessary part, a demanded part – "woe to me if I do not preach the gospel." It was a role that would require every talent and insight and skill and gift and strength I had, to be spent without question, without stint, and yet in the humbling knowledge that only that part of it would be made use

> of which fit into the immeasurably greater plan of the relentless, pursuing God whose will on the world not be thwarted. The lion is God.[118]

The primary question for us as we end this chapter is not so much one of others – those Muslims, that Qur'ân – as one of ourselves. We began this chapter by asking, "Is the God of the Qur'ân the same as the God of the Bible?" We have looked at the term *Allâh*, at language about God, at theological comparisons and at missiological intent. We close this chapter with a different question, asked from "within" as it were – within a framework that presupposes that God has been making overtures towards Muslims long before we arrived on the scene: "Where has God already been – in the Qur'ân, among the Muslims – long before we turned up?" Do we have humble eyes, like O'Donovan, to gradually discern those traces of the divine or does our prejudged answer to the question of qur'ânic "God" and biblical "God" blind us to any Spirit-given insight?

Interlude

If you were God, how would you convince Muslims that – all along – they had a special place in your divine heart?

The Essential Ingredient

Lady Macbeth evidently knew that if it is the best ointment or perfume that you are after, Arabia is the place to go for it. In her famous "Out, damned spot!" speech, she goes on to declare:

> Here's the smell of blood still;
> all the perfumes of Arabia will not sweeten this little hand.
> (*Macbeth*, Act 5, scene 1)

Murder proved too strong a stench for even the pungent aroma of Arabia's purest spices to dispel.

Myrrh is a pale yellow gum that derives from a shrub growing in Arabia, Somalia and Ethiopia. From the hardened drops of the fragrant resin found in the bark of the myrrh bush, a powder, called stacte, is produced. Onycha is another powder produced in the same part of the Middle East from the horny shell of a clam-like mollusc found in the Red Sea. When burnt, this powder emits a penetrating aroma. Galbanum is a brownish, pungent resin that exudes from the lower part of the stem of a ferula (giant fennel) plant. It is found around the Mediterranean Sea. It has a musky, pungent smell and acts as a binding agent, preserving the scent of a perfume mixed from different spices. Frankincense is a resin obtained from the *Boswellia* tree. Native to India, this tree is also widespread in the Middle East and North Africa. Frankincense is still today one of the most highly valued incense gums in the area with a beautiful fragrance of balsam (Figure 38). When the people of Israel came to worship in the tabernacle, they were required to use such resins and spices as part of their worship:

Then the Lord said to Moses, “Take fragrant spices – gum resin [stacte], onycha and galbanum – and pure frankincense, all in equal amounts, and make a fragrant blend of incense, the work of a perfumer.” (Exodus 30:34–35)

Figure 38
Frankincense and myrrh

Such unguents were not obtainable in Israel. They had to be procured from the people of the east – from non-Jews, from Ishmael’s children. For King Solomon’s temple, cedar, pine and algum logs were required from Lebanon. Most of the skilled labour needed to work the gold, silver, bronze, iron, stone, wood, yarn and fine linen that would go into the splendid structure was overseen by Huram-Abi (mother from Dan and father from Tyre) who was assigned to Solomon’s project by Hiram, king of Tyre. The famous Queen of Sheba provided spices for worship in the temple. We are informed that "there had never been such spices as those the queen of Sheba gave to King Solomon" (2 Chronicles 9:9)! Still later, at Jesus' birth, magi from the east conveyed gifts of gold, frankincense and myrrh to offer in worship to the son of Mary (Matthew 2:11).

In other words, cooperation with the people of the east was consistently required in order for Israelite worship to be truly pleasing to Yahweh. At the time of both tabernacle and temple, the cloud of incense would not rise before the Holy One of Israel without the inclusion of blended spice grown and processed by eastern hands. When the Holy One came himself to earth in incarnation, one of the few infant reminiscences recorded in the Gospels tells the inclusion again of gifts from the east. Those presents spoke louder than words about divinity, glory, suffering and death. Worshippers from the east predict the Gospel story with their own – oh so significant – offering for the worship of the Christ-child.

Uncomfortable Cousins?

Chapter 5 "Befores" and "Afters"

Jewish and Gentile ways of being "Christian"

When Christianity first emerged in the wake of Jesus' resurrection and the outpouring of the Holy Spirit on the day of Pentecost, it looked like a very Jewish affair. Its initial protagonists were Jews who had never thought of themselves as other than Jews. On the day of Pentecost, Peter addressed the tantalized crowd as "Fellow-Jews" (Acts 2:14) and "Brothers" (Acts 2:29). Those members of his audience whose hearts were impressed, appealed for help to Peter and the other apostles as fellow-Jews: "Brothers, what shall we do?" (Acts 2:37). At the end of many years of mission, church-planting and evangelism, the Apostle Paul still defined himself as a Jew (Acts 21:39) and offered his testimony to "Brothers and fathers" in Jerusalem (Acts 22:1), reiterating to them that "I am a Jew" (Acts 22:3). Early believers in Christ still gathered in the temple courts within Jerusalem, still kept the food laws of Judaism, still worshipped on the Sabbath. Many former priests swelled their number, and faith in Christ was seen to represent the fulfilment of the Jewish longing for Messiah. Explanations of the gospel were offered in strongly Jewish terms with extensive reference to Old Testament texts. Stephen, on trial in front of the high priest, began his impassioned exposition of scripture with Abraham, forefather of the Jewish people. He reached as far as Solomon before his slant on Jewish history enraged his hearers. Saul went looking in the Jewish synagogues of Damascus for followers of Jesus (Acts 9:2), and ironically ended up preaching that Jesus was the Son of God in those same synagogues (Acts

9:20). The point is that the early believers in Christ were to be found in the synagogues. They were Jews, after all.

It would take a major revision in the attitude of several of the leading apostles before they could even admit that God might welcome Gentiles also into the salvation that Jesus brings. Peter, slow though he proved to be, was still quicker at grasping this than most of his contemporaries (see Figure 39). The rumour preceded him from Caesarea to Jerusalem that he had gone into a Gentile home there. Inside the house, moreover, he had dared to eat with uncircumcised people. This disturbing development was what really concerned the apostles and brothers throughout Judaea when they heard that the Gentiles "had received the word of the Lord" (Acts 11:1–3). Where would such abandoning of Jewish purity laws lead?

Figure 39
Continuity and discontinuity between Judaism and Christianity

Messenger		Gospel thought-form		Audience		Church character
❒ Jews of dispersion (Acts 11:19)	+	❒ Jewish	+	❒ Jews only	=	❒ Jewish
❒ Jews from Cyprus and Cyrene (Acts 11:20)	+	❒ Jewish	+	✦ Greeks also in Antioch	=	❒✦ Jewish/Gentile
❒ Saul/Paul and Barnabas (Acts 13, 14)	+	✦ Greek	+	✦ Gentiles mostly	=	❒✦ Gentile/Jewish
❒ Paul (Acts 15:12 onwards)	+	✦ Greek	+	✦ Gentile	=	✦ Gentile

Key: ❒ *Jewish* ✦ *Greek*

The Jewish believers who dispersed from Jerusalem because of persecution arising out of the Stephen incident, ended up travelling as far as Phoenicia, Cyprus and Antioch. They told their message, however, "only to Jews" (Acts 11:19). They were Jews on the run, sharing the gospel with their own people. Some of them, however – Jewish followers of Jesus hailing from Cyprus and Cyrene – reached the cosmopolitan city of Antioch. There they began to tell the good news about the Lord Jesus to Greeks as well as to Jews (Acts 11:20). They found themselves, good Jews, speaking about a Jewish Messiah to a Gentile audience. And God spoke through them! Gentiles as well as Jews were converted. The believing community in Antioch took on a mixed ethnic form – Jews and Gentiles.

The mother group with the apostles in Jerusalem eventually heard about this radical development in Antioch, and Barnabas (of Cypriot origin) was sent north to investigate. Having assessed the situation in Antioch, Barnabas acted quickly. He thought he knew just the man for the job at hand and fetched Saul from Tarsus to oversee the burgeoning new church in Antioch. Antioch soon became the mature and secure base from which Saul and his companions set off on missionary journeys – journeys to the Gentiles around the northern Mediterranean coast. On these expeditions Saul used the Roman version of his name – Paul – and adapted his presentation of the good news of Jesus according to whether his audience was Jewish or Gentile.

After the end of the first missionary journey, Paul and Barnabas returned to base camp in Antioch. Once home, they soon became embroiled in a controversy provoked by visiting Jewish believers from Judaea who insisted that the new Gentile believers in Antioch should be properly circumcised in order to be saved. Paul and Barnabas were subsequently deputed to represent the Christians of Antioch at a council in Jerusalem. The critical issue before that council was whether the newly believing Gentiles needed to become Jewish proselytes in order to be proper disciples of the Jewish Messiah, Jesus Christ. Gradually at Jerusalem this delicate matter was thrashed out, with input from Paul, Barnabas, Peter and James. The council's decision was that Gentiles could become genuine followers of Jesus Christ without having to become Jewish proselytes en route. It would take many years for this important concession to be thoroughly welcomed and worked through by the Jewish Christians. The Holy Spirit had, however, charted a vital way forward in terms of how the gospel might be preached. Jewish apostles and evangelists discovered that God gladly authorized the proclamation of his salvific acts in Gentile thought-forms to Gentile audiences resulting in Gentile churches. The infiltration of Gentile society had begun.

Parting of the ways

With the rapid growth of Gentile Christian churches and with the destruction of Jerusalem in AD 70 plus the eclipsing of the Jewish faith in the Roman imperial world, Christianity came to take on an increasingly Gentile feel. If Matthew had put together his text about Jesus Christ for a Jewish readership, John constructed his account in order to communicate with people of a Greek mind-set. The Apostle Paul crafted his message for Gentile audiences very differently from the manner in which he spoke to Jews. With the Gentiles he emphasized the role of God in creation and judgement. He sometimes quoted from his Gentile audience's own philosophical tradition. One can discern from the epistles of the New Testament that the Gentile-dominated churches increasingly adopted Graeco-Roman authority structures for their own self-ordering. The authority of a bishop came soon to mirror the paterfamilias focus of authority in Roman society. Christians no longer worshipped at temple or synagogue but in their own, distinctive places of meeting. Nor did they meet on the Sabbath but on Sunday, the day of resurrection. Christians were not required to be circumcised, but underwent baptism into Christ. Greek, rather than Aramaic, became the language of Christian faith-expression, and apologists like Justin Martyr strove to reclaim the Greek philosophical world for Christ. Gradually, the Gentile Christians came to look on those Jewish Christians who attempted to remain within Judaism as heretics. Different groups of Ebionites, as they were called, lived on into the second half of the fourth century. Some were discovered by Pantenus in "India" – most probably indicating South Arabia.[119]

The Christian movement remained largely underground for many decades out of necessity. It was seen by the authorities as a threat to stability – at first as a sub-theme of Judaism, then distinctively as a separate Christian faith. The Christians were, of course, dismissed as "atheists" in the view of the Romans who had their own precious gods. Eventually, the blood of the martyrs, the hellenizing of the Christian message and the unseen work of the Holy Spirit took the Christian faith to the heart of empire. When the top Roman was converted, Christianity became a political force in its own right. By the beginning of the fourth century, hardly anyone would expect a "Christian" also to be a Jew.

Continuing the tradition

A similar kind of tension surrounds the origin and early development of Islam though the shift from identification with the "parent" tradition to differentiation from it was crammed into far fewer years. Prophet Muḥammad thought of himself initially as standing firmly in the line of the People of the Book:

> The same religion has He
> Established for you as that
> Which He enjoined on Noah –
> The which We have sent
> By inspiration to thee –
> And that which We enjoined
> On Abraham, Moses, and Jesus ... (Sura 42:13)

It followed that Muḥammad understandably expected the contemporary People of the Book to respond favourably to his call to them to receive his message:

> O ye People of the Book!
> Believe in what We
> Have (now) revealed, confirming
> What was (already) with you ... (Sura 4:47)

Confirmation, not contradiction, constitutes the tenor of the early Islamic message as far as Jews and Christians are concerned. Muḥammad is himself positively instructed by God to refer to the former scriptures if he is in any sense doubtful about his own experience of inspiration. The custodians of those earlier revelations will be well placed to encourage Muḥammad about the material he is now receiving from God:

If thou wert in doubt
As to what We have revealed
Unto thee, then ask those
Who have been reading
The Book from before thee:
The Truth hath indeed come
To thee from thy Lord:
So be in no wise
Of those in doubt. (Sura 10:94)

It is strongly suggested, in these late Meccan and even Medinan suras, that the word or Book being presented through Muḥammad comes as an affirmation of previous scriptures:

That which We have revealed
To thee of the Book
Is the Truth – confirming
What was (revealed) before it ... (Sura 35:31)

The sense of progression from former scriptures to this scripture is thus, initially, one of strong continuity. Indeed, it is reasonable to conclude that Muḥammad understood the Qur'ân to be sent down in order to shame his people, the Arabs, into faith. The Arabs could now no longer offer the excuse that they did not know what God wanted because the scriptures had never appeared in their language. An Arabic Qur'ân puts paid to that evasion as the following (late Meccan) verses insist!

Lest ye should say:
"The Book was sent down
To two Peoples before us,

And for our part, we
Remained unacquainted
With all that they learned
By assiduous study;"
Or lest ye should say:
"If the Book had only
Been sent down to us,
We should have followed
Its guidance better than they." ... (Sura 6:156–157)

We have earlier noted Muḥammad's affinity with the *ḥunafâ'* and his association, for support, with Khadîja's Christian cousin Waraqa. In Mecca, there were Jews, it is claimed in the Qur'ân, who knew Muḥammad's message "as they know their own sons" (Sura 6:20). They knew it because it stood in the tradition of what was previously revealed through prophets of Jewish origin. Such learned Jews, it is further stated, accepted that the prophecy that Muḥammad brought rang true (Sura 26:197). Even in Medina, some Jews evidently accepted Muḥammad and his revelation (Sura 7:159). After Muḥammad's eventual, angry break with the People of the Book, moreover, he could still insist that Law and Gospel both predicted his coming. He refers to God's response to a prayer of Moses in which God promises to extend mercy towards:

"Those who follow the Apostle
the unlettered Prophet,
whom they find mentioned
in their own (Scriptures), –
in the Law and the Gospel ... " (Sura 7:157)

The qur'ânic Jesus, we learn, goes so far as to offer a foretelling of Muḥammad's actual name:

And remember, Jesus,
The son of Mary, said:
"O Children of Israel!
I am the apostle of God
(Sent) to you, confirming
the Law (which came)

Before me, and giving
Glad Tidings of an apostle
To come after me,
Whose name shall be Ahmad." ... (Sura 61:6)

The early Islamic revelation found expression within a mind-set that saw it as contiguous with what had previously been revealed to and through the People of the Book.

Contradicting the tradition!

A contrasting sense of discontinuity arose quite abruptly after Muḥammad had shifted with his followers to Medina. There, the majority of Jews dissociated themselves from his message and tried to resist his growth in power. In the end, two of the three Jewish tribes in Medina were expelled and the third was punished with execution and enslavement. The Qur'ân comes to express a sense of radical discontinuity between the prophet of Islam and the People of the Book:

It is a wish of a section
Of the People of the Book
To lead you astray.
But they shall lead astray
(Not you), but themselves,
and they do not perceive!
Ye People of the Book!
Why reject ye
The signs of God,
Of which ye are (Yourselves) witnesses?
Ye People of the Book!
Why do ye clothe
Truth with falsehood,
And conceal the Truth,
While ye have knowledge? (Sura 3:69–71)

As we have observed, the direction of prayer for Muslims was abruptly changed from Jerusalem to Mecca. The timing of the community fast was altered. Islam emerges in Medina as an

Arab entity with a holy book in Arabic. Although Muḥammad's earliest community of believers put religious allegiance above tribal or clan ties – a major counter-cultural act – Islam has tended ever since to retain a sense in which its Arab identity outweighs its embrace of other cultures and languages. All Muslims are required to read or listen to their sacred text in Arabic. All Muslims have to worship in Arabic. All Muslims must pray facing towards Mecca. Pilgrimage is sited on Mecca and Medina. In Medina, Prophet Muḥammad's émigré community was transformed into the engine for a wholly new society, one that would attempt to swallow up the lands of the People of the Book.

Parallel processes

In the early development of both Christianity and Islam, issues focusing on continuity and discontinuity from previous religious communities or ideals were faced with initial reluctance and later difficulty. It was assumed at first in each case that continuity was the fundamental reality underlying the current development. Discontinuity became unavoidable when it was realized that what was new could not be accommodated by the old. A different identity was sought as the new expression of each faith grew more established. Christianity became a predominantly Gentile faith, disassociated from its origins within Judaism and finding its place in a Greek-oriented world. Islam became a predominantly Arab-focused faith, disconnected from its roots in Judaism and Christianity. Successful establishment gradually meant (for Christianity) or speedily meant (for Islam) a shift from being an underground movement, working at the fringes of society to becoming a strong religio-political force in its own right. Both religions, it might be argued, changed in essential character at that point: after a long 300 years, Christianity became the culture of an empire while Islam, after a mere twelve years, became the ideology of a Medinan state.

Christian theologizing

Christianity may have become the established faith of the Roman Empire with Constantine's conversion, but how was such a faith to find meaningful expression within the world with which it now came to be so strongly identified? How was connection with the Old and New Testament scriptures to be maintained during an active engagement with the Greek philosophical world? Who was to speak for "Christianity" in, say, the matter of affirming the doctrine of the Trinity?

The formulation of a doctrine of the Trinity constitutes an attempt to draw out the implications of the biblical revelation of God as Father, Son and Holy Spirit. Such a doctrine is not formally contained in the Bible but it is strongly present by implication (see Figure 40).

Figure 40
"Trinity" in the Bible

Reference	Verse	Comment
Genesis 1:26 Deuteronomy 6:4	Then God said, "Let us make man in our image, in our likeness ... " "Hear, O Israel: The Lord our God, the Lord is one."	*'elôhîm*, plural noun God is one
1 Timothy 3:16	God ... appeared in a body	incarnation of Son
John 10:30 John 15:8–11	"I and the Father are one." "I have obeyed my Father's commands ... "	Jesus as one with, yet distinct from, Father
1 Peter 1:2	... foreknowledge of God the Father, by the sanctifying work of the Spirit, for obedience to Jesus Christ ...	naming together of Father, Son and Holy Spirit

The early Christians continued to own the Jews' uncompromising belief that "the Lord our God is one God". They also testified, however, that "Jesus Christ is Lord." They applied to

Christ the Old Testament passages referring to Yahweh, and they worshipped Christ as God.

The problem was how to *explain* that God could be both one and more than one. Jews quickly accused Christians of having two gods. Later on, pagans made the same accusation. The problem was particularly difficult to resolve because the Greek concept of unity carried a sense of perfect or literal oneness, excluding any internal distinctions.

By AD 300, as the Christian movement expanded, three major models for thinking through doctrine had developed (Figure 41). Those theologians using what might be labelled the "Greek model" felt at ease using the categories of thought of the Hellenized world to express Christian truth. Christians ema-

Figure 41
Models for theologizing AD 150–400

Greek model	"Bridge" model	Roman model
use of categories of thought of Hellenized world to express Christian truth	some appeal to Greek thought some appeal to ecclesiastical tradition	rejection of Greek philosophical categories appeal to dogma and enhanced ecclesiastical tradition
Alexandria especially	Gaul	Rome/Carthage axis especially
Justin Martyr (100–167) Clement (taught in Alexandria 190–202) Origen (186–255)	Irenaeus (130–200)	Tertullian (160–220) Cyprian (200–258) Augustine (354–430)
e.g. Justin: Plato in agreement with the truth of Christianity *e.g. Origen: truth is founded in Plato and revealed in the Scriptures*	*e.g. Irenaeus: influenced by Justin in his thinking but appeals to dogma versus the Gnostics*	*e.g. Cyprian: list of bishops of Rome. Authority of church: "he cannot have God for his Father who does not have the Church for his mother"*

nating from a Greek philosophical background maintained a continuity of thought with their traditional heritage in working out their salvation. Justin Martyr, for example, had been brought up in the Greek cultural tradition and possessed a strong background in philosophy. He felt that Christian teaching fulfilled the essential mission of philosophy, which was to explore the divine. He believed that the divine *Logos* as "seminal word" (*logos spermatikos*) was active in the Greek philosophers: you could (vaguely but essentially) hear the voice of God speaking through them. He wrote his famous *Apology* in about AD 150. His aim in this work was to explain Christian faith to the Greek mind.

The two major theologians utilizing the "Greek model" for explaining Christianity were Clement and Origen. Clement taught in Alexandria during the years AD 190–202. He was heavily influenced by Philo, a Jewish philosopher who in effect amalgamated Jewish monotheism and Greek philosophy. Origen (AD 186–255) became head of the catechetical school in Alexandria. He was trained in Greek philosophy but also knew Hebrew. He used his background in Greek philosophy to present Christian truth in a way that Gnostics could easily accept. In Alexandria, the categories of thought of the Hellenized world were unashamedly used to express Christian truth.

Not everyone, however, thought so highly of Greek philosophy. A "Roman model" was preferred by those who rejected Greek philosophical categories and instead appealed to dogma and ecclesiastical tradition. Tertullian (AD 160–220) was a lawyer from Carthage who converted to Christianity. He wrote in Latin and in fact the word "Trinity" originates with him – his famous phrase was *trinitas: una substantia, tres personae*; "Trinity: one substance, three persons"! For Tertullian, there was nothing in common between pagan (Greek) thought and Christian thought. While Gnostics relied on secret traditions, Tertullian concretized the handing down of faith in rigid customs maintained and passed on by bishops. Over the first three centuries, bishops had gradually assumed responsibility for specific geographic areas, or dioceses – a pattern of institutionalisation modelled on the organization of the Roman army. Cyprian (died

AD 258) and Augustine (AD 354–430) followed in Tertullian's mould. The Carthage/Rome axis espoused strong discontinuity from the Greek world of the time. Their maxim was in effect: "Don't try to think the Christian faith through in those pagan, Greek categories; just declare it in our Roman, churchy ones."

A third model for doing theology can also be discerned in these early years. It was a sort of "bridge model" in which there was some appeal to Greek philosophy and some appeal to Roman ecclesiastical tradition. This model emerged especially in Gaul with Irenaeus as its chief proponent. Irenaeus (AD 130–200) came from Asia Minor (possibly Smyrna) and ended up as Bishop of Lyons. In his major work *Against Heresies*, Irenaeus used mental images taken from Greek philosophy but appealed to scripture and tradition to show how those images should be understood. At the same time, Irenaeus stressed the importance of bishops as teachers maintaining a continuity of the rule of faith.

By the fourth century, then, there were very different models amongst Christians for thinking through doctrine. Those models produced contrasting starting-points for assessing, for example, the Christian conviction about God as Trinity. The Rome/Carthage axis theologians (Tertullian, Cyprian, Augustine) adopted a monist starting-point.[120] The unity of the Godhead was the touchstone of their orthodoxy. The overriding interest of the Roman-minded theologians was to discern from scripture the identity of Father and Son in revelation and redemption. The Alexandrian theologians (Clement, Origen) adopted a pluralist starting-point, based upon a Platonic interpretation of Christianity. For them, the *Logos* as distinct from the Father is important; later the Spirit as distinct from Father and Son would be seen as important. The overriding interest of the Greek-minded theologians was to reconcile Christianity with Hellenism (see Figure 42).

At both edges of the axis, there developed tendencies towards extremes. Thus, for example, at the monist edge a perspective dubbed "monarchianism" or "modalism" or "Sabellianism" took "unity" too far. This perspective emerged in Asia Minor and was transported by Praxeas, Sabellius and others to the

Figure 42
Wrestling with "the Trinity"

Extremes in forms of MONISM	**Western orthodoxy**	**Eastern orthodoxy**	**Extremes in forms of TRITHEISM**
Monarchianism (Sabellianism) God existed in different modes at different times	unity of the Godhead emphasized *Tertullian/ Augustine*	uniqueness of the persons of the Godhead emphasized *Justin/Origen*	**Subordinationism** reduced status of the Son as compared with the Father *e.g. Arius*
Economic trinitarianism dispensations for the purposes of creation and redemption	Father and Son identified in revelation and redemption *una substantia, tres personae*	co-presence of two (later three) distinct entities within the Godhead Father and Son are two in *hypostasis*, one in harmony and identity of will	**Binitarianism** absorbed the functions of the Spirit in the Son

west, where it flourished. Its holders claimed that the one God existed in different modes, but in only one mode at any one time. God's different names – Father, Son, Holy Spirit – described the different modes or roles he played at different times. At the other extreme, on the tritheist edge, a perspective known as "subordinationism" took "uniqueness" too far. Arius (in the fourth century), for example, said that the Son was essentially different from the Father in the sense that the Father was ingenerate while the Son was generate. So the Son was not fully God. Arius even argued that there was a time when the Son was not.

Theologians wrestled with such complex issues from their different linguistic backgrounds and philosophical constructs. They found it difficult to hear one another, let alone think what kind of a legacy they might be leaving for non-Christians to have to come to terms with. Of course, it was the controversies arising from differently conceived theological statements or from overcorrections to on-the-edge views that would later provide Muḥammad with his misunderstandings of what Christians believed about the Trinity or the nature of the Son![121]

Islamic theologizing

Islam, as we have already noted, has also known its different theological emphases and arguments. We will leave to the following chapter a consideration of the major split between Sunnî and Shî^ca expressions of Islamic faithfulness. Here, we need to recognize the existence of a historic tension in Islam – that between ethical ideals and legal rules. This tension emerged strongly within 200 years of the death of Prophet Muḥammad, at a time when the formalized, politically supported expression of the faith appeared to be losing its integrity.

In principle, a good Muslim is a person who seeks to fulfil God's will in terms of obeying specific commands and following the example of Prophet Muḥammad. Schools of jurisprudence came gradually to be established in which such specific commands were elucidated and the Prophet's example made concrete. From the Qur'ân, then the *ḥadîth*, then expert opinion and consensus, the law in Islam grew to assume a huge size and importance. In a way, it came to be considered an extension of "scripture", for *sharî^ca* law interprets how scripture is to be applied and obeyed. It is the law's strong connection with the Qur'ân that gives it such powerful sanction. By the middle of the tenth century, four significant schools of jurisprudence had developed though there also existed many independent scholars with smaller personal schools. By AD 1300, only the four major schools of Ḥanîfa, Shâfi^cî, Mâlik and Ḥanbal remained as influential. Their interpretations continue to provide the authorized source of jurisprudence for Muslims today. The principle of *ijtihâd*, or independent reasoning, however, was also accepted as valid by the Ḥanbalis and some of the Shâfi^cî theologians. Such validation has meant that qualified legal scholars have been continuously encouraged to apply independent judgement in addressing new legal questions. The law, as a result, has continued to evolve and grow. Even with such continuance and growth, however, the law is not always precise nor does it necessarily cover every contingency. Some actions, it determines, are required, others recommended; some are forbidden, others discouraged. In some instances the law remains neutral. In many cases, the law does not provide sanctions and so its application is left up to personal conscience. Local custom may or may not accommodate various requirements of the law. Ira Lapidus summarizes the prolific but limiting nature of law as the sole regulator of proper Islamic living:

> The law took the form of a vast reservoir of case materials and precedents which could be used as the basis of judicial decisions but no longer offered a rigid cadre of rules for the regulation of social, familial, and commercial matters. The numerous jurists combined with the discretion of judges in the application of the law gave Islamic law almost boundless flexibility in practice.[122]

What is more, although the authority of law might be conceived as absolute, it was often not strictly adhered to in practice, even by supposed upholders of the Islamic faith. Umayyad Islam in Damascus, especially, presented the image of a very compromised "Islam". The Umayyads take their name from Muᶜâwiya, son of Abû Sufyân, one of the leading Companions of Prophet Muḥammad. Muᶜâwiya became caliph in AD 661. In the compromised environment of the Umayyad caliphate, an alternative approach to "obeying God" gradually took root and spread widely. Sufism, a mystical genre of Islam, sought to get around the uncertainties inherent in the development of *sharîᶜa* by seeking the spiritual growth of the soul in anticipation of a direct experience of God's reality. Focus was deliberately placed on developing a visionary, ecstatic knowledge of God himself rather than on elaborating a practical obedience to his commands. Sufism tended, as a result, to devalue worldly things rather than emphasize their importance as part of humankind's trust under God. Perhaps the earliest Ṣûfîs were inspired by the

Christian asceticism flourishing in contemporary Syrian and Nestorian churches. It is from the wearing of wool (*ṣûf*), rather than the silks and satins of decadent Muslim rulers, that Sufism derives its name. Early pioneers, such as Ḥasan al-Basrî, Râbiᶜa of Baghdad, and al-Muhâsibî – in the eighth and ninth centuries – engaged in rigorous self-discipline as training for the soul.

Ṣûfîs lived within both Sunnî and Shîᶜa expressions of Islam as proponents of a unique kind of philosophy or "spirituality". Their vision of what true religion might mean derives from an appreciation of Prophet Muḥammad himself as an ascetic, a mystic, a contemplator. Was not that how the Qur'ân first came to be revealed? In a state of trance or ecstasy, the mountain-top meditator had been squeezed into reciting God's word, had he not? Resembling Muḥammad in this sense, then, is at least reasonable if not actually required. Sufism allowed a view of the world that held out as valid the possibility of human religious ascent towards union with God. Saints well on their way to such lofty heights displayed miraculous powers and were viewed as mediators with God on behalf of ordinary believers.

While the law brought Muslims to submission by rules and regulations, the Ṣûfî vision was of an obedience achieved out of love for God. *Sharîᶜa* is designed to bring conformity of behaviour to theologically discerned legal requirements. Sufism aims at the purification of the heart for the love of God. In both approaches to inducing true *islâm*, there developed extremist views (see Figure 43).

In the world of law, Aḥmad ibn Taymiya (AD 1263–1328) was a forceful proponent of making the ulema – theologian-jurists like himself – the interpreters and measurers of Muslim submission to God. Ibn Taymiya was born in Harran, Mesopotamia but fled from there to Damascus to avoid the Mongol invaders. He emerged as a renowned Ḥanbali scholar of the Qur'ân and the *ḥadîth*, and first came to fame in AD 1293 when he orchestrated a campaign to punish with death a Christian who was accused of insulting Prophet Muḥammad. In his view, the caliphs were to be simply executors of the will of God as elucidated by the ulema. He wrote a major treatise outlining why it was legitimate for the Muslim Mamluks to attack the Muslim

Figure 43
Contrasting models of theologizing in Islam AD 800–1300

Islamist model	"Combination" model	Ṣûfî model
literalist interpretation of *sharîʿa*; scholasticism	Ṣûfî experience plus *sharîʿa* discipline	esoteric view of meaning of verses of Qur'ân; quest for ecstatic union with God
Ibn Ḥanbal (780–855)	Al-Ghazâlî (1058–1111)	Al-Bistami (d. 873) Al-Ḥallâj (d. 922) Al-Junayd (d. 911)
Ibn Taymiya (1263–1328)		Ibn al-ʿArabi (1165–1240) Jalal al-Din Rumi (1207–1273)
e.g. ibn Taymiya: *It is for this reason that Imâm Ahmad b. Hanbal and other religious leaders used to motivate the instruction to dye the beard by (the general reasoning for) differing. Ibn Hanbal said: "I heard Abû ʿAbdullâh say, 'I wish everybody to change his gray hair and not to be like the Scripturaries, in view of the Prophet's words:* Change gray hair and do not become like the People of the Book!' "	*e.g. al-Ghazâlî:* His *Niche for Lights* (*Mishkat al-Anwar*) is both a commentary on the famous "light verse" of the Qur'ân and a rendering of its allegorical or esoteric meaning. God is the Light of the heavens and the earth. The parable of His Light is as if there were a Niche and within it a Lamp: the Lamp enclosed in glass: the glass as it were a brilliant star: Lit from a blessed Tree, an Olive, neither of the East nor of the West, whose Oil is well-nigh luminous, though fire scarce touched it: Light upon Light! God doth guide whom He will to His Light. (Sura 24:35) For al-Ghazâlî, the "lamp" has to be experienced as well as known about.	*e.g. Rumi:* *One went to the door of the Beloved and knocked.* *A voice asked, "Who is there?"* *He answered, "It is I."* *The voice said, "There is no room for Me and Thee."* *The door was shut.* *After a year of solitude and deprivation he returned and knocked.* *A voice from within asked, "Who is there?"* *The man said, "It is Thee."* *The door was opened for him.*

Mongols. He also exposed many of the excesses of popular religion that tended to live alongside Sufism in a famous tract entitled *The Necessity of the Straight Path against the People of Hell.* Ibn Taymiya is the theologian, above all others, to whom appeal is made in the writings of recent Islamists such as Sayyid Qutb and ᶜAbd al-Salâm Faraj. Ibn Taymiya's treatment of the theme of *jihâd* and his justification for waging war on fellow Muslims are seen as critical arguments for contemporary Islamist insistence on the use of armed struggle as part of faithful obedience. The interpretations of Ibn Taymiya and current Islamists provide examples of the radical application of law to living and fighting. I have described something of the variety and consistency of the Islamist mind-set, especially as it found expression in the twentieth century, in *Holy War: Why do Some Muslims become Fundamentalists*?[123] The Islamists comprise extremists at the literalist end of the spectrum of interpreting how Islam should find expression.

In the Ṣûfî world also, extremists made their appearance. Al-Ḥusayn ibn Mansûr al-Ḥallâj, executed at Baghdad in AD 922, constitutes one of the better known such radicals. Al-Hallâj lived as a preacher-mystic in Khurasan and Afghanistan. He perceived the world of being as comprising a dichotomy between humanity (*nâsût*) and divinity (*lâhût*). His goal as a Ṣûfî was to experience a unification of these two realms through "passing away" or annihilation (*fana'*). The divine and the human were to be brought together through an esoteric reading of the Qur'ân, discovering its hidden meaning. This kind of thinking was, of course, diametrically opposed to the traditional concept of *tawḥîd* or divine unity, in which the divine and human realms are posited as essentially different. It was also far from the received idea of "submission". Al-Ḥallâj expressed his vision in poetic words:

> Praise be to Him who revealed the mystery of His resplendent divinity (*lâhût*) in His humanity (*nâsût*); to appear subsequently in the form of one hidden and one apparent: in the form of man who eats and drinks.[124]

Praise leads to prayer to become like "Him". Surrender involves not just man's will but his very self:

> My ego (I-ness) keeps coming between me and You; by thy self! Eliminate this I-ness from in between us.[125]

Al-Ḥallâj's experience of the elimination of "I-ness" and his consequent sense of unity with God led him to proclaim "I am the Truth." He was assured that he had accomplished his "repentance" and had returned to God. He also reputedly performed miracles and claimed an authority greater than that of the ulema and the caliphs because his was, he said, the authority of the divine presence. All this amounted to a step too far. He was prosecuted for heresy and eventually executed. The "speculative Sufism" of later centuries categorized Ṣûfî "saints" according to the prophet whose model of spirituality they followed. Al-Ḥallâj was viewed as the most famous of the "Christic" saints – a saint in the tradition of Christ. Louis Massignon, twentieth-century French Islamicist, was specifically attracted to al-Ḥallâj because of his echoes of Christ. Massignon's *magnum opus* comprised a four-volume study of al-Ḥallâj.

Muhyi al-Dîn ibn al-ᶜArabi (AD 1165–1240) was born in Spain and grew up within the Ṣûfî tradition. He travelled widely throughout North Africa and the Middle East, settling eventually in Damascus. This Spanish (Andalusian) Arab was to have a huge and lasting influence upon the developing Ṣûfî movment. He is revered by his disciples as "the Great Master". Ibn al-ᶜArabi studied under a Spanish woman Ṣûfî, and evidently experienced trances or unique psychic states at various times. Some of his own compositions came to be written while he was in a trance. Such inner experiences constituted the essence of what Ibn al-ᶜArabi tried to convey to others, often through the medium of poetry. Sometimes, such poems might appear on the surface to be love stories, even erotic, but Ṣûfîs found within them insight into inner reality. Ibn al-ᶜArabi's philosophy is fundamentally monist – all reality is one, for everything that exists is, ultimately, God. Yet all manifestations that reveal God also act like veils to conceal him – he is beyond them. They are but symbols of the divine reality, of "the Truth". The person who grasps or experiences this true nature of reality and the unity of all existing things is the perfect saint. Ibn al-ᶜArabi saw himself as just such a person. Ibn al-ᶜArabi's approach to religiosity diminished, at least by implication, the importance of observing Islamic law and Muslim ritual. His personal emphasis upon trances and other forms of psychic awareness increased the significance of dreams, visions and the experience of ecstasy. The theosophical doctrines of Ibn al-ᶜArabi tended to lead to the idea that contemplative, miraculous and magical means could induce oneness with God. The veneration of saints and the making of pilgrimages to the tombs of saints was given strong rationale within Ibn al-ᶜArabi's approach to spirituality. The "Great Master" considered himself to be the spiritual heir to both Jesus and Muḥammad, converted (in a vision) by Jesus in order to reflect Muḥammad's mission in bringing God's mercy to ordinary people.[126] With Ibn al-ᶜArabi, Sufism reached quite an extreme expression, both in terms of its philosophical convictions and in terms of its outworking in popular, devotional practices.

Between the men on the extreme literalist and esoteric edges of theologizing stands al-Ghazâlî, proponent of what might be labelled a "combination" model. Muḥammad al-Ghazâlî is immensely respected within Islam as the person who managed to combine acceptance of the transcendence of God plus the authority of the Prophet and the historical tradition of the community – concerns of the orthodox theologians – with the experience and authority of the Ṣûfî master. Sufism and *sharîᶜa* came to be conjoined by him in a manner that has remained definitive within Islam.

At the time of al-Ghazâlî's birth in AD 1058, the Saljuq Turks had just conquered Baghdad and overrun Asia Minor. Al-Ghazâlî was born at Tûs, near the modern city of Mashhad in north-east Iran. In AD 1063, Alp Arslan became Sultan of Nishapur. He would be succeeded by his eldest son Malik Shah in AD 1072. Al-Ghazâlî's autobiographical work *Deliverance from*

Error (*al-Munqidh min al-Dalâl*) is the main source for much of what is known about his life.

Muḥammad al-Ghazâlî was orphaned at an early age and brought up by Ṣûfîs. In his teenage years, the youthful al-Ghazâlî felt increasingly estranged from his native faith. The bonds of mere authority (*taqlîd*) and inherited beliefs lost their hold on him, "for I saw that Christian youths always grew up to be Christians, Jewish youths to be Jews and Muslim youths to be Muslims".[127] So how could Islam claim to be universalist? What could be its "beyond confessional" basis for being accepted as true? Al-Ghazâlî eventually made himself ill through his quest for a reliable basis for human knowing, especially knowing about God. He decided to take up the life of a wandering dervish and for twelve years pursued that path towards enlightenment. His experience of the Ṣûfî way successfully brought al-Ghazâlî to certain, though internal, knowledge of God, and such certain knowing returned him to the authority of given scripture and tradition. In his major treatise *The Revivification of the Religious Sciences* (*Ihya' ʿUlum al-Dîn*), al-Ghazâlî gives his considered reflection upon the ideal relationship between the "outer" and "inner" life for a Muslim. Much of the treatise deals with common religious duties resembling a sort of monastic rule. Al-Ghazâlî certainly sought to demonstrate the inner meaning of such canonical duties, but he strongly insisted on their requirement in the life of every Muslim. He upheld (contrary to some Ṣûfîs before him) that the beginning of a truly Ṣûfî style of life was focused in a faithful observance of *sharîʿa* law. He thus disarmed the more conservative theologians in their mistrust of the Ṣûfî movement while at the same time shifting Sufism away from a purely esoteric, non-grounded experience towards orthodoxy of belief and practice.

At the heart of al-Ghazâlî's dynamic renewal of religious experience and practice lies his view of the nature of man. Al-Ghazâlî held that the essence of the human being is the soul, a positive, spiritual substance referred to as "heart" (*qalb*), "spirit" (*rûh*), "soul" (*nafs*) or "reason" (*ʿaql*). In its original state (*al-fiṭra*), before being joined to the body, this soul is pure and eternal. Most especially in al-Ghazâlî's view, the soul has the capacity for the knowledge of God. The soul becomes joined to the body because the body is the designated vehicle for carrying the soul on its journey to God. However, the given carrier (the body) constitutes a kind of "poisoned chalice", for the body inevitably tends to corrupt the pure state of the soul it is conveying. The powerful emotions of desire and anger plus an inclination to evil (*shaytanîya*) war against the spiritual qualities of a person. The goal of human existence becomes the perfecting of the soul so that the spiritual or divine elements prevail over the material and satanic elements. How can such a goal be achieved? With the help of Sufism! The Ṣûfî path is designed to lead a person away from attachment to sense perception, away from sexual passion and worldly ties. A ritual of *dhikr*, the repetition and remembrance of the name of God, helps empty the mind of all distracting desires. Certain knowledge of God becomes possible through this internal route. An external consistency, however, is also required in order for this internal reform of the heart to be valid. That external consistency is achieved through good actions – the prescribed actions of the law. So *sharîᶜa* and Sufism combine to make possible true knowledge of God and true submission to him. In such terms, as well as in the example of his own life, al-Ghazâlî brought together the burdens of Sufism and *sharîᶜa* and made the combination normative for orthodox, Sunnî Islam. Cragg applauds the effect that al-Ghazâlî had in bringing a mystical element into Islamic orthodoxy:

> Something of the starkness of transcendence was corrected and man's knowledge of God became a ground of communion with God ... Perhaps we may say that, for al-Ghazâlî, the Muslim confession: "There is no god save God" had come near to meaning: "Whom have I in heaven but Thee? There is none upon earth that I desire beside Thee" (Psalm 73:25).[128]

Perhaps Cragg states his wistful case too strongly, for al-Ghazâlî certainly maintained an adherence to a view of "strict transcendence" throughout his life and writings. It is rather, surely, his opening up of the possibility of experiencing the knowledge of the divine through mysticism that was accepted within orthodoxy. The divine person, God, remains throughout an inscrutable mystery.

Just as in the developing Christian world of state religion there emerged different ways of thinking through the faith, so in the Islamic world of established religion there developed alternative concepts of the Muslim way of life. In both faiths, extremists flourished toward the edges of the alternative views but somewhere in the middle a broad space for orthodoxy and orthopraxy was maintained.

Crossing the culture barrier?

The delicate question of sharing or expressing faith across cultural or worldview divides is as much an issue today as it has been in previous Christian or Muslim history. We have explored in this chapter some of the powerful and dynamic processes involved for Christians from different backgrounds wrestling with the mystery of "Trinity". We have observed a major rewriting of what constitutes faithful *islâm* arising out of the interaction between different mind-sets, each the proponent of a discrete way of growing in submission.

Here we return to our start-of-the-chapter interrogation of how Jewish disciples of Jesus gradually learned to make their new-found faith understandable and attractive within a Greek-minded world. Some of the major protagonists of the book of Acts grasp the significance of adapting the message to the recipients' context. Jews like Peter, and especially Paul, struggled heroically with the implications of conveying the "good news" to Gentiles. Luke stands out as the only Gentile author whose carefully compiled material is included in the New Testament. In his Gospel we discover an emphasis on the universality of the message of the kingdom – from Luke's highlighting of the "good Samaritan" to the centurion with incredible faith to a concern for "the times of the Gentiles". The non-Jew Luke compiles for a Roman official a well-researched cameo of Jesus' life. In the book of Acts, Luke records the carrying of the gospel by Jesus' disciples across the culture barrier to

Samaritans and then to Gentiles. The carrying, however, is all done by Jews. It is only after the time of the first apostles that we discover Gentiles rethinking and expressing anew the gospel in Greek mode. What should the gospel look like when served up to a Hellenistic world? What constitutes acceptable belief and behaviour? Where does the gospel affirm or challenge the mind-set of people like Justin Martyr and his contemporaries?

Questions of contextualization arise every time the gospel traverses a culture. Debates occur over terminology and meaning as categories of thought current in the receptor culture are made to serve the purpose of conveying Christian concepts. What does it mean to say that Jesus is God? How can Christ be conceived as both fully divine and fully human? What degree of miscommunication might occur when Greek-speaking Hellenists argue with Latin-speaking imperialists about theology? How much might different degrees of theological emphasis reflect alternative ways of thinking or of using language?

Equivalent questions arise at the cutting edge of Christian mission to Muslims today. Indeed, it appears that issues concerning "contextualization" are probably debated with the most passionate intensity of any contemporary mission matter. At heart is the question of communication. Cragg challenges us precisely on this point, in the context of sharing the gospel with Muslims:

> The Gospel of the Word made flesh must be intelligibly told. Those who tell it must be prepared to reckon with the mental world of other men in which it is understood or – as often as not – misunderstood. From that world, the listener's world, comes the framework of ideas within which, at least initially, the new thing is judged.[129]

So what words or terms communicate best – indigenous ones or ones seen as foreign? Words spoken in the heart language of the receptor or words spoken in an unfamiliar tongue? Is worship to be expressed via indigenous forms or via imported ones? Is there a way in which "mission to Muslims" can be reconceptualized so that unnecessary "foreignness" is removed?

For many years, any tentative exploration of contextualized communication of the gospel was strongly refused, for a variety of reasons. For communities of Christians living as minorities in Muslim societies, the adoption of Muslim identity or language would prove far too compromising of their own community's integrity. It would also be potentially open to misinterpretation by their Muslim fellow-countrymen. Missionaries, maybe, brought messages strongly wedded to their own Western worldviews and cultural forms – a long way from anything that might be vaguely audience-oriented. In the way that they had themselves received the gospel, was how they knew to pass it on.

Recently, in various countries and among many Muslim communities, however, a contextualized approach to faith-sharing and church-growing has, to varying degrees, become much more the norm. David Penman, missionary in Pakistan and the Middle East before becoming Archbishop of Melbourne in 1984, describes some of the changes made in Pakistan that reflected a move away from "the Latin/Victorian captivity" of the church towards a more indigenous model:

> In the city of Peshawar some thoughtful and creative Christians realised that if Christ was to be born into their society, and to become a turning point of their culture, then there was an urgent need for buildings to reflect appropriate aspects of local architecture. The church they built had several minarets, a pulpit like a niche in the wall, and water basins for ritual ablutions ... The struggle was real and the price very high.[130]

The major question in such contextualized approaches remains hotly contested: just how far is it right to go?

John Travis,[131] a long-term mission partner working among Muslims in Asia, has formulated a categorization of increasing stages of contextualization to be found among communities of Christ-followers in Islamic contexts. He calls it the "C1 to C6 spectrum". The spectrum defines the kind of believing community most likely to come to expression where different degrees of contextualization are applied (Figure 44).

Figure 44
John Travis's spectrum of contextualized communities of believers in Christ

	Type of Community	Degree of Contextualization
C1	Traditional church using outsider language	Orthodox, Catholic, Protestant. Many found in Muslim countries. Big cultural gap to majority Muslim community. C1 believers call themselves "Christians".
C2	Traditional church using insider language	Same as C1 except for language, but religious vocabulary is still distinctively Christian. Big cultural gap. Majority of churches located in the Muslim world are C1 or C2. C2 believers call themselves "Christians".
C3	Somewhat contextualized Christ-centred communities using insider language and religiously neutral insider cultural forms	Forms may include local folk music, ethnic dress etc. with Islamic elements filtered out. C3 congregations consist of a majority of Muslim background believers. C3 believers call themselves "Christians".
C4	Contextualized Christ-centred communities using insider language and biblically permissible cultural and Islamic forms	Biblically permissible Islamic forms and practices are utilized: dietary practices, fasting, Islamic terms, dress etc. C4 communities comprised almost entirely of Muslim background believers. C4 believers call themselves "followers of ᶜIsâ the Messiah" or equivalent.
C5	Christ-centred communities of "Messianic Muslims" who have accepted Jesus as Lord and Saviour	C5 believers remain legally and socially within the Islamic community. Aim is to cause a turning to Christ from within Islam. Messianic mosques/C5 believers are viewed as Muslims by the Muslim community and refer to themselves as "Muslims who follow ᶜIsâ the Messiah".
C6	Small Christ-centred communities of secret underground believers	C6 believers worship Christ secretly. C6 believers are perceived as Muslims by the Muslim community and identify themselves as "Muslim".

Travis analyzes elements of language, culture, worship forms and religious identity in an effort to assess the degree of indigenization or contextualization going on. At one end of the spectrum (C1/C2, even C3) occurs the kind of traditional Christian expression found in many Muslim nations. Believers identify themselves as Christians and live culturally, liturgically, religiously far away from their Muslim neighbours. At this end of the spectrum, a Muslim who wants to follow Jesus has to become totally dislocated from his family and community in order to join the "Christians". He has no choice but to become a "foreigner" to his own people and take to himself the strange thought-forms and mores of national Christians or Western missionaries with whom he now associates. The majority of churches in the Muslim world are C1 or C2. Travis asks whether the extractionist, one-way approach that produces such kinds of churches is really reflective of Jesus' incarnational commitment to communication?

At the other end of the spectrum (C5) are communities of believers in Christ who identify themselves as Muslims and are perceived as Muslims by their neighbours. Worship of Jesus takes place secretly or in mosques or home gatherings. Contact with national Christians, should any such people exist, is discouraged. At this end of the spectrum difficult ethical issues arise over the question of "deceit": for example, should Christians be labelling themselves "Muslims" in order to reach Muslims? Should Christians be attempting renewal movements within Islam – making Muslims better Muslims – blurring the edges of the counter-cultural claims of the cross of Christ? C5 workers respond, of course, that Jesus commanded us to make disciples, not converts. Many Christians working at this degree of contextualization insist that no one from a Christian background may take an identity further than C4 – no Christian should be presenting himself as a "Muslim". Only those who are raised as Muslim within a Muslim family might want still to be known as "Muslim". Such a person, after all, may legitimately see himself as far more "Muslim" than "Christian" even though he disagrees with the Islamic line on the corruption of the Bible or the non-crucifixion of Jesus. He does not dress, speak, eat, pray, worship like a Christian but like a Muslim. In that way, it might be perfectly honest for him to identify himself as a "Muslim" follower of Jesus. C6 believers are strongly distinguished from all others in that their faith in Jesus is not made public. For reasons of personal hesitation or potential persecution, some Muslim believers in Christ begin or remain secret in their discipleship. Who of us dare judge them?

Between the two extremes lie C4 communities of believers from a Muslim background. Phil Parshall, with fellow missionaries in Bangladesh, experimented in the 1970s with seeking to develop such kinds of fellowships of "followers of ᶜIsâ". His theological and missiological principles he identified in a book, *New Paths in Muslim Evangelism.* Biblically permissible Islamic forms or practices were accepted as valid in the developing communities of believers. Such "Messianic Muslims" developed a church life separate from the other Christian communities in the country. The production of Muslim-sensitive scriptures and the miraculous provision by God of indigenous apostles and leaders (often eventually martyrs) has led in some situations to massive growth in such Muslim-oriented believing communities. Joshua Massey claims that by the end of the twentieth century, "C4 is today probably the most common approach used by new missionaries to Muslims".[132]

Elizabeth Brooks provides a fascinating contemporary example of a person struggling with issues of contextualization in a C4 setting. She works as a Christian witness among a large Turkic-speaking, Muslim people group in Central Asia. As the number of Christian believers from this background increases, the question of what to do about certain indigenous practices becomes critical. She illustrates the problem with an examination of *may puritix* or "praying into smoking oil". This form of invoking the spirits of dead relatives is pervasive and performed almost entirely by women. Cooking oil is heated until it smokes and into the smoke prayers are breathed on behalf of deceased relatives. The ritual is expected regularly of widows or daughters who thereby declare their faithfulness and reliability of character to all observers. The aim of the ceremony is to enable merit to accrue to those who have died. The practice is part of the religio-cultural matrix in which Muslim women of this Turkic people group are immersed. The question that Brooks explores is whether the practice contradicts biblical standards, whether it might be transformable and "redeemable" or whether it needs to be completely abandoned and replaced. Her conclusion, in regard to this practice, is that both the practice and the concepts lying behind it need to be replaced. They should not be accepted or transformed, in order "to avoid syncretism and the dangerous lure of demonically-inspired efforts to interact with the dead".[133] Syncretism comprises the mixing of old patterns of religious belief and practice with new ones. In this case, Brooks feels that the new Christian faith of such Muslim background believers would be seriously compromised if they continued with any kind of "reinterpreted" *may puritix* practices. Brooks does include a caveat to her conclusion in her suggestion that trying to work through the matter of how the *may puritix* syndrome might be healthily contextualized is still, in her view, a fluid process rather than a fixed decision.

The contextualization debate, as with Brooks's example, raises urgent questions about the possibility of syncretism (see Figure 45). Where there are low levels of contextualisation there are likely to be few risks of syncretism – of mixing Islam with Christian believing. But there is likely to be little indigeneity of communication or "church" forms either. At this end of the spectrum, moreover, there is likely to be engendered a radical hostility towards Islam in former Muslims who have converted to Christ. Zwemer is quoted by a Muslim researcher into Christian missionary methods as saying: "The aim of missionary work is not to bring a Muslim into another religion; it is to bring him out of Islam, so that he may become its opponent and staunch enemy."[134] As increasing contextualization is promoted, the risk of syncretism grows. Cragg, after summarizing the radical difference between Islamic and Christian concepts of revelation, God, prophethood, humanity and salvation, still strongly affirms the need for the gospel to be preached as an "insider" affair: "the nature of the Gospel is such that the impact of Christ is not totally to displace, but paradoxically to

Figure 45
Contextualization and syncretism

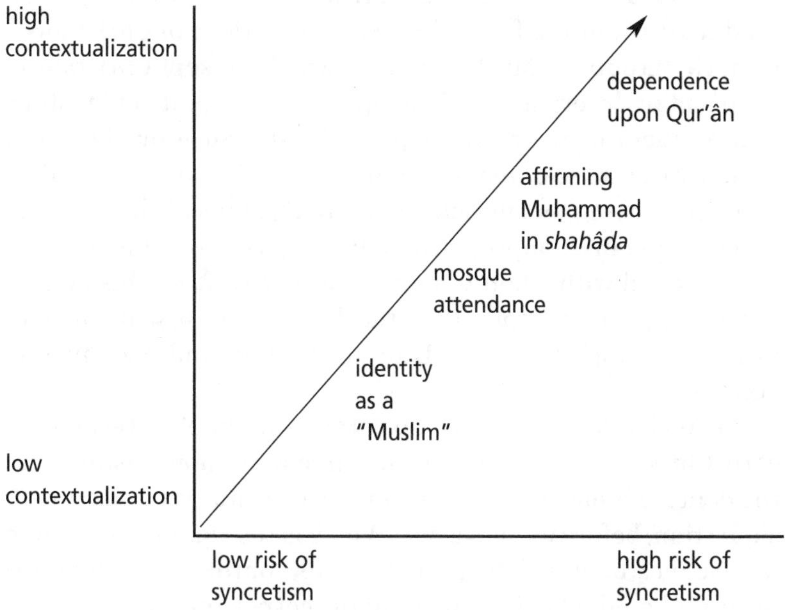

fulfil, what is there".[135] At what point does the resulting "Muslim–Christian" faith become something other than reflective of the gospel of Jesus Christ?

In a situation of high contextualization, a Muslim is going to sense strong continuity between his Islamic inheritance and his faith in Christ. Maybe this can be viewed as parallel to the Gentiles in the post-apostolic era discovering that "Christian" did not have to equate also with "Jewish". Twice in the book of Acts, the jarring, unexpected phrase "Gentile believers" explodes out of the pages – in Acts 15:23 and 21:25. How would such terminology have been received by a Jewish reader in the first century? Critics of a C4 or C5 approach suggest that the terms of the gospel are being unacceptably watered down in order to make it more palatable for Muslims to accept. Their concern is reminiscent of the Judaizers' insistence at Antioch that Gentile followers of Christ had to be circumcised "in order to be saved" (Acts 15:1). These visiting brothers saw the matter as a salvation issue – that is, an ultimate issue.

In a situation of low contextualization, a Muslim is going to sense strong discontinuity between his new faith in Christ and his previous Muslim heritage. Critics of a C1 to C3 approach tend to discount the faithful role of generations of Christians – minority groups in Muslim lands – who have kept Christianity alive and in different ways held open the possibility of Muslims joining them in their expressions of faith. Such brothers and sisters are accused of making it unnecessarily hard for Muslims to enter the kingdom of God. Yet C1 to C3 kinds of churches are precisely the most appropriate fellowships for Muslims who are disillusioned with Islam to join. It has been within this kind of fellowship, for example, that the large post-1979 turning to Christ of Muslims from Iranian background has mostly occurred.

This chapter has thrown up parallels in the New Testament, early Christian, early Muslim and current missions history over the delicate issue of continuity and discontinuity. I close it with a question, before we move on: "Who has the right to determine the balance between the pulls towards continuity or discontinuity?" Should it be the bringer of the gospel, the receiver of the gospel, the Holy Spirit or a combination of all three?

Chapter 6 Set Free or Set Fast?

In this chapter we take up our consideration of "success" in prophethood. We have noticed that for many of the biblical prophets, "success" and "failure" were ironically intertwined. The prophets' words "failed" in the sense that, over and over again, the Israelite kings and people and religious leaders refused to heed them. The word from God was not accepted in the hearers' hearts. The warners warned but the audience would not be warned. Yet the prophets' words "succeeded" in the sense that the consequences that they predicted, should the people take no notice of God's repeated declarations, actually happened. The Assyrians did come and destroy Samaria! The Babylonians did come and destroy Jerusalem! God's warnings were fulfilled. The prophets were vindicated, and in that they might be counted successful.

Hijra and exodus – what next?

Prophet Muḥammad endured thirteen years of being a warner. He prophesied in Mecca, at first privately but then publicly and with increasing confidence about his message. He delivered to the Meccans what the angel had vouchsafed to him. He looked for a renewal of worship and obedience directed towards the one God. He expected others to experience the same dissatisfaction and emptiness that had driven him up Mount Ḥirâ to meditate and pray. He anticipated that his message – from God himself – would be received with eagerness. Instead he got mockery, refusal, threat and even persecution. He had to send some of his early converts to Abyssinia for their own safety. Only the protection afforded him by his powerful uncle Abû

Ṭâlib (who, incidentally, never became a Muslim) shielded Muḥammad from the extremes of personal abuse. Muḥammad tragically lost both his wife and his uncle-protector in the same year. At that point his position in Mecca became untenable.

The solution to Muḥammad's difficult predicament was found in *hijra*, or exodus. He transferred with his followers to Yathrib/Medina and in that city a new day dawned for him. He and his disciples found liberation from their powerful critics. In Medina the prophet could be successful in the fullest sense – what he said went. What he declared on God's behalf was obeyed. What he commanded as leader of the community of faithful was fulfilled. We have noted that there is considerable discussion among commentators as to whether or not Muḥammad himself underwent a major character change as he shifted from Mecca to Medina. What certainly did arise was an opportunity for the Muslim community in that city to hold high their heads and work out the details of their faith in everyday living.

The pattern of faith-development for the Muslims newly arrived in Medina is reminiscent of the experience of Moses and the people of Israel after their exodus from Egypt. The memory of that change in fortune would tower over the Jewish national consciousness throughout subsequent centuries. An oppressed minority was led in an ultimately successful emigration that freed them from Pharaoh's tyranny and made possible their being transformed into a nation. Moses stood his ground with Pharaoh – enabled to do so by Yahweh – and then became the representative of God on earth in constructing a community built around obedience to the Lord. The Law was delivered via him on Sinai and the people covenanted to live in submission to it. Moses explained to them what that meant in terms of economic, judicial, religious and family relationships. Dietary restrictions and calls to warfare in God's name were part and parcel of being Moses' people. In fact, the prophet wore himself out trying to make the theocracy work and Jethro the Midianite, his father-in-law, had to step in to help him manage affairs properly. In the words of John Bright: "The notion of a people of

God, called to live under the rule of God, begins just here, and with it the notion of the Kingdom of God."[136]

For some 200 years after the conquest of Canaan by the people of Israel, the nation remained a tribal league, a racial and religious body rather than a strictly geographical or political one. Leadership was exercised by charismatic individuals marked for responsibility by God. The faithfulness of such (mostly) men facilitated the direct rule of God over his people. Israel remained for those many years a tribal theocracy, deliberately spurning any idea of monarchy.

With the growth of the Philistine threat and the eventual debacle of the Ark's capture, however, the people of Israel experienced dramatic military and spiritual humiliation. In the face of this emergency the first tentative steps towards statehood occurred. Saul was made "king". He was still a leader (reluctantly) chosen by God but, for various reasons – explained in terms of his failure to honour God – his intervention proved negligible in changing Israel's fortunes. The Philistines regained control and their garrisons again spread throughout the land. David, also chosen by God, led the people of Israel out of subservience to the Philistines – but he also led them into the realities of "monarchy" and its tendency towards dynastic rule. The tribal league gave way to the formation of a state centred in a king. A state-sponsored religious machine came to be created that ran the danger of placing itself at the service of its sponsor over against its duty to yield primary allegiance to God. The history of the kingdom of Israel under David and Solomon and their successors tells the tale of what happens when charismatic leaders who lived by obedience to God become replaced by dynasties whose major goal is to hold on to power by whatever means.

The theocracy that Muḥammad introduced in Medina all those centuries later underwent a similar transformation. The first caliph after the Prophet was Abû Bakr – he ruled for only two years before he died in AD 634. His major achievement was to pacify an Arabia that had risen in revolt. ᶜUmar ibn al-Khattab, the second caliph, was assassinated in AD 644 after ten years of rule. During that decade, the Arab conquests extended well beyond the frontiers of Arabia and the seeds of the formation of an Arab empire were securely sown. Under ᶜUthmân ibn Affan (AD 644–656), the third caliph, the conquests continued eastwards. The era of the fourth caliph, ᶜAlî ibn Abû Ṭâlib (AD 656–661) saw the internal tensions within the Muslim community, long since growing, burst into the open. We shall return to this ugly matter later in this chapter. A sort of civil war ensued in which Muᶜâwiya triumphed; he became the next caliph.

The establishment of Muᶜâwiya's caliphate eventuated in a different process for handing on leadership. Each of the four first caliphs had been selected by a small electoral body. The community then ratified the choice, swearing an oath of loyalty to the chosen leader. From Muᶜâwiya onwards, the caliphate became hereditary, the property in effect of a particular family (see Figure 46). The caliphate remained with the Umayyad family (named after Umayya, one of the pre-Islamic Quraysh leaders in Mecca) for about 100 years. We have already examined some of the frustrations that loyal Muslims had with the quality of Umayyad leaders in Damascus – frustrations that contributed to the espousing of a Ṣûfî approach to religiosity. A revolt eventually overthrew the Umayyads. The dynasty that replaced them comprised caliphs descended from an uncle of Muḥammad named ᶜAbbas – hence the designation ᶜAbbassid that is given to the new caliphate. The following 500 years saw the end of the political unity of the Muslim world as various provinces of the Arab empire gradually gained or regained their independence.

Powerless to powerful

Probably the closest Christian equivalent to the change that occurred for Muḥammad as he shifted from being a persecuted prophet to becoming a powerful statesman was the conversion of Constantine. The pagan Constantine, following the policy of his father Constantius Chlorus (a monotheist who had died in AD 306), chose not to be antagonistic towards Christians in his dominions. In AD 312, Constantine invaded Italy with the aim of ousting Maxentius, the opportunist usurper of Rome. When he

Figure 46
From charismatic to dynastic leadership

Judaism		**Islam**
Moses	prophet	Muḥammad
Joshua the judges Saul David	charismatic/ appointed leaders	Abû Bakr ʿUmar ʿUthmân ʿAlî
David ↙ Solomon ↙ ↘ northern kingdom of Israel — southern kingdom of Judah	dynastic leaders	Muʿâwiya → Umayyad caliphate ↓ ʿAbbassid caliphate ↓ Turkish Ottoman supremacy

came to face up to Maxentius, Constantine grew worried because Maxentius reputedly relied on pagan magic for protection and power. Constantine evidently felt the need for an equivalent power. He later told the historian Eusebius that while praying one afternoon, he had a vision of a cross of light in the sky that bore the inscription "Conquer by this!" The daytime vision was confirmed by a dream that same night in which God appeared to Constantine with the "cross" sign, telling Constantine to make a likeness of it. Constantine's surprisingly easy victory over Maxentius at the Milvian Bridge near Rome confirmed him in his faith in the efficacy of the cross-emblem. By virtue of the victory, Constantine emerged as emperor of the whole western half of the Roman Empire. In AD 313, through the Edict of Milan, initial declarations of official tolerance of Christians were made by both Constantine and his eastern rival Licinius.

With the emperor's overnight espousal of the Christian

faith, wonderful though that was, Christianity underwent a drastic evolution. Until then it had existed at the peripheries of the Roman world. It had transformed individuals and communities slowly, from the edges. It had been truly counter-cultural. Christians were continuously persecuted. Emperors tried to destroy the Bible. The major power-holders of the day resisted the faith vehemently – until the most influential power-holder got converted. Overnight, Christianity became a state religion. It eventually emerged as the only official cultus of the Roman Empire. All the weight of political authority would now be brought to bear in its cause. Apart from a brief reaction under Julian, Christianity was continuously given the support of the government. Bishops received tax exemptions and donations in gold, plus great prestige. Some of them gained influence in the imperial court itself. Artists now painted icons of Christ sitting on a heavenly throne surrounded by wealth and the trappings of power, just like the emperor. The church, moreover, came to be modelled on the organization of the state.

As a consequence of this dramatic shift in fortune, human power quickly muddied the waters of something God-given, just as had happened with the dynastic development in Judaism. What came to be done in the name of Christ, by Christians to Christians, by Christians to Jews and Muslims, would be unforgivable and inexcusable but sadly predictable. The harnessing of human power to deliver truth – "our truth" – has been as much the internal heritage of the Jewish and Christian religions as it has of Islam. Emperor Constantine's conversion to Christianity ensured that the politicians would be increasingly involved in affairs of the church, while church leaders would have controlling voices in important political decisions.

Truth and power in Christian history

Constantine had another dream that led him to believe that God was telling him to found a new capital for the eastern half of the empire. Byzantium was the place of his choice and it soon became known as the emperor's city or "Constantinople". In AD 324, Constantine ended up on the Bosphorus, having defeated his rival Licinius. Constantine was now sole emperor. He wanted to visit the holy land and be baptized in the river Jordan. Emperor Constantine never made his pilgrimage, however, because of an argument going on in the eastern church – an argument about who exactly Jesus was.

By AD 300, there were groups of allied churches both within and without the Roman Empire (see Figure 47; note that this figure needs to be read from the bottom up). The relatively young Armenian church, for example, existed outside the empire. Constantine's eastern colleague Licinius (with whom he had agreed upon religious toleration in AD 313) was a pagan, and as suspicions rose between Constantine and Licinius, Constantine tried to enlist the support of fellow-Christians to the east. He managed to encircle Licinius by making an alliance with the Armenians. When Licinius harassed Christians near the Armenian border and prohibited synods, Constantine was pleased to have an excuse for a war against Licinius. The fighting culminated in Constantine's victory. In AD 324, as we have stated, he emerged as sole ruler of the empire. Incidentally, other churches outside the Roman Empire existed in Persia, Ethiopia and India.

Within the Roman Empire, five church groupings had emerged over the first 300 years after Christ. They were known as the "Pentarchy" – the church in five regional administrations, each self-governing or "autocephalous" – and comprised the patriarchates of Rome, Antioch, Jerusalem, Alexandria and more recently Constantinople. Constantinople became the new capital of the Roman Empire in AD 330 and it was then that Christianity was made the official religion of the state. The five groupings of churches, each independent, were united as equals in a fellowship of shared communion. In that communion, an honorary preference was given to Rome and Constantinople.

Over the five centuries from AD 300, various political, cultural and theological issues were addressed and supposedly resolved in numerous councils of bishops (see Figure 48). Four of these councils – Nicaea (AD 325), Constantinople (AD 381), Ephesus (AD 431) and Chalcedon (AD 451) came to be called "ecumenical" or universal councils, binding upon the whole church

Figure 47
Developing church: councils and splits

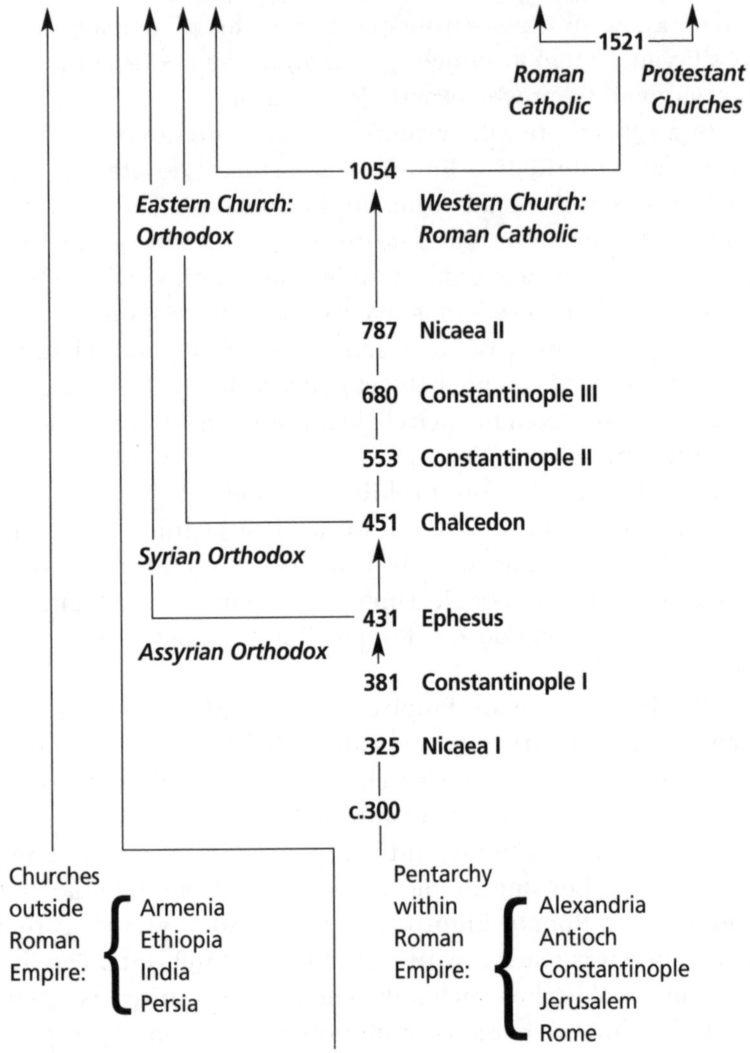

– though that did not mean that everyone agreed to be bound by the decisions taken at them! Three subsequent councils – Constantinople (AD 553, 680) and Nicaea (AD 787) – were general councils but they influenced Western Christianity less. There were plenty of other councils or synods of bishops in the intervening years.

Figure 48
The ecumenical councils

Arena	Issues
Politics	The role played by the emperor in church affairs
Ecclesiastics	The roles of bishops of Rome, Constantinople, Alexandria: who has what authority? The influence of the schools of Antioch and Alexandria with their different approaches to being Christian in a Hellenized world: who is right?
Theology	Questions about the person of Christ

During the fourth to the sixth centuries, in the newly acclaimed Christian Byzantine area of the world, various theological debates took place over issues to do with the Trinity, the nature of the person of Christ, the role of the Spirit and so on. At one level these debates may be read as important theological or Christological enquiries (Figure 49). Take, for instance, the theological debates over the person of Christ. There were two major questions to be resolved. Firstly, how is Christ, the Son of God, himself God? Secondly, how is Christ both human and divine, both man and God? At another level the debates may be seen as the waving of theological "flags" declaring peoples' distance from one another and – especially – their distinction from the dominant religio-political authority of the day. At heart they have to do with the clashing of people from different cultures who saw the world differently from one another.

It might be argued, for example, that in political terms the Arianism of the Germans helped maintain in the Goths a sense of separateness from the mass of Catholics whom they had subjugated (see Figure 50). Or, perhaps the monophysitism of Egypt, Syria (which at first inclined to Nestorianism) and Armenia served to pronounce the separateness of those Christians from overbearing imperial lordship.

In the following paragraphs we look briefly at questions

Figure 49
Theological debates

Argument known as ...	Critical issues ...
Arian controversy	Was God the Father quite separate from God the Son (the Arian view)? Was one merely an aspect of the other (the Sabellian view)? Were they at once distinct and similar (the orthodox view)?
Monophysite/Nestorian controversy	In Christ were the human and divine components completely fused (the Monophysite view)? In Christ were the human and divine components completely separate (the Nestorian view)? Were they at once separate but co-mingled (the orthodox view)?
Donatist controversy	Can one remain faithful to the "church of the martyrs" and accept as leaders those who have lapsed under persecution (Donatists said "no")? Can one ally the church with the power of the state in order to deal with one's ecclesiastical opponents (Augustine said "yes")?
Pelagian controversy	Does human nature, both in Eden and in the current world, participate in the wholeness and goodness of the original creation (the Pelagian view)? Does human nature, changed forever by the "fall" of Adam, pass the taint of "original sin" via conception to each human being (the Augustinian view)?

Figure 50
Culture bloc and theological "flag"

Culture bloc	Theological "flag"
German	Arianism
Spanish	Adoptionism
Egyptian, Syrian, Armenian	Monophysitism
Persian, Mesopotamian	Nestorianism
Roman, Latin	Catholicism
Byzantine, Eastern	Greek Orthodoxy

about Christ. Not only do the debates over Christology illustrate the strange mix of theology and politics but they have a direct bearing on the manner in which Islam came to consider Jesus.

How is the Son of God really God?

Arius (AD 250–336) was a senior presbyter in charge of one of the twelve "parishes" of Alexandria. He was a charismatic preacher with a fan-club of clergy and ascetics. He was in effect a popularizer of Christianity. Around AD 318, Arius clashed with his bishop, Alexander of Alexandria. Arius claimed that the Father alone is really God. The Son is essentially different from his Father. So, the Son did not exist before he was begotten by the Father; yet, as creator of the rest of creation, the Son existed "apart from time before all things". Neither did the Son know the Father perfectly. In many ways, the Son was "less" than the Father. Arius' view was strongly subordinationist.

Arius was trying to make the Christian faith palatable to the secular Greek mind. He believed that the *Logos* took the place of the human soul in the earthly Christ and that the *Logos* was united only with a human body, not with a full human nature. It was more acceptable to the Greek mind that the *Logos* might be associated with contaminating human flesh if the *Logos* were gently lowered to the status of a "perfect creature" or "honorary god". In his *Logos* theory, Arius was taking a half-step towards those who tried to explain the Christian faith within a Greek mind-set. In a way, he paralleled Origen in his similar concern for expressing Christianity in a Hellenized way, earlier in the same city of Alexandria.

A local council of Egyptian and Libyan bishops at Alexandria soon excommunicated Arius, along with a dozen other clergy and two bishops (in AD 318). Arius, however, quickly found friends elsewhere. He won the support of former fellow-pupils of Lucian of Antioch, an influential teacher who had been martyred a few years earlier. Those pupils included Eusebius, Bishop of Nicomedia, home to the imperial headquarters on the Asian side of the Bosphorus. Another Eusebius, of Caesarea, the famous church historian, rallied support for Arius in his region. Constantine, now emperor of east as well as west, was dismayed to discover in AD 324 that his new territories were split over what he dismissed as a "theological trifle". His religious adviser, the Spanish Bishop Ossius, was dispatched to Alexandria but failed in his attempts to reconcile the parties. Eventually Constantine summoned a general assembly of bishops to meet under him in Nicaea. Either the emperor himself or Bishop Ossius chaired the discussions around the Arian question when it came up, though more is known of the outcome of the council than of its proceedings.

Arius was quickly condemned by his own words. Three bishops previously banned, including Eusebius of Caesarea, were cleared. To exclude Arian error, the council produced its own creed – known as the Creed of Nicaea in order to distinguish it from the "Nicene creed" that was produced at the Council of Constantinople in AD 381 (see Figure 51).

Significant phrases were inserted to pointedly counteract what Arius was saying. "Begotten ... from the substance of the Father" indicates that the Son was not created. "Very God from Very God" shows that the Son is fully God. The anathemas at the end declare that the Son is neither metaphysically nor morally inferior to the Father and that the Son does not belong to the

Figure 51
Creed of Nicaea

We believe in one God, the Father, Almighty, maker of all things visible and invisible;

And in one Lord Jesus Christ, the Son of God, begotten of the Father, only-begotten, that is, from the substance [*ousia*] of the Father; God from God, Light from Light, Very God from Very God, begotten not made, of one substance [*homoousios*, consubstantial] with the Father, through whom all things were made, both in heaven and on earth; who for us men and for our salvation came down and was incarnate, was made man, suffered, and rose again on the third day, ascended into heaven, and is coming to judge the living and the dead;

And in the Holy Spirit.

And those who say: "There was a time when he was not", and: "He came into being from nothing", or those who pretend that the Son of God is "Of another substance [*hypostasis*], or essence [*ousia*]" (than the Father) or "created" or "alterable" or "mutable", the catholic and apostolic church places under a curse.

created order. The creed, however, contained certain ambiguities. What was really meant by "of one substance" [*homoousios*]? The Greek word could describe two coins made from the same metal, giving the possible interpretation that the Godhead might be split in substance. And how do you handle a text like John 14:28 – "If you loved me, you would be glad that I am going to the Father, for the Father is greater than I" – that seems to affirm that the Son is in some manner subordinate to the Father?

Arianism by no means disappeared. Arius was banished to the provinces of Illyria (the Balkans), but a couple of years after the Council of Nicaea, Constantine came himself to favour the Arian view and ordered him home to Egypt. By then, Athanasius (AD 295–373) was Bishop of Alexandria. He had been present at the Council of Nicaea as a deacon and had succeeded to the patriarchate of Alexandria in AD 328. Athanasius was certainly no friend of Arius! Indeed, he later said that Arius' unexpected death on the day before he was due to be reinstated to his position of presbyter was the result of divine providence. Maybe

Arius had been poisoned! Athanasius became the most vocal defender of the non-Arian (pro-Nicene) view in the fourth century and ended up annoying Constantine and Constantine's son Constantius – so much so that he was himself sent into exile five times!

During the reign of Emperor Constantius (AD 337–361), numerous eastern synods made a variety of declarations of faith, many of them somewhat sympathetic to the Arian position. A synod held at Constantinople in AD 360, for example, rejected all previous declarations of faith and affirmed that "the Son is like the Father" rather than consubstantial with him. This view constituted the official version of what became known as "Arianism", especially among the barbarians on the fringes of the Roman Empire. What if Theodosius – a supporter of the Nicene view – had not become emperor in AD 379? Maybe the Arian view would have become the "orthodox" view. As it was, two years after being crowned emperor Theodosius made "heresy" a crime against the state. The two sons of Theodosius, moreover, reigning after his death in AD 395 as emperors of East and West, continued their father's policy of withdrawing patronage from Arian Christian leaders. Perhaps for that very reason the Visigoths and other Germanic tribes adopted the "heretical" view, and established themselves as Arian Christians.

How is Christ both human and divine?

Once the divinity of the Son was firmly established (the Arian controversy), the question of how Christ can be both fully divine and fully human rose to the surface. How could "God" be born a baby, "grow in wisdom", suffer thirst and grief and die? One way of handling the question was to suggest that the eternal Word of God "accommodated" himself to the conditions of humanity. The theologians in Alexandria tended to reason in such a way. The case, however, could be overstated – and it was, in the 360s, by Bishop Apollinarius of Laodicea in Syria. In an extreme anti-Arian reaction, Apollinarius asserted that Christ's human nature differed from that of other men in one important respect: the divine Word or *Logos* replaced the human mind in Christ. In this conception, Jesus was not fully human, so his "human" experiences constituted a kind of play-acting. The virgin birth marked the difference between Christ and everyone else. Humanity became the "sphere", not the "instrument" of salvation. Christ was "one nature composed of impassible divinity and passible flesh ... one enfleshed nature of the divine Word". In the union, Christ's flesh accordingly took on a divine character. In other words, Apollinarius strove to keep the "God aspect" of Christ well away from contaminating, human flesh.

Apollinarius' view was attacked by his old friend Athanasius, Bishop of Alexandria. When Athanasius died in AD 373, others took up the opposition to Apollinarius' undermining of the "human aspect" of Christ. Famous protagonists were the Cappadocian Fathers – Basil of Caesarea, Gregory of Nazianzus and Gregory of Nyssa. Apollinarius' views were conclusively condemned in the west by a Roman council in AD 377 and in the east at the Council of Constantinople in AD 381. This latter council was called by imperial authority and an official edict later promulgated by the Emperor Theodosius in AD 388 settled the issue against Apollinarius. "What is not assumed [by the Word] is not healed" said Gregory of Nazianzus. In other words, if God in Christ did not lay hold of our full humanity, then our full humanity cannot be saved.

Soon, the challenge arose of dealing with those who seemed to overstate the "human aspect" in Christ. In responding to people like Apollinarius, such theologians appeared to imply that Jesus was less than fully divine (see Figure 52). A focal point of discussion was found in the role of Mary in the processes of incarnation. Apollinarius had held that the virgin birth was more than just an act of grace – there was profound truth in the title "Mother of God" or *theotokos* (God-bearer), which was generally applied to Mary. Remember, Apollinarius wanted to emphasize the "God aspect" of Christ. Diodore, Bishop of Tarsus (died AD 390) and his disciple Theodore of Mopsuestia (died AD 428) reacted to Apollinarius' views, emphasizing that the redemption of humanity surely depends on the perfection and obedience of Christ as man. In a strong response to

Figure 52
Jesus Christ: divine and human

Orthodox

Christ is fully human ← → Christ is fully divine

Non-orthodox

← →

	overstressing the "human" element in Christ	*overstressing the "divine" element in Christ*
1st – 3rd centuries	**Ebionites** Jesus not God, but a deified man, e.g. the Christ descended on Jesus at his baptism	**Docetics** Jesus not really human, but a divine being walking the earth in disguise
4th century	**Arians** Jesus not fully divine; not eternal but created, intermediate between God and the world	**Apollinarians** Jesus had a human body and soul but his mind (*nous*) was divine, the divine *Logos* occupied the place of the human mind
5th century	**Nestorians** the two natures were so different that Jesus was really almost two persons, only united "in good pleasure", not in essence	**Eutychians (Monophysites)** there was only one nature because the divine had "swallowed up" the human at incarnation

Apollinarius, these Antiochene churchmen stressed – overstressed! – Christ's humanity. They believed, in effect, that in Jesus there was a union of two distinct natures – the human and the divine. Jesus' identity with God consisted in the "living accord" between his human will and the Father's. Pushed to the limit, this teaching could seem to imply that there were two Christs, one of them being only a man who was adopted by God.

Theodore strongly influenced a monk from Antioch called Nestorius. In AD 428, Nestorius was made Patriarch of Constantinople. Nestorius, faithful to the current Antiochene view, rejected the term *theotokos* of Mary. At most, he offered, he could think of her as *christotokos* ("Mother of Christ" or "Christ-bearer"). After all, how can "God" be a baby? Nestorius, it appeared, was promoting the Antiochene implication that Christ was constituted of two persons. He did not deny the deity of Christ, but in emphasizing the reality and integrity of his humanity, he pictured the relation between divine and human as a merging of wills rather than an *essential* union.

There was strong objection to Nestorius' perspective, and to the Antiochene sources from which it developed. The chief opponent, Cyril, Bishop of Alexandria (375–444), wrote three letters to Nestorius rebuking his teaching. To the final letter he attached twelve anathemas against Nestorius. The anathemas condemned anyone who denied Mary the title of *theotokos*, anyone who separated the words and acts of Christ between divine and human natures, and anyone who failed to confess that the Word of God suffered in body, was crucified in body and tasted death in the body. Cyril's anathemas from Alexandria were received as an insult in Antioch and a pamphlet war started between the two centres.

Eventually, the harassed Emperor Theodosius II summoned a council of bishops to congregate at Ephesus in AD 431 to sort out the argument. When John, Bishop of Antioch arrived with his retinue four days late for the council, he discovered that Cyril's group had already condemned and deposed Nestorius. John's group immediately convened a rival council that condemned Cyril who in turn castigated them from his council! The two groups appealed to the emperor to ratify their respective judgements – and the emperor responded by arresting all three protagonists: Nestorius, Cyril and John! Cyril bribed his way back to Egypt and Nestorius was allowed to return to his monastery in Antioch. A reconciliation was eventually brokered between Cyril and John in AD 433 in which both were forced to compromise. The formula they agreed became the basis for the "definition" later approved by the Council of Chalcedon in AD 451 (see Figure 53).

Despite the agreed compromise, the Alexandrian party – after the death of Cyril – began to champion the more extreme views of Eutyches (378–454), an elderly monk and abbot of

Figure 53
The "definition" of Chalcedon

> Therefore, following the holy Fathers, we all with one accord teach men to acknowledge one and the same Son, our Lord Jesus Christ, at once complete in Godhead and complete in manhood, truly God and truly man, consisting also of a reasonable soul and body; of one substance [*homoousios*] with the Father as regards his Godhead, and at the same time of one substance with us as regards his manhood; like us in all respects, apart from sin; as regards his Godhead, begotten of the Father before the ages, but yet as regards his manhood begotten, for us men and for our salvation, of Mary the Virgin, the God-bearer [*theotokos*]; one and the same Christ, Son, Lord, Only-begotten, recognized in two natures, without confusion, without change, without division, without separation; the distinction of natures being in no way annulled by the union, but rather the characteristics of each nature being preserved and coming together to form one person and subsistence [*hupostasis*], not as parted or separated into two persons, but one and the same Son and Only-begotten God the Word, Lord Jesus Christ; even as the prophets from earliest times spoke of him, and our Lord Jesus Christ himself taught us, and the creed of the Fathers has handed down to us.

Constantinople who exaggerated the "divinity aspect" of Christ in his condemnation of the Nestorians. Eutyches had suggested, by way of analogy, that Christ's humanity was absorbed by his divinity like a drop of wine in the sea. Eutyches agreed that the original components for the incarnation were the divine Word and an integral human nature, but in the union of the two natures he held that the former "swallowed up" the latter. In effect, then, Christ ends up with only one nature – the divine one. Eutyches, as chief proponent of this "single-nature" (monophysite) view, was summoned in AD 448 to a synod at Constantinople to answer charges of heresy. Eutyches was condemned but he made appeal to Leo, the Bishop of Rome. The Roman bishop was not sympathetic, however, and wrote back supporting Flavian (Archbishop of Constantinople) who had condemned Eutyches. The Emperor Theodosius II (AD 408–450) called another council at Ephesus under the presidency of

Dioscorus, successor to Cyril in the see of Alexandria. At that controversial council (AD 449, sometimes nicknamed the "Robber Council") Eutyches was upheld and Flavian deposed. The monophysite view was vindicated. The following year Theodosius died. Under a new empress and emperor (Pulcheria and Marcian), a new ecumenical council was called at Chalcedon (AD 451). This council was attended by over 400 Greek bishops and included representatives from Rome. In its sessions, Nestorius' views were disowned, and so was the monophysite perspective as put forward by Eutyches. The Council of Chalcedon officially approved the "Tome of Leo", praised patriarch Flavian, and put out a composite "definition" (Figure 53).

A year later, Chalcedon's decrees became imperial law. The church in Egypt, however, where Cyril had been a great churchman, rejected the official line, seeing it as essentially Nestorian. Within the patriarchates of both Alexandria and Antioch there were sizeable majorities whose voices were raised against Chalcedon. Neither Emperor Justin I (AD 518–527) nor Justinian (AD 527–565) was able to heal the deep divisions of the east that had developed over these "theological" arguments. The Christians of Egypt, the Syrian Jacobites, the Egyptian-won Christians in Ethiopia and the Armenians became and remained monophysite in their view. After the later condemnation of Theodore of Mopsuestia at the second Council of Constantinople in AD 553, a separate Nestorian Church took a more discernible form, finding a home in the Persian kingdom.

Such were some of the major doctrinal controversies pursued from the historic centres of Christian faith in Alexandria, Antioch, Jerusalem, Rome and Constantinople. Emperors convened councils and settled doctrinal disputes by imperial decree. Underneath the theological words lay power struggles between bishops in different sees. Representatives of different views, and power bases, anathematized one other. Simmering rivalries quickly erupted when one group or another gained the ear of an emperor. Mutual suspicion of church leaders' motives was fuelled by resolutions such as the one made at the Council of Constantinople in AD 381 affirming that the Bishop of Constantinople should have rank immediately after the Bishop of Rome because Constantinople constituted the "New Rome". This offended Rome – had it previously been primary simply because it was the secular capital of the empire? The affirmation also enraged the Alexandrians who were not considered for first or second place. The Alexandrians could now expect assistance in their attacks on theologians in Constantinople from cities in Asia Minor like Ephesus, where church leaders were hostile to the powerful prelates at the imperial capital. The Alexandrians also received support (in the case of the Nestorian controversy) from Jerusalem, which was hostile to Antioch, the Nestorian home-base. A complex matrix of political alliances and theological arguments underlay and gave ever-changing expression to issues that were really about the relationship between "truth" and "power".

What did all this "politicking" mean for the mass of the Christian faithful? Their comprehension of the issues involved was probably minimal, and any expectation that they might change their beliefs after their leaders had been anathematized quite naïve. They held to what they knew.

Christians in Syria, as we have seen, tended to end up as monophysite – emphasizing the "divine" element of Christ's nature. As a result, the reference to Christ as divine and to Mary as *theotokos* or "God-bearer" was common. What did ordinary Christians make of that? If Mary was "mother of God" and Christ was more divine than human, then was it not fair to deduce that God and Mary together produced Jesus? The Trinity must be Father and Mary plus their Son.

Christians in Mesopotamia and Persia tended to end up as Nestorian – overemphasizing the "human" element of Christ's nature. ʿAlî ibn-Rabbân al-Tabarî (died AD 855) was an educated Nestorian Christian physician from Baghdad. He converted to Islam at the age of 70. Perhaps his Nestorian view of Christ made him open to the Muslim perspective: Christ was really an ordinary man, wonderfully used of God. Al-Tabarî set out to show in his book *Refutation of the Christians* that Christian belief about Jesus being both divine and human is contradictory and consequently in error.

Emerging from the battles between opposing, Christian

schools of thought – as promoted by different, self-assured power bases – came some of the concepts that would have a direct bearing on the kind of understanding of Christianity that lies behind some of the pronouncements of the Qur'ân.

Truth and power in Islamic history

When Prophet Muḥammad died, he had no son to succeed him. He did have a surviving son-in-law who was also his cousin and father to the Prophet's only grandsons, Ḥasan and Ḥussein. That son-in-law's name was ᶜAlî ibn Abû Ṭâlib and he was married to Fâṭima, one of the daughters of Muḥammad by Khadîja. ᶜAlî had been an early believer and companion to the Prophet. There was a strong suggestion by some of ᶜAlî's supporters that on his deathbed Muḥammad named ᶜAlî as his successor. Others claimed that during Muḥammad's farewell pilgrimage to Mecca, Gabriel appeared again to the Prophet and instructed him to name ᶜAlî as his legal successor, something that he did – they insisted – on the way back to Medina. In the event, the leadership passed to Abû Bakr, then to ᶜUmar, then to ᶜUthmân before it came finally to ᶜAlî.

Even then, ᶜAlî's succession to the caliphate was not uncontested. ᶜAlî and his supporters were opposed by a group in which Prophet Muḥammad's widow, ᶜÂ'isha, occupied a prominent position. There were violent clashes and even an armed battle. ᶜAlî was victorious at the "Battle of the Camel" (AD 656) but soon found a superior rival in the person of Muᶜâwiya, the governor of Syria. Muᶜâwiya was the son of Abû Sufyân, a tribal leader who, 40 years previously, had strongly opposed Muḥammad right up to the truce of Ḥudaibiya. Muᶜâwiya had not involved himself in the conflict between ᶜÂ'isha and ᶜAlî, but with ᶜÂ'isha he demanded the punishment of Caliph ᶜUthmân's assassins – ᶜUthmân was his cousin, after all. Caliph ᶜUthmân, a Meccan aristocrat of the Umayya clan (Abû Sufyân's clan), had been murdered in AD 656 by a band of about 500 Arabs from Fustat. It was with the support of these Arabs that ᶜAlî finally succeeded to the caliphate. The consequent civil strife continued throughout ᶜAlî's rulership. Eventually the opponents met at the Battle of Siffin (AD 657) where moderate voices in both camps managed to negotiate an agreement to arbitrate the question of whether ᶜUthmân's murder was justified. Some of ᶜAlî's supporters – known as the Kharijîs or "Secessionists" – turned against him as a result of his willingness to go to arbitration. They were defeated in battle. The arbitrators met in AD 659 and concluded from their deliberations that the murder of ᶜUthmân had not been justified. ᶜAlî rejected their conclusion, but unfortunately for him his own coalition of forces was beginning to unravel. He himself was assassinated by a Kharijî and Muᶜâwiya declared himself caliph.

The civil war "ended" with the caliphate firmly established in the hands of the Qurayshi Umayyad family. Muᶜâwiya moved the seat of the caliphate to Damascus, thus considerably marginalizing Mecca and Medina. The power of the Muslim community now lay with the historic Arabian tribal leaders rather than with the early Muslim elite. The civil war began a dispute that in one sense has never really "ended": who has the legitimate right to occupy the caliphate? Is it those who accepted the succession of Muᶜâwiya and the historical sequence of caliphs following him or is it ᶜAlî and his descendants? Sunnî or Shîᶜa? Incidentally, the Kharijîs (who survive with descendants until the present time and whose theological convictions support a radical interpretation of Islam) held that the caliph should descend from neither family, but should be elected by the community of Muslims at large, and should only remain as caliph for as long as he discharged its responsibilities honourably.

The significant point for our interest is that Sunnîs, Shîᶜas and Kharijîs developed different versions of Islam. It appears to be the case in Islam, as well as in Christianity, that different theologies acted as flags for other, cultural or political differences. For Shîᶜas, a strong sense of solidarity has found focus in their continuing loyalty to the Caliph ᶜAlî plus the conviction that the caliphate could only proceed within his family's lineage. Since the Shîᶜa denied the legitimacy of the Sunnî succession of caliphs, an independent *ḥadîth* (tradition) and law was sought in which ᶜAlî might be promoted as the most important authority. At the same time, the Shîᶜas' political misfortunes forced them to face up to the issue of "failure" or "suffering". The catalyst for such reconsideration revolved around a critical confrontation at Karbalâ'. The two sons of ᶜAlî, Ḥasan and Ḥussein, Muḥammad's only surviving male line, each fell victim to enormous tragedy. Ḥasan, the elder, was persuaded to abdicate in favour of Muᶜâwiya after only a few months as caliph in succession to his father. He was killed in mysterious circumstances – possibly poisoned by his own wife at the instigation of Muᶜâwiya's son Yazîd – in Medina in AD 669.

Ḥasan's younger brother Ḥussein attempted to challenge Yazîd for the caliphate in Damascus when the Caliph Muᶜâwiya (Yazîd's father) died in AD 680. The people of Kufa sent a message to Ḥussein saying that they would recognize him as the new caliph instead of Yazîd. Ḥussein accepted the call and set out for Kufa. On the way, he was surrounded by a vastly superior force and both he and his small retinue were massacred at Karbalâ', in lower Iraq, on the "tenth of Muḥarram". That tragedy is recalled in Shîᶜa communities on that date in an annual passion play, retelling the story of Ḥussein's martyrdom. Sometimes, the re-enacting is accompanied by processions in which real or symbolic acts of self-flagellation occur. For several years, while living in Lebanon, I would go with friends to observe the commemoration hosted at Nabatieh, a town in the Shîᶜa-dominated south of the country. Many men would process round the town's neighbourhoods after the performance of the passion play, cutting themselves with razors or swords, returning to the staged area in the main square soaked in blood. They wore white gowns over their clothes, symbolic of their willingness to be martyred in the tradition of Imam Ḥussein.

In the passion play, Ḥussein is presented as innocent, a man stricken with suffering for others. The drama re-enacts the preparation for battle of the heroic campers on the day before the fight and then their cruel slaughter on the following day. Ḥussein seeks the safety of his followers in return for his own surrender. His seeking is in vain and so he spends the night in prayer:

The next morning both sides prepared for the slaughter. Husain first washed and anointed himself with musk, and several of his chief men did the like; and one asking them what it meant, Husain replied pleasantly, "Alas! There is nothing between us and the black-eyed girls of Paradise but that these troopers come down upon us and slay us!" Then he mounted his horse, and set the Qur'ân before him, crying, "O God Thou art my confidence in every trouble and my hope in every adversity!" and submitted himself to the judgment of his companions before the opened pages of the sacred volume. At that his sisters and daughters began to weep ... the fight began on both sides. It raged, chiefly in a series of single combats, until noon-day, when both sides retired to prayer, Husain adding to the usual office the "Prayer of Fear", never used but in cases of extremity. When shortly afterwards the fight was renewed, Husain was struck on the head by a sword. Faint with the loss of blood, he sat down by his tent and took upon his lap his little son Abdullah, who was at once killed by a flying arrow. He placed the little corpse upon the ground, crying out, "We come from God and we return to Him. O God, give me strength to bear these misfortunes." Growing thirsty, he ran toward the Euphrates, where, as he stooped to drink, an arrow struck him in the mouth. Raising his hands, all besmeared and dripping with blood, to heaven, he stood for awhile and prayed earnestly. His little nephew, a beautiful child, who went up to kiss him, had his hand cut off with a sword, on which Husain again wept, saying, "Thy reward, dear child, is with thy forefathers in the realms of bliss." Hounded on by Shamer, the Syrian troops now surrounded him; but Husain, nothing daunted, charged them right and left. In the midst of the fighting, his sister came between him and his slayers, crying out to Amer, how he could stand by and see Husain slain. Whereupon, with tears trickling down his beard, Amer turned his face away; but Shamer, with threats and curses, set on his soldiers again, and at last one wounded Husain upon the hand, and a second gashed him on the neck, and a third thrust him through the body with a spear. No sooner had he fallen to the ground than Shamer rode a troop of horsemen over his corpse, backwards and forwards, over and over again, until it was trampled into the very ground, a scarcely recognisable mass of mangled flesh and mud.[137]

Ḥussein is perceived as an offerer of vicarious merit because of his suffering and martyrdom as an innocent man. The Umayyad army and its general are vilified as symbols of all that is evil. In the killing of Ḥussein, not only is justice denied and innocence violated, but the physical lineage of Prophet Muḥammad is wiped out. The passion play offers a construct on reality that is in strong contrast to the (Sunnî) "God's people are always successful" variety. Shîᶜa Islam has at its core some sympathy for a redemptive view of suffering. As Cragg summarizes: "All sorrow is Husain's sorrow and all sin is in his murderers."[138]

The reconstruction of Islamic faith in Shîᶜa hands went deeper still. As we have noted, the critical issue for Shîᶜa Muslims was not so much law (or for the Shîᶜa Ṣûfîs, mysticism) as loyalty to the Caliph ᶜAlî, and the consequent conviction that the true caliphate should only descend within his family lineage. Out of this conviction arose a reinterpretation of the idea of "caliph" or leadership of the community. The Shîᶜa theologians gradually developed their distinctive concept of the "imamate". The Qur'ân provided their starting-point:

> And remember that Abraham
> Was tried by his Lord
> With certain Commands,
> Which he fulfilled:
> He said: "I will make thee
> An Imâm to the Nations."
> He pleaded: "And also
> (Imâms) from my offspring!"
> He answered: "But My Promise
> Is not within the reach
> Of evil-doers." (Sura 2:124)

According to Shîᶜa theologizing, this passage shows that the imamate (the caliphate) is a divine institution. The words about that imamate not being within the reach of evil-doers is interpreted to mean that the divinely appointed leader must be without sin. ᶜAlî was consequently "refashioned" so that he emerged as having been created by God, along with

Muḥammad, Fâṭima, Ḥasan and Ḥussein, before the creation of Adam, prior to there being heavens and earth, paradise and hell. He thus exhibited this exceptional quality of not being an evil-doer and the imamate could be safely assigned to his family. Jaᶜfar al-Ṣâdiq (died AD 765), the sixth imam in the line of ᶜAlî, taught that the true ruler of the Muslim community descended in the line of ᶜAlî through the handing on of an internal, secret knowledge along with authority to interpret the Qur'ân and the *ḥadîth*. By the ninth century, Shîᶜa concepts of the imamate came to embrace the idea that the imam was in fact a sinless and infallible guide to religious truth. As has been sometimes deduced, the Roman Catholic expression of the Christian faith has developed some convictions – such as the infallibility and unquestionable authority of the pope – that mirror aspects of the Shîᶜa view of the imamate. When the physical line of imams came to an end in the closing years of that century, the theory of a hidden or occulted twelfth imam came to be developed. This imam will return as Mahdi or Messiah at the end of time. His hiddenness makes him a figure of mystery and promise. His representatives on earth, *mujtahids* or instigators of *ijtihâd*, exercise governance on his behalf. That is why Imam Khomeini could speak with such authority during the years following the Islamic revolution in Iran. He represented the Hidden Imam and when he spoke on a matter, there was an end to it. Shîᶜa Islam lives with the hope that the Hidden Imam will one day disclose himself.

The development by Sunnî and Shîᶜa Muslims of separate theologies and political structures began in a dispute about succession to Prophet Muḥammad. Early disagreement was exacerbated by murder, intrigue, massacre and a power struggle over authority within the house of Islam. The differences came to be increasingly concretized in theological constructs that justified different ways of being Muslim. Ethnic distance between Arabs and Persians fed suspicion and hostility. Today, the major Shîᶜa expression of Islam is found in Iran, though there are significant Shîᶜa communities in Iraq (constituting the major Arab concentration of Shîᶜa), in the Indian subcontinent, in East Africa and in Lebanon. The chief centres of pilgrimage are connected with Ḥussein or the imams and lie in Iran and Iraq: Karbalâ', Najaf, Qum, Mashhad and Kazimain.

Within Islam, the delicate interrelation of truth and power has been demonstrated in *fatwâ*-fighting and cruel wars, in the reinterpretation of history and radical theological reconstruction. The early development of the Islamic faith bears many parallels, in this respect, to the experience of Christians in the period after that faith became the official cultus of an empire.

We have spent most of this chapter considering the relationship between truth and power as it has found expression within the historical development of both Christianity and Islam. The history of each faith seems to have been concerned with, even dominated by, that relationship. How truth and power come to be entwined expresses and exposes the very human nature of both religious groups. Orthodox belief and practice in each are constantly deemed to require some sort of external sanction. We need now to ask whether such a process was a requirement or expectation of Jesus or Muḥammad. What relationship between truth and power came to find expression in their lives and leadership?

Jesus, Muḥammad and power

Jesus, as he himself recounted, was sent primarily to recover the lost house of Israel to God. The "house of Israel" that he found in and around Jerusalem and Judaea proved "lost" in many senses. During three years of public ministry a tale largely of conflict between Jesus and the Jewish leadership developed. Matthew in his Gospel, especially, describes the life and ministry of Jesus in such terms. An ironic subplot within this most Jewish Gospel is focused on the aggressive hostility shown towards Jesus by the Jewish leaders. That hostility eventually leads to the strong language of Jesus in chapter 23, where he repeatedly accuses the teachers of the Law and the Pharisees of being hypocrites, blind leaders of the blind! That hostility leads also to the arrest, trial and execution of Jesus, as instigated and manipulated by those offended leaders.

After the Babylonian exile of the Jews and especially during the Maccabean revolt, the powerful Jewish Hasmonean family gained control of the high priesthood. The leaders of this family came to operate what amounted to a theocratic state (see Figure 54). The Hasmoneans were strongly opposed by the

Figure 54
Jewish Hasmonean power-holders

Name	Years
Jeshua, son of See	3 BC – AD 6
Joazar, son of Boethus	6
Annas, son of Seth	6–15
Ishmael, son of Phiabi I	15–16
Eleazar, son of Annas	16–17
Simon, son of Kami	17–18
Joseph Caiaphas	18–36
Jonathan, son of Annas	36–37

Pharisees who despised the priestly family for abandoning, in their view, Israel's ancient traditions. Other radical dissident groups, such as the Essenes, also despised the high priestly family and its allies. The 6,000 or so Pharisees comprised officials who, as custodians of the Law, knew the Jewish data of revelation. They understood God's will, or thought they did. So their knowledge constituted a form of power. They proclaimed on behalf of God, they defined orthodoxy and orthopraxy for the faithful. If their theology was ever questioned, or if their power looked as if it might be undermined, they would fight tooth and nail to retain their tight grip on both. In the process of Jesus' public ministry, these various, often opposed, groups came increasingly together to oppose his challenge to them.

The life and ministry of Jesus, presented by Matthew in

terms of him being the "Teacher of Israel", brought Jesus into constant conflict with such leaders who saw themselves as authority figures ordained by God to guide his people Israel. Those religious leaders interacted with the political rulers of the land in such a way that they maintained themselves in office and guaranteed a quiet life for the imperial administrators (see Figure 55). Jesus of Nazareth emerged as a threat to both sets of powerful people. Matthew's presentation of Jesus'

Figure 55
Roman power-holders

Procurators	Dates: AD	New Testament
Coponius	6–10	
Ambivius	10–13	
Annius Rufus	13–15	
Valerius Gratus	15–26	
Pontius Pilate	26–36	Luke 3:1; 23:1
Marcellus	36–38	
Marullus	38–41	
no procurator: Herod Agrippa I king over Judaea and Palestine	41–44	Acts 12
Cuspius Fadus	44–46	
Tiberius Alexander	46–48	
Ventidius Cumanus	48–52	
M. Antonius Felix	52–59	Acts 23 – 24
Porcius Festus	59–61	Acts 24:27
Albinus	61–65	deals with complaint that high priest Ananus II condemned Jesus' brother James to death
Gessius Florus	65–70	*Jerusalem destroyed*
Vettulenus Cerialis	70–72	

life and ministry describes the rejection of the Teacher by his own people, plus the inclusion by that Teacher of the Gentiles in his offer of reconciliation. In the process of Jesus' being rejected and suffering ignominy, Matthew (in contrast to Mark, say) emphasizes that, all along, Jesus is perfectly in control. He is not passive. It is his choice to accept such a path of suffering.

Ultimately, Jesus comes to Gethsemane. Walking in the footsteps of most of the biblical prophets before him, Jesus discovers that very few people heed his voice. The secular power-holders and the religious power-holders certainly will not listen to him. They combine to silence him. In Gethsemane, Jesus faces a choice. It is a choice concerning how he judges truth to be related to power. He, of all people, knows what constitutes truth. In his own words, "I *am* the Truth." Should not the Truth be vindicated, be seen to be successful? Such a route is certainly possible for him. "Do you think," he asks his stunned and fearful disciples as he is being arrested, "I cannot call on my Father, and he will at once put at my disposal more than twelve legions of angels?" (Matthew 26:53). Even here, Matthew is at pains to emphasize that Jesus is making active choices about his life and death. Jesus tells his followers to put away their swords. He chooses not to relate truth and power in a physically violent way. He will allow human power to "succeed", to have its sway, to enjoy its heyday in nailing him to a cross.

Yet, even in the time of death, another power speaks on Jesus' behalf. The crucifixion scene is unnaturally dark and supernaturally eerie. While Jesus' cry of abandonment goes unanswered in Mark's Gospel, Matthew describes several miraculous, apocalyptic occurrences: the splitting of rocks in an earthquake, the rising of dead people from the tombs. In Mark's Gospel at this point, one man recognizes in Jesus someone divine, but in Matthew's Gospel all who are with the centurion at the site of crucifixion are terrified, confessing that Jesus is the Son of God (Matthew 27:54).

A few nights later, while the Jewish and Roman power-holders are sleeping, something divine occurs within the deathly hush of a grave – marked again by a supernatural earthquake – and Jesus is discovered risen! His resurrection life is liberated to pulsate its way through the lives of humankind – yeast, vision, holy resource for eternal change. Such is Jesus' way of combining truth and power. He willingly offers himself to death, secure in the knowledge that that is the way to ultimate victory for himself and for all who will put their trust in him to deliver them. It is a way of looking at power that is in character with Christ's style of appearance on earth, his incarnation. Paul describes the choreography of that event as divine Son deigns to become earthly Man. It is a kenotic dance, a movement of self-emptying. God's way of sorting out human sin and injustice in a world gone awry is to convey his Truth. Essentially, in Christ, his Truth comes in the guise of a vulnerable, woman-born baby. From the date of that particular birth, that point in the dance, the Christian calendar begins.

Prophet Muḥammad takes a different route. Emigration away from persecution in Mecca leads to the possibility of him becoming the designer, himself, of a civilization in Medina. The Battle of Badr felt a bit like the powerless people of Israel emerging as victors over mighty Pharaoh and all his forces. At Badr, a handful of Muslims resoundingly beat a much larger force of Meccans. God gave them a resounding victory. *Hijra* led to the establishment of a state in which the statesman was an intermediary between God and man. As prophet, he was vindicated by God. The Muslim reversal at Uḥud was quickly explained; the followers of the Prophet needed to commit themselves to proper obedience. Over a ten-year period, God's way of going about things was exegeted by Prophet Muḥammad. With qur'ânic approval, Muḥammad's responsibility changes from simply having a duty to convey the message that God gave him (Sura 42:48) to defining for his community how they are to live in God's favour. Emigration led to emirship. The Muslim calendar is dated from that point, from the time of the shift from persecution to power.

Our brief look at the connection made between truth and power in the developing histories of both Christianity and Islam reveals a complex web of motive and attitude. Too often, in each faith's history, truth has been shackled to the service of political power. Cragg pointedly asks, concerning the more recent confessional violence in Lebanon, "has not the voice of faith been almost silenced by the travesties of the faithless 'faithful'?"[139] Different theologies have evolved, in both faiths, as dissident groups have tried to assert their distance from the current power-holder. As a result, atrocious things have gone on in the name of religion, things that will need closer inspection in chapter 8 of this book.

One might argue that, in the wrong use of "power" to defend or export "truth", Christians are the more culpable, the more blameworthy. After all, what is the heritage that each faith community derives from its prophetic source on this matter of truth and power? For Prophet Muḥammad, the use of weaponry to achieve God's goal was not only permitted; it was commanded. It is as a result of the qur'ânic command to use force to achieve supremacy that the discussion goes on in Muslim circles today about the nature of *jihâd*. The Islamists claim, with considerable justification it seems to me, that "using the sword" literally means using force where that is commended in the Qur'ân. Prophet Muḥammad certainly made that his interpretation in his own lifetime. For Jesus, such an approach to the appropriation of physical force was an option he consistently refused to take. In Islam, the progression from preacher to powerful ruler was legitimized by God himself. In the words of Cragg: "Islam has the built-in instinct to abjure the tragic and to take 'manifest victory' as both appropriate to truth and indicative of God's presence."[140] In Christianity, the call is continually for Christians to have that mind in them that was in Christ Jesus – to walk the way of humility and vulnerability. The cross was, for Christ, a symbol of his decision to absorb violence rather than to inflict it. For Christians, then, to fail in following their Lord in this essential attitude makes them the more accountable for any violence of spirit or body perpetrated in Christ's name.

Chapter 7 Do It in Public?

Lord of all, or not at all

In the name of God,
Most Gracious, Most Merciful.
Praise be to God,
The Cherisher and Sustainer of the Worlds;
Most Gracious, Most Merciful;
Master of the Day of Judgment.
Thee do we worship,
And Thine aid we seek.
Show us the straight way,
The way of those on whom
Thou hast bestowed Thy Grace,
Those whose (portion)
Is not wrath,
And who go not astray. (Sura 1:1–7)

The major petition of the opening sura of the Qur'ân – called the *Fâtiḥa* or "Opener" – is expressed as a prayer for guidance. The sura begins with praise and worship and then moves on to petition: "Show us the straight way" (literally, in Arabic, "Guide us to/in the straight way"). The prayer is one for guidance. The Qur'ân itself is often referred to as *hudâ* or "guidance". Indeed, Islam itself, can be referred to as "guidance":

> Islam is a complete way of life. It is the guidance provided by Allah, the Creator of the Universe, for all mankind. It covers all the things people do in their lifetime. Islam tells us the purpose of our creation, our final destiny and our place among other creatures. It shows us the best way to conduct our private, social, political, economic, moral and spiritual affairs of life.[141]

Learning how God wants humankind to live and committing to live accordingly is the purpose and aim of being a Muslim. In such a manner, "guidance" is received. Islam as a faith focuses strongly on the will of God, declaring it and explaining it so that humans may submit to it. Hence, as we have seen, Islam places a major emphasis on law. Muslims see in nature a world of harmony and order as creation works according to the laws that God has established. For humans, also, God has a law, a way of order and harmony that humanity should accept to live by. By submitting to God and obeying his law, human beings may experience true peace. The Islamic way of life meshes with what is deeply desired by all human beings – peace and harmony and wholeness of life. It offers, to all who will yield, the equivalent of the Hebrew idea of *shalôm*.

The concept of "worship" in Islam contains far more than simply a piety element. It amounts to a total surrender of the human being in all facets of living. This emphasis is richly expressed in many verses of the Qur'ân:

> Say: "Truly, my prayer
> And my service of sacrifice,
> My life and my death,
> Are (all) for God,
> The Cherisher of the Worlds ... " (Sura 6:162)

Indeed, human beings are set apart from all other created beings (except that species of spirits known as jinn) in possessing this capacity to truly worship God:

> I have only created
> Jinns and men, that
> They may serve me. (Sura 51:56)

According to this well-known verse, jinn and humankind are ready made to serve God. The Arabic verb translated "serve" gives the noun "service" or *ᶜibâda* (plural *ᶜibâdât*). This is a significant term connoting "worship-in-obedience". The concept of *ᶜibâda* in Islam is comprehensive in its embrace. It includes all activities of life if those activities are performed to please

God. Right attitudes in prayer are important, not just the prayer itself. Obligatory rituals and beliefs constitute part of the worship. Everyday behaviour, also, can be assessed as right or wrong conduct in front of God. Sometimes the noun *ᶜibâdât* is used to refer to the last four of the "five pillars" of Islam (see Figure 56).

Figure 56
The "five pillars" of Islam

Collective term	Pillar	Explanation
	shahâda	declaration of faith
ᶜibâdât	*ṣalât*	five compulsory daily prayers
	zakât	welfare contribution
	ṣawm	fasting during Ramaḍân
	ḥajj	pilgrimage to Mecca

In introducing his discussion on these main "acts of worship" in Islam, Mawdûdî explains them in the following terms:

> The Arabic word defining these acts of worship is *ibadat*. This is derived from the word "abd" which means submission. "Abd" also can be defined as something "owned" by someone else. What all this really means is that God is your Master and you are His servant and whatever a servant does in obeying his Master, whatever he does for the pleasure of his Master, is an act of worship. This Islamic concept of worship is very wide. If you remove from your speech false, malicious, and abusive things, and speak the truth and talk about good and helpful things; if you do all this because God Almighty has told you to, this constitutes a form of worship. They are acts of worship no matter how secular their appearance might be. If you obey the law of God across the board in your commercial and economic affairs, if you use it in your dealings with your parents, relatives, and friends, clearly these activities become acts of worship. If you help the poor and handicapped,

> feed the hungry and serve the ailing, and if you do all this not for any personal gain, but to seek the pleasure of God, they are nothing short of acts of worship. Even your money earning activities – your jobs – the activities you undertake to earn your living and feed your dependents – are acts of worship if you remain honest in performing them and observe the law of God. In short, all your activities and your entire life are acts of worship if your heart is filled with fear and love of God while performing them. Your entire life is worship if your ultimate objective in life is to seek the pleasure of the Great and Wonderful God.[142]

True submission means moulding one's entire life according to the patterns of Islam. Formal acts of worship help set the tone, but *ᶜibâda* is about making the whole of life an act of worship in obedience. That is why law (*sharîᶜa*) is so important in Islam. Law declares what should be happening when "the rubber hits the road", as it were. Law gives direction to obedience. In effect, law constitutes what religion is about. Cragg emphasizes this point in his contention that law has to take precedence even over theology in Islam:

> Law, rather than theology, has the prior emphasis in Islam. Broadly, it is obedience to the will of God, rather than fellowship in the knowledge of God's nature, which is paramount. Revelation is for direction of life, rather than disclosure of mystery ... Islam is essentially submission, rather than "communion".[143]

As a consequence of this view of "worship", there has tended to develop very little distinction in Islam between the sacred and the secular. Such a distinction has, of course, manifested itself historically in some places, especially where outside colonizers or internal religious and political leaders of Muslims have allowed piety to become divorced from everyday life for whatever reason. Turkey under Atatürk, for example, underwent a deliberate secularization of its society after World War I – but the Turks have subsequently never freed themselves from the internal tension that that secularizing movement brought to their society. The twentieth century saw in Turkey a see-sawing of opinion shifts as the secularists and the Islamic traditionalists took turns to gain the upper hand. Iran, also, was deliberately secularized under the two Shahs – but the battle about what Islam means for that country was decisively won by Imam Khomeini and the Islamists in the Islamic Revolution there. Those who wanted to continue to divorce piety from everyday living ended up dead or in exile. For that is not the Islamic way.

For Muslims, there are no areas where the will of God does not extend. God has a view on everything. The point of Islamic law, or *sharîʿa*, is to bring that view out. How does God want inheritance matters handled? How should a family function? What constitutes faithfulness in the world of banking and commerce? Those and similar questions it seeks to address.

One rule for all

There is consequently a strong horizontal feel to any Islamic community, and to the Islamic constituency as a whole, for the law of God instructs Muslims as to how they should relate to one another. In prayer, all Muslims turn towards the same spot on earth. In pilgrimage, all Muslims wear the same simple apparel. In reading God's word, all Muslims learn the same text in the one language. In decisions about trading or sexual intercourse or making war, all Muslims are subject to the same divine sanctions. God says that certain foods or drinks are shameful and that's an end to the discussion – for all Muslims. The whole community concurs on these matters. They are questions of faith.

Islam is thus deliberately inclusive in terms of its acceptance of people of different ethnic or linguistic background. The mosque becomes the melting-pot where a microcosm of diverse humanity may find meaning and mutual support. This ability of Islam to bind together people of different ethnicity was demonstrated most forcefully in the 1994 massacres in Rwanda during which, in the course of two months, some 800,000 men, women and children died. The great majority of the killed, and the killers, were Christians. The small Muslim community in Rwanda proved its ability to overcome traditional Hutu and Tutsi enmity:

> The only faith which provided a bulwark against barbarity for its adherents was Islam. There are many testimonies to the protection members of the Muslim community gave each other and their refusal to divide themselves ethnically ... Muslims are often socially marginal people [in Rwanda] and this reinforces a strong sense of community identification which supersedes ethnic tags, something the majority Christians have not been able to achieve.[144]

Muslims find solidarity together.

A major area of tension arises for Muslims where the law of God, for whatever reason, remains unobeyed. Maybe it is because Muslims in religious or political authority have abandoned their *islâm*. Such is certainly the angry diagnosis by Islamists of the sort of contaminated, half-hearted Islam that was upheld in ex-colonized Muslim countries in the second half of the twentieth century. The indigenous leaders of the newly independent nations, themselves educated in the secularized West, oversaw a muddied mixture of Islamic law and Western constitutional law instead of leading their societies into a true submission to God's desires.

Maybe the law of God remains unobeyed because individual Muslims select the degree to which they will allow God's law to mould their lives. The purpose of Mawdûdî's preaching in the years prior to partition in the Indian subcontinent was to prepare an elite of Muslim leaders who would guide the Muslim community in India into a faithful obedience to *sharîʿa* law. When the Muslims opted for a separate homeland, Mawdûdî agitated for the adoption of an Islamic state as their political expression. In the event, the secularists under Jinnah won the ideological battle and many Pakistani Muslims in the years since 1947 have chosen the degree to which they have allowed *sharîʿa* law to impinge on their lives.

Maybe the law of God remains unobeyed because Muslims live as minorities in Western secular societies where the prevailing worldview will not countenance as valid a perspective that wants to involve "religion" in all the details of life. The French made their secularist point in the 2004 banning of headscarves as part of the apparel of Muslim girls going to state-run schools.

Back on their feet

One of the striking changes in the make-up of the world in recent decades has been the widespread, deeply motivated renewal of Islam as a faith community. That renewal process has once again allowed Muslims to see themselves as significant on a global scale. The rapid changes on the world scene in the years after the end of World War II provided the backdrop for such renewal.

From AD 1750 to AD 1950, most Muslims in the world lived under non-Muslim military or civilian rule. The Western (European) imperial powers did not, for the most part, involve themselves in details of piety. Muslims were permitted to worship in their mosques, to keep their fast of Ramaḍân, to make their pilgrimages to Mecca, and to live openly as confessing Muslims. By the "piety" test, Muslims remained free to practise their faith. The "piety" test, however, is a Western or secular humanist construct, reflecting the kind of separation of sacred and secular domains to which the post-Enlightenment Western world is wedded. Piety, for Muslims, amounts to nothing without the political power to order all of life in conjunction with God's desires. Medina is looked back to with such exaggerated idealism precisely because there the Prophet was able to be statesman as well as preacher. The long history of the caliphate until its demise at the end of World War I – however unfaithful in its many particulars – was at least "correct" in the sense that Muslims were politically responsible for their own destinies. Caliphs and dynasties may have been aberrant in the manner in which they functioned, but *that* they functioned was an important principle of the way God wants society to work. Ever since Muḥammad's exodus from Mecca to Medina, religion and rule have for Muslims been bound into one, holistic enterprise.

Under European colonial tutelage, then, Muslims lacked the opportunity for proper *islâm* in being denied independent political power. They were unable to truly serve their Lord.

They were not allowed to be fully Muslim. A searching of the Islamic heart took place in country after country, often provoked by Islamists like Mawdûdî, al-Bannâ', Qutb and others.[145] The abolition of the caliphate itself came as an enormous shock to Muslims, symbolizing the shutting down of the political or "power" aspect of being Muslim. The emotional pain of Muslims finding themselves ruled by non-Muslims is parallel to the agony faced by Jewish exiles from the land of Israel in the years after the fall of Samaria in 722 BC and the razing to the ground of Jerusalem in 587 BC. How could the exiled Jews sing the Lord's songs in a foreign land? Such was their constant lament. How, in the twentieth century AD, could Muslims hold their heads high when prevented from proper *islâm* by the foreign occupiers of their lands? The call from the early Islamists, along with many other Muslim activists, was for Muslims to take their destiny into their own hands, to reclaim control of the institutions of their societies so that they could determine once again the ethos and pattern of their public, communal existence. From AD 1945 to AD 1960, Western imperial powers receded from Muslim – and other – lands. The period of colonialism was over. Muslim states emerged as independent and autonomous entities throughout Asia, Africa and the Middle East. Political power was returned to Muslims for them to exercise on behalf of their own communities.

How such power was subsequently used became the subject of constant debate throughout the Muslim world in the second half of the twentieth century. The Islamists especially have been dissatisfied with how their political and religious leaders – since independence – have failed, in their eyes, to be radically Muslim. Only in a few situations has an Islamic state been willingly introduced as the political context in which Muslims may work out their "service". Independence tended to mean the establishment of Muslim nation-states rather than the creation of an Islamic entity. The caliphate has not been revived. Indeed the idea of nationality has proven a much stronger ideal than the (political) concept of *umma* – or Islamic community. Areas of Muslim majority in the subcontinent of India chose to become Pakistan at partition. Bangladesh preferred to become a separate nation from Pakistan, via Indian assistance, in 1971. The Islamist version of a single Islamic state for all Muslims seems a long way from public implementation. Despite such questions concerning how "Islamic" Muslim nations really are, the point I wish to make here is that the arguments have been made by Muslims themselves about their *islâm*. It has constituted an *internal* debate.

Against this backdrop, the renewal movement within Islam as a world faith has found expression and gained momentum:

> during the latter half of the 1970's, Islam dramatically re-emerged in Muslim politics across the Islamic world; in General Zia ul-Hak's *coup d'état* in Pakistan in 1977 and his call for establishment of an Islamic system of government (*Nizam-i-Islam*); in the Iranian "Islamic revolution", in the seizure of the Grand Mosque in Mecca, in the assassination of Anwar Sadat in Egypt, and in the bloody suppression of the Muslim Brotherhood in Hama by the Syrian government. Islam has played a more active and widespread role in Muslim politics from North Africa to Southeast Asia. However, this political phenomenon has been rooted in a deeper, widespread and more profound religious revival which has encompassed both the personal and the political sphere. The personal aspect of the Islamic revival is reflected in increased emphasis upon religious observances (mosque attendance, Ramadan fast, outlawing of alcohol and gambling), religious programming in the media, the proliferation of religious literature, the rebirth of the Muslim Brotherhood, the rise of new Islamic associations, the success of Muslim student associations in university elections, and the vibrant *dawah* (missionary) movements which seek not simply to convert non-Muslims but to "Islamize" the Muslim population, i.e. to deepen their knowledge of and commitment to Islam.[146]

Such Muslim resurgence has been much more noticeably put under the spotlight of universal observation since the collapse of the Marxist option on the ordering of man and society. A self-confident Islam provides one of the widely perceived – if not popularly understood – approaches to being human and societal at the beginning of the twenty-first century.

Controller of my own destiny

In Western societies, the divorce between the sacred and secular worlds has been established for well over a century. The deliberate substitution of man-made law for divine law was succinctly expressed in the *Declaration of the Rights of Man and Citizen* passed by the French National Assembly on 26 August 1789:

> Men are born free and equal in rights. Law is the expression of the general will. All citizens have the right to take part personally, or by their representatives, in its formation. Liberty consists in the power to do anything that does not injure others; accordingly, the exercise of the natural rights of each man has no limits except those that secure to other members of society the enjoyment of these same rights. These limits can be determined only by law.

Notable by its absence in the declaration is any reference to a higher power or authority.

In our Western view of the world, the prevailing "norm" has come to be that of secular humanism. Such a norm declares that human beings rule the world! People are rendered free to decide their own destinies, and are expected to live with the consequences of their success or failure in managing themselves and the world aright. Moreover, it is as secular beings that Westerners rule the world. There is no more to us humans than meets the eye. We are not inherently religious. A small minority of individuals may choose to be religious; that is their right. Whatever religious choice they make is also their right: to be a Christian or Taoist or Muslim or whatever. The working hypothesis of Western culture is, however, that a human being is not intrinsically a religious being. He or she is a secular being and lives in a secular society. Individualism counts for a lot in the Westerner's world! Any attack upon an individual's right to control his or her own destiny is strongly resisted. The fundamental role of authority in society is consequently that of protecting individuals' rights. Personal morals and public ethics may be of virtually any variety so long as they do not impose negatively on others' basic human rights. The "freedom" of individuals to live according to the norms they choose is paramount. A variety of societal engagements are possible in the secular humanist perspective, but in all of them secularism remains supreme. When we choose to register with a local GP, we want to know that that person is a well-qualified and competent physician. Whether he or she is divorced, living with a same-sex partner, an elder of the local Baptist church or an atheist hardly comes into the equation.

Such a secularist view of reality is true for Britain (and the rest of Europe) today. Yet, despite the steady erosion of a more holistic view of all of life as religious, Christianity still continued until fairly recently to infuse British public culture. The tenets and ethos of Christianity were still owned by British individuals – whether churchgoers or not – well into the second half of the twentieth century. The worldview of British people might indeed have become secularized, but still there was strong sympathy for the lingering traces of Christian religious norms as "our" religious norms, should British people think of themselves as espousing a religious identity. The English language was saturated with biblical and Christian imagery. Speaking, for example, about "the return of the prodigal" or referring to someone as "a doubting Thomas" was part of common parlance. Callum Brown argues strongly in his book *The Death of Christian Britain* for the thesis that a short, sharp, cultural revolution in the 1960s altered the fundamental character of British people.[147] After the 1960s, the concept of a "Christian Britain" was no longer truly reflective of society.

The cultural revolution of the 1960s caused a deepening secularization of British society in a manner inconceivable, suggests Brown, prior to World War II. Brown holds women to account for this radical change in British religiosity in recent decades. Through what he calls a discursive history – a story of people's self-description – Brown charts not only the demise of British people's commitment to the structures of Christian faith, but also the radical reconstruction of what they think life is all about (see Figure 57).

Brown demonstrates with considerable evidential support that it was women who had been the bulwark of popular support for organized Christianity between AD 1800 and AD 1963, and that it was women who cancelled their relationship to Christian

Figure 57
The changing face of British religiosity according to Callum Brown

1956–1973 decline in ...	Concerns of the 1960s onwards ...
church membership	environmentalism
communicants	gender equality
baptisms	racial equality
religious marriage	nuclear weapons and power
Sunday school participation	vegetarianism
	well-being of body and mind

piety in the 1960s "and thereby caused secularisation".[148] British women secularized the construction of their identity in that decade and the next, and the churches started significantly to lose them. Perhaps this was as much due to the churches' failure to recognize and promote the ministries of women within their male-dominated structures as to the growing influence of feminist convictions. The result of British women's exodus from the churches, for whatever reason, has been a crisis of membership for the denominations and a deep secularization of the worldview of British people:

> Whereas previously, men and women were able to draw upon a Christian-centred culture to find guidance about how they should behave, and how they should think about their lives, from the 1960s, a suspicion of creeds arose that quickly took the form of a rejection of Christian tradition and all formulaic constructions of the individual.[149]

Now, when it comes to religion, we in Britain live with some major paradigm shifts compared with 50 years ago. The holding of religious faith is very much the mark of an individual's choice rather than a feature of community. There is no expectation that people should be "religious" and certainly no expectation that, if someone is, their expression of religiosity should be of one particular, “national” kind. As a vicar in multi-ethnic south-west London, I have become used to being asked by parents of infants being brought for “christening” if a godparent of the child may be a Muslim or Hindu friend. There is, in such requests, a healthy openness towards people of different faith traditions, something refreshing and non-bigoted. But, in the context of what is actually being affirmed in baptism, such openness comes with not an inkling of recognition that Muslim or Hindu and Christian commitments might be mutually incompatible. The potential godparent is chosen as a friend who is “religious” and thus able to offer the child some support in an area in which the parents feel inadequate or lost. Secular society is not necessarily anti-religious; it just insists that matters of faith be a private and optional matter. At the same time, our secular humanist mind-set holds that all belief systems are equally valid or equally suspicious. No single set of beliefs can be universally and completely “true”. Tolerance of one another is the key issue for society as a whole and for religious groups in particular. The demonstration by any religious community of anything other than tolerance – in belief or in practice – is despised and mistrusted. It is an anachronism today to suggest

Figure 58
Religion in Britain in the third millennium

"Secularized" religion means ...
privatized faith
pluralism of beliefs
marginalization of religion
relativizing of values

that Britain is a “Christian country”, unless by that term one accepts a strongly emaciated biblical content (see Figure 58).

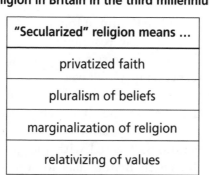

Faith is deliberately excluded from the public domain in Britain. In fact, as we shall see, it is mostly Muslims in this nation who have had the greatest influence with "politically correct" politicians or newspaper editors in reining in ethically questionable medical practices or religiously offensive media material. In our secular society, values have as a whole become relativized and consequently are not really open to question. The most important, though usually unstated, values that currently provide the motor for our national life include an overriding concern for human "rights" (see Figure 59). Such values take the place of values more deliberately linked in previous

Figure 59
"Values" of secular society

"Secularized" values include ...
preoccupation with various human rights
elevation of individual over community
wealth as a sign of blessing/achievement
pursuit of personal fulfilment/happiness
separation of religious motivation from social concerns

generations with the Ten Commandments of the Old Testament or the Beatitudes of the New Testament.

In the last decades of the twentieth century, "respect" has chased away "respectability". Power issues focusing on the "rights" of individuals have displaced agreed-upon community mores that used to define "normal" behaviour. One result of this sharp shift has been that today, any proclamation of "absolute" convictions is treated with the greatest suspicion. The Christian church in Britain has for the most part been found wanting in living out a counter-cultural alternative that has not been perceived as bigoted, reactionary or irrelevant in this massive transformation of societal ethos in the last 50 years. Maybe for the reason that Brown persuasively suggests, the very process of increasingly deep secularization has proceeded so quickly precisely because church people (women of the 1960s and beyond in his view) have opted out of the Christian/church constructs in order to develop alternative "post-Christian" views of the world.

Islam in Britain

One of the major changes that has taken place in British society in the last three decades has been the coming of age of Muslim communities in our midst.

Muslims living in Britain feel themselves connected to a wider fellowship or brotherhood of believers – something parallel to the Christian concept of the kingdom of God. They consequently find themselves benefiting from the global patterns of Islamic resurgence – described earlier in this chapter – that elevated the self-understanding of Muslims in the second half of the twentieth century. As such, British Muslims at the end of the twentieth century are very different people from the believers who turned up in this country as part of the new economic workforce of the 1950s.

Most Muslims in Britain originate from the Indian subcontinent, but there are also substantial numbers from the Middle East, Africa, south-east Asia and parts of central Europe. A large variety of local, regional and national Islamic organizations plus many hundreds of mosques exist in our country. Muslims are British citizens either by naturalization or registration or, for the most part, because they have been born in Britain.

In the 1990s, a book authored by a man born an Indian Muslim, but who by then had lived for many years in Britain, caused uproar – both in Britain and around the globe. The Salman Rushdie affair helped to project the concerns of this fairly small minority within our society into the centre of the political and media worlds. Since then, other international affairs concerning Muslims have served to maintain a high profile fascination at national level with followers of Islam.

In his book on the Salman Rushdie incident, Shabbir

Akhtar (at that time a community relations officer in Bradford and a member of the Bradford Council of Mosques) put his finger on what the affair was about, from a Muslim perspective:

> By a complex process of events, the defence of Salman Rushdie and his novel has, mistakenly, become a defence of Western values. The scenario is certainly stranger than fiction: a virulently anti-Islamic book is written by an Indian apostate living in Britain, and an Iranian cleric orders his execution ... Mrs Thatcher's government, condemned as racist by the author, leaps to his defence. The Islamic world and the Western world become ideologically polarised almost overnight.[150]

Now why? Why the strong polarization? Says Akhtar:

> It seems to me that the Muslim response over the Rushdie affair challenges the cultural imperialism implicit in the occidental outlook. Why should the West dictate the mental and moral fashion for the rest of the civilised world? Only Muslims have dared to ask that question .... The Rushdie affair is, in effect, part of an ideological battle between Islam and the West.[151]

I think Akhtar is correct. With the growing self-confidence of the Muslim community worldwide, and within Britain, that ideological battle is one that will not go away. The starting-points for Westerners/Britishers and Muslims in their outlook on life are far apart; they always have been. It's just that now the Muslims are standing up in the modern political world, the education world, the media world, the health world, the justice world, and in national and international forums and they are saying: here is an alternative way of viewing life and going about things, authored by God himself!

What do British Muslims want?

What are Muslims in Britain after? Some say that they want control of this country in order to turn it into a Muslim nation. David Pawson has defended in print his strong premonition that "Islam will take over this country". In *The Challenge of Islam to Christians*, he raises the question of whether the foreseen takeover will come about by a process of simple demographic change as the Muslim population grows biologically more speedily than the rest of the population, or by increasing numbers of indigenous British people converting to Islam.

Doubtless there are some Muslim groups for whom *daᶜwa* or mission is their primary objective. They would like to see Britain become an Islamic state. The *Hizb ad-Tahrir* group, set up in Jerusalem in 1953 as a breakaway from the Muslim Brotherhood, is centred today mainly in Britain. It is attracting an increasing number of followers, mainly among young British Muslims. It is opposed to freedom and democracy, rejects any participation in the British political system, and even condemned the huge London march that took place to demonstrate against the taking of Britain into a war against Iraq in 2003. The primary enemy of this Islamist youth movement is the value system of secular Britain, though its strategy for attacking and replacing that system does not include the use of violence. Since its ideology is centred on the restoration of the legitimate caliphate, it regards the rightful caliph as the only person authorized to wage a valid *jihâd* or holy war. How far such a movement will achieve its avowedly Islamist aims while it rejects any use of the democratic processes available for political expression in Britain remains to be seen.

Other Islamist groups work within Britain in a more integrated manner. The *Jamâᶜat-i Islâmî* (Islamic Organization, founded by Mawdûdî), for example, entered Britain from Pakistan via migrants and gave rise to four major organizations here: the UK Islamic Mission, Young Muslims UK, the Islamic Foundation and the Muslim Educational Trust. Khurram Murad of the Islamic Foundation has advocated the need for Islam to become contextualized within the United Kingdom in order for *daᶜwa* to proceed more effectively. He wants to see British Muslims being led by white converts with English being used as the main language for communication of the faith. His vision has been finding some expression in recent years. Stuart Robinson gives pen to the thoughts of a visitor listening to Muslim proselytizers at Speakers Corner in Hyde Park, London in the 1990s: "As I moved from speaker to speaker I was challenged that at the heart of a nation that once spearheaded the proclamation of the Gospel around the world, Islam was boldly proclaimed, not by immigrants but by a former Christian."[152] An association for British Muslims was refounded in 1978 and today claims to have 50,000 to 80,000 members.[153] The 2001 census revealed that "White" and "Black Caribbean" Muslims then numbered about 184,000. Converts to Islam include women who have adopted Islam upon marrying Muslims, and young intellectuals who have discovered in Islam what was lacking in their experience of secular humanism or Christian church life. Some British converts to Islam have taken the Ṣûfî route, becoming followers of the various Ṣûfî discipleship groups.

Some Muslim youth are active in mission to non-Muslims, distributing literature especially in universities and colleges, inviting staged "dialogue/debates" with Christians and arranging "Islamic festival" weeks to promote their faith. The construction of more purpose-built mosques, rather than the adapting of other buildings like redundant churches, may also be promoted by Muslims as a form of witness. While the Christian faith in Britain is portrayed as dying, Islam's hour for this country has evidently arrived. Here is another new mosque to prove it! One British Muslim expressed in an edition of *The Muslim News* the aim of his society as "the transformation of the UK from *Dar al-Kufr* to *Dar al-Islam*" (from being a country of non-believers to being a Muslim nation). That, he said, "must be our goal, or we have no business being here ... ".[154] Sheikh Omar Bakri Muhammad, official spokesperson for the (recently dissolved) Muslim political organization *al-Muhajiroun*, has similarly predicted that if such a goal "is not accomplished from outside, through invasion of the West by an Islamic state, we will be its army and soldiers from the inside. We will wage an ideological attack ... "[155] The sheikh has elsewhere stated that his personal ambition is to see the Islamic flag flying over Downing Street. The equally infamous, hook-handed Abû Hamza of Finsbury Park Mosque connection has spoken in like manner of his prior commitment to an Islamist perspective: "Do I see myself as British? ... I live here and have a British passport. It is a superficial identity. The true identity lies in the heart and spirit ... This identity is Islam."[156]

Ahmed Deedat is on record as asserting, during a speech in Bradford, that only engagement in *daʿwa* legitimizes Muslim migration to the West. Jay Smith suggests that "radical Muslims" today make up roughly 25 per cent of the United Kingdom's Muslim population, a suggestion based on the results of polls by Gallup and Q-News in 2002. He claims that in September 2001 such radicals made up only 15 per cent of their community and he postulates that the fallout from the Iraq war will have moved the figure higher still:

> It does us no good to dismiss them as simply irrelevant extremists, representing a small minority of Muslims. The statistics ... show they are growing in numbers and ability, and are prepared to die for what they believe, and take as many as possible with them.[157]

Yet it is obvious that for most Muslims in Britain, *daʿwa* was never their motivation for coming to this country, nor is it the *raison d'être* of their remaining here. In fact, it is usually Christians who raise the spectre of a potential takeover of this country by Muslims. Ron George, for example, makes the point that *hijra* or flight as experienced by Prophet Muḥammad has been interpreted as a "symbol of hope" for many Muslim revolutionaries like al-Afghani, Khomeini, and even Idi Amin. Though they experienced banishment, they could look back to the *hijra* and take comfort that they also would be given, in God's providence, the power and opportunity to return. George suggests:

> When Muslims make up a minority in a society they tend to be peaceful and appeal to logical debate and reason to promote their faith à la Meccan period. On becoming a significant percentage of a community they move over to Medinan mentality in taking up the sword and seeking to overthrow the host community and impose Sharia law. This can be seen in Lebanon and Sudan and could well be seen in Europe in days to come.[158]

Peter Brierley, a former government statistician who is executive director of a company named Christian Research, has compared "piety trends" of Christians and Muslims in Britain. He predicts that, if present processes continue, "the number of active Muslims will outstrip practising Anglicans in about 2013". In fact, *The Times* announced at Easter 2004 that 930,000 Muslims attend a place of worship in this country at least once a week, as against 916,000 Anglicans. By Brierley's further calculations, practising Muslims would be expected to outnumber all Christians in Britain who attend Sunday services by AD 2039. Brierley's predictions certainly make for sombre reading, though he contextualizes his comparisons in a way not done in September 2001 by Cardinal Cormac Murphy-O'Connor (leader of Roman Catholics in England and Wales) who declared that Christianity was close to being "vanquished" in Britain. Brierley's figures are predictions drawn from one measurement of piety – church or mosque attendance. He goes on to admit that in this country, considerably more than 70 per cent of the population still describes itself as at least nominally Christian, compared with 3 per cent who say they are Muslim.

Other warners of the "threat of Islamic takeover" appear to promote a picture of Islam in Britain as a homogeneous, monolithic, highly motivated population of Islamist missionaries bent on unitedly bringing post-Christian Britain to its knees. As far as I can discern, Pawson does not answer his question as to how the prophesied Islamic takeover will occur.

Why Muslims?

When did Muslims come to live in Britain? Prior to 1914, some Muslims had arrived in this country and they settled in Liverpool, London and Woking. By 1939, further groups of Muslims had settled in Britain; some were students or businessmen but most were sailors. After 1945 more Muslims, serving in the colonially recruited armed units, were demobilized in Britain. Unfortunate individuals fleeing the confessional massacres that accompanied partition in the Indian subcontinent (1947) as the British pulled out of its former colony, ended up in Britain. During the 1950s immigration (especially of Pakistanis) grew steadily. The significant Muslim communities that came into being during the period AD 1960 to AD 2000 formed part of the larger post-World War II flow of migrants from former British colonies. They were welcomed to this country to reignite the exhausted industrial base of the economy. In the 1960s and 1970s families of earlier migrants from the Indian subcontinent joined their worker relatives in the United Kingdom. The immigration of East African Asians (many originating from the Gujarat region of India) after their expulsion – from Uganda especially – included many Muslims. The history of the multiplication and consolidation of Muslim communities in this country is demonstrated in the dramatically rising curve of mosque registrations (see Figure 60). Today, there are in Britain approximately 600 or 700 mosques and between 3,000 and 5,000 other Islamic centres and Qur'ân schools.

Figure 60
Mosque registration in Britain

Year	Number registered
1966	18
1977	136
1985	338
2002	c.600

According to the 2001 census, the Muslim population of Britain was at that date about 1.5 million: 68 per cent had their origins in Bangladesh, India and Pakistan, 18 per cent had their origins from elsewhere in Asia or Africa, and 14 per cent were White or White mixed.[159] The statistics of the more recent censuses show a changing dynamic within the Muslim communities in Britain. A comparison of the total number of Britons of Pakistani and Bangladeshi descent present in this country with the percentage of them that were born in the United Kingdom gives substance to Muslims' insistence that they are "British Muslims" (Figure 61).

Figure 61
Britons of Pakistani and Bangladeshi descent born in the United Kingdom

Year	Total number	Percentage born in UK
1951	5,000	0%
1991	640,000	47%
2001	995,659	53%

The Muslim community in Britain is not an internally integrated community. The fact that its major evolution occurred as a result of a search for work means that it is a relatively young community. The kind of work sought has affected the class structure of the community and where such work was available has determined the regions in Britain in which Muslims have settled. Specific factors in the originating countries have meant that the migration has started from very limited regions (95 per cent of the Bangladeshis in Britain, for example, come from Sylhet district in the north-east of Bangladesh). Muslim immigration to Britain has followed a pattern similar to that in other parts of Western Europe, except that it started five to ten years earlier. As a result, the shift to family reunion in this country took place some ten years earlier. In Britain, moreover, a significant educated middle class has developed among Muslim immigrants. Such immigrants are, in this reading of recent history, not part of a plot to take over Britain but ordinary people, subject to the vagaries of politics, economics, national and international relations.

Neither do Muslims in Britain form a united, monolithic community. One of the ongoing difficult questions for Muslims living in this country is precisely that of whether or not they constitute a "community". Four decades of Muslim immigration to Britain have seen profound changes of perspective, both among Muslims themselves and in the worldview of British society. Initially, immigrants came to Britain for economic reasons. Theirs was a work-related migration whose purpose in their eyes was to help their families back home. "Back home" was the major focus of life and ethos for those early migrants. The 1962 Commonwealth Immigration Act limited the numbers permitted to come to Britain but allowed dependants to join Asians already in employment here. At this point, many families joined workers already in Britain. With the removal of families to Britain in the 1960s and 1970s a major change of focus occurred. The nub of economic activity and sociocultural identity shifted from the villages of the Punjab and Sylhet to the inner-city areas of London, Birmingham and Bradford. With the arrival of the families, the centre of religious identity plus Muslim worship and practice needed to relate to the British context. The question quickly arose: how is a Muslim to be a Muslim in Britain? At the same time, the rules of immigration meant that it was not the whole extended family (that is, including the grandparents) but the horizontally extended family (just brothers, sisters, cousins) who decamped to Britain. Patterns of employment tended to disperse such horizontally extended families in different locations. Moreover, the climate in the United Kingdom necessarily tended to force the whole family indoors, with big consequences for women.

> When it is not possible to see the sister-in-law or cousin's wife by going out the back door [that is, into a common courtyard], when everybody in the neighbourhood is a stranger, and leaving the house therefore has the same connotations as visiting another village, the *purdah* has ceased to be a protection and source of security. It has become a prison cell.[160]

With the father of the family occupied at work and with the mother isolated and often illiterate, children (who learned English) frequently had to act as mediators and interpreters between the institutions of British society and their families.

In such a complex, alien world, Islam has played a major role in offering some corporate sense of identity, and in reinforcing traditional values within a disoriented community. Such a role, however, has also brought its own problems in that imams have tended to be brought over to Britain from villages in the subcontinent for five years or so at a time. Such leaders have tried to maintain a culture of the "home village" without any understanding – or addressing – of the vagaries of living in inner-city Britain. This has proved especially frustrating to members of the second and third generations who live with the tension of inhabiting at least two totally different worlds. Is it surprising that some of these youngsters have opted out of their parents' traditions and have hoped through self-chosen marriage to take control of their own destinies? Is it any wonder that others of these "intermediate" generations have become easy recruitment targets for some of the extremist Muslim groups?

Organizing the Muslim community on a national basis has proved signally difficult. Early attempts were mainly made along national and ethnic lines. Ṣûfî orders (especially the ᶜAlawiyya Order with which Yemenis were associated) also provided some early forms of organization. Later, other orders associated with the Indian subcontinent (Naqshbandiyya, Qâdiriyya and Chishtiyya) became active. They tended, however, to operate primarily through the personalities of their *shaykhs* rather than through the associations of mosques, so remained personal rather than national in their constituency links. Gradually, various politico-theological organizations began to make their appearance. The foundation for the development of such associations was laid in the late 1960s when Muslim families came to settle in Britain. With them came the ideological and cultural heritages of their societies of origin. Such heritages included the various religious movements that had developed back home in response to imperial rule and the spread of European culture. Foremost among them have been the Deobandi and Barelwi movements, whose rivalry has at times contributed to open conflict when control of individual mosques has been at stake. Perhaps 20 per cent of Britain's Muslims follow the more conservative, Islamist-oriented teachings of the Deobandi sect. Some 20 colleges currently teach its hard-line interpretation of Islam. Also significant are the *Tabligh-i Jamâᶜat* movement, with a college established in Dewsbury, West Yorkshire, and the Islamist group *Jamâᶜat-i Islâmî*.

The concerns of British Muslims at a national level appear to be of two major kinds. Firstly, how can the best possible conditions for Muslims to live their faith in this country be achieved? Issues include access to facilities for worship, the status of Islamic family law, *ḥalâl* food and dress code in institutions, plus sensitivities to Muslim requirements in health care and so on. Secondly, how can the survival of the faith into the next generations of Muslims in Britain be ensured? Concern is especially expressed over matters of education and the relationship between Muslims and the British state school system. Pressure continues to grow for more Muslim schools to be established within the state system. In the mid-1980s, representatives of Muslims living in Birmingham and representatives of Birmingham schools managed to agree a document that was called *Guidelines on Meeting the Religious and Cultural Needs of Muslim Pupils*.[161] Whilst the *Guidelines* document was considered a step forward in terms of handling some of the "hot potatoes" of school life – things like assemblies, collective worship, prayer facilities, religious holidays, respect for modesty, segregation of sexes, teaching of music, dance, drama and sex education, and provision of *ḥalâl* food – most of the Muslim members of the working party were dissatisfied with the end result because of a more fundamental concern. They felt that the ideological basis of British schooling is incompatible with an Islamic worldview. Such incompatibility is a problem recognized by most Muslims in Britain, but little understood by British secular humanists. It has, at heart, to do with the separation in British society of the sacred and the secular. A Muslim from Birmingham expressed the problem in terms of the teaching of history:

> "teaching history must aim to show the effects on society of diverting from divine teaching; the idea of responsibility to the creator must be promoted in the teaching of all subjects."[162]

Another Muslim makes the same point with regard to the subject of economics:

> "Islam views life as a compact whole and does not divide it into many separate and conflicting parts. The economic aspect is one of the most important parts of our life ... The Islamic system is balanced and places everything in its right place. Islam has given detailed regulations for the conduct of ... economic life ... "[163]

Such views, which seem to pull the whole of life and learning under a religious umbrella, appear reactionary, unenlightened, even dangerous to a secular humanist worldview that has abandoned any commitment to one overarching "metanarrative". People who want to think in those terms are quickly – though falsely – labelled "fundamentalist".

For Muslims in Britain, the argument can often seem lost before it is even begun. Misunderstood by secular-minded British outsiders to its faith, it finds itself at the same time caught up in the processes and consequences of a worldwide Islamic resurgence – itself a process of discovery and reassertion of distinctive identity in a world dominated by the West. It is so easy for Muslims in Britain to be stereotyped as representing the most extreme examples of that faith community, accused of setting about to destroy with bombs the fabric of the society that has nourished them for many decades. At the same time, Muslims in Britain are subject to strong calls from within their community for "getting their act together" as Muslims. Different groups make strong calls for a purification of Islam from its illegitimate accretions. Much of the invective of British Islamist or other reform movements is directed at the local Muslim community. That invective often comes across as a critique of the values and traditions that Muslim villagers, migrated to Europe, hold dearest. At the same time, it has to be acknowledged that the process of migration has brought together in British cities Muslims of a variety of cultural backgrounds. The experience of meeting other modes of Islamic cultural expression raises questions as to the sole legitimacy of any one particular mode. Traditions that have been defended historically as "Islamic" become problematical when other Muslims defend different traditions as equally "Islamic".

The Muslim community of Britain is "settled" only in the

sense of living historically in this country. It is not settled in the sense of being a community in which the constituent parts are at ease with each other, nor is it agreed in its interpretation of some of the current international tensions that involve members of the Islamic faith. It is certainly not an overwhelmingly Islamist community, but it has struggled until recently to put forward voices that can redress the more outrageous views of the media darlings like Abû Hamza or Omar Bakri Muhammad. At the same time, most Muslims do have a deep problem with the secular humanist worldview that marks indigenous British society – for them, life is perceived much more holistically in a single, religious explanation and requirement. The hedonistic ethos and the lax morality of Western society are feared as powerful and contaminating, so every effort is made to try and protect their children and youth from being ruined by them. Unfortunately, because of the Islamic non-separation of the sacred and secular worlds, it is too easily assumed by Muslims that the immorality displayed by the host culture in Britain may be equated with Christianity. The current state of "Christian" Britain is taken to prove how degenerate has become the holy word that Jesus was originally given to declare. In Muslims' minds, Christians are certainly grossly mistaken in their Christianity if current, "Christian" Britain amounts to its proper expression.

Real Christian faith?

Sadly, therefore, Muslims in Britain find little excitement or comfort in the prospect of considering, or allowing their children to consider, the vital Christian alternative to secular humanism that is on offer in many Christian communities up and down this land. Maybe the placing of their children in church schools – where at least there is expected to be a religious ethos – is viewed as better than immersing them in the "godless" state education system. But usually that is as far as any identification with Christian faith might go. Khalda came to England with her parents in the early 1960s and settled in the Midlands. Her parents were Kashmiris. The majority of Muslim Pakistanis in Britain come from the Mirpur District of

Azad (Free Kashmir). She comments that "Kashmiris are warm and very hospitable people, they appreciate the gains they have made in coming to England but are painfully aware of the cost of losing their children to western social values."[164] Khalda grew up, like other Pakistani children, in two worlds: that of English society and culture at school and that of traditional Muslim culture at home. "I knew the two worlds could never be compromised (a conflict felt by most Muslim youths growing up in the West, especially girls) ... they were centuries apart," she reflects.[165] Not only did Khalda live in this dichotomized world, but she gradually became attracted to following Jesus. She had been taught to read the Qur'ân (in Arabic) and grew up with a fear of God. Through her sister, she became exposed to the Christian gospel. Her father's angry reaction, when her sister became a follower of Jesus, was to take the girls back to Mirpur to teach them a painful lesson. Khalda made her own decision to follow Jesus, knowing that she would have to live with her parents' response to their sense of bearing disgrace in front of their extended family. The cost of such a decision has been huge and only the grace of God has upheld Khalda in her commitment to Jesus. Finding meaning and purpose in Christ constitutes a fairly rare possibility for contemporary British Muslims.

One of the healthy processes occurring among committed Christians in the decades surrounding the turn of the third millennium is an active agitation for the reconnecting of the sacred and secular spheres. Christians believe increasingly passionately that God has a view about all aspects of human living – not just piety. In the arts, in science, in medicine and politics and economics, Christians critique the secular humanist worldview and, in many instances, work with people of other faiths in Britain to try and restrain contemporary society from its headlong tumble into moral and ethical chaos.

Theoretically, at least, a renewed, vibrant and engaged Christianity might seem to offer a positive stepping-stone by which Muslims could find friendship, understanding and cooperation in many of the concerns that worry them. After all, both faith communities seek to uphold a religious ethos in the face of rampant secularization.

Why has such friendship, understanding and alliance been so slow to develop? Why have the "Khaldas" proved to be the exception rather than the rule? Why, indeed, is such a strong sense of shame felt by Muslims when a member of their religious community – with its expression of monotheistic faith – embraces Christianity – with another such expression? To that question we turn in the next part of our exploration of Islam and Christianity.

Interlude

If you were God, how would you convince Muslims that – all along – they had a special place in your divine heart?

Eastern Relatives

There are plenty of examples in the Old Testament of "people of the east" who demonstrated a remarkable relationship with God, though they lived outside the powerful covenant that God made with Abraham and Isaac.

Enoch

Enoch was obviously an ardent rambler! He lived in the era just prior to the birth of his great-grandson Noah (Genesis 5:21–32), a righteous man living in dangerous, extremely violent times. Enoch was "taken away" or "removed" by God. And how! He evidently walked with God into the divine presence.

Job

Job, it seems, lived during the time of the patriarchs in the land of Uz. The precise location of Uz is uncertain, although there are some clues. Maybe the designation was originally derived from the individual Uz, son of Aram and grandson of Shem (Genesis 10:23; 1 Chronicles 1:17). Is that where the man of that name lived? One of Job's friends, Eliphaz, came from Teman (Job 4:1) which is situated in Idumaea – where the Edomites lived. Elihu came from among the Buzites who lived next to the Chaldeans in north-east Arabia. Uz was subject to attacks from Sabeans and Chaldeans (Job 1:15,17) so must have been at least a fairly close neighbour to those peoples. The Septuagint version of the Old Testament refers to Uz as the land of the Aistai, a people whom Ptolemy located in the Arabian desert adjacent to the Edomites of Mount Seir. Uz certainly had to have had fertile pastures in order to be able to sustain all of Job's animals.

It had a least one major city, too, since Job sat at the city gate. It would seem fair to conclude that Uz was probably located either in Arabia, east of Petra (modern north-west of Saudi Arabia) or in Bashan, east of the Sea of Galilee and south of Damascus (today's western Jordan or southern Syria). The literary form of Job is similar to documents going back to the second millennium BC. And Job uses Arabic words. Gleason L. Archer Jr raises the suggestion that, if the timing of the story is pre-Mosaic, it "gives rise to the possibility that it was originally composed in some language other than Hebrew, whether in a North Arabian dialect or possibly in Aramaic, as some have suggested".[166] The patriarchal family-clan organization and the lack of reference to the Law reflect the time of Abraham rather than some time after the exodus. Job functions as a priest in offering sacrifices for his family (Job 1:5), like Abraham (Genesis 12:7). Job's longevity, moreover, is typical of the patriarchs. Rabbinic tradition does not attempt to identify the author other than suggesting that the writer must have preceded Moses.

An eastern locale and a date prior to Moses would account for the comparative rarity of the name Yahweh in most chapters of the book. Job prefers to use the pan-Semitic term *'elôah* or *'elôhîm* for God. Interestingly, the title *Shaddai*, the Almighty, occurs no fewer than 31 times in Job (and only 16 times in the rest of the Old Testament). Such a manner of referencing "God" would seem to confirm the theory of a non-Israelite background for Job. Whatever date, origin or ethnic background is accurate, Job was evidently a man about whom God could boast. He is described in the Bible as "the greatest man among all the people of the East" (Job 1:3). Did God choose to hold up to Satan, as someone in whom he could boast, a faithful representative of the people of the east? Not the Aramean (Abraham), but an unknown contemporary from the Arabian desert! This was the person who, above all others, truly feared God and shunned evil (Job 1:8). What was God trying to say, here?

Melchizedek

Melchizedek is presented in Genesis 14:18 as King of Salem and priest of the Most High God. He, definitely, was a contemporary of Abraham. The Jewish historian, Josephus, depicts Melchizedek as the founder and first priest of the city of Jerusalem, whose name derives from him. O. Michel suggests that in Genesis 14 we are offered a glimpse of an ancient Palestinian tradition.[167]

Whatever the historical or textual origins of "Melchizedek", the point for our study is that this character stands completely outside the Abrahamic tradition. And outside that tradition he is depicted as one greater than Abraham. Psalm 110 refers to the Genesis anecdote in a strongly Messianic context. Hebrews, in the New Testament, takes up the Messianic theme. Melchizedek's very name points to the Messianic gifts of righteousness and peace (Hebrews 7:2). The absence of any genealogy suggests a miraculous origin (Hebrews 7:3). No mention of birth or death indicates the eternal and imperishable quality of his "priesthood" (Hebrews 7:3). The author of Hebrews goes on to make his point that despite these lofty conclusions, Melchizedek constitutes only a pale reflection of the Son of God. For our purposes here, however, the incredible message is given that Genesis 14:17–20 declares that Melchizedek is greater than Abraham and Levi – far superior, in other words, to the Jewish Law and cultus. In this Palestinian priest-king who stands outside the tradition belonging to Abraham, Moses and Aaron, God projects upon earth a wonderful hint of what Christ will be like.

Jethro

Jethro was priest and chief of the clan of Kenites, part of the tribe of the Midianites. We shall consider him more fully in our next interlude, *Helps along the Way?*

Good outsider?

Outside of the people of Israel, then, there is evidence in the Old Testament of a rich spiritual heritage. It is a theme that is reflected by Jesus in his interaction with his disciples. It finds potent expression in Jesus' juxtaposition of the "good outsider" with the "bad insider". Too often, persons on his discipleship team display less faith, less "godlikeness", than folk from non-Jewish backgrounds who do not have a place within the holy group. Jesus often holds up the faith he finds in outsiders and compares it with the faithlessness displayed by those who share life and ministry with him.

In the difficult dialogue sequence of Mark 9, Jesus illustrates his attitude of being on the lookout for faith arising anywhere beyond the boundaries of expectation. John complains to Jesus about the ministry of a maverick exorcist. The man is exercising his ministry in Jesus' name but is not part of the in-group. John's objection, it would seem, has to do with insecurity and a desire to control. It appears as hugely ironic in the light of the disciples' own failure in exorcising, only just recently exposed (Mark 9:14–29)! Jesus offers three reasons why the disciples must not hinder the exorcist. Firstly, anyone who is using Jesus' name in such a dynamic way cannot quickly speak badly of him (verse 39). Secondly, those not against Jesus and his disciples are in fact for them (verse 40) – we remember that, very soon, Peter will speak against Jesus and the rest of the disciples will abandon him. The third reason is the most important, introduced by the heavy word "Amen". In Jesus' eyes, a person who shows the simplest act of hospitality to anyone bearing the name of Christ will receive due recognition in the kingdom. In other words, disciples or "insiders" have no monopoly on relating to God. There are others, outsiders, who in being compassionate towards followers of Christ will inherit their reward.

Jesus goes on in the same chapter of Mark (9:42–50) to raise the possibility that an "insider" might prove to be "bad". Stumbling blocks can come from within the community of faith – Judas is a case in point. Apostasy is an awful possibility and will incur God's wrath. How can a faith community's solidarity be strongly maintained while at the same time resisting the temptation to become hard-heartedly exclusive? By affirming the good from "outside" and eliminating the bad that is "inside" would seem to be Jesus' suggestion.

In the Old Testament, there occurs strong affirmation of non-Jewish people with whom God is well pleased. We have mentioned a few briefly. The genealogy of Jesus Christ reveals more, including non-Israelite women. Jesus in his ministry seems to reinforce this possibility, this way of looking at people. People who are turned towards him, though standing outside the covenant or kingdom, need to be affirmed, while those of us who count ourselves "in" need to be self-critical and humbly vigilant about our faith-status.

Competing Cousins?

Chapter 8 A Tainted Past

Why is it so difficult for Muslims and Christians to trust one another? Quite simply: the waters of time have been constantly muddied by unhelpful interactions between the two faith communities. Across many centuries, the negative encounters of members of the two faith communities seem to have outweighed by far the positive ones. As Albert Hourani suggests:

> It is easy to see the historical relationship of Christians and Muslims in terms of holy war, of Crusade and *jihad*, and there is some historical justification for this. The first great Muslim expansion in Christian lands, Syria, Egypt and North Africa, Spain and Sicily; the first Christian reconquests, in Spain, Sicily and the Holy Land; the spread of Ottoman power in Asia Minor and the Balkans; and then the spread of European power in the last two centuries: all these processes have created and maintained an attitude of suspicion and hostility on both sides and still provide, if not a reason for enmity, at least a language in which it can express itself.[168]

Muslim "conquest"

The Byzantine Empire constituted the main political expression of Christianity at the time of the Arab Muslim conquests. The fourth century had seen a triumph of the Christian church. At the start of that century, Christians were still being persecuted. By the end of the century, it was inconceivable that an emperor would adopt any religious allegiance other than a Christian one. The idea of "Christendom" as a territorial entity came to find expression. Armenia emerged as the first

Christian state in AD 303, and the Roman Empire followed suit in AD 337. In the last half of the fourth century, the "new" religion spread to the German tribes. In the fifth and sixth centuries, Nubia and Abyssinia became Christian. Byzantium, supremely, brought the power of secular might to bear on its theological constructions, persecuting those who differed from what it considered normative faith. As we have seen, the theological issues at stake mostly concerned the nature of Christ. The doctrinal formulations of the ecumenical councils of the fourth and fifth centuries found expression in Greek philosophical terms, terms that were unfamiliar or not acceptable to those from other backgrounds. Egyptians, Syrians and Persians – representative of such other Christian populations – preferred to express their faith in alternative, more indigenous, terms. As a result, in the century of Muslim expansion after the death of Prophet Muḥammad, the Muslim armies came upon a divided Christendom in which some of the Christians, especially the Copts in Egypt, expressed a preference for new Muslim overlords instead of long-standing Byzantine oppressors.

The experience of Christians living under Muslim rule varied from place to place. In some situations, Christians and other non-Muslims with valuable skills or experience came to occupy significant positions. Nestorian Christians, especially, contributed to the growing Islamic civilization with translations of classical works from Greek into Arabic. In Baghdad, for example, the ninth-century caliph al-Ma'mun constructed the "House of Wisdom", reputedly the first institution of higher learning in the Islamic and Western worlds. In Spain, mutual exchange between Muslim and Christian cultures facilitated a fairly informed Christian encounter with Islam. Cordoba became home to some 70 libraries, indicative of the intellectual fervour that drew from the resources of different communities and faith histories. According to Irshad Manji, "secular Hebrew poetry poured from the pen of Shmuel ha-Nagid, the rabbi and amateur bard who served as prime minister in the Spanish courts of two Muslim monarchs".[169] In most areas where Islam expanded, local Christian communities tended to decline. Large-scale conversion to Islam in North Africa, for example, left hardly any indigenous Christian presence there. Kate Zebiri comments that Byzantine Christian writings on Islam tended to be more polemical than those of Arab Christians. This, she suggests, was because the Byzantines were freer to express open hostility, not being directly under Muslim rule. Islam tended to be characterized by them, not as a heretical cousin of Christianity, but as a completely false religion inspired by the devil. Western Christian views of Islam may well have been early informed by such polemics:

> Muhammad was sometimes seen as a figure inspired by Satan or even identified as the Antichrist; among other things, it was said that he encouraged sexual promiscuity and suffered from epileptic fits, that Muslims were idolaters, and that the Qur'an was a jumbled collection of materials from biblical and non-biblical sources.[170]

The expansion of Islam into the heartlands of Europe was stopped only through battle – at Poitiers in AD 732 by Charles Mantel and his Frankish cavalry. Despite internal dissensions, the Islamic enterprise grew until it extended from the Pyrenees to the Indus river. Growth, however, produced its own drawbacks. In later years, the Muslim world was no longer ruled by one caliph. In the east, the Saljuq Turks overthrew the ᶜAbbassid dynasty based in Baghdad. In the centre, a Fâṭimid dynasty controlled that area of the Islamic domain from its base in Cairo, while in the west, the Almoravids ruled in the Maghreb and Andalusia (Spain). The Spanish connection, as we have suggested, offered the possibility of comparatively positive communication between Muslims and Europeans – an exception to the general rule. Moses ben Mamon (Maimonides), a Jewish philosopher, rabbi, physician and ethicist, published almost exclusively in Arabic from his home base in Cordoba until he had to flee for his life in the mid-twelfth century. Arabic translations of Greek philosophers plus the works of such Muslim philosophers as Ibn Sina (Avicenna, died AD 1037) and Ibn Rushd (Averroes, died AD 1198) began to be translated into Latin. Some of the intellectual fervour arising from such interaction contributed to an intellectual awakening in Europe that culminated in the Enlightenment.

From the end of the thirteenth century, the Ottoman Turks established an empire that again reached into Europe. From the first Battle of Kosovo in AD 1389, Slavic resistance to the Turks in the Balkans proved non-existent. Only Hungary and Venice stood between the Turks and Europe. Constantinople, the last great bastion of eastern Christianity, fell to the Turks in AD 1453. Its capture was celebrated by Sultan Mehmet's soldiers in three days of savage pillage. We learn that, as a result, "the blood ran in rivers down the steep streets" of that hilly city.[171] In succeeding years, the pressure of an expansionist Ottoman empire extended into the Balkans. By Martin Luther's day, even the great city of Vienna was besieged by the Ottomans (AD 1529). It is only fair to note that the Turkish expansion at this late stage was actively encouraged by Francis I of the French house of Valois, who saw it as a way to harm his rival Charles V of the Austrian house of Hapsburg.

In the middle of this long period of steady Islamic expansion there occurred a 200-year interval in which the attention of Christian Europe became fixated on convulsive attempts to wrest the holy places from the "infidel". It was the turn of the Christians to conquer at Muslim expense.

The Crusades

The Crusades provide an example, in the history of the Western Christian world, of the strong identification of "truth" and "power". All Crusades were announced by preaching and undertaken by Christian warriors in fulfilment of a solemn vow. Each fighter received a cross from the pope or his representative and was considered a soldier of the church. Crusaders were granted indulgences and temporal privileges, such as exemption from civil jurisdiction. The giving/receiving of a cross gave the name to the military expeditions: "crusade" derives from the Latin word (*crux*) for cross. The aim of the Crusades, or at least the famous eastern Crusades, was to deliver the holy places from Muslim control (see Figure 62).

Figure 62
The Crusades

	Dates AD	Protagonists & places
1	1095–1101	Bohemond, Godfrey, Raymond of Toulouse, Robert of Normandy, Pope Urban II; Jerusalem captured and Latin Kingdom established
2	1147–1149	Conrad III, Louis VII, Pope Eugene III; after loss of the Principality of Edessa
3	1188–1192	Richard Lionheart, Frederic Barbarossa, Philip Augustus, Pope Gregory VIII; after the fall of Jerusalem to Salah al-Din (Saladin); recaptured Acre
4	1204	Pope Innocent III; to consolidate Christian territory in the holy land and aimed at Egypt, Saladin's base; Constantinople ransacked and taken over by crusaders
5	1217–1219	conquest of Damietta
6	1228–1229; 1239	Frederick II, Thibaud de Champagne, Richard of Cornwall
7	1249–1252	Louis IX of France after Jerusalem again in Muslim hands
8	1270	Louis IX, Edward I; failed to capture Jerusalem

A pivotal battle on Friday 19 August AD 1071, which took place near the town of Manzikert (close to Lake Van), dramatically altered the dynamics of power in the Middle East. The emperor, Romanus Diogenes, decided to lead a military expedition to safeguard the eastern border of his empire from incursions by local Muslim warriors. The Saljuq sultan, Alp Arslan, reacted by leading his army from Syria to defend what he saw as his interests in the border area. Each protagonist viewed their involvement in the consequent clash as a defensive measure. At the critical confrontation, the Saljuq Turks destroyed the Byzantine army, defeating it in battle and taking the emperor prisoner. Facing no organized opposition, the various groups of Muslim invaders were quickly able to roam westwards from the border area and overrun the whole peninsula. They thus crippled the empire's ability to function by depriving it of its source of manpower in Asia Minor. The Muslim victory left just a European rump on the west side of the Bosphorus, plus a few coastal districts on the east of the Bosphorus, to imperial rule. Turkish tribes migrated into the vacuum created by the overthrow of the imperial army and "Turkey" became Muslim. By AD 1092, not one of the great metropolitan sees of Asia remained in the hands of the Christians.

The Saljuqs had earlier squeezed the Fâṭimids out of Syria, taking Jerusalem in AD 1070, a year before Manzikert. Unlike the tolerant Fâṭimids, the newly converted, zealous Muslim Saljuqs refused to allow Christian pilgrimage to the holy land. Byzantium, in desperation, appealed to the Christian West for mercenaries despite the huge rift between Eastern and Western churches that had exploded into being in AD 1054. Meanwhile, in the West, Sicily and parts of Spain had by now been reclaimed from Islamic rule and there was a conviction among rulers in Europe that the time had come to turn back the "infidel" tide elsewhere as well.

Pope Urban II (1088–1099) acted decisively. He himself addressed assembled crowds at Clermont in AD 1095, exhorting them to go and exterminate the "vile race" (of Muslims) from the holy land and give aid to the Christian inhabitants there. Fulcher of Chartres, chronicler of the Crusade, records the strong language used by the pontiff.[172] The appeal fell on fertile imaginations in Europe and soon marauding bands were making their way eastwards, murdering Jews in German cities as they went. Even the four better-disciplined, principal armies that rendezvoused in Constantinople did as much harm as good to Latin–Orthodox relations by their conduct. Eventually Antioch was captured and quarrelled over before Jerusalem was finally reached in AD 1099. The armies soon "liberated" it and the Crusaders went on a rampage, killing everyone they met. Muslim survivors took refuge in the Dome of the Rock, but a group of Crusaders broke in and slaughtered everyone inside. The Jews of the city fled for safe refuge into their synagogue. That was set on fire so that everyone inside died. The various chroniclers tell of streets running with blood and of horses splashing blood up onto their riders' leggings.[173] All the Jews and all the Muslims of Jerusalem died. The looting of sacred shrines and the slaughter of innocent people confirmed the general Muslim view that the Westerners were savage barbarians, unbelievers with no faith at all except in blood and wealth. The Muslim world would never forget nor forgive the Crusaders' behaviour. A Latin Kingdom of Jerusalem was established in AD 1100 that lasted until AD 1187 when Saladin reconquered the area.

Other crusades followed the first, most of which were dismal failures if not downright disgraceful affairs. One of them, the infamous fourth Crusade, did not even get as far as the holy land, turning aside en route to plunder the city of Constantinople, the final bastion of the Eastern Empire. The Crusades failed in their major goals of freeing the holy land, reuniting Christian East and West and halting the advance of Islam. They did, incidentally and ironically, contribute to a bringing of rich Arab knowledge to the West, and to an increase in trade between the two regions. From the perspective of Western Christendom at the time, and especially in the view of the popes who called for them, the Crusades were conceived as defensive wars. From the perspective of Muslims, then and thereafter, the Crusades were seen as the essential, undiluted representation of "Christianity". The cross became the symbol, above all things, of crusade. A desire for hegemony, an innate barbarism and a lust for blood are viewed as the bottom line in Christian attitudes to the world. "Christianity" equals "the Crusades".

As Zebiri rightly comments: "The Crusades have had an impact on mutual perceptions of Muslims and Christians which has been disproportionate to their direct political effect."[174]

Mahmoud Ayoub, a Muslim commentator, agrees: "The Crusades in themselves were not a very important chapter in Muslim history. They have been, however, crucial in providing the pattern for and spirit of the long history of conflict and mistrust between Muslims and Christians."[175] In the second half of the twentieth century, the Crusades were still being invoked and "crusader language" being used by Islamists keen on winning the argument for their particular Islamic vision for Muslim nations. Sayyid Qutb, inspirer of many of the armed Islamist groups of Egypt, wrote the bulk of his avidly read material while in prison during Nasser's rule. Qutb's call to his own contemporaries in Egypt was to wrest control of the government in Egypt and elsewhere in order to apply the Islamic vision that he espoused. In Qutb's view, government was wrongly in the hands of men who had been seduced by the false ideology of Arab nationalism. Political leaders in the Islamic world had been colonized in their hearts and minds by Europe and America, aided and abetted by compromised clerics of Islam. Such leaders refused to concede the possibility of establishing a nation on the basis of religion – of Islam. Yet Qutb posited the example of Israel as a nation specifically formed on the basis of religion rather than nationality – supported in the process by the British, funded by the Americans and accepted by the Russians! His conclusion was therefore that Western objection to the formation of an Islamic government in the Arab world was not founded on a hesitation about a nation based on religion per se. Rather, that objection was based on a deep sense of inadequacy (within the Western worldview itself) and a fear of an Islamic success. Time and again Qutb returns in his writing to rail against the West. In doing so he plays the "Crusades" card. Typical is the following statement from his commentary on the Qur'ân:

> This is the reality of the battle which the Jews and the Christians initiate in every land and at all times against the Islamic community … It is the battle of doctrine that is raging between the Islamic camp and these two armies who may fight among themselves … however, they always cooperate in the battle against

> Islam and the Muslims ... They did not announce it a war in the name of doctrine – as it is in reality – fearing the zeal and emotion of the doctrine. Rather, they announced it in the name of land, of economics, of politics, of military bases ... [176]

International Zionism, international communism and international crusaderism – Qutb's terms – were all signs of this essential conflict disguised as other issues. Qutb called on his fellow Muslims to stop patterning their lives on the West. The source of that Western model came via the discredited and despicable People of the Book. Muslims may only pattern themselves after the mind of God as revealed in the Qur'ân. Egypt's humiliation in the Six Day War, less than a year after Qutb had been executed for his Islamist views, won Qutb's argument for him. The many Arabs had lost against little Israel because they had abandoned living according to God's will. Listen to Sayyid Qutb and you will realize that the Crusades are still being fought. It's just that they occur in another guise in the late twentieth century.

When another Islamist, Usama bin Ladin, replaced *Ḥizbollah* International out of frustration at a softening attitude towards the West by some of the Iranian leadership, he named his new organization "The International Islamic Front for the Struggle against Jews and Crusaders" (*al-Jabhah al-Islamîyyah al-ᶜAlamîyyah li Qital al-Yahûd w'al-Salabiyyîn*). Bin Ladin also played the "Crusades" card. "Jews" and "Crusaders" are identified by him as the enemy. Why? Because Muslims generally see a sinister alliance between modern Western colonialism, or "new world crusaderism" as they call it, and "world Zionism". In February 1998 the Front issued its famous "kill Americans everywhere" *fatwâ*. The *fatwâ* began with a statement of three complaints. Firstly, the United States had been occupying the lands of the Arabian Gulf for seven years, using their bases there as staging posts for bombing Iraq, a Muslim nation. Secondly, the Americans were threatening to take apart the Iraqi regime, thereby humiliating Muslims again. Thirdly, the Americans' motive in such threatened aggression was obviously to serve the Jewish state and divert everyone's attention from the Israeli occupation of Jerusalem. Such "crimes and sins" by the Americans were interpreted as a clear declaration of war on God, his messenger and Muslims.

After the tragic events of September 2001 in New York and Washington DC, President George W. Bush inadvertently justified the Islamist perspective on tensions between the West and Islam. Bush spoke initially about the need for a "crusade" against terror. He was evidently unaware that that word immediately triggers the most hostile thoughts about Western, Christian, ethnocentric religious hegemony in the minds of most Muslims. It certainly would not help the President of the United States of America win the moral argument at international level, and his advisers soon persuaded him to change his choice of language.

The Crusades have left a powerful pall over Muslim–Christian relations, lasting until today. Some Christians have recently sought to do something about that negative legacy. Reconciliation marches were organized in the 1990s by some creative, Western Christians to coincide with centenary remembrances of earlier crusading actions. Representatives of Western Christian missions and churches walked through Muslim lands to Jerusalem, retracing the rough route of the first Crusade. Their aim was to express repentance and to seek forgiveness for atrocities committed all those centuries previously in the name of Christ. In encounter after encounter with various Muslim officials, these twentieth-century Christians dissociated themselves from the kind of Christianity represented by their forebears. In many places and by many Muslims, the marchers were warmly received. Their humble stance was strongly appreciated and wide, local media coverage of their expressions of sorrow was given. In two major respects, however, the twentieth-century expressions of repentance and reconciliation were somewhat compromised. Firstly, the original Crusades were called for by popes. The marchers of the twentieth century, unfortunately, included no official Vatican representatives. Secondly, local, indigenous Christians in the Middle East felt bypassed and marginalized by the activities of the Western marchers. Living today in the shadow of

Islam and isolated from many Christian communities in the West because of the latter's support for the state of Israel, Arab and other Middle Eastern Christians felt that the reconciliation marches took no account of the persecutions inflicted upon them, down through the centuries, by powerful Muslim groups. It was thus, in their eyes, a pretty one-sided, non-costly kind of reconciliation that was being effected.[177]

The *Reconquista*

By AD 650, the initial, rapid expansion of Islam had spent itself, except in the west of North Africa. There, the conversion of the Berbers gave renewed force to the Muslim expansion and the remaining Byzantine provinces were overrun. The conquerors swept on into Spain in AD 711, and the defeat there of the Visigoths delivered the whole peninsula with the exception of a northern strip (that contained the independent Basques and others) to Islam (Figure 63). The invaders also took over the Visigothic corner of France and began to enlarge it until they were stopped at Poitiers in AD 732 by Charles Martel.

Figure 63
Spain in the seventh and eighth centuries

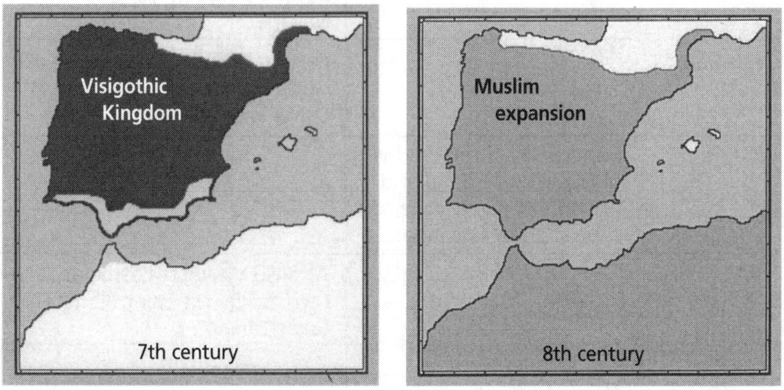

The Moors who conquered Spain were a mixture of Arabs and Berbers. They often fell out with each other and tended to fight out their arguments in Spain, often allying with Christian families or contracting Christian forces to fight for them. Moreover, although the Umayyads were comprehensively overthrown as rulers of the Arab empire in AD 750, one of the few Umayyads to survive (Abd al-Rahman) managed to establish himself as emir (or ruler) of independent Cordoba from AD 756. His success came after a bitter struggle that gave the Christians of northern Spain under Alfonso I the opportunity to win back and refound the kingdom of Galicia. The "*Reconquista*" refers to the medieval Christian reconquest of the Iberian peninsula that followed over the next few centuries (Figure 64).

Figure 64
Significant events of the *Reconquista*

Date AD	Muslim successes	Christian successes
711–718	Muslims invade Iberia (Spain) and push inland.	
718		Pelayo defeats the Muslim army in Alcama and the "reconquest" begins.
791–842		Alfonso II conquers a number of strongholds and settles the lands south of the river Duero.
905–926		Sancho I Garces creates a Basque kingdom centred on Navarre.
930–950		Ramiro II, king of Leon, defeats Abd al-Rahman III at Simancas, Osma and Talavera.
981	Ramiro III is defeated by al-Mansur at Rueda and obliged to pay tribute to the caliph of Cordoba.	
1065–1109		Alfonso VI unites Castile and Leon under his sceptre and takes Toledo.
1086	The Muslim kings of Granada, Seville and Badajoz call in the Almoravids.	

1102	The African Muslims occupy the peninsula as far as Saragossa.	
1118		Alfonso I of Aragon conquers Saragossa.
1151	The Almohads, who have displaced the Almoravids, retake Almaria.	
1195	The Almohads defeat the Castilians at Alarcos.	
1212		Alfonso VIII of Castile, Sancho VIII of Navarre, Pedro II of Aragon plus troops from Portugal and Leon win the Battle of Las Navas de Tolosa.
1217–1252	Granada survives as the sole independent Muslim kingdom.	Fernando III, king of Castile and Leon, conquers Cordoba, Murcia, Jaen and Seville.
1309		Fernando IV takes Gibraltar.
1492		Isabel and Fernando take Granada.

Towards the end of the eighth century, Charlemagne attempted unsuccessfully to conquer Spain. In AD 800, however, he took Barcelona and by AD 811 had gained control of the Catalan area. During these years, Benedictine monasteries were founded in the reclaimed areas and pilgrimage to Santiago de Compostela was revived. Indeed, St James (patron saint of Spain) became known as "*Santiago Matamoros*" or "St James the Moor-killer". At the beginning of the tenth century, Abd al-Rahman III restored and extended the *al-Andalus* empire, pronouncing himself the first Spanish "caliph" (AD 912–961). His long reign was followed by that of Hisham II (AD 961–976) under whose prime minister – al-Mansur – the entire Iberian peninsula was conquered by the Muslims. During Abd al-Rahman's rule, and that of his two successors, the Umayyad dynasty centred on Cordoba "took its place as the most cultured city in Europe and, with Constantinople and Baghdad, as one of the three cultural centres of the world".[178]

Towards the close of his caliphate, Abd al-Rahman III was

repeatedly defeated in battles with Ramiro II, king of Leon. From the peak of its success in the tenth century, the Umayyad caliphate of Spain rapidly unravelled. Civil war between Arabs and Berbers continued unchecked and although the caliphate lingered on until AD 1031, it became an impotent spectator of events beyond its control. Berber emirs proclaimed their independence in the south and west of Spain and in Morocco; the eastern seaports soon followed suit. As the Muslim states in Spain disintegrated in the eleventh century, so the Christian kingdoms – Castile, Leon, Navarre, Aragon and so on – expanded. During his papacy, Pope Gregory VII (died AD 1095) turned the reconquest into a religious duty for Christians. Military orders, such as those of Santiago and Montesa, were founded. The capture of Toledo by Alfonso VI of Castile in AD 1085 was a significant moment. This former capital of Visigothic Spain, for many years a centre of Muslim civilization, returned to Christian hands.

The Christian success forced the Muslim rulers of Granada, Seville and Badajoz to call to their aid the Almoravids, a Muslim Berber dynasty based in Morocco. The Moroccan Almoravid army crossed the straits, defeated Alfonso VI and then returned to Africa. A few years later (in AD 1090) they came back to seize control of the Muslim-dominated areas of Spain so that from 1090 to 1145 the Almoravids ruled Spain as a province of Marrakesh (Figure 65). That rule was repressive, typified by their exiling of Ibn Rushd, their burning of the works of al-Ghazâlî and their suppression of the Ṣûfîs. The Almoravid military machine expanded Muslim rule into Valencia.

In the early twelfth century, the kingdom of Aragon began its own offensive against the Moors, and its union with Catalonia in AD 1140 gave it additional military strength. During the 1150s, another Berber dynasty – the Almohads – defeated the Almorovids and took control of all their former territories, including the Spanish "province". They were not able to hang on to their newly acquired colony for long. Regional anarchy plus Christian pressure – promoted by Pope Innocent III who proclaimed a full crusade against the Moors – led to the Almohads being defeated in AD 1212 by the combined

Figure 65
Spain in the twelfth century

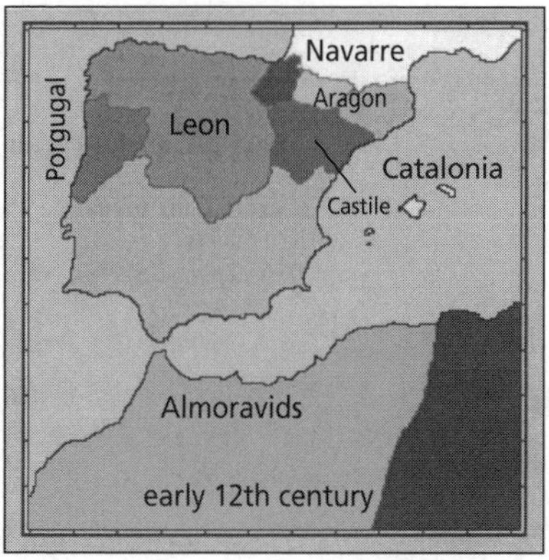

forces of Leon, Castile, Navarre and Aragon under Alfonso VIII at the Battle of Las Navas de Tolosa. Castile captured Cordoba in AD 1236 and Cadiz in AD 1262.

By the middle of the thirteenth century, only Granada remained in Muslim hands. Alfonso XI began a fight for Granada in AD 1312: it lasted for a quarter of a century. He defeated the Spanish and Moroccan Muslims in the Battle of Rio Salado. The African threat to Spain was ended. A union of Castile and Aragon through the marriage of Isabel I of Castile and Fernando II of Aragon in AD 1469 led to the uniting of Spain and the reconquest (in AD 1492) of Granada, the last Muslim possession in Spain (Figure 66).

The gradual reconquest of Muslim Spain by Christians did not extinguish the Muslim presence from Spain, at least not immediately. That outcome did, however, become a national objective over the next century. "Morisco" is the term used for Moors (Muslims) who stayed on in Spain after the fall of Granada in AD 1492 and who were baptized unwillingly. In AD 1501, Spanish law offered Muslims a choice between conversion or exile. Many converted but remained secretly loyal to Islam. In AD 1556 Arab and Muslim dress was forbidden in Granada, and a decade later Philip II decreed that the Arabic language could no longer be used. Finally, in AD 1609, Philip III expelled the Muslims from Spain. Between 1609 and 1615, the last of the

Figure 66
Spain in the late fifteenth century

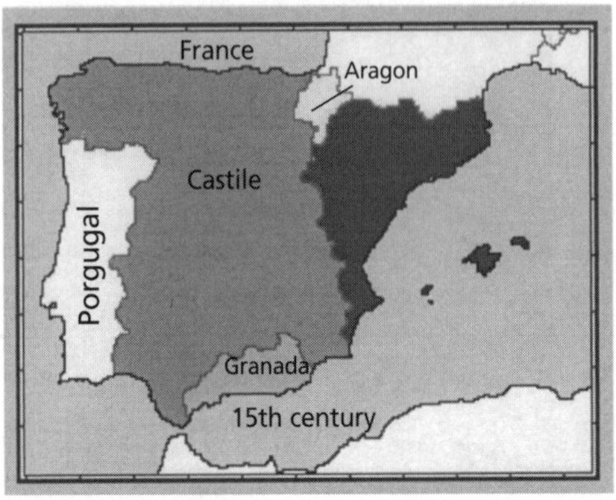

Moriscos, the crypto-Muslims, were deported, mostly to North Africa and Istanbul. A similar process had taken place in the fifteenth century with regard to Jews living in Spain; virtually the entire Jewish population was expelled. The Christian requirement for religious homogeneity meant that Jews and Muslims had either to assimilate or be expelled.

According to one modern Muslim scholar and diplomat, the loss of Spain by the Muslims left a "permanent scar" on the Muslim psyche. Its effect, he claims, has continued to recent times.[179] The expulsion of the Moors, moreover, perhaps provoked a significant shift in the convictions of deportee Muslims concerning their Prophet. Gerard Wiegers has examined the polemical writings of some of the Moors expelled from Spain during this period. He notices that "one of the new concepts appearing in such polemical writings is the idea that *Muhammad is the Messiah* ..."[180] Perhaps in the maelstrom of the expulsion of the Moors lies the origin of *The Gospel of Barnabas*, a work that similarly presents Muḥammad as Messiah. One wonders whether out of such mistreatment of Muslims by Christian Europeans has arisen a document that is repeatedly referred to in Muslim polemical works of the late twentieth century. Maybe the acts of aggression in one Christian generation have come back to haunt a later generation. As we shall see, the *Gospel of Barnabas* is a major player in relations between

Christians and Muslims at the beginning of the twenty-first century.

The conquest (by Muslims) and reconquest (by Christians) of Spain typifies the unhelpful history that both faith communities inherit with regard to their previous interaction. The memory of each community has been scarred by serial experiences of territorial loss and communal humiliation. Potent reminders of such uncomfortable experiences tended to remain visible long after the memories of specific atrocities faded. At one end of the Mediterranean sat the former mosque – La Mezquita – at Cordoba, converted to a church by Christians. At the other end of the Mediterranean sat the previous church of Hagia Sophia, in Constantinople, converted to a mosque by Muslims. Such visible scars of Muslim and Christian violence toward one another have kept suspicion, if not outright enmity, alive. As Peter Riddell and Peter Cotterell summarize: "Such scars have contributed profoundly to ongoing strains in the relationship between Christianity and Islam down through the ages."[181]

European imperialism

By the eighteenth century, a worldwide variety of Islamic societies had come into being. The highly centralized Ottoman Empire in the Middle East and the more relaxed Mughal Empire of the Indian subcontinent offered alternative models of constituting an Islamic polity. South-east Asian Islamic societies were different again. During the eighteenth and nineteenth centuries these various societies were strongly affected by European intervention. By this time, European peoples had been experiencing major changes within their societies. Now they began to flex their muscles on the world scene. Technological inventiveness coupled with the capacity to generate economic wealth and military power culminated in a rapid transfer of global political and commercial dominance to Europe. Such dominance meant that approximately 90 per cent of the Muslim world came to be ruled by Western colonizing nations at one stage or another during the period AD 1700 to AD

1960. By the beginning of the twentieth century, the European powers (and China) had carried out their conquest of almost all the Muslim world.

European ascendancy took a cultural as well as a political and economic form. The Enlightenment period had resulted in a strong process of secularization within European society so that political and economic institutions came to be freed from religious requirements or vetoes. "Religion" was relegated to the narrow sphere of piety or private faith. The scientific mind engendered confidence that nature, society and even the human personality could be rationally understood without recourse to religious myth. Throughout the Muslim world, European dominance came to mean the imposition of the latter's institutions and cultural concepts upon indigenous peoples. In schools and universities founded by missionaries, curricula were set according to the priorities and requirements of each mission's homeland. "Modernization" became the name of the political, educational, economic and cultural game in the Muslim lands under "Christian", European rule.

From the late eighteenth century to the early twentieth century, the Muslim state systems collapsed under the imposition of European military, political and commercial domination. Eventually, the twentieth century saw the gradual formation – under European tutelage – of national states ("Muslim nations") through which the Muslim leaders of their peoples tried to give a modern political identity to their societies. This phase of nation-building began after World War I and continues until today. The consolidation of national states, especially after the realization of their independence from the colonial experience, has resulted in conflict throughout the Muslim world over the direction of their current development and the role, within that direction, of Islam.

In looking back at the experience of being under colonial rule, many Muslims feel aggrieved. They suggest that the rule by force of outsiders constituted a human rights violation. They argue that imperial powers indulged in the economic rape of their nations' resources. They came to smart under an aggressive political subjugation whereby the manner in which their societies cohered was deliberately changed to mirror the "Western" way. They count the cost in lost lives of being drawn into the Western military argument about democracy, fascism and communism that eventuated in World War II. Many of them rue the secularizing of their societies and lots of them view the experience of political imperialism as including a form of religious domination. Christian missionaries frequently followed on the coat-tails of political and military success to share their message about Christ and serve Muslim populations in the areas of health and education. Although, in lots of cases, altruistic Christian missionaries found themselves opposed to the kind of attitudes and activities of fellow-Westerners who were ruling the "natives" they were seeking to serve, Christian missionaries are nevertheless still viewed as a powerful secularizing force in many of the societies that they entered. A common perception of Muslims "on the receiving end" of Western colonizers, missionaries and orientalists was that the attitude of the Westerners towards Muslims and their faith was "one of disdain and insensitive paternalism".[182]

Dr Zaki Badawi, chairman of the British Council of Mosques, summarizes the sort of feeling evoked by the ever-present memory of having been, so recently, under Western domination:

> We feel deeply the humiliation, the marginalisation of the whole Muslim world. Muslim countries are so divided, so small, so irrelevant ... We are the most backward among nations, and the poorest. Almost the whole of Islam belongs to the Third World. Part of the Middle East may have enormous oil resources, but, even there it is the West that ultimately controls them.[183]

The State of Israel

Parshall suggests, correctly in my opinion, that "throughout the Muslim world, the greatest ongoing deterrent to peaceful coexistence between the 1.2 billion Muslims and the West is the Palestinian issue".[184] At the core of Middle Eastern tensions, and probably of global tensions also – if the American "war on terror" is linked to issues of continuing injustice involving Palestinians – lie two apparently irreconcilable claims. Both Israeli Jew and Palestinian Arab assert historic right of ownership to the same small strip of land as their homeland.

Chronic instability, regional wars, *intifâda* or "uprising", suicide bombings, eviction from and destruction of homes – deep personal suffering for millions of "innocents" has resulted over the past 50 years. From both Israeli and Palestinian sides the conflict has been turned into a religious issue, so that both advocates of Jewish settlement along with the displacement of Palestinians, and Islamists who want to see the State of Israel cease to exist, are motivated by strong religious belief. At all stages in the development of the State of Israel and in the inability to resolve the resulting dilemma at the heart of the Middle East, Western nations have been involved. Many Muslims perceive the Western involvement to be motivated, not so much by a will to see a Jewish state created, as by a desire to see a destabilizing factor maintained in the Arab world.[185]

The end of World War I brought the final break-up of the Ottoman Empire and the establishment of a number of Middle Eastern states whose boundaries were determined by France and Britain. In AD 1922 the League of Nations gave Britain a Mandate for Palestine that incorporated the text of the Balfour Declaration. In the eyes of Arab leaders, that document (the Balfour Declaration) broke the promises previously made to them by the British government during the war. The Mandate empowered Britain to secure the establishment of a Jewish National Home, though without prejudice to the civil and religious rights of the rest of the population.

At the end of World War II, Britain resigned its Palestinian Mandate to the United Nations. The European Holocaust precipitated a strong surge of world opinion supporting the idea that the Jews should be made secure within a state of their own. In 1947 the UN General Assembly voted for the establishment in May 1948 of a Jewish state on part of the land still called Palestine. Arab inhabitants were not consulted. War resulted. By its end in January 1949, almost 750,000 Palestinian Arabs

(Muslims and Christians) had either fled or been expelled – they were now refugees.

The next two decades saw the rapid consolidation of the State of Israel on the one hand, and on the other hand the failure of the Arab states and the Palestinians either to launch a war against Israel that they could win or to agree on terms for a peace settlement with Israel. Western interest in the region revolved mainly around maintaining vital supplies of oil from the Gulf and containing any spread of Soviet influence. The United States consistently refused to negotiate officially with the Palestinian Liberation Organization and did not really involve itself positively in attempts at conflict resolution until the Camp David Accords of 1979, which settled territorial issues between Israel and Egypt. Despite some further progress made via the Madrid Conference (1991), the Oslo Accords (1993), the Peace Treaty between Jordan and Israel (1994) and the Wye River Agreement (1998), the emergence of Ariel Sharon of the Likud Party as prime minister since early 2001 has slowed – even stalled – positive steps towards peace and reconciliation in Israel/Palestine. With the emergence after 1991 of the United States as the only superpower in the contemporary world, that nation's perceived hypocritical stance with regard to Iraq and Israel as non-compliers with UN Council resolutions has served to underline Muslims' negative view of the West.

The United States of America is probably the only power in the world today that has the political and economic clout to achieve some positive steps towards a resolution of the Israeli/Palestinian problem. Its refusal to use its influence in such a way does not help Muslims to countenance positive relations with the "Christian" West. Indeed, as Bell points out, "one of the biggest blockages to gaining the trust of Muslims today is the fact that they perceive the West (including the Christian Church) to be endorsing and financially supporting the State of Israel".[186] Certainly, the American government's annual aid package to Israel is massive. Chapman describes the ability of the Christian dispensationalist and Zionist view of world history to affect how politicians in the White House approach contemporary policy-making in the Middle East. In the view of such American (and other) Christians, the biblical land of Zion and the modern Zionist State of Israel are equated. The latter regime is therefore to be supported by Bible-believing Christians.[187] Chapman's study – *Whose Promised Land?* – of the continuing crisis over Israel and Palestine well documents some of the historical processes lying behind the conflict there. It also explores the theme of "the land" in Old and New Testaments and suggests some legitimate and illegitimate ways of reading the Bible in relation to the Middle East situation. Chapman is quite clear that this long-standing, profound war over worldview, religion and land at the heart of the Middle East has been a major factor contributing to the anger and resentment finding recent expression in outrages like 11 September 2001. David Grossman, an Israeli writer, is also quite clear that the only chance of a resolution to conflict in Palestine/Israel lies with outside pressure-bringers:

> Only a miracle or a catastrophe will change the situation. If you don't believe in the first and fear the latter, you realize that the only practical hope for saving Israel and the Palestinians from mutual slaughter is heavy international pressure on both of them.[188]

If a powerful, Western, "Christian" nation – the only potential outside pressure-bringer – is perceived as being (religiously) predisposed to one partner in the conflict, it is not surprising that Muslims mistrust Christians. It looks, at the beginning of the third millennium, as if there is no possibility of ever sorting out the "dagger in their heart" that Muslims currently feel concerning the continued existence, in its present shape, of the State of Israel.[189]

Other wars

Recent conflicts in the Balkans have resulted in a strong alienation of Muslims from Christians. It was in those conflicts that the horrible term, "ethnic cleansing", came into common currency. In 1989, Slobodan Milosevic travelled to Kosovo with over a million Serbs to mark the 600th anniversary of the great Battle of Kosovo of AD 1389. At that famous battle, as noted earlier, the Serbs had been defeated by the Ottoman forces and, as a result, were subjected to Ottoman rule for nearly five centuries. Milosevic's symbolic pilgrimage in 1989 was made against the background of a shifting demographic balance in the region. The Albanians were demanding that Kosovo be given the status of a Yugoslav republic. The Serbs and the Yugoslav government resisted, afraid that once Kosovo had the right to secede it would do so, maybe merging with Albania. "Ethnic cleansing" became the name of the cruel game in the 1990s as minority Serbs and Croats in Bosnia-Herzegovina strove to redress the expansion in the region of the Muslim population. In Bosnia, over the next months and years, the gruesome and pervasive reality of native, white, European Muslims being raped and massacred – by native, white, European Christians – was displayed to a disbelieving world. It seemed to the Muslims to take forever for the international bodies to act against Milosevic's forces. By then, Islamists from around the Muslim world had joined the battle, introducing their concept of *jihâd* or holy war to the Balkans.

The conflict quickly came to be seen as ethno-religious, both by the parties themselves and by outside observers. The Croats (Roman Catholic Christians) saw themselves as guardians of the West against Orthodoxy and Islam. The Serbs (Orthodox Christians) saw their enemies – Bosnian Croats and Muslims – as stooges of the Vatican and the Turks. The Bosnian Muslims identified themselves as victims of genocide, sidelined by the West for religious reasons and requiring the support of fellow Muslims from around the world. Events in the north-east Bosnian city of Zvornik illustrate the point. There, in April to June 1992, the Serbs "cleansed" the area of its 40,000 Muslims. They planted a cross on the site of the Ottoman tower they had blown up – the tower had been built to replace the Orthodox church that had been destroyed on that site by the Turks in AD 1463. The destruction of mosques, monasteries and churches, and the "cleansing" of people from other religious or ethnic backgrounds, sullied Muslim–Christian relations catastrophically in the Balkans and beyond at the end of the twentieth century.

The Gulf War of 1991 and the Iraq War of 2003 have not helped Western democracies regain the trust of Muslims around the globe. Such Muslims wonder why one nation of the Middle East should be held to account for its acts of aggression by the international community while another should not. Why was Iraq forced to abandon its pretensions in Kuwait while Israel was not required to return occupied land in Israel/Palestine? The "Desert Storm" of 1991 saw Muslims defeating Muslims with the help of non-Muslims, an unhappy state of affairs compared with the brilliant defeat of infidel, Soviet forces in Afghanistan by combined Muslim-only efforts. Saudi Arabia, home of the most holy Islamic sites on earth, suddenly became infested with American soldiers – men, women, Jews! The aftermath of that war served to confirm the diagnosis made concerning the ills of the world by the Islamists. The "Christian" nations were only really concerned about access to Middle Eastern oil and the containment of Iran. Issues of international justice in the Middle East were hardly on their agendas.

The questioning of the 2003 war against Iraq has been far stronger. Why should America, Britain, Spain and Italy take it upon themselves to remove a regime in a Muslim country without United Nations support? Whatever the evils of Saddam Hussein – and few Middle Eastern Muslims saw in him anything other than a ruthless, secularizing dictator – with what justification did Western, "Christian" nations single-handedly dispose of him? It feels like the Crusades all over again, dressed up in different clothing. It is reminiscent of the break-up of the Ottoman Empire when Western powers scrambled for influence and control.

... and terrorism

In this book I have tried for the most part to help Western Christians see themselves and the history of the development of Christianity vis-à-vis Islam from a perspective different from their own inherited one. I have questioned whether that history "on the ground" truly reflects the attitude and priorities of Christianity's founder, Jesus Christ. I need to say at this point that the rise of Islamism (Islamic fundamentalism) raises – or should raise – an equivalent soul-searching by Muslims. Is such an approach to gaining political power really what Prophet Muḥammad would have encouraged? I have explored this issue in depth in *Holy War*. Here, we need to take note that the use of terror against civilians (men, women and children) is a highly questionable procedure from an orthodox Islamic perspective. The mass murder in North America in September 2001, the continuing slaughter of Israeli citizens through suicide bombings, the blowing up of commuter trains in Madrid or the taking of child hostages in Ossetia have tragically become part of the canvas depicting "what Islam means" for most contemporary world citizens. Those terrible acts by some Muslims may be the end-result of long and angry frustration over issues of injustice, but they also constitute totally unacceptable ways of expressing such frustration in the modern world. Unless orthodox, non-Islamist Muslims bend over backwards to communicate the abnormality – in their view – of such terrorist atrocities, the blood left on that current "canvas" describing Islam will blot out other, more valid, expressions. The committing of acts of terror by Islamic extremists has hugely coloured how those of other cultures or faiths now view Islam. It will be a virtually impossible task to persuade such observers that the terms "Muslim" and "terrorist" do not necessarily go together. Blood upon the canvas has produced bad blood between peoples and nations.

Bad blood

In his editorial commentary on the World Council of Churches' evaluation of Christian–Muslim dialogue, Richard Rousseau begins by admitting that that element of interfaith relating has not progressed nearly as far as Christian encounters with Jews or Christian encounters with the "religions of the east". He suggests that history explains a good bit of the reason why that should be:

> From the days of the original Islamic imperial surge, reaching to the Pyrenees in Spain and briefly penetrating France, through the drawn out frustrations of the Crusades, the gradual decay of the Islamic powers, the colonial era and, in these latter days, the OPEC and Iranian revolutions, the Christian West and the Islamic East have been antagonists.[190]

Surprisingly, Rousseau does not mention the Israel/Palestine issue directly. And the Bosnian, Gulf and Iraq wars were still one or two decades away! If Rousseau could characterize Christian–Muslim relations in the early 1980s as "antagonistic", what would he call them today? There is evidently more ground to be made up in the race to undo prejudice before catastrophic international events make any efforts at rapprochement nigh on impossible.

Breaking stereotypes

I believe that there are ways towards mutual understanding and rekindled trust. Those ways begin at a personal level in the breaking of stereotypes that Muslims hold of Christians and Christians of Muslims. There are plenty of resources to assist Western Christians in that process. Bell's helpful manual is appropriately entitled *Friendship First*.[191] His aim is to offer an easy-to-read publication that helps ordinary Christians discuss the good news with ordinary Muslims "in an atmosphere of friendship". Margaret Burness attempts a similar goal for Christian women in her *What Do I Say to my Muslim Friends?*[192] And there are plenty more helps, some of them listed in the bibliography at the end of this book. The starting-point is found in being human, making friends. That is surely something that we all can do!

There are also appropriate ways for Christians to hold to account the political leaders of their own nations. In democracies we are offered the right to make our views known. We in Britain can write to our members of parliament, to government officials, to the prime minister's office. We can lobby and march in protest at actions that we do not want performed in our name. I might not agree with everything that the American author and film-maker Michael Moore stands for, but he does appear to be a person who can see through stereotypes. Aside from the crudeness of his rather blunt style in *Stupid White Men*,[193] he creatively offers some positive suggestions as to ways out of the current impasse over Israel and Palestine. Congress, he suggests, should inform Israel that it has 30 days to end the bloodshed perpetrated in its name or lose the $3 billion per annum it receives from the United States. Israel should be given a year to work out a plan with the Palestinians to create a nation called Palestine. The new nation of Palestine must then present a constitution prohibiting aggression against Israel and guaranteeing democratic rights to all Palestinians. The United States should subsequently donate double to Palestine the amount that it is donating to Israel. And to the then living President Arafat, Moore writes a letter guaranteeing success in his aims for an independent Palestinian state if he would only take a route that has never yet failed – mass, *non-violent*, civil disobedience.[194]

As Christians we need to ask careful questions about the view we hold of Muslims. Just how prejudiced are those views? How does our reading of scripture inform our outlook on followers of Islam? Are such people sidelined because we believe that God is working out a prearranged plan in the land that Israelis and Palestinians fight over – and the non-Muslims have, therefore, to be the winners? Or do we recognize that the Bible does not give any encouragement to believe that one people has a divine right to that small piece of "holy" land? Chapman, for example, asserts:

> Jews and others have presented convincing *historical, political and psychological* arguments to justify the creation of a Jewish state in the land in the twentieth century. But on the basis of the New Testament understanding of the relationship between Jews and Gentiles ... it is hard to see how *Christians* can produce convincing *theological* arguments based on the Bible for the appropriateness and necessity of a Jewish state in the land.[195]

Our integrity as Christians is brought into question by the complex matrix of contemporary Muslim–Christian relations at a global level. What does it really mean – in the messy world of politics and international relations – for us to be followers of Christ? What possibility might there be, especially, for Christians (and Muslims?) from the "developing" world to act as mediators, advocates of peace with justice in some of the hotspots of the contemporary world where conflict has become so strongly entwined with religious allegiances?

The heritage of bad blood between Muslims and "Christian" West is chronic and runs deep. It makes it doubly difficult for Muslims and Christians in today's international climate to begin to trust one another. It prejudices attempts to address issues of historic and persisting injustice. It makes harder any kind of encounter except one that is hostile in nature – whether that encounter is being pursued in the realm of politics, interfaith relations or personal witness.

Chapter 9 Meeting Head-on

It seems to be the case among human beings that those seemingly similar or sharing a common vocabulary often find the greatest difficulty in communicating successfully. Both Islam and Christianity have a strong sense of mission – they are each missionary faiths. This facet of their belief and practice derives from the highest source in each case. For Christians, mission is directly commanded by Jesus Christ. For Muslims, the Qur'ân explicitly commands the propagation of the faith (Figure 67).

Figure 67
Mission imperative

Islam	Christianity
It is He Who hath sent His Apostle with Guidance and the Religion of Truth, to proclaim it over all religion, even though the Pagans may detest (it). Sura 9:33	"Therefore go and make disciples of all nations, baptizing them in the name of the Father and of the Son and of the Holy Spirit ... " Matthew 28:19

The fact of this common emphasis on missionary outreach has hardly helped Muslims and Christians accommodate one another. Rather it has contributed to the sense of competition and mutual hostility already complicating their relationship:

> Among religions, the interrelationship between Christianity and Islam is of particular interest. Accounting for approximately half of the world's population between them, both are missionary religions with mutually exclusive claims to universality and finality,

> and this inherent conflict of interests is compounded by a long history which has often been fraught with conflict and antagonism. Even the common ground which they share as participants in the Abrahamic monotheistic tradition has frequently been a cause of discord rather than harmony.[196]

The century from AD 1900 to AD 2000 saw the world's population increase from 1.6 billion to 6.0 billion, roughly a fourfold increase. During that same period, the world's Christian community increased at the same rate, from 558 million in AD 1900 to 2 billion in AD 2000. The overall Muslim population, by contrast, grew at a much faster rate from a much smaller base – from 200 million in AD 1900 to 1.2 billion in AD 2000 (see Figure 68).[197] In the 30 years from AD 1970 to AD 2000, the Muslim population increased by some 114 per cent, compared with 62 per cent for the Christian population and 64 per cent for the world population. The figures, and the rates of growth, underline the sense of increasing competition between these two major, mission-oriented world faiths.

Figure 68
Growing faith communities

Year	World population	Muslims	Christians
1900	1,620 million	200 million	558 million
1970	3,696 million	554 million	1,236 million
2000	6,055 million	1,188 million	2,000 million
(2025 projected)	(7,824 million)	(1,785 million)	(2,617 million)

Making disciples ...

The history of Christian mission has been told elsewhere. In so far as that history impinges on Muslims, and their consequent view of Christianity, a major bone of contention has been the role of force in the propagation of Christian faith. Since the conversion of Constantine, the issue for Christians has not been simple, especially if by "force" is understood more than just sword or gun. Other forms of domination have found expression in political, economic or cultural – as well as military – power.

In AD 1500, Christianity had shrunk to being almost wholly a European religion. During the following century the Jesuits especially spearheaded an expansion of Roman Catholic Christian mission in Asia and Latin America. Ships of trade and conquest carried in their cabins Christian missionaries. Those missionaries would enjoy their governments' protection in their evangelizing work. The eighteenth century saw upheavals in the Roman Catholic missionary enterprise due mainly to the French Revolution, the dissolution of the Jesuits (AD 1775) and the decline of Spain and Portugal as world powers. The Russian church, however, became strongly involved in mission during this century. Then, at the end of the eighteenth century, the first significant Protestant missionary societies began to emerge.

The massive movement of Protestant Christian missionaries around the globe in the eighteenth to early twentieth century was largely made possible by colonizing European powers. In the early 1800s the first burst of Protestant missionary societies occurred with the formation of the Baptist Missionary Society (1792), the Church Missionary Society (1799) and the British Foreign and Bible Society (1804), amongst many others. This initial spurt was followed by a second wave after AD 1865 with strong North American participation following the end there of the Civil War. The Americans tended to form centralized, denominational mission groups. The faith missions of Hudson Taylor's ilk came into being in the second half of the nineteenth century. A Catholic resurgence in missions also occurred during the nineteenth century after the Jesuit order was re-established in AD 1814. The White Fathers, many of whom worked in Muslim contexts, started their mission work in AD 1868. Within the Russian Orthodox community, a renewal in piety resulted in an awakened mission consciousness.

Makary Glucharev, for example, worked amongst the Kalmaks, producing a book entitled *Thoughts on the Methods to be Followed for a Successful Dissemination of the Faith among Mohammedans, Jews and Pagans in the Russian Empire*. The *Pax Britannica* facilitated the global work of many such Christian missionaries, a significant proportion of whom were women.

As a result of the faithful and costly witnessing of Western Christian missionaries, there arose a Christian presence in virtually all the world. That presence remains until today, making Christianity a truly global phenomenon. As we have earlier mentioned, the relationship between missionaries and colonial administrators was not always straightforward or positive. The foreign rulers sometimes sought to restrict Christian missionary activity for fear of it inciting religious unrest. At the same time, many missionaries held a less ethnocentric view of the nationals who became their "brothers and sisters in Christ" than did the upholders of imperial control. Nevertheless, in many situations it was assumed by all the foreigners – administrators and missionaries alike – that the exporting of Western culture and societal mores was part and parcel of what they were there for and, in itself, a "good thing", even a "Christian thing".

Patterns of paternalism and assumptions about Western cultural superiority were more likely to go unquestioned when the missionary fraternity belonged to the race ruling the "natives". It is a mark of the transforming work of God that significant numbers of missionaries did develop more healthy attitudes to indigenous cultures and their peoples. Maybe this was partly due to their learning the language of the folk they were trying to reach for Christ. Through language-learning, the worldviews of the different people concerned began to be appreciated. Missionaries learned new concepts of reality, different but valid ways of viewing life and religion. The "converts", moreover, were encouraged through this process with a sense of national or ethnic pride – a major contributor to some of the independence movements that would later challenge the continuation of colonial rule!

Christian missionaries became agents of significant change

in many of the countries where they worked. They were a major secularizing force through their strong and long involvement in the fields of literacy and education. For many years, the leadership of the mission groups lay firmly in the hands of Western Christians. Mission headquarters were located in the home nations and the funding for missionary activities "overseas" derived from there. The World Missionary Conference that was convened at Edinburgh in AD 1910 took as its slogan "The evangelising of the world in this generation". It was a conference of Western mission agencies and leaders. Over the next decades, despite World War I, success in evangelism around the world would lead to new churches being formed. Gradually the leadership of such mission churches became indigenized. By AD 1933 over 60 per cent of Roman Catholics in Asia were being led by indigenous clergy. Protestant schools, hospitals and other philanthropic institutions were increasingly directed by national personnel. Missionary councils gradually transformed themselves into church councils and church councils eventually combined to become national church councils.

After World War II, the World Council of Churches was constituted at Amsterdam in AD 1948. All five continents were represented at its inauguration. From 1910 to 1961 the shift of emphasis from "mission" to "church" at the national level reflected the success on the ground of the Christian movement. At the international level, also, delegates to meetings tended increasingly to be national church leaders rather than foreign missionaries. The internationalization of the world after World War II, along with the abandoning of the "imperial" mind-set and the confrontation with people of other faiths, led to a major shift in Christian theology and ecclesiology. In AD 1961, at New Delhi, the International Missionary Council that had been formed in AD 1910 was subsumed under the World Council of Churches in its Commission for World Mission and Evangelism. Ecumenism became the important focus for Christian relationships at world level and Christian ecumenists took increasingly a "dialogue", rather than a "mission", approach to relating to people of other faiths.

Daᶜwa

> Islam ... aims at bringing its message to all corners of the earth. It hopes that one day the whole of humanity will be one Muslim community, the "Umma".[198]

Muslims living in the West often express the hope that the West will one day be won over to Islam through peaceful persuasion, by means of *daᶜwa* ("invitation" to Islam). The "religion plus power" quality of Islam – the combination of sacred and secular aspects of living – means that mission in Islam amounts to both the conveying of the truth (*tablîgh*) by word of mouth and the invitation (*daᶜwa*) to the straight path by persuasion and explanation. Such a view of mission is authenticated in the life and example of Prophet Muḥammad. The use of economic, political or military power in the cause of establishing or making the truth prevail is openly validated. In the West, of course, this kind of approach is no longer seen as acceptable – except that one might argue that certain Western nations have decided that "might" is a fair contemporary deliverer of democracy (a particular political ideology) to a nation like Iraq, even if the United Nations would not countenance that kind of application of force.

Interestingly, the spread of Islam in many instances has had far less to do with the use of the sword than is commonly supposed. Apart from the tiredness of Egyptian Copts with Byzantine overlords that led them in those early years of Muslim expansion to welcome the armies of Islam, in many parts of the world it has often been members of the Ṣûfî orders or Muslim merchants who have carried their faith to non-Muslims. In India, for example, voluntary conversions to Islam at tribal levels took place far more frequently and with much greater consequence than forced conversions. The egalitarian actions of Muslim conquerors attracted lower caste or non-caste Hindus to the fold of Islam. More recently, some of the Ṣûfî-influenced reformist movements in the Indian subcontinent have won vast numbers of non-Muslims to Islam. In the "Malay" world of south-east Asia, it was mostly Indian Muslim traders who gradually brought Islam to the people. A similar combination of Ṣûfî order and itinerant trader represented the cutting edge of Islam as it expanded in West Africa.

In March 1924, a new Turkish national assembly abolished the more than 1,200 years-old institution of the caliphate. The assembly's secularizing constituents sent Abdul Majid II of the Ottoman dynasty into exile in Paris. The Islamic world seemed to have had its political heart excised. How now to organize the community at international level? What new "centre" – symbolic or practical – could be found for Islam? In 1926, King Abdul Aziz ibn Saud convened at Mecca a Muslim conference to which were invited representatives of the Islamic community from around the world. Out of the king's conference developed the Islamic World Congress, proposed symbol of unity for the whole, modern Muslim world. A significant facet of the emerging Islamic World Congress was its "lay" constituency. It was neither controlled nor led by the ulema. Indeed, while that initial meeting was proceeding, ulema at al-Azhar in Cairo were finding it difficult to come up with a united response to the calamity of the caliphate's abolition. The movement deriving from the Saudi king's initiative became largely responsible, in the twentieth century, for generating a search for a new Muslim identity in the contemporary world. A significant milestone in that redefinition was reached in March 1972 when, in Jeddah, the Organization of the Islamic Conference was founded (see Figure 69).

In areas of religion, culture and care for Muslims scattered in non-Muslim lands, the Organization of the Islamic Conference has worked closely through its secretariat in Jeddah with two international, Muslim religious organizations: the Muslim World League and the Islamic World Congress. The Muslim World League is a powerful body at the international level in the Muslim world. An Islamic religious organization only obtains legal status if it is approved by the Muslim World League. Linked with the Muslim World League are various groups including an international association for *daʿwa* and the propagation of Islam. The Islamic World Congress has had as one of its official tasks the care of Christian–Muslim dialogue. Linked with the Organization of the Islamic Conference are

Figure 69
Objectives of the Organization of the Islamic Conference

	Detail
1	To promote Islamic solidarity among member states.
2	To consolidate cooperation among member states in economic, social, cultural, scientific and other fields.
3	To seek to eliminate racial segregation and colonialism in all its forms.
4	To support international peace and security founded on justice.
5	To safeguard holy places of Islam and support the struggle of the Palestinians.
6	To safeguard the dignity, independence and national rights of all Muslims.
7	To promote understanding and cooperation among member states and with other countries.

other international institutions carrying special responsibility for mission. These include the Islamic Solidarity Fund, the Islamic Development Bank, the Islamic Broadcasting Service Organization and so on.

Other transnational organizations incorporating *daᶜwa* as one of their aims, besides the Muslim World League, include the World Islamic Call Society and the Islamic Council of Europe. While in the past, *daᶜwa* has most often been directed at lax or heterodox Muslims, it is now increasingly being targeted at non-Muslims, especially in the Western context.

Some of the significant motor force for *daᶜwa* or mission within Islam has come from Muslims living in the subcontinent of India. Perhaps this is because Indian Muslims, living in an area that never ceased to be predominantly Hindu, despite the prolonged Muslim rule over the larger part of it, have always been conscious of constituting a community with a distinctive mission and message. Pressed up against a non-yielding community of other-faith Indians, Muslims asked early on in India why they had not managed to be "successful". Shah Wali Allah (AD 1703–1763) of Delhi first began to analyze and explain this failure. He especially focused on seeking to get rid of Hindu accretions that had become part and parcel of Islam as expressed in India. He also encouraged the hope that Muslim government would be restored in the subcontinent. His thinking came to influence many of the Muslim reform movements that came after him.

Abû'l-ᶜAlâ' Mawdûdî (AD 1903–1979) picked up on Wali Allah's complaint that the root cause of Muslim decline was to be found in the widespread departure from Qur'ân and *sunna* (following Prophet Muḥammad's example), and in the corresponding shift from the rule of righteous caliphs who feared God to the reign of nominally Muslim kings. Mawdûdî formed *Jamâᶜat-i Islâmî*, or the Islamic Organization, in AD 1941 with the aim of educating a small and disciplined elite who would work to capture social and political leadership in the country and bring it back to true Islam. At partition in AD 1947, Mawdûdî ended up in the newly formed nation of Pakistan, campaigning within it for the establishment there of an Islamic state. *Daᶜwa* is one of the eight main objectives of the Islamic Organization founded by Mawdûdî. With the dispersion of members of the Islamic Organization to the West, that group, with its mission objectives, entered British (and European) society.

Mawlânâ Muhammad Ilyas (AD 1885–1944) was a second Indian Muslim who looked to Shah Wali Allah for inspiration. Descended from a respected Ṣûfî background, Ilyas was inspired to start a *Tabligh-i Jamaᶜat* or "faith movement" among the people of his home region. In the 1930s this movement spread widely. Ilyas called every committed Muslim to leave his home and work for a period in order to practise and preach the faith in an intense but simple manner. The ensuing revival of faith was manifested in the building of mosques and the establishment of Qur'ân schools with trained reciters and teachers. Gradually the movement spread to other parts of India and

Pakistan and beyond, including Britain. Annual gatherings in Lahore of members of *Tabligh-i Jamaʿat* number over a million, comprising the largest annual gatherings of Muslims after the *ḥajj*. In the year of his death, Ilyas gave a summary of his vision for faith renewal at a meeting in Delhi. "Success", in his view, depends upon the complete adoption of Islam and strict obedience to Muḥammad (see Figure 70).

Figure 70
Collective Muslim "success"

Means	Support
The inculcation of a missionary spirit	Say thou: "This is my Way: I do invite unto God – on evidence clear as the seeing with one's eyes, – I and whoever follows me". Sura 12:108
The acquisition and transmission of knowledge	O Apostle! Proclaim the (Message) which hath been sent to thee from thy Lord. Sura 5:70
Enjoining the right and forbidding the wrong	Ye are the best of Peoples, evolved for mankind, enjoining what is right, forbidding what is wrong, and believing in God. Sura 3:110
Mutual cooperation	The Believers are but a single Brotherhood: so make peace and reconciliation between your two (contending) brothers. Sura 49:10

Ilyas contends strongly for a performance of duty out of a sense of renewal within heart and soul rather than as the result of force. His emphasis is on individual moral and spiritual reform as the precondition for any properly Islamic endeavour in the world of public life. The *Tabligh-i Jamaʿat* has consistently been an apolitical movement – indeed, political discussion among the members of a preaching group is forbidden. In Britain, the Deobandi seminary established in 1982 at

Dewsbury acts as the European centre for the *Tabligh-i Jamaᶜat*. Every Christmas it hosts a huge gathering attracting Muslims from across Western Europe.

Success in mission?

Christians convert to Islam. Thousands have done so and continue to do so. Perhaps this is as a result of intellectual or spiritual interest, perhaps it is the result of a marriage. Sometimes it may have to do with a desire to stop being a second-class citizen in a majority Muslim society. In AD 1981, at Minakshipuram in the Tirunveli district of Tamilnadu, India, 1,500 persons converted to Islam. Nearly all came from one Dalit caste known as the Pallars; many of them were small landowners, daily harassed by the Shudra castes just above them. Islam offered the possibility, especially for the younger generation, of reception into a faith in which equality of treatment is promoted, plus active protection from oppression.[199] Since AD 1981, other Christians in the same district have become Muslims:

> Mohammed Sultan [a new Muslim in Kanday village] grew tired of casteism in the community and church. He instanced that the only higher-caste Christian family in the vicinity would not allow Dalits into their home. He wanted to make improvements for his children, if not for himself. He had witnessed the funeral of a new Muslim elsewhere and the respect shown pushed him to invite Muslims to come to the village. His wife found things less easy, he admitted, but she had to accept. But equality remained at the center, and he quoted the high-profile marriage of a new Muslim to the daughter of a rich Muslim businessman.[200]

Muslims also convert to Christianity. Again, this can be for a number of reasons, not necessarily all "spiritual". In Indonesia, for example, after Dutch rule for several hundred years, millions of people had become Christians. In AD 1965, when communists were attempting to take control of the government of the country, there erupted an upsurge of anti-communist activity and many people with communist sympathies were killed.

The government decreed that everyone must have a religion. Millions of people, including many Muslims, decided at that point to join the Christians, for they had not taken part in the massacres. A similar, though much smaller, movement to Christ amongst Muslims in some areas of Algeria in more recent days seems to be partly the result of the terrible bloodshed inflicted by Muslim upon Muslim in that country. The following article appeared in the Algerian Arabic daily *El Youm* in December 2000:

> In Kabylie, people of all ages are converting to Christianity ... The (Protestant) church of Ouadhias has played an important role in the proliferation of the number of conversions in Kabylie ... The deterioration of the image of Islam during the crisis has played its part in this rise of conversions to Christianity and the adoption of its principles. What is happening and what has happened in Algeria, such as the massacres and killings in the name of Islam, has led many, when asked what the difference, in their view, was between Islam and Christianity, to declare: "Christianity is life, Islam is death."[201]

People leaving Islam are viewed as "apostates", and consequently, "blasphemers". The Qur'ân speaks strongly about such renegades, affirming their strong punishment in the hereafter:

> And if any of you
> Turn back from their faith
> And die in unbelief,
> Their works will bear no fruit
> In this life
> And in the Hereafter;
> They will be Companions of the Fire
> And will abide therein. (Sura 2:217)

Some of the *ḥadîth* bring punishment for apostasy forward to this life. It is quite clear in such traditions that the requirement of Prophet Muḥammad for apostates is that they be killed now:

> Narrated ᶜIkrama: ᶜAlî burnt some people and this news reached Ibn ᶜAbbâs, who said, "Had I been in his place I would not have

> burnt them, as the Prophet said, 'Don't punish (anybody) with Allâh's Punishment.' No doubt, I would have killed them, for the Prophet said, 'If somebody (a muslim) discards his religion, kill him'."[202]

Even if the death penalty is not enacted by family members or others, converts from Islam to Christianity often find themselves in legal jeopardy. Some Muslim background, Christian believers in Egypt published an open plea for the right to freedom of belief and worship in that country in October 2003. This plea was made in response to the arrest earlier that month of 22 converts, and those who assisted them in trying to obtain new "Christian" identities in Alexandria (see Figure 71).[203]

Figure 71
Declaration by Muslim background, Christian believers in Egypt

IN THE NAME OF THE FATHER, THE SON AND THE HOLY SPIRIT

For many years, we have been struggling for the simplest of our human rights, the freedom of belief and the freedom of worship. We have been imprisoned, tortured, followed by the security police and subjected to all forms of abuse for our faith in Jesus Christ as Lord and Saviour. But in Jesus, our lives and behaviour are so much better. Many among us were terrorists, Islamist fundamentalists. We were burning churches, killing, treating our whole society as apostates. But after we put our faith in Jesus, we became pacifists, bonded to our nation, living in the best way we could.

But despite this change for the better, our Islamic government does not accept the changing of our religion from Islam to Christianity. This right is accepted by the Constitution of Egypt, but rejected by Islamic Law (Sura 2:217). Islamic law is the main source for the Egyptian Constitution, Article 2: "Islam is the state religion, Arabic the official language, and the principles of Islamic Law the main source of legislation." According to this legislation, we as converts are considered apostates. We need to repent within three days, or we will be killed. But al-Azhar was "merciful" to us, and changed the punishment to repentance to be carried out for the rest of the apostate's life. So, he will be imprisoned for life, under surveillance, threatened – for the rest of his life! We are between the jaws of the Constitution and the legislation. To solve this dilemma of the freedom of belief guaranteed in the Constitution, and the judgment for apostasy in Islamic Law, they put us between the jaws of an illegal law. The Penal Code states that whoever blasphemes or disdains a heavenly religion must be brought before the courts. By "heavenly religion" here, they mean Islam! But how, and why? No one knows. Is it logical that the person who chooses a religion other than Islam is accused of blasphemy, and the opposite is not applied?

We as Christian converts therefore declare:

1) We claim our rights, as given by the Egyptian Constitution and by all the international declarations and treaties of human rights worldwide. We ask the Egyptian Government not to treat its citizens in an unequal way. Just as it deals with the Christian embracing Islam, giving him the right to change his faith, his name, his identity and all his official papers in less than 24 hours, we as converts claim the same right – the citizenship right by which we are subject to the same rights and the same duties. Here Christians are not persecuted, because they have the freedom to change their faith; but Muslims are persecuted, because they are not enjoying that same right!

2) We ask that all cases of falsification of documents against the converts to Christianity be dropped, with no conditions. The Egyptian Government is itself responsible for this illegal action, because it has deprived us of one of our basic legal rights, to embrace a new faith and change our name, our identity and our official papers. Give us our rights, and we will not falsify these things.

3) We ask the Egyptian Government and all human rights organizations all over the world to stop the torture, illegal detention, security surveillance and incitement of families against religious converts. It is unbelievable in the 21st century that the tribunals of inquisition are still controlling our consciences, hearts and minds.

4) We declare to the Egyptian Government that it has been playing for time for many years now, while we have had to spend our

lives, our dreams and ourselves behind bars, kept in prisons and under detention. In the face of the rising number of converts, the government has no choice but to respect the desire of thousands of Muslims to embrace Christianity. We do not want this to be only an inner, secret faith, but a totally embracing one, so that we will be able to worship freely our Lord and Saviour Jesus, and be allowed to raise our children in all the boundless grace of Jesus Christ our Lord and Saviour.

Finally, we believe that "In the world you shall have tribulation: but be of good cheer. I have overcome the world." "For I reckon that the sufferings of this present time are not worthy to be compared with the glory which shall be revealed in us."

THE CHRISTIAN CONVERTS OF EGYPT

Such "open letters" to an international audience appear to be the only recourse for minorities of Muslims who convert to Christianity. The public embarrassing of their governments offers hope of protection from execution or extreme torture. It amounts, however, to a highly risky and not necessarily effective procedure. Shenk's response to Kateregga's exposition of the *Umma* in their Christian–Muslim dialogue is to plead for two rights in situations where Muslims rule: the right of Christians freely to worship and witness, and the right of Muslims to become Christians should they so choose.[204] Those rights – especially the second – are a long way, today, from being permitted, let alone promoted.

Conclusion

Perhaps the contrasting approaches to mission made by the two faiths is best encapsulated in the activities of Muslims in establishing Qur'ân schools and of Christians in translating the Bible into the local language. The goal of the former is to bring uniformity of belief and practice to all who come into the Islamic fold. All Muslims are required to rote-learn the Arabic text, whether or not they understand it. The philosophical direction of spirit is centripetal – all Muslims are to relate to the centre.

A common law will determine for them how to live and behave. The goal of Christians in Bible translation, by contrast, is to allow there to be direct communication between God and the people concerned. The philosophical direction of spirit is centrifugal – dispersing responsibility for faith from the centre to the peripheries. The Spirit of God is invited to work with new Christians to determine how the kingdom of God is to find expression in the particular culture concerned.

The fact that both Islam and Christianity are global faiths with worldwide aims ensures that their missionary activities are often in conflict with one another. At the beginning of the twenty-first century, Africa south of the Sahara constitutes a major area in which the two faiths compete in acute and urgent manner. At present, Muslims constitute the overwhelming percentage of the population in such states as Mauritania, Senegal, Guinea, Mali, Niger and Somalia. They form the majority in Nigeria, Sudan and possibly Tanzania. They make up significant minorities in countries such as Ivory Coast, Ghana and Sierra Leone. Severe conflict has recently marked the lot of many of these nations where Muslims do not comprise the overwhelming majority of the population. Samuel P. Huntington predicts the prevalence, in the twenty-first century, of what he calls "fault line" wars. Such wars amount to conflicts between states or groups from different civilizations – and, in Huntington's view, "religion" constitutes the core element defining "civilization". Fault line wars, according to Huntington, share the prolonged duration and high levels of violence of other communal wars, but they almost always occur between peoples of different religions and they tend to recruit the support of fellow-religionists, thus internationalizing local conflicts. He summarizes a few fault line conflicts involving Christian Serbs and Croats in the former Yugoslavia or Buddhists and Hindus in Sri Lanka, but then suggests that the Islamic civilization has, in this regard, the most "bloody borders":

> The overwhelming majority of fault line conflicts, however, have taken place along the boundary looping across Eurasia and Africa that separates Muslims from non-Muslims. While at the macro or

> global level of world politics the primary clash of civilizations is between the West and the rest, at the micro or local level it is between Islam and the others.[205]

If Huntington is correct, the focal points of "mission" – Christian and Muslim – are going to be found at such cross-roads of tension or civilizational fault line during the first part of the twenty-first century. Countries like Indonesia, the Philippines and many African nations in the part of that continent that is south of the Sahara will discover themselves at the forefront of controversy over ethnic and religious commitment. Mission, once again, is inevitably going to be strongly attached to and compromised by the military and political intentions of protagonists seeking to assert their authority along those fault lines. Mission, as espoused by Muslims and Christians in such delicate areas, is likely to be very messy, very costly. Blood, for cross and crescent, is still going to be freely spilt.

Interlude

If you were God, how would you convince Muslims that – all along – they had a special place in your divine heart?

Helps Along the Way?

The covenant between God and Abraham's descendants through Isaac was at significant points kept on track by the involvement or intervention of people from outside that covenant – especially eastern relatives.

The Ishmaelites

God used Ishmaelites, for example, to rescue Joseph from his hole in the ground (Genesis 37:12–36). The jealous brothers of the ornamented robe-wearer at first planned to murder young Joseph and dispose of his body in a cistern. Reuben persuaded them not to take his life immediately, but to incarcerate him in the cistern. Reuben played for time in order to be able to work out a less drastic expression of their anger. He searched for a solution that would not completely destroy their father Jacob. During the meal break that they then took, some of the brothers ended up bargaining with a passing caravan of Ishmaelites from Gilead. The cameleers were conveying spices, balm and myrrh to Egypt. They were persuaded by the brothers to buy a new slave – young Joseph. The Ishmaelites, defined more particularly as Midianites, quickly sold Joseph in Egypt to Potiphar, one of Pharaoh's officials. In Potiphar's household, Joseph's Egyptian saga began.

The Midianites were descended from Midian, one of Abraham's sons by Keturah. Through Joseph's adventures in Egypt, God found a way to save the whole of Jacob's family (the progenitors of the twelve tribes of Israel) during a period of sustained and devastating famine. Here is Joseph's later perspective on his turbulent life: "Don't be afraid," he encourages his brothers. "Am I in the place of God? You intended to harm me, but God intended it for good to accomplish what is now being done, the saving of many lives" (Genesis 50:20). The children of Ishmael/Midian featured significantly in God's overarching intention for good in the life of Jacob's family.

Pharaoh's household

The irony of the story of Moses' birth and protection is wonderfully told in the Bible. After the high drama involving two named Hebrew midwives, Shiphrah and Puah, pitting their wits against an unnamed Pharaoh of Egypt, Moses is born and successfully hidden. When the baby reaches the age of three months, his mother realizes that she can conceal him no longer. She delivers him to the river Nile, though not in the manner that Pharaoh had ordered! His instruction had been that Hebrew male infants should be thrown into the river to drown. Moses' mother entrusts her son to the river to be saved. Already in the story of Moses' life, the gods of the Egyptian world – including the Nile god – were being proved subject to the Israelites' God. Then that same sovereign God arranges that Moses should be spotted, loved, and adopted by none less than the daughter of the king who had required the baby's drowning! In Pharaoh's household, Moses is named, protected, educated, nurtured and prepared for being a commander of men. The leadership qualities of Moses' later life surely owe much to how his character was formed in the Egyptian palace environment. God, it appears, arranged for the best that Egypt could offer to be available for the preparation of the man to whom he would later entrust rulership and control of his people.

Jethro

Jethro, "priest of Midian", plays a significant role in keeping the Abrahamic covenant on track. Jethro is a chief of the clan of Kenites, part of the tribe of the Midianites – evidently a monotheistic tribe. Jethro, over many years, provides Moses with a refuge and a wife, and sustains him in hope and wisdom.

During the long period of time during which Moses lived and worked keeping Jethro's flocks, Moses learned about desert life. He spent 40 years in the Sinai wilderness *before* returning to Egypt to confront Pharaoh. As a result, he was well prepared to spend another 40 years there during the wilderness journey of the people of Israel. His training was accomplished through Jethro the Midianite.

Moses married Zipporah, one of Jethro's seven daughters (Exodus 2:21). He had two sons by her: Gershom and Eliezer (Exodus 18:3–4).

Jethro was a follower of the one God. Maybe Jethro's faith in the one God kept alive Moses' belief in that same God, despite his having to flee for his life from Pharaoh.

Jethro was supplier of wisdom to Moses when the latter became overwhelmed trying to sort out the details of ruling over the people of Israel.

Ruth

Ruth is a Moabitess, a daughter from among the people of the east. This "foreigner" becomes significant in the genealogical line to Messiah, and represents for us other women with equivalent roles. In a quiet story of ordinary life, strong in its contrast to the war and strife described in the pages of Judges, the book of Ruth focuses on a tale of personal faith and loyalty. The new-found faith of a Moabite girl, and her sacrificial love for her mother-in-law – both of them women who find themselves at the margins of their societies – are woven into the colourful tapestry of God's plan of salvation. Descended from Ruth will be King David, from whose line will emerge the Messiah.

Not always helpful

Sometimes the people of the east appear in opposition to the people of Israel. Uzziah, for example, fights against the Arabs (2 Chronicles 26:7), and Arabs oppose the rebuilding of the temple in Nehemiah's day (Nehemiah 4:7). In significant ways and at critical points in Old Testament history, however, God recruits the expertise or faith of eastern people to keep his plan of salvation on track.

Cousins in Hope?

Chapter 10 Dust and Divinity

Spirit of God plus putrid clay?

In one sense, the Qur'ân comes across as mainly a book about humankind. Of course, its primary voice is God's, but it is "sent down" to humanity. It is revealed as a "guidance" to enable humankind to walk the "straight path", to live in a way that pleases the sovereign creator. And that is the first point to make here about man in the Islamic view – he is a created being:

> Man We did create
> From a quintessence (of clay);
> Then We placed him
> As (a drop of) sperm
> In a place of rest,
> Firmly fixed;
> Then We made the sperm
> Into a clot of congealed blood;
> Then of that clot We made
> A (foetus) lump; then We
> Made out of that lump
> Bones and clothed the bones
> With flesh; then We developed
> Out of it another creature.
> So blessed be Allah
> The Best to create! (Sura 23:12–14)

The Qur'ân clearly declares the creaturehood of man. He is not an autonomous being, not chance-bred but God-formed. Various apologetic writings make much of this passage from Sura 23, plus other similar passages, asserting that it accurately describes – miraculously, given the time of the revelation – the biological process of procreation from conception to gestation to birth. Bucaille, for instance, comments that "it is difficult not to be struck by the agreement between the text of the Qur'ân and the scientific knowledge we possess today of these phenomena".[206]

Why did God create humankind? Five passages in the Qur'ân openly declare the purpose of the divine act of creation. Four of those passages suggest that God's motive is to show his justice. The fifth passage elucidates God's motive in the following manner:

> I have only created
> Jinns and men, that
> They may serve Me. (Sura 51:56)

We have noted this verse before and commented on the significance of the verb "serve" (a word with the same root as *ʿibâda*, conveying the sense "obey" or "worship"). Relationship is obviously intended, even if that relationship is one between Master and servant rather than Father and child:

> When my servants
> Ask thee concerning Me,
> I am indeed
> Close (to them): I listen
> To the prayer of every
> Suppliant when he calleth on Me:
> Let them also, with a will,
> Listen to My call,
> And believe in Me:
> That they may walk
> In the right way. (Sura 2:186)

With "servants" God still wants a mutual listening, and he wills to be close to them. The promise of such a relationship in faith is that servants may walk in a way designed for them by their Lord.

In nine suras of the Qur'ân, Adam is mentioned. His life is

given purpose and meaning in God's making him his "vice-regent" or *khalîfa* ("caliph"). The same mission that God himself has in the cosmos, man must perform on earth as vice-regent. God shares this original idea with the angels:

> Behold, thy Lord said to the angels: "I will create
> A vice-regent on earth." They said:
> "Wilt Thou place therein one who will make
> Mischief therein and shed blood? –
> Whilst we do celebrate Thy praises
> And glorify Thy holy (name)?"
> He said: "I know what ye know not." (Sura 2:30)

The angels question God's wisdom in making man his vice-regent on earth. They suggest that while they (the angels) appropriately worship God, humankind is unfortunately likely to engage in bloodshed, crime and sin. Is God sure about what he is proposing? God replies to the hesitant angels that he knows something that they do not know. And with that he sets about the task of creating humankind. Incredibly, to the angels at least, God takes a very lowly substance – sedimentary clay or earth – and from it fashions a vice-regent for himself. The clay is infused with some of God's own spirit and man is thereby created. God's vice-regent on earth is a compound of base mud and divine spirit or breath. There is mystery here in the making of man. How is it possible for man to be constructed in such a way and yet *not* display God's image or likeness? After all, it is the spirit of God alone that makes the vital difference for this portion of earthly dust.[207] There is, indeed, at least one *ḥadîth* that alludes to this possibility: "Narrated Abû Huraira: The Prophet said, 'Allah created Adam in His picture ... ' "[208] Perhaps if such a mystery is allowed to Islam, a parallel mystery in Christian conviction – for example, Jesus being both fully divine and fully human – might equally be permitted (Figure 72).

The angels are commanded to fall down in prostration before this human creature, despite their inherent superiority to man – after all, they are created of light while he is created of mud.[209] The angels baulk at this command so God devises a

Figure 72
Mystery in Islamic "Adam" and Christian "Christ"

Mystery in Islamic "Adam"	Mystery in Christian "Christ"
Adam is putrid clay + divine spirit, yet he is not made in the image or likeness of God	Jesus is fully divine + fully human, equal to God and subject to God

quiz: angels versus Adam! He asks the angels first to "name the names", to define what is what in creation. They cannot of course, but Adam can because he knows them. God's secret weapon in man is revealed. The thing that God earlier knew – that the angels did not know – was that God would himself teach man "the names". God teaches Adam the nature of all things, so that Adam can truly represent him.

The concept of *khilâfa* (trusteeship) is evidently not that of a person deputizing for someone who is absent or incapacitated. Rather, it is the rulership of a person who takes on some of the characteristics of the one he represents. This is especially presented in the Qur'ân in terms of the vice-regent being given knowledge. Man is set apart from the beasts by his ability to acquire knowledge. Man is even set apart from the angels, not because of his lineage, but because of his knowledge. Three sources of knowledge are specified, within the proviso that the overarching giver of knowledge is God himself. Man derives knowledge from within himself, from outside himself (that is, from nature) and from history (see Figure 73).

Man is also set apart from the beasts by his exercise of will. The world is entrusted to him by God and man has the power to use or abuse that trust. What will man will to do with his knowledge?

> We did indeed offer
> The Trust to the Heavens
> And the Earth
> And the Mountains;
> But they refused
> To undertake it,

Being afraid thereof:
But man undertook it ... (Sura 33:72)

Figure 73
"Man" and knowledge

All knowledge comes from God as ...	*He Who taught (the use of) the Pen, – taught man that which he knew not.* (Sura 96:4–5)
knowledge from within	Soon will We show them Our Signs ... in their own souls ... (Sura 41:53)
knowledge from nature	Soon will We show them Our Signs in the (furthest) regions (of the earth) ... (Sura 41:53)
knowledge from history	... teach them to remember the Days of God." Verily in this there are Signs for such as are firmly patient and constant. (Sura 14:5)
Knowledge without discernment of heart is valueless	*Do they not travel through the land, so that their hearts (and minds) may thus learn wisdom and their ears may thus learn to hear? Truly it is not their eyes that are blind, but their hearts which are in their breasts.* (Sura 22:46)

The heavens, the earth, the mountains – that is, other creatures of God – refused to undertake a "trust" or responsibility on behalf of their creator. They chose to remain free from the burden of having to make moral choices about good and evil. Man, however, undertook the trust, the *amâna* – the moral responsibility – and in that undertaking he finds himself accountable to God. Man, uniquely in creation, is in a position to know what is right and what is wrong and can choose to act freely in accordance with such knowledge (Sura 91:7–10).

In such senses, then, God's breathing into man his spirit finds definition. Mankind owns the faculty of godlike knowledge and will. For mankind, there is no inherent compulsion. He, alone in the world, owns the faculty of choosing to conform or not conform to God's will. He is free to be good or evil, to resemble mud or to resemble God. Freedom thus brings danger. Man may keep his soul pure as God made it or he could choose evil and make himself an enemy of God. Man is further responsible for the fulfilment of a divinely trusted mission in this world, for he is the bearer of God's *amâna* in the world and in nature. Man, therefore, holds his own destiny and that of the world in his hands.

Man is set apart from the beasts, finally, by his capacity to have faith, to believe. The sense of *îmân* conveyed in the Qur'ân is more tightly defined than the English words "faith" or "belief", both of which carry intimations of doubtfulness or non-sureness. *Îmân* is a more sure thing, something manifestly shown, something to do with man's knowledge of himself and of the world around him:

> And say: "Truth has (now)
> Arrived, and Falsehood perished:
> For Falsehood is (by its nature)
> Bound to perish." (Sura 17:81)
>
> Let there be no compulsion
> In religion: Truth stands out
> Clear from Error: whoever
> Rejects Evil and believes
> In God hath grasped
> The most trustworthy
> Hand-hold, that never breaks ... (Sura 2:256)

There is no room for compulsion in religion because religion does not need it. Truth and error have been so clearly shown up that it is obvious where faith lies. It is a matter of man being willing to grasp what God has clearly made manifest. To do less than this brings man deservedly to punishment. To go with God brings a flawless support into human lives, plus God's protection. The Qur'ân therefore addresses the totality of human experience, dealing with piety and ethics on the one hand and inheritance law and procedures for warfare on the other. Prophet Muḥammad illustrates the holism of an integrated life – he is constantly engaged in political and military struggle against enemies while at the same time exemplifying what it means to be a man of prayer and devotion.

The reality of human response to God is that, consistently, humankind has not lived up to what God expects of it. From the very first, this falling short has been a facet of our relationship with God. In Islam, however, such falling short is in a sense to be expected, in that humankind is created "weak":

> God doth wish
> To lighten your (difficulties):
> For man was created
> Weak (in flesh). (Sura 4:28)

The three detailed accounts in the Qur'ân concerning Adam eating the forbidden fruit in the Garden of Eden emphasize that the devil, or Iblîs, is the source of evil. He is also a "strong cause" of Adam and Eve's disobedience: he "makes them slip" (Sura 2:36). The "fall" of Adam is, as it were, an accident or mistake, not a deliberate choosing to disobey his creator. Kateregga summarizes the Islamic perspective on this original falling short:

> The Muslim witness is that Iblis, who disobeyed Allah even before the creation of man, is the source of evil. Although the first man Adam and his wife Hauwa sinned, it was not a deliberate desire to disobey their Creator. They were tempted by the master of evil – Iblis. They sincerely confessed to Allah, Who granted them pardon.[210]

Adam and his wife are removed from the garden, but not from the possibility of a relationship with God. Guidance will still come to them from God, and if they or any of their descendants follow that guidance, they will not lose their way or fall into misery. Adam's "fall", then, did not constitute a "fall" for the whole human race. It was not "original" in any biblical sense. Divinely given law and divinely offered forgiveness are sufficient remedy for any human being's disobedience. The Qur'ân avers that guidance did come after Adam and Eve's failure and that Adam did learn:

Then did Satan make them slip
From the (Garden), and get them out
Of the state (of felicity) in which
They had been. We said:
"Get ye down, all (ye people),
with enmity between yourselves.
On earth will be your dwelling-place
And your means of livelihood –
For a time."
Then learnt Adam from his Lord
Words of inspiration, and his Lord
Turned towards him; for He
Is Oft-Returning, Most Merciful. (Sura 2:36–37)

Interestingly, in the verses describing God's ordering humankind out of the garden, a plural form of the verb is used:

(God) said: "Get you down,
With enmity between yourselves.
On earth will be your dwelling-place
And your means of livelihood, –
For a time." (Sura 7:24; made more explicit in Sura 2:36, above: "all ye people")

In Arabic, verbs have singular, dual (referring to "you two") and plural forms. If only Adam and Eve were being expelled from the garden, the dual form would have been used. Perhaps the plural form means that Iblîs is included with Adam and Eve in the expulsion; that is a common Muslim interpretation. Perhaps one might detect a hint here that in Adam, all of humankind is included in the fall from grace.

Evil, then, amounts in effect to ignorance, or at least to non-willed falling short – and such evil can be dispelled by the sending/receiving of "guidance". Unrepented evil, or remaining in opposition to "guidance", ensures that a person is heading for a state of divine damnation. In that case, on each person's head be it: "They shall reap the fruit of what they did, and ye of what ye do!" (Sura 2:134).[211] Each individual stands accountable for his or her own obedience or disobedience. There is no legacy from Adam's original sin, no inheriting the weight of the sins of one's forebears. A person's good deeds (living by guidance) or evil deeds (abandoning that guidance) will alone weigh against each other at Judgement Day. Everyone thus has an equal possibility for acquiring heaven in that each person starts his or her life, as it were, with a clean slate before God:

> So set thou thy face
> Steadily and truly to the Faith:
> (Establish) God's handiwork according
> To the pattern [*fiṭra*] on which
> He has made mankind:
> No change (let there be)
> In the work (wrought)
> By God: that is
> The standard Religion:
> But most among mankind
> Understand not. (Sura 30:30)

The "pattern" (*fiṭra*) after which God has made humankind conveys the idea that God has programmed each new baby with an inclination towards God, towards true religion. Each human being is, by God's intention, born to be Muslim. Kateregga goes so far as to say that "all people are born as true Muslims, innocent, pure, and free" (Sura 30:30; quoted above).[212] People are pulled away from realizing that intention by the schemes of the devil, by pollution emanating from contact with non-Islamic faiths or by deliberately turning their backs on Islam. Al-Bukhârî offers a tradition – alluded to earlier in our consideration of al-Ghazâlî's theology – supporting such a perspective: "No child is born except in the state of natural purity (*fiṭra*) and then his parents make him Jewish, Christian or Magian."[213]

Sin as original?

In AD 417, rioters took to the streets of Rome in order to bash each other into Christian agreement about just how bad Adam's sin in Eden had been. On the one side were partisans of Pelagius, a British monk who had been declared orthodox by two councils of bishops in Palestine some two years previously. On the opposing side were supporters of Augustine, a North African bishop, at whose instigation fellow bishops from Africa had twice condemned Pelagius. Augustine, moreover, had persuaded two bishops of Rome (Innocent and Zosimos) to agree with him. The argument between Augustine and Pelagius was conducted within the imperial palace at Constantinople as well as on the streets of Rome. Augustine's fellow African bishop Alypius lobbied at the imperial court against Pelagius – 80 Numidian stallions for the emperor constituted part of Alypius' persuasive argument! In AD 418, Pope Zosimos excommunicated Pelagius while Emperor Honorius fined him, expelled him from office and exiled him along with his supporters. Pelagius died soon afterwards, but his thesis was taken up by one of his students, a young Italian bishop, Julian of Eclonum. Julian and Augustine argued over "Pelagianism" during the last twelve years of Augustine's life.

The theological debate concerned the material covered in Genesis 1 – 3. Did that material affirm the possibility of human freedom to choose good or evil, or did it rather tell a story of universal human corruption and bondage? All involved in the debate agreed that Adam's sin brought suffering and death upon humankind. But, while Julian insisted that each of Adam's offspring was left free to make his or her own choice for good or evil, Augustine insisted that Adam, as a corporate personality, irrevocably contaminated with sinfulness the whole human race for as long as it continued. Julian saw Genesis as affirming that human beings possess free moral choice, being made in God's image, while Augustine read the same text as demonstrating that the whole human race inherited from Adam a nature damaged by sin. Such damage, Augustine contended, is passed on via conception, through the semen – except, of course, to Jesus Christ, who was conceived without the involvement of semen.

The issue that lay at the heart of this debate was what came to be known as the doctrine of "original sin" – a term not found in the Bible, of course, but first mooted, it would seem, by Augustine himself. "Original sin" is a distinctively Christian concept. Judaism knows no such doctrine. The Jewish rabbis had never read Genesis in Augustine's way, and Jewish commentators on Genesis today are still usually quick to point out that the word "sin" is not directly connected with the biblical story of Adam and Eve. Instead, it appears first in the Bible within the following chapter where the sad history of Abel and Cain is told. God warns Cain: "sin is crouching at your door ..." (Genesis 4:7). Sibling rivalry, or jealousy, or envy, gives way to fratricide. For Jewish theologians, fratricide is the original human relational sin as described in the *Torah*. That same *Torah* ends with Deuteronomy where two other brothers, Aaron and Moses, learn to live mutually supportive lives despite the fact that the younger brother becomes the more prominent of the two. Their relationship becomes a model, as it were, of the *Torah* mending the wrong relating (ending in death) of Cain and Abel. In Jewish theologizing, as a consequence, there is a recognition of an evil impulse (*yetzer ha-ra*) active in human beings from birth, and a good impulse (*yetzer ha-tov*) that comes with the age of discretion and the ability of an adult to feed on the Law and control the former, evil impulse.

The Christian doctrine concerning "original sin", expounded by Augustine, arose out of Christian reflecting on what Christ's death and resurrection had achieved. It was informed most strongly by Paul's discussion of the human condition in Romans 5:12–21 – the only place in that letter where Adam is explicitly mentioned. In Augustine's view, Paul is seeking to get across two arguments about sin and death in this passage. The first contention is that Adam transgressed a prohibition that carried with it an explicit death penalty – so death came into the world, and everyone since Adam has had to live under its shadow. The second contention is that, quite apart from the divine sentence over this particular transgression, sin and death are intimately connected – from the moment envy distorted desire (humans wanting to be like God), desire has pulled human beings towards death. Thus the passage Romans 5:12–14 is retranslated or interpreted in the following manner by James Alison in his helpful study of the doctrine of original sin, *The Joy of Being Wrong*:

> Therefore just as through one man the sinful state of affairs was brought about in the world, and through this sinful state of affairs, the reign of death, so did the reign of death penetrate all men, involving them all in the sinful state of affairs. The world indeed lived in a sinful state of affairs before the Mosaic law; however, while there was no law no sort of moral assessment was possible, but that did not stop the reign of death dominating, in the period between Adam and Moses, over those also whose active involvement in the sinful state of affairs was not in the likeness of the transgression of Adam, who is the type of the one who was to come.[214]

Such a restatement of the point that Augustine was making – arising from Paul's words in Romans concerning the entry of sin into the world – illustrates the shift that Augustine made from theologians prior to him (highlighted in Figure 74 by comparing Augustine with Chrysostom). For those earlier interpreters of Paul in Romans 5, the sense was much more that the reign of death involved all humankind because all humankind were involved in sin. Elaine Pagels constructs an interesting case for the proposition that Pelagius, following Irenaeus, Tertullian, Clement of Alexandria, Chrysostom and other pre-Augustinian Christians, discovered above all else in Genesis 1 – 3 a manifesto of human liberty. Pelagius and company encouraged one another as free human beings, made in the image of God, to choose their own faith and life against all the opposition of the Roman imperial machine. Augustine, however, was born into a church that already had imperial power on its side. Plus, as a younger man, he had personally pursued a vigorous "exploration" of sin – he was under no illusion as to a human being's potential for depravity. His view of the endemic sinfulness of all humankind, including Christians – derived from Genesis 1 – 3 – justified the use of force to protect "orthodoxy" and punish "heretics". Control of naturally-evil people, especially as personified in the Donatists of North Africa, led Augustine to favour the use of military might to suppress such non-orthodox Christians.[215]

While the Christian church was surviving and growing as a persecuted minority, it evidently espoused a conviction about

Figure 74
Interpreting Romans 5:12

<table>
<tr><td colspan="2">"Therefore just as through one man sin entered into the world, and through sin, death; so also to all men death passed, inasmuch as all sinned" (King James Version).</td></tr>
<tr><td>John Chrysostom read this in Greek and took it to mean that Adam's sin brought death into the world, and so death came upon all because ["for that"] "all have sinned":

"[Paul] enquires whence death came in, and how it prevailed. How then did death come in and prevail? 'Through the sin of one.' But what means, 'for that all have sinned?' This; he having once fallen, even they that had not eaten of the tree did from him, all of them, become mortal." (Homily 10 on Romans 5:12)

In other words:
(a) sin came into the world via one man;
(b) in consequence of sin came death;
(c) because of the causal relationship between sin and death, the latter extended itself to all for the reason that
(d) all sinned.</td><td>Augustine read this in Latin and took it to mean that through Adam death came upon all men, in whom [i.e. in Adam] all sinned:

"In the first man, therefore, there existed the whole human nature, which was to be transmitted by the woman to posterity, when that conjugal union received the divine sentence of its own condemnation; and what man was made, not when created, but when he sinned and was punished, this he propagated, so far as the origin of sin and death are concerned." (De Civitate Dei, book 13, chapter 3)

"For we all were in that one man, since we all were that one man, who fell into sin by the woman who was made from him before the sin. For not yet was the particular form created and distributed to us, in which we were to be propagated; and this being vitiated by sin, and bound by the chain of death, and justly condemned, man could not be born of man in any other state." (De Civitate Dei, book 13, chapter 14)</td></tr>
</table>

human nature, drawn from Genesis 1 – 3, that encouraged the hope of freedom in a cruel, Roman world. That conviction was not dissimilar to the Islamic view as described in the first paragraphs of this chapter. Human beings are made "good" ("in God's image" in the Christian version) and have the freedom to make moral choices. In this positive reading of human "origins", even if human beings are stained by sin – whether Adam's or their own – baptism, or incorporation into Christ, cleanses the believer from all sin. Pelagius' followers further argued that God, being just, would not have punished anyone but Adam for what Adam had done. Julian argued that Augustine was wrong to suggest that a physically transmitted, hereditary sinfulness infected the whole of human nature (and nature itself) as a result of Adam's "fall". Death (mortality) and sexual desire were, according to Julian, natural and normal components of life for Adam and Eve in Eden, before they sinned. Adam did not die physically on the day of his punishment for disobedience; he began to die morally and spiritually. That was the nature of the "death" introduced by Adam into human experience. In other words, disobedience and sinfulness are very serious, but they are very serious for each one of us – we each are accountable to God for the moral and spiritual choices we make.

Augustine argued that through an act of will, Adam and Eve did indeed alter "nature", both their own and that of the natural world. Death arose and thorns arose! Neither had been present before the "fall". Men ever since Adam have had to labour in their work while women after Eve have certainly had to "labour" in theirs. Nature has been permanently blighted because of human sin. Augustine finds evidence of this catastrophic alteration to human nature after Adam and Eve's "fall" in the ogres of infancy (some babies are born deformed), sexuality (it seems to have its own, wanton, life) and mortality (the sting of death pierces us all). For Augustine, Adam's sin was "original" and it altered forever what "human nature" and "the natural world" might be. Human beings are without exception tainted at conception with the effects of Adam's sin. Augustine reiterated this theological perspective, with reference to Romans 5:12, in a later work called *The Retractations*:

infants, who assuredly possess human nature, inherit original sin because in the first man human nature has sinned, and for this reason, "Sins harm only the nature of him who commits them." Indeed, "by one man" in whom all have sinned, "sin entered the world".[216]

Julian and Augustine debated the "Pelagian" issue for more than twelve years, as we have indicated, until Augustine died. In the long wake of his death, the church gradually came to decide in favour of Augustine's perspective. In Pagels' words:

> From the fifth century on, Augustine's pessimistic views of sexuality, politics, and human nature would become the dominant influence on western Christianity, both Catholic and Protestant, and color all western culture, Christian or not, ever since. Thus Adam, Eve, and the serpent – our ancestral story – would continue, often in some version of its Augustinian form, to affect our lives to the present day.[217]

A less drastic reading of Genesis 1 – 3, somewhat akin to the qur'ânic view on the events of Eden, is nevertheless part of our Christian heritage. Not that sinfulness is any less serious in this reading. It is just that each of us is held responsible for our turning away from God. Death claims us because we indeed prove ourselves sinners.

Sorting sin out

There are intimations, within the Islamic perspective, of different grades of seriousness in human sinfulness:

> Those who avoid
> Great sins and shameful deeds,
> Only (falling into) small faults –
> Verily thy Lord is ample
> In forgiveness ... (Sura 53:32)

Reflection by Muslims on this and other qur'ânic references to sin has led to some major debates. One such debate has been about which sins will remain unforgiven by God unless the sinner repents. Another debate has been about whether some sins are more serious than others – are there major and minor sins?[218] Differing perspectives are offered by theologians of the Sunnî, Muᶜtazilî and Kharijî traditions. My purpose here is not to describe the intricacies of those various perspectives, but to point out that, as a result of them, Muslims tend to feel strongly that there are grades of sin, even if they are not all agreed as to which sins fit which grade. The point I wish to make is that, by and large, the Muslim concepts of "worst-grade sin" are different from (Western) Christian concepts of "worst-grade sin".

Thus, attributing partners with God (the sin of *shirk* or polytheism), murdering a Muslim or abandoning one's faith (the sin of *kufr* or unbelief) are considered virtually unforgivable acts. The harshest penalties – both on earth and in eternity – result from their commission. "Big sins" for Muslim societies include disrespect for Prophet Muḥammad, ungratefulness for the creator's bounty and rebellion against one's parents – all minor or non-issues within Western societies. Do Western Christians really see their neighbours' atheism as "sin"? We may grieve at peoples' easy use of the words "Jesus Christ!" as a form of swearing, but do we expect Westerners to become convicted of sin for such misuse of Jesus' name? Lying, cheating, stealing – "big sins" for Western cultures – are not treated as so shameful in many Muslim societies, perhaps with qur'ânic justification.

It seems to me that the Bible itself challenges Western norms as to what is considered "greater" or more serious sin. Think about the temptations of Jesus in the manner that Luke, for example, describes them. Western readers find it somewhat difficult to relate to these "temptations" that Jesus undergoes. For us, temptation is usually perceived as having to do with a yielding to indulge in "bad acts" – like lying or stealing or committing adultery. Breaking those commandments that were inscribed on Moses' *second* tablet is what temptation tends to be about for Westerners. Jesus' tests in the desert were strongly focused on the *first* tablet of Moses' ten commandments, and especially on the first commandment of that tablet. Loyalty to

God, honouring of God, holding no other idol in one's heart before God – such was the focus of trial for Jesus. Yielding to that kind of temptation seems also to constitute the genre of "unforgivable" or "serious" sin as enunciated in the Qur'ân (see Figure 75).

Figure 75
Serious sins and mild sins

Mild sins		Serious sins	
sexual impurity	Sura 24:2	not believing in the one true God	Sura 39:3; 67:6
abuse of slaves	Sura 24:33	intentional killing of a believer	Sura 4:93
dishonesty in inheritance	Sura 89:19	preferring the life of this world; ungratefulness	Sura 79:35; 7:16
gossip, scandalous talk	Sura 104:1–9	**Unforgivable sins**	
killing female babies	Sura 81:8–9	attributing of partners with God	Sura 4:116
indulgence in alcohol; eating forbidden foods	Sura 2:173	rejecting Muḥammad and accusing him of lying	Sura 58:20
theft	Sura 5:42	apostasy	Sura 3:90

Muslims and (Western) Christians thus tend to find it hard to feel the force of the other's views of "mild" sins, let alone "big" or unforgivable ones! Little wonder, then, that they also find it difficult to comprehend one another's legal systems. Within Islam, the penal system takes its lead from the theological definitions of sin or transgression that the Qur'ân proposes. Crimes – transgressions of God's law – require a legal punishment. Again, different schools of law reflect variously upon different theological definitions of major or minor sin. If unbelief or *kufr* is considered a virtually unforgivable sin, it should not be surprising that punishment for expressions of that sin find extreme form. "Unbelief" takes many shapes including apostasy, not acknowledging Muḥammad as God's Prophet and blasphemy. For such "sins" death is required as punishment. For the sin of murder, the death penalty is required but it can be avoided through an act of forgiveness by aggrieved family members. Adultery also carries a likely death penalty.[219] Of course, the Sinaitic Law earlier prescribed capital punishment amongst the people of Israel for sins equivalent to those just defined within the Islamic penal system (see Figure 76).

"Sin", for both Jewish and Islamic worlds, brings temporal repercussions. Many contemporary Muslims posit the view that Western societies today are disintegrating so rapidly – rotting from within – precisely because on these major issues (except perhaps murder), let alone on a whole host of less major ones, such societies have abandoned their creaturehood. Instead of listening to God, Westerners have enthroned themselves (as we have seen in our earlier discussion concerning secularization). As a result, blasphemy is rife while moral and sexual licence run riot.

According to the Gospel accounts, Jesus' concern for these three "major" sins is very strong. But constantly he seeks to get behind the externals of the law or the mechanics, as it were, of sinning, to the spirit of the person involved. Anger within a person can be the equivalent of murder in Jesus' eyes. Lust within a man can be the equivalent of adultery. Living by the letter of the law can equate to a form of blasphemy, of denying God himself. By Jesus' standards, we all fall far short!

For many Muslim societies, ceremonial purity is a major issue, defining how a man or a woman might live cleanly before God. It also constitutes another aspect of looking at life-before-God that Western Christians find difficult to appreciate. Defilement occurs easily, both deliberately and accidentally. Killing an animal in the wrong way or having a monthly period may each lead a Muslim to defilement in front of God. "Sin"

Figure 76
Sins leading to capital punishment in Sinaitic and Islamic law

Sin	Sinai	Qur'ân/*ḥadîth*
"unbelief", e.g. blasphemy	Say to the Israelites: "If anyone curses his God, he will be held responsible; anyone who blasphemes the name of the Lord must be put to death. The entire assembly must stone him. Whether an alien or native-born, when he blasphemes the Name, he must be put to death." Leviticus 24:15–16	And remember Moses said to his people: "O my people! Ye have indeed wronged yourselves by your worship of the calf: So turn (in repentance) to your Maker, and slay yourselves (the wrong-doers); that will be better for you in the sight of your Maker." Sura 2:54[220]
murder	Show no pity: life for life, eye for eye, tooth for tooth, hand for hand, foot for foot. Deuteronomy 19:21	O ye who believe! The law of equality is prescribed to you in cases of murder: the free for the free, the slave for the slave, the woman for the woman. But if any remission is made by the brother of the slain, then grant any reasonable demand, and compensate him with handsome gratitude ... Sura 2:178
adultery	"If a man commits adultery with another man's wife – with the wife of his neighbour – both the adulterer and the adulteress must be put to death." Leviticus 20:10	The woman and the man guilty of adultery or fornication – flog each of them with a hundred stripes ... Sura 24:2 Narrated Ibn ᶜAbbâs: ᶜUmar said, "I am afraid that after a long time has passed, people may say, "We do not find the Verses of the Rajam (stoning to death) in the Holy Book", and consequently they may go astray by leaving an obligation that Allah has revealed. Lo! I confirm that the penalty of Rajam be inflicted on him who commits illegal sexual intercourse if he is already married and the crime is proved by witnesses or pregnancy or confession." al-Bukhârî, *al-Ṣaḥîḥ*, vol. 8, book 82, chap. 16, trad. 816, pp. 536–537

often amounts in such an environment to a breaking of the ritual purity code. As a result, shame ensues. With Adam and Eve, in both biblical and qur'ânic telling, shame over nakedness preceded any conviction or accounting for disobedience (Genesis 3:7; Sura 7:22). Al-Tabarî, in his commentary on the Qur'ân, quotes the Jewish convert Wahb ibn Munabbih's explanation of such shame. Adam hides in a tree, according to Wahb ibn Munabbih, and refuses to come out when the Lord calls him because "I feel ashamed before You, O Lord".[221]

Much of the Sinaitic Law handed down to the people of Israel had to do with defilement and its prevention or cure. In a strong way, the *Torah* drew attention to the constant condition of defilement in which the people of Israel found themselves. Jesus, in declaring all foods clean (Mark 7:18–23), was not so much setting aside the food laws themselves as emphasizing that the real issue of cleanness is focused in our spiritual condition, not in the food. The force of Jesus' healing of lepers lay in their then reporting to the priest and being pronounced "clean"! The word of Jesus is a cleansing word. When Jesus "touched" a corpse or was troubled by a haemorrhaging woman, the potency in the incident is focused in his being able to absorb or handle ceremonial uncleanness. Jesus releases ordinary people from such contaminating sins and their all-enveloping shame.

According to the Qur'ân, a human being's soul is "prone to evil" (Sura 12:53) but evil is not inherent in human nature. Adam repented of his disobedience and God forgave him (Sura 2:37). Theologians from the various schools have argued extensively over the meaning of "repentance". What constitutes "sincere" repentance (Sura 66:8) and does the expression of it guarantee forgiveness by God? Can an act of repentance automatically nullify punishment for a particular sin? And so on.[222] People become sinners by rejecting God, by disobeying God's law. Anyone can follow the straight path so long as God guides him to it and strengthens him "with a spirit from Himself" (Sura 58:22). At the final judgement, a person will be saved if his good deeds outweigh his evil deeds. Human beings, then, are not so much in need of someone to save them as of teachers and guides who will give them God's commandments and warn them of the consequences of non-submission. It is therefore in terms of prophethood and the sending down of God's word that "salvation" finds its meaning in Islam – for that is how the straight path is conveyed to humankind (see Figure 77).

The actual word "salvation" occurs only once in the Qur'ân:

> "And O my People!
> How (strange) it is
> For me to call you
> To salvation while ye
> Call me to the Fire!
> Ye do call upon me
> To blaspheme against God,
> And to join with Him
> Partners of whom I have
> No knowledge; and I
> Call you to the Exalted
> In Power, Who forgives
> Again and again!" (Sura 40:41–42)

The context of these verses in the Qur'ân is a bit complicated. At the time of Moses, a believer declares these words to his contemporaries. How odd, he protests, that while he is seeking their good, they are seeking his damnation! He is calling them to submission to the one God who gives forgiveness upon repentance while they are trying to get him to acknowledge Pharaoh as divine and indulge in the whole blasphemous cultic life of Egyptian religion – a cultic life that brings no real forgiveness. "Salvation" lies in relationship with the "Exalted in Power", one who "forgives again and again".

A Muslim is assured of a positive accounting before God on three or four grounds (see Figure 78). If he has appropriately responded to God's "signs", then the balance on Judgement Day will swing in his favour (Sura 7:8–9). If he has shown his love for God in following the *sunna* of the Prophet, then God will love him and forgive his sins (Sura 3:31). Surprisingly perhaps, the Qur'ân realistically suggests that most people reject right guidance and do not love God: "Most men are not believers" (Sura

Figure 77
"Salvation" in Islam and Christianity

Islam		Christianity
↙	God as creator	↘
↓		↓
shows his sovereignty in creation		shows his character in creation
↓		↓
sends his guidance via books; prophets point to scripture		sends his guidance via Christ; scriptures point to Christ
↓		↓
deals with evil via judgement; jinn and humankind judged		deals with evil via cross; Satan and death defeated
↓		↓
accepts that creation is contaminated but can be mended by humankind's *islâm*		accepts that creation is contaminated by fall of humankind but will be transformed in new creation
↓		↓
forgives the repentant sinner and judges works on the Day of Judgement		comes to earth to reconcile man to himself; "saves" repentant sinners
↓		↓
looks for a rule of righteousness on earth		looks forward to a new heaven and new earth
↓		↓
↘	God as sovereign	↙

12:106). Although people are born in a state of natural purity, the majority of them appear to negate that as soon as they reach the age of accountability. The qur'ânic witness is that "if God were to punish men for their wrongdoing [*ẓulm*], he would not leave, on the (earth), a single living creature" (Sura 16:61). Humanity is in a pretty desperate state! Even someone as pure as the prophet Joseph recognizes a problem at the core of human nature when he is faced with the temptation imposed on him by Potiphar's wife. Instead of blaming Iblîs or the temptress herself, Joseph confesses that "the (human) soul is certainly prone to evil" (Sura 12:53). The third ground for a positive accounting lies in the fact that ultimately, God is God and may forgive whom he pleases and may punish whom he pleases (Sura 5:18). A fourth ground is developed in the *ḥadîth* as opposed to the Qur'ân: it is found in the effectual intercession on behalf of the believer by Prophet Muḥammad.[223] Interestingly, Muslim theologians who hold different views as to what it might mean for Muslims to sincerely repent – and thus be granted forgiveness on the Day of Judgement – nearly all agree that the Prophet's intercession at that time will be effectual. Muḥammad's worth and compassion for his followers is especially celebrated in popular poems and songs of devotion during the annual commemorations of the Prophet's birthday.

In the qur'ânic story of the near-sacrifice by Abraham of his (unnamed) son, a tale of redemption is recounted. Abraham receives a vision – when he is either in or near Mecca, according to Islamic tradition – in which he learns that he is to offer his son in sacrifice. His son commits himself to cooperate, and both father and son are commended for their willing submission to God. The sacrificial act is interrupted by God, however, who announces that in terms of intention the vision has already been fulfilled:

> We called out to him,
> "O Abraham!
> Thou hast already fulfilled
> The vision!" – thus indeed
> Do We reward

Those who do right.
For this was obviously
A trial –
And We ransomed him
With a momentous sacrifice. (Sura 37:104–107)

Figure 78
Hope in judgement?

Grounds	Verse
responding positively to God's "signs" (Sura 7:8–9)	The balance that day will be true (to a nicety): those whose scale (of good) will be heavy, will prosper: those whose scale will be light, will find their souls in perdition, for that they wrongfully treated Our Signs.
following the *sunna* of the Prophet (Sura 3:31)	Say: "If ye do love God, follow me: God will love you and forgive you your sins: for God is Oft-Forgiving, most Merciful."
God may forgive whoever he wills (Sura 5:18)	Wherewith God guideth all who seek His good pleasure to ways of peace and safety, and leadeth them out of darkness, by His Will, unto the light, – guideth them to a Path that is Straight.
The Prophet's intercession may be effective (al-Bukhârî)	"I will raise my head and praise Allâh with a saying (invocation). He will teach me, and then I will intercede. He will fix a limit for me (to intercede for) whom I will admit into Paradise … "

It is breathtaking to realize here that in the intention to perform the act, God sees the vision fulfilled. The importance of intention is, of course, daily emphasized in the experience of Muslims at the beginning of acts of formal prayer. All times of prayer in Islam have to be prefaced by the *niyya* or "intention". The same is true of the other obligatory acts of Islam. With prophets Abraham and Isaac, God read their intention of heart as equivalent to the physical act. One might confidently argue that with Jesus, in his intention to submit to dying – in the midst of the clamour to take him to crucifixion – God sees that particular "vision" fulfilled. We shall look more closely at the crucifixion narratives in the following chapter. "Fulfilment" in this intentional sense frees God in the Abrahamic instance to instigate something wonderful. It enables him to put in place a ransoming of Abraham and his son. The patriarch is to be saved from seeing his beloved son lying broken and lifeless before his eyes. It is emphasized that God himself does the ransoming. He is a ransoming God.

What does the "momentous sacrifice" mean? Does it point to the fact that God provides a substitute – a fine sheep or ram? Such a sense is certainly strongly commemorated in the annual ritual of *ᶜÎd al-Aḍḥa* when hundreds of thousands of sheep are sacrificed throughout the Muslim world, especially at Arafat on the tenth day of the pilgrimage at Mecca. A "momentous sacrifice" – instead of Abraham's son – by this interpretation, involves blood being shed and a life given for a life. Or perhaps the "momentous sacrifice" is more a reference to Abraham and his son's willing submission to God. That is what saved them – their willingness to offer themselves in self-sacrifice. By this interpretation, the intended sacrifice of Abraham's son is what makes possible the continuing relationship of God with Abraham – and hence with all Muslims. Such is certainly an interpretation understood in the Shîᶜa world, where Imam Ḥussein is seen as the supreme example of offering up one's life unto death. His martyrdom at Karbalâ' provides the wellspring for the continuation of the true faith. Both interpretations offer hints of the kind of meaning that Christians place upon this patriarchal symbolism.

Mindful of whom?

There are, as we have seen, several points of contact between the qur'ânic view of human beings and a biblical one. There are also considerable differences of concept (see Figure 79).

The Bible has a high view of humanity as created in the

Figure 79
"Man" in Qur'ân and Bible

Qur'ân	Bible
born weak	born sinful (since Adam)
God's vice-regent, ruling the world according to the declared laws of God	God's representative, learning to direct life according to the Spirit of God
by intention Muslim	made in God's image
knowledge and will lead to submission	conscience and will lead to repentance
"guided" in right path	"born anew" to relationship with God
servanthood/submission to God	friendship/intimacy with God
Satan a hugely powerful tempter	Satan powerful but not overpowering

image and likeness of God, plus a correspondingly low view of human beings in their deliberate choice for disobedience. The demonic figure in the biblical Eden is limited to the role of a suggester of evil. Eve and Adam themselves make the fateful decision to want to be like God. As a result of their consequent "fall", the image of God in humankind has become marred, plus all humans find themselves subject to death. Adam and Eve's sin is seen, especially since Augustine, as "original", affecting their whole progeny. All men and women are born tainted, with a tendency towards evil. John Donne subtly expresses this sad diagnosis or tendency in his poem "I am a Little World":[224]

> I am a little world made cunningly
> Of Elements, and an Angelic spright,
> But black sinne hath betraid to endlesse night
> My world both parts, and (oh) both parts must die.

The Qur'ân has a lower view of humanity as created from a mixture of base clay and spirit of God, plus a correspondingly higher view of human beings in their falling for Iblîs' temptation. The qur'ânic Adam, with Eve, is in effect manipulated into disobedience by Iblîs, but the punished human beings are forgivable and able to live in obedience to God again. There is no stain on their progeny. That progeny, moreover, is born "weak" and understandably easily led from the straight path. Iblîs remains a powerful player in humankind's experience of life.

One might propose that the biblical account revels in the wonder of humankind being made in the image of God, able to enjoy fellowship with its creator, while the qur'ânic account is much more reticent about any kind of communion between an absolute creator and a shapely bit of dust. On the other hand, the Qur'ân takes very seriously the reality and power of Iblîs in opposing God's purposes – and making use of Eve and Adam to do so. His is an awesome power and responsibility to so seek to shift God's vice-regent on earth into a state of disobedience. The Bible, by contrast, emphasizes the responsibility of both Eve and Adam for their dishonouring of God and, in a sense, diminishes the serpent with the strong prediction of its destiny as crushed under the heel of the promised seed from Adam. In a shorthand way, we could say that the biblical account focuses on "God/humankind-made-in-God's-image/Satan", while the qur'ânic account concentrates on "God/Iblîs/humankind-made-from-clay".

Given such difference of emphasis concerning the nature of humankind and the diagnosis of what is wrong with humanity vis-à-vis God – and who is responsible for that – it is not surprising that the person and ministry of Jesus Christ is distinctly presented in the two faiths. To those presentations we now turn.

Chapter 11 Made-up Messiah

The essential picture of Christianity that one deduces from the pages of the Qur'ân is that it constituted in its original form a faithful conveying of God's eternal message to the children of Israel at a particular time of history. The conveyor in this instance was the Jewish prophet Jesus. He was a true messenger-prophet in the tradition of Moses and David and took his place in the line of faithful *muslim* (submitted) leaders that would eventuate in the coming of Muḥammad. Jesus is described in the Qur'ân with very little allusion to the context in which he lived and preached. His immediate disciples are delineated as characters willing to stand out in their generation as believers in God. They, like Jesus, are *muslim* and declare as much:

> When Jesus found
> Unbelief on their part
> He said: "Who will be
> My helpers to (the work
> Of) God?" Said the Disciples:
> "We are God's helpers:
> We believe in God,
> And do thou bear witness
> That we are Muslims." (Sura 3:52)

Gradually, however, the historical followers of Jesus moved away from his original message. They lost the plot – or at least the revelation.

Three suras of the Qur'ân speak in detail about Jesus: "The Family of Imran" (Sura 3 – Medinan), "The Table" (Sura 5 –

Medinan), and "Mary" (Sura 19 – late Meccan). More than 90 references in all appear in 15 different suras of the Qur'ân, though the majority of the references occur in Medinan suras. The imbalance in proportion between Meccan and Medinan suras probably reflects the fact that it was in Medina that Muḥammad came into confrontation with both Jews and Christians.

Jesus is consistently called ᶜÎsâ in the Qur'ân. The Arabic word probably reflects an acquaintance at some stage with the Greek *Iesous*. Jesus is also referred to as *al-Masîh* meaning Messiah or Christ. Often the name ᶜÎsâ is linked with the phrase "son of Mary", emphasizing the fact that he had no earthly father.

Jesus is introduced in the Qur'ân via his mother, Mary. The childhood of Mary is described. She is the daughter of "a woman of ᶜImrân". The story of Mary reflects some of the emphases of Christian apocryphal material (see Figure 80).

It is striking that Mary is the only woman whose name stands alone in the Qur'ân. Joseph, her husband, is not mentioned. All other women are designated in relation to their husbands: "wife of Adam", "wife of Noah" and so on. Mary is a special case. The angel Gabriel announces to Mary the coming virgin birth of Jesus. Both Qur'ân and New Testament relate the annunciation in a similar way (see Figure 81).

The purpose of the birth story in the Qur'ân is, of course, to get across the message that Jesus is the son of Mary and not the Son of God (Sura 43:57–67). As we have noted, "Jesus the son of Mary" becomes the most important name for Jesus in the Qur'ân and serves continually to emphasize his humanity.[225] The miracle of virgin birth is confirmed by another miracle as Jesus speaks from the cradle:

> He said [from the cradle]: "I am indeed
> A servant of God:
> He hath given me
> Revelation and made me
> A prophet;
> And He hath made me

Figure 80
Mary in the Qur'ân and in Christian apocryphal books

Sura 3:35–37	*Protevangelium of James* chapters 4 & 8	*Gospel of the Nativity of Mary* chapters 1 & 7
Behold! A woman of ʿImrân said: "O my Lord! I do dedicate unto Thee what is in my womb for Thy special service: so accept this of me: for Thou hearest and knowest all things."	And Anna said: "As the Lord my God liveth, if I beget either male or female, I will bring it as a gift to the Lord my God; and it shall minister to Him in holy things all the days of its life."	The blessed and glorious ever-virgin Mary, sprung from the royal stock and family of David, born in the city of Nazareth, was brought up at Jerusalem in the temple of the Lord.
When she was delivered, she said: "O my Lord! Behold! I am delivered of a female child!" – and God knew best what she brought forth – "And nowise is the male like the female. I have named her Mary, and I commend her and her offspring to Thy protection from the Evil One, the Rejected."	And her months were fulfilled, and in the ninth month Anna brought forth. And she said to the midwife: "What have I brought forth?" and she said: "A girl." And said Anna: "My soul has been magnified this day." And she laid her down. And the days having been fulfilled, Anna was purified, and gave the breast to the child, and called her name Mary.	"For I am that angel who has presented your prayers and alms before God; and now have I been sent to you to announce to you that thou shalt bring forth a daughter, who shall be called Mary, and who shall be blessed above all women."
Right graciously did her Lord accept her: He made her grow in purity and beauty: to the care of Zakarîya was she assigned. Every time that he entered (her) chamber to see her, he found her supplied with sustenance. He said: "O Mary! Whence (comes) this to you?" She said: "From God: for God provides sustenance to whom He pleases, without measure."	And Mary was in the temple of the Lord as if she were a dove that dwelt there, and she received food from the hand of an angel.	For daily was she visited [in the temple] by angels, daily did she enjoy a divine vision, which preserved her from all evil, and made her to abound in all good.

Sura 19:23–25	*Gospel of Pseudo-Matthew* chapter 20
And the pains of childbirth drove her to the trunk of a palm-tree: she cried (in her anguish): "Ah! Would that I had died before this! Would that I had been a thing forgotten and out of sight!" But (a voice) cried to her from beneath the (palm-tree): "Grieve not! For thy Lord hath provided a rivulet beneath thee; and shake towards thyself the trunk of the palm-tree: it will let fall fresh ripe dates upon thee."	And it came to pass on the third day of their journey, while they were walking, that the blessed Mary was fatigued by the excessive heat of the sun in the desert; and seeing a palm tree, she said to Joseph: Let me rest a little under the shade of this tree. Joseph therefore made haste, and led her to the palm, and made her come down from her beast. And as the blessed Mary was sitting there, she looked up to the foliage of the palm, and saw it full of fruit, and said to Joseph: I wish it were possible to get some of the fruit of this palm. And Joseph said to her: I wonder that thou sayest this, when thou seest how high the palm tree is; and that thou thinkest of eating of its fruit. I am thinking more of the want of water, because the skins are now empty, and we have none wherewith to refresh ourselves and our cattle. Then the child Jesus, with a joyful countenance, reposing in the bosom of His mother, said to the palm: O tree, bend thy branches, and refresh my mother with thy fruit. And immediately at these words the palm bent its top down to the very feet of the blessed Mary; and they gathered from it fruit, with which they were all refreshed.

> Blessed wheresoever I be,
> And hath enjoined on me
> Prayer and Charity as long
> As I live;
> (He) hath made me kind
> To my mother, and not
> Overbearing or miserable;
> So Peace is on me
> The day I was born,
> The day that I die,
> And the day that I
> Shall be raised up
> To life (again)." (Sura 19:30–33)

Perhaps we smile at the idea that Jesus-as-speaking-baby might thus be recruited to confirm the miracle of what was going on in his being "sent" by God. But how do we imagine the biblical Jesus to have carried off his dual nature as a boy or youth?

Figure 81
The annunciation in Qur'ân and Bible

Qur'ân	Bible
Relate in the Book (the story of) Mary, when she withdrew from her family to a place in the East. She placed a screen (to screen herself) from them; then We sent to her Our angel, and he appeared before her as a man in all respects. She said: "I seek refuge from thee to (God) Most Gracious: (come not near) if thou dost fear God." He said: "Nay, I am only a messenger from thy Lord, (to announce) to thee the gift of a holy son." She said: "How shall I have a son, seeing that no man has touched me, and I am not unchaste?" He said: "So (it will be): Thy Lord saith, 'That is easy for Me: and (We wish) to appoint him as a Sign unto men and a Mercy from Us': It is a matter (so) decreed." So she conceived him, and she retired with him to a remote place. Sura 19:16–22	In the sixth month, God sent the angel Gabriel to Nazareth, a town in Galilee, to a virgin pledged to be married to a man named Joseph, a descendant of David. The virgin's name was Mary. The angel went to her and said, "Greetings, you who are highly favoured! The Lord is with you." Mary was greatly troubled at his words and wondered what kind of greeting this might be. But the angel said to her, "Do not be afraid, Mary, you have found favour with God. You will be with child and give birth to a son, and you are to give him the name Jesus. He will be great and will be called the Son of the Most High. The Lord God will give him the throne of his father David, and he will reign over the house of Jacob for ever; his kingdom will never end." "How will this be," Mary asked the angel, "since I am a virgin?" The angel answered, "The Holy Spirit will come upon you, and the power of the Most High will overshadow you. So the holy one to be born will be called the Son of God. Even Elizabeth your relative is going to have a child in her old age, and she who was said to be barren is in her sixth month. For nothing is impossible with God." "I am the Lord's servant," Mary answered. "May it be to me as you have said." Then the angel left her. Luke 1:26–38

The one gospel insight we are given – where Jesus forgoes returning to Nazareth with his family and stays instead at the temple in Jerusalem to "amaze" his audience with his understanding and answers (Luke 2:41–51) – suggests that bringing up this unique person was no easy matter for his parents. Carol Ann Duffy, a contemporary Scottish poet, has the young Jesus speaking in babyhood in her poem entitled “The Virgin Punishing the Infant”. In a piece that probes beyond sentimentality to the harsh realities of communal village life, Duffy describes Jesus the infant from the perspective of a (female) village neighbour. While other babies are murmuring “googoo goo” at their mothers' breasts, this baby is insisting “*But I am God*”. He gets smacked for his cheek![226] It is a disturbingly imaginative cameo positing the enigma of “baby Jesus” as “God”. Rhys Prichard (AD 1579–1644) similarly used poetry to convey that enigma, though he identified the “God” element of Jesus as “Father”:[227]

> Let us go to see the daughter [maid] who is a mother,
> The mother who is a maid [daughter], peaceful and spotless:
> The daughter [maid] nursing her Father in his wrappings,
> The Father sucking a child's breasts.

Beyond this qur'ânic incident of speech in infancy, the further miracles performed by Jesus with the permission of God are described in Medinan suras (see Figure 82). They include giving life to clay birds, curing lepers and blind people, raising the dead, seeing hidden things and securing from heaven a table laden with food. Again, many of the qur'ânic miracles are reminiscent of incidents described in the canonical and apocryphal Gospels.

Not much is said in the Qur'ân about what Jesus taught, although he is described as confirming the scriptures that came before him. He warned his followers against idolatry and promised them the assurance of paradise if they died fighting in the way of God. Importantly, he foretold the coming of Muḥammad, performed the ritual prayer (the *salât*) and gave alms (*zakât*).

Almost incidentally, one can derive a very positive witness to Jesus from the Qur'ân despite the qur'ânic emphasis on Jesus' mere humanity and its refusal of some of the core Christian convictions about Jesus as Lord and Saviour (see Figure 83). Jesus is given a number of honorific titles and, in some important respects, is set apart from all other prophets. He is

Figure 82
Miracles of Jesus

Sura	Event	Reminiscent of ...
19:30; 3:46	Jesus speaks as baby in Sura 19:30–33: He said: "I am indeed a servant of God: He hath given me revelation and made me a prophet."	*Arabic Gospel of the Infancy of the Saviour* chapter 1: We find what follows in the book of Joseph the high priest, who lived in the time of Christ. Some say that he is Caiaphas. He has said that Jesus spoke, and, indeed, when He was lying in His cradle said to Mary His mother: "I am Jesus, the Son of God, the Logos, whom thou hast brought forth, as the Angel Gabriel announced to thee; and my Father has sent me for the salvation of the world."
3:49; 5:113	Sura 5:113: "... And behold! thou makest out of clay, as it were, the figure of a bird, by My leave, and thou breathest into it, and it becometh a bird by My leave ... "	*Arabic Gospel of the Infancy of the Saviour* chapter 36: Now, when the Lord Jesus had completed seven years from His birth, on a certain day He was occupied with boys of His own age. For they were playing among clay, from which they were making images of asses, oxen, birds, and other animals; and each one boasting of his skill, was praising his own work. Then the Lord Jesus said to the boys: The images that I have made I will order to walk. The boys asked Him whether then he were the son of the Creator; and the Lord Jesus bade them walk. And they immediately began to leap; and then, when He had given them leave, they again stood still. And He had made figures of birds and sparrows, which flew when He told them to fly, and stood still when He told them to stand, and ate and drank when He handed them food and drink. see the *Gospel of Thomas* chapter 2
3:49; 5:113	cures the blind and lepers	reminiscent of Bartimeus and the ten lepers?
3:49; 5:113	raises the dead	reminiscent of Lazarus or the son of widow of Nain?
3:49	sees hidden things	reminiscent of Gospel accounts of Jesus knowing peoples' thoughts?
5:115–118	causes a "table prepared" to come down from the sky	reminiscent of the feeding of the 5,000/4,000 or the Last Supper? The Arabic verb is related to the word *tanzîl*, suggesting the heavenly origin of the food or "sacrament" referred to

Figure 83
Positive witness to Jesus in the Qur'ân

Sura	Information about Jesus
3:45	birth announced by an angel as good news
19:20	born of a virgin
19:19	is holy, faultless (sinless)
4:171	an apostle (messenger); Word of God; a spirit from God
5:113	creator of life; healer of the blind; raiser of the dead
43:63	came with clear signs
19:21	a sign to humankind and a mercy from God
21:91	a sign to all people
3:45	of honour in this world and the next; the Christ/Messiah
4:158	raised to heaven; he is alive
43:61	will come back for judgement

described as Messiah, as God's word and as "a spirit from Him". In his mission he is strengthened by the "holy spirit" (Sura 2:87).

Three times Jesus is designated as a "Sign" (in Suras 19:21; 23:50–52; 21:91), usually in the context of his manner of birth. The "sign" aspect of Jesus' birth is that he is born without a human father. The two major "birth passages" are found in Sura 19 (Meccan) and Sura 3 (Medinan). In them the main protagonists are "Our spirit", the "angels", Mary and Jesus. The angels are witnesses to the choice of Mary as vehicle for the conception of Jesus by an act performed by God's spirit towards Mary. That act is described in various verses by the words "bestow", "cast into" or "inbreathe". Whatever the mechanical details intended in these passages, they all add up to give the strong impression of God himself (or his spirit) being intimately involved in the producing of Jesus in the womb of Mary. So much so that Jesus is himself identified as a "spirit" (Sura 4:171) – incarnated spirit, might we wonder? For the most part, "spirit" in the Qur'ân refers to the angel Gabriel, and Muslims tend to think of that archangel when mention is made of the "Holy Spirit". Jesus, however, is also uniquely "spirit" in some sense: something of God himself was transferred to Mary, or through Mary to Jesus.

Interestingly, the Qur'ân nowhere explicitly states that Jesus is a man, in contrast to its declaration concerning Muḥammad. It does not even stress the humanness of Jesus over against the claim of some that he was divine, though it might easily have done so. Through the qur'ânic witness, Jesus appears as different from all other human beings. It is as if the Qur'ân cannot admit real "incarnation" as such – God becoming man in Christ Jesus – but by its very description of the uniqueness of Jesus' birth allows some such process as a possibility. This cumulative, positive witness to Jesus that is expressed in the Qur'ân is filled out in the Traditions (the *ḥadîth*). There Jesus is portrayed as sinless, humble, otherworldly, ascetic, perceptive and witty, willing to suffer and possessing a personal relationship with God. No wonder that many Muslims have found in the "shadowy figure" of the Islamic Jesus someone whom they might begin to seek out and approach:

> Gradually, my praying changed until I was praying over and over between [formal] prayer times, on each bead, "Oh Jesus, Son of Maryam, heal me." The more I prayed, the more I was drawn to this shadowy, secondary figure in the Holy Quran, who had power that Mohammed himself never claimed. Where was it written that Mohammed healed the sick and raised the dead?[228]

Of course, the Qur'ân is very clear on what Jesus is *not*! Primary denial is made of the Christian concept of Trinity and Christ's part in it. God is one and one means singular. Jesus is not divine – he was no different from other prophets who brought God's message to their people. Jesus Christ is not the "Son of God", for he was created by God. The crucifixion did not happen – God could not have allowed one of his prophets to be outmanoeuvred and defeated, especially by Jews (see Figure 84).

Figure 84
Negations about Jesus in the Qur'ân

Sura	Correctives concerning Jesus
4:171; 5:76, 78; 5:119	God cannot be a Trinity
5:75, 78; 5:19; 5:120; 9:31	Christ is not divine
10:68; 3:59; 2:116; 21:22–26; 19:88–93;19:35	Jesus Christ is not the Son of God
4:157–158	The crucifixion of Jesus did not happen

With all four of these denials, major though they are, there appears, on closer examination, to be more than initially meets the eye. It seems likely that Muḥammad understood the Christian concept of Trinity to refer to God, Mary and Jesus. Perhaps this was due to the reference being made by some contemporary Christians to Mary as *theotokos* or "God-bearer". There was, as we have explored in chapter 6, a vigorous debate among Christians about how Jesus Christ could be conceived as both fully divine and fully human. Theologians tended in turn to overemphasize one or the other of these two facets of Jesus' make-up. Mary as *theotokos* was enunciated as part of the corrective to those who overemphasized Jesus' humanity. Mary was the person who bore God to earth in giving birth to Jesus. Mary the "God-bearer", however, quickly became popularized as Mary the "Mother of God". Someone evidently got the idea from this phrase that God indulged in sexual intercourse with Mary to produce a son, Jesus. It is such blasphemy that Muḥammad was seemingly reacting against. In several suras of the Qur'ân, Muḥammad appears to accept that normative Christianity is monotheistic, not polytheistic. We have already noted the strong statement of Sura 29:46 that "our God and your God is One". Elsewhere, the Qur'ân acknowledges that some Christians truly honour God's word and worship him (Sura 3:113–114).

Jesus' divinity is denied in the Qur'ân on the basis that he was no different from other prophets who brought God's word to their peoples. But the qur'ânic denial of Jesus' divinity is quite specifically expressed: "They do blaspheme who say: 'God is Christ the son of Mary'." (Sura 5:75) Who was saying "God is Christ"? Some of the proponents of an extreme monophysite Christology (Julianists and Gaianists) were not only attributing divine nature to Christ but identifying "God" with Christ. As we have seen, the definition of Chalcedon affirmed not that "God is Christ" but that "Christ is God". The Qur'ân surely makes a fair point here in denying the first clause, even if it will not allow the second. Such non-allowance (of the second clause) is quietly softened by qur'ânic admission that Jesus was significantly different from all other prophets in several respects, and in some respects uniquely so – for example, in his sinlessness and his "deathlessness". The designation of Jesus as "a Word from Him: his name will be Christ Jesus" (Sura 3:45) further softens such non-allowance. The English words "his name" or "whose name" translate a masculine personal pronoun in the Arabic intimating that "a word" does not refer to a simple word of language but to a person.

Divine sonship is denied in the Qur'ân because Muḥammad rejected the idea that Jesus was the product of a physical act of intercourse between God and Mary. There are two main Arabic words for son: *walad* and *ibn*. Both appear in the Qur'ân. *Walad* is a noun that refers to the physical boy who results from the sexual union of a man and a woman. *Ibn* is a title of relationship. It appears, for example, in Sura 2:215 where reference is made to charity offered to family members, to orphans and to "wayfarers". A "wayfarer" is, literally, "a son of the road" or "*ibn sabîl*". The Qur'ân, in speaking of Jesus as "son", consistently uses the word *walad* rather than *ibn*. In the one (Medinan) verse denying the sonship of Jesus that uses the word *ibn* (Sura 9:30), the context is one of comparing Christians' elevation of Jesus as parallel to the Jewish elevation of Ezra as a son (*ibn*) of God. To give a human being such prestige or honour is not in the prerogative of Christians or Jews. The denial of Christ's sonship coheres almost exclusively in a disgust at the idea of Jesus as the physical product (a *walad*) of sexual union between God and Mary. One might argue that the Qur'ân does not really deny the sonship of Christ in terms of his unique status with God (the essential *ibn* sense). If a "wayfarer" can be a "son of the road" in a non-physical manner, could not Christ be "son of God" in a non-physical sense?

Similarly with the crucifixion, various veins of interpretation run through the qur'ânic recounting. The overriding concern seems to be that the Qur'ân will not allow that a prophet sent by God could be "unsuccessful". Where did Muḥammad get the idea that crucifixion amounted to a "failure" that Christ successfully avoided? Well, there were plenty of sources potentially available to him. Some of the options under discussion in quasi-Christian circles in the centuries prior to the rise of Islam are summarized in Figure 85.[229]

Cragg is famous for his sensitive attempts at theological "retrieval". He tries to retrieve the essential Christian gospel from within the text and context of the Qur'ân. With regard to his analysis of the Qur'ân's dealing with the crucifixion, Cragg begins by acknowledging that so much is at stake in the matter including the Islamic understanding of God, its view of evil, of providence, of forgiveness and its interpretation of divine power. Cragg argues that the Qur'ân admits certain facets of the biblical crucifixion incident. The intention to crucify is stated – that is what the Jews intended to do to Jesus. The will to crucify is also allowed in that God promises to be involved in the process, taking Jesus to himself (Sura 3:55). Somehow also, there can be discerned from the Qur'ân that God has a will in the very process of crucifixion, a will expressed in the famous words:

> That they [the Jews] said (in boast)
> "We killed Christ Jesus
> The son of Mary,
> The Apostle of God;" –

Figure 85
Theories of non-crucifixion

Source	Details
Cerinthus: mid to late first century	At the time of crucifixion the divine Christ flew away and the human Jesus suffered, died and rose again. Irenaeus and Jerome say that John wrote his Gospel primarily to refute Cerinthus.
Docetists: from *dokesis* meaning "semblance" or "illusion"	Asserted that Christ's human body was a phantasm and therefore that the crucifixion was an illusion: "If he suffered he was not God; if he was God he did not suffer." Ignatius of Antioch wrote against the docetists.
Basilides: AD 125–150	Suffering implies sinfulness. Christ, the divine *nous* or intelligence could not have suffered. Irenaeus summarizes Basilides' view: "Wherefore he [Christ] suffered not, but a certain Simon, a Cyrenian, was impressed to bear his cross for him; and Simon was crucified in ignorance and error, having been transfigured by him, that men should suppose him to be Jesus, while Jesus himself took on the appearance of Simon and stood by and mocked them … "
Gnostic Nag Hammadi documents: e.g. *Coptic Apocalypse of Peter* AD 150–333	"After he [Jesus] had said these things, I [Peter] saw him as if he was seized by them, and I said: 'What is it that I see, O Lord? Is it you yourself whom they take, and are you grasping me? Or, who is the one who is glad and who is laughing above (?) the wood [the cross]? And do they hit another one on his feet and on his hands?' The Saviour said to me: 'The one whom you see glad and laughing above (?) the wood, that is the Living One, Jesus. But the one into whose hands and feet they are driving the nails is his fleshly part, which is the substitute. They put to shame that which has come into existence after his likeness. But look at him and at me'."

> But they killed him not,
> Nor crucified him,
> But so it was made to appear to them … (Sura 4:157)

God takes Jesus towards crucifixion and in the event achieves his divine goal. That goal is expressed in the Arabic words *shubbiha lahum* or "so it was made to appear to them"; more literally "they were brought under the illusion that … " The question that Cragg asks of the text is "What constitutes the illusion?" Is it that "he [that is, Jesus] was resembled to them" (this is the traditional Muslim interpretation) or is it that "it [that is, crucifixion] was made to seem so to them" (this is the less orthodox, Ahmadîya interpretation)?[230] In effect, the Ahmadîya support a swoon theory, for according to them, Jesus later revived and made his way to India. Both possibilities are permitted by the Arabic. Is it possible that the text allows for the crucifixion itself to seem an illusion, though not in the Ahmadîya "swoon theory" manner? Could the text allow that the act of crucifixion did not amount to what the Jews intended it to be, but rather to what God intended it to be? Sobhi Malek certainly takes up this last possibility. He examines the Qur'ân's comment on the famous Battle of Badr when the few troops under Muḥammad defeated an overwhelmingly large force of Meccans. "It was not you that killed them," declares Sura 8:17, "but God. And when you threw (a handful of dust at the enemy), it was not you, but it was God." Although the odds were greatly against Muḥammad and his men, the Quraysh were defeated. How? By God's intention and involvement in the action. So, perhaps, with Sura 4:157, suggests Malek:

> What if this same interpretative principle were to be applied to the controversial verse of sura 4:157? In that case, the verse could read like this: "The Jews said, 'We killed Christ Jesus, son of Mary, the messenger of God.' Yet, it was not the Jews who acted at Calvary, it was God. They did not kill him nor did they crucify him, but it was made to appear to be so. Rather, it was God who prepared him for this very purpose; God sent him to die![231]

Some such interpretation actually fits best with the three other qur'ânic statements that speak explicitly about Jesus' death, two of which place the death of Jesus before his resurrection or ascension (see Figure 86). The Qur'ân asserts, moreover, that some prophets are indeed wrongfully killed (Sura 4:155; 2:87). So why not Jesus? As part of another argument, it is furthermore suggested that should God choose, for whatever reason, to destroy Christ the son of Mary, no human being would be able to stop him (Sura 5:19). The force of the argument here is admittedly that Christ is only human, not God, so God does not absolutely need him. But the possibility of God being responsible for the death of Jesus is expressed. Tobias Mayer (until recently lecturer in Islamic philosophy at the School of Oriental and African Studies in London) suggests that the qur'ânic reference to the crucifixion is in reality "highly ambiguous and does not necessarily contradict the Gospels in itself".[232] He quotes some Muslim theologians, such as Wahb ibn Munabbih and Qâsim ibn Ibrâhîm, who accepted the crucifixion at face value and he critiques the reliability of *ḥadîth* usually offered in support of the "standard" interpretation of the end of Jesus' earthly life. According to Malek also, some Islamic scholars point out that the Qur'ân does not say that Jesus was not killed, nor does it say that he was not crucified. What it does say is that the Jews did not kill or crucify him.[233] The events of Calvary, by this reading of the Qur'ân, are not necessarily to be denied.

However much might be retrievable from the qur'ânic references to the death and resurrection of Jesus, Islamic theology has consistently interpreted Sura 4:157 to mean that the crucifixion did not happen historically. Other concerns from the Islamic worldview impinge on this narrative, making denial of the historical event the only conceivable option. After all, as we have seen from our previous chapters, the crucifixion has no redemptive requirement. God can just say "Be!" and something is. God can just say "I forgive" and someone is forgiven. There is no requirement for a payback, for any kind of atonement. What is more, the crucifixion should not need to happen, in a moral sense, to Jesus. Why should he die when he had commit-

Figure 86
Verses about Jesus' death

Reference	Verse	Comment
4:157	That they [the Jews] said (in boast), "We killed Christ Jesus the son of Mary, the Apostle of God"; – but they killed him not, nor crucified him, but so it was made to appear to them ...	who/what really happened? • a substitute for Jesus on cross • a non-dying of Jesus on cross • a divinely contrived affair
3:55	Behold! God said: "O Jesus! I will take thee and raise thee to Myself ... "	the verb "take thee" is used only of God (as subject) and indicates death
19:33	[Jesus speaking] "So Peace is upon me the day I was born, the day that I die, and the day that I shall be raised up to life (again)"!	the sequence supports birth/death/resurrection, not birth/ascension/death

ted no sins? Each person is responsible for his own life. The moral inclination, here, is to expect all the more that an innocent Jesus should be vindicated. Despite non-crucifixion, or rather because of it, Jesus is conceived of as having a significant eschatological role. He is alive at the moment and will return to earth at the end of the world. At that time he will be associated with the Mahdi, the ruler who will appear on earth in the last days. Indeed, in the view of some, Jesus may well be the Mahdi. Either way, he is coming again.

In a way, the major differences between Islam and Christianity as they apply to Jesus lie more in what Islam asserts as false than in what it asserts as true. And in its understanding of what is false, most Christians would agree with a great deal. The concept of Trinity does not refer to God, Mary and Jesus. Jesus is not the physical "son" of God and Mary. Jesus is not divine in the sense of being a separate "god" from God (Christians do not believe in tritheism). And the denial of incarnation and crucifixion in the Qur'ân is almost made in passing. It is hardly focused on and, indeed, it would seem possible to retrieve from the Qur'ân an alternative (closer to Christian) reading or interpretation.

We shall consider, in a moment, whether there might be some more positive or accessible ways of conveying Christian conceptions about Christ to a Muslim audience. Firstly, however, we need to note two major issues that tend to make communication about Christ more, rather than less, difficult in current times. On the one hand, Christian hesitations about using the Arabic Muslim name for Jesus make it hard for Muslims to begin to hear anything at all about Christ that they might accept. On the other hand, the appeal by Muslims to the so-called *Gospel of Barnabas* serves to concretize an "Islamic" view of Jesus as being equivalent to the alleged, original, uncontaminated Christian perspective.

At which name of Jesus?

We have already noted Christian hesitations over referring to God as *Allâh* despite the fact that millions of Arab Christians relate to him as such on a daily basis. When it comes to the name Jesus, however, most Arab Christians find themselves on the other side of the argument. Historically, Christians in the Arab world have used the word *Yasû^c^a* to refer to Jesus – a word derived originally from the Hebrew *Yeshua^c^* via the Syriac *Yeshû^c^*. The Muslim term, *^c^Îsâ*, would seem to have derived originally from the Greek form of the name, *Iesous*. In many Muslim countries where there is a minority Christian population, the Christians have used *Yasû^c^a* for "Jesus" while Muslims have used *^c^Îsâ* – except Turkey, for example, where the Christians have consistently referred to Jesus as *İsa* in Turkish.

The Christian objection to using *^c^Îsâ al-Masîh* is based on two major arguments. The first is that the *^c^Îsâ* of the Qur'ân is not the same Jesus as the person whom we meet in the Bible. The second is that the Bible has long since been translated into Arabic and an established Christian tradition has developed that knows Jesus only by the non-Muslim name. Some Muslims express a degree of sympathy for at least the first of these reasons. Ahmad Azhar, for example, comments that viewing "the

Jesus of the Christian Gospels and the Isa of the Quran" as absolutely distinct from one another frees Muslims from what he calls a "pseudo-Islamic respect for the Christian Jesus".[234]

In terms of opportunities for communicating the gospel to Muslims, it must surely be significant that God has overseen a considerable amount of "writing into" the Qur'ân of truth about the person of Jesus. While Muslims have to work hard to uncover a reference to Muḥammad in the Bible, Christians are offered in the Qur'ân a wealth of biblically accurate information concerning Jesus Christ. Why lose all that for the sake of a name? L. Bevan Jones argues the case for using the name *ᶜÎsâ*, concluding:

> we should gratefully receive, and without hesitation use the name for Jesus which the Muslims offer us and fill it, for their sakes, with a new content.[235]

John Travis similarly argues that Christians need to be the flexible people in this matter of terminology, in line with Paul's desire that we become "all things to all men so that by all possible means some might be saved" (1 Corinthians 9:22).[236] Whether such an option is possible in contexts where there exists a historic, Arabic-speaking, Christian population remains a delicate issue. In those situations, perhaps, the principle of not offending or causing a brother or sister to stumble becomes the overriding concern.

A convenient gospel?

At the beginning of the eighteenth century a researcher from Holland unearthed a manuscript written in Italian that contained a text purporting to be *The Gospel according to Barnabas (Gospel of Barnabas)*. The manuscript was acquired by the National Library in Vienna (where it remains today). Since then, a Spanish text has been discovered in Sydney, Australia. A few scholars believe that the Spanish text is the more original. In 1907 a Protestant pastor and his wife, Lonsdale and Laura Ragg, published the Italian text with an English translation and introduction. The English introduction strongly suggested that the manuscript dated from sometime after AD 1575 – it was composed on a distinctive kind of paper that began to be made at that date. The introduction also suggested that the text itself could not have dated from much earlier than the paper it was written on. It was either composed completely from scratch or else was a revision of a slightly earlier work. There were certain anachronisms dating from the medieval period that were included in the text. Wooden casks are mentioned at one point (chapter 152); these were invented much later than Jesus' day, in Gaul. Mary is said to have given birth to Jesus without pain – this goes against the qur'ânic account but in accordance with medieval legend. The wise men from the east are identified as three in number (chapter 6) while the fruit tasted by Eve and Adam is classified as an apple (chapter 40); these interpretations come much later than the first century AD. Jesus himself is described as being presented with a book when he is 30 years old (chapter 10). The presenter of the book is Gabriel, and the book itself descends into the heart of Jesus. The description tells the story of the "sending down" of the *Injîl* in the vocabulary of the later sending down of the Qur'ân to Prophet Muḥammad. The author of the text, whoever that person was, clearly had little understanding of the geography of Palestine. Nazareth (high in the hills), for example, is placed on the shores of Lake Galilee (chapter 20). The "Barnabas" behind this material is in no way connected with the author of the *Epistle of Barnabas*, an apocryphal book dating from the second century.[237]

A translation into Arabic of the *Gospel of Barnabas* was made and published in AD 1908 – though without the critical introduction. The text, anachronisms notwithstanding, retells the story of Jesus in 222 chapters in the form of a "gospel harmony". In its preamble, the author of the "gospel" introduces himself as "Barnabas, apostle of Jesus the Nazarene, called Christ". He is writing this gospel, he declares, because many of his contemporaries "being deceived of Satan, under pretence of piety, are preaching most impious doctrine, calling Jesus son of God, repudiating the circumcision ordained of God for ever, and permitting every unclean meat: among whom also Paul hath been deceived ... " In the text, Jesus repeatedly denies that he is the Son of God (chapters 13 and 93, for example), and the supposed origin of the belief that Jesus is Son of God is explained (chapter 91). Jesus foretells the coming of Muḥammad, actually naming him (chapter 97). Judas is substituted for Jesus when crucifixion looms large (chapter 216). Adam is said to have seen the Muslim *shahâda* (the brief confession of faith) in a vision and to have persuaded God to engrave it upon his thumbnails (chapter 39). Specifically Muslim observances, like ablutions before prayer (chapters 36 and 61), are identified. In many chapters the falsification of Jewish and Christian scriptures is asserted (for example, in chapters 44, 58, 71 and so on).

The material in the *Gospel of Barnabas* is now widely referred to by Muslims in their conversation with Christians. The English version of the Italian text has been translated into Arabic, Urdu, Persian, Indonesian, Turkish, German, Dutch, modern Italian and even Spanish! It provides grist for the mill of those Muslims who are aware that there was a rift at one point between the biblical Paul and Barnabas. That rift, it is suggested, was over the nature of the true gospel that Jesus brought. Paul seemingly won the day and, after him, a distorted version of Jesus' gospel became the inheritance of the Christian church. The *Gospel of Barnabas* reinstates the truth. The picture of Jesus that is given in this text is close to the traditional Islamic one (see Figure 87). Abûl-ᶜAlâ' Mawdûdî, father of the twentieth-century Islamist movement, made significant use of the *Gospel of Barnabas* in his commentary on the Qur'ân (on Sura 61:5, where Jesus announces the coming of Aḥmad) and in his biography of Prophet Muḥammad. Muhammad ᶜAta ur-Rahim, among other contemporary Muslims, makes substantial apologetic use of the *Gospel of Barnabas*, even claiming that it was accepted as a canonical Gospel in the churches of Alexandria until the beginning of the twentieth century. He uses the *Gospel of Barnabas* as the main source for his book *Jesus – a Prophet of Islam*.

The central theme of the *Gospel of Barnabas*, however, runs quite contrary to the witness of the Qur'ân. As we have seen,

Figure 87
Jesus in the *Gospel of Barnabas*

Jesus ...	Text
... not the son of God	Then Jesus, having lifted his hand in token of silence, said: "Verily ye have erred greatly, O Israelites, in calling me, a man, your God. And I fear that God may for this give you heavy plague upon the holy city, handing it over in servitude to strangers. O a thousand times accursed Satan, that hath moved you to this!" (chapter 93)
... predicts Muḥammad by name	Jesus answered: "The name of the Messiah is admirable, for God himself gave him the name when he created his soul, and placed it in a celestial splendour. God said: 'Wait Mohammed; for thy sake I will to create paradise, the world, and a great multitude of creatures ...'. Mohammed is his blessed name." (chapter 97)
... carried up to heaven	When the soldiers with Judas drew near to the place where Jesus was, Jesus heard the approach of many people, wherefore in fear he withdrew into the house. And the eleven were sleeping. Then God, seeing the danger of his servant, commanded Gabriel, Michael, Rafael, and Uriel, his ministers, to take Jesus out of the world. The holy angels came and took Jesus out by the window that looketh toward the South. They bare him and placed him in the third heaven in the company of angels blessing God for evermore. (chapter 215)
... replaced by Judas	Judas entered impetuously before all into the chamber whence Jesus had been taken up. And the disciples were sleeping. Whereupon the wonderful God acted wonderfully, insomuch that Judas was so changed in speech and in face to be like Jesus that we believed him to be Jesus. (chapter 216)
... not crucified but Judas	So they led him [Judas looking like Jesus] to Mount Calvary, where they used to hang malefactors, and there they crucified him naked, for the greater ignominy. Judas did nothing else but cry out: "God, why hast thou forsaken me, seeing the malefactor hath escaped and I die unjustly?" Verily I say that the voice, the face, and the person of Judas were so like to Jesus, that his disciples and believers entirely believed that he was Jesus ... (chapter 217)

Jesus names Muḥammad as Messiah in the text of the *Gospel*. He denies that he, Jesus, is the Messiah: "'As God liveth, in whose presence my soul standeth, I am not the Messiah whom all the tribes of the earth expect'" (chapter 96). Jesus is portrayed rather in the role traditionally occupied by John the Baptist as forerunner of the Messiah (in chapters 42 and 96). Yet the Qur'ân never refers to Muḥammad as Messiah but does consistently give that title to Jesus:

> Behold! the angels said:
> "O Mary! God giveth thee
> Glad tidings of a Word
> From Him: his name
> Will be Christ Jesus, [the Arabic is *al-masîh* or "Messiah"]
> The son of Mary, held in honour
> In this world and the Hereafter
> And of (the company of) those
> Nearest to God ..." (Sura 3:45)

Eleven times the Qur'ân refers to Jesus as *al-masîh*. In Muslim tradition, Jesus is the only person to be given the title "Messiah".

We have hinted in chapter 8 at the possible source, in the Iberian peninsula, of the idea that Muḥammad is Messiah. Luis F. Bernabé Pons is convinced of the Moorish origin of the *Gospel of Barnabas*. He argues that the *Gospel* was parallelled by a series of Morisco recreations of early Christian writings, found in Grenada at the end of the sixteenth century, and referred to as "the lead books of Sacramento".[238] In these "books", Christian themes are presented with distinctively Islamic overtones.[239] Bernabé Pons finds explicit reference to the *Gospel of Barnabas* in a document dating from AD 1634, and illustrates how Ibrâhîm al-Taybilî, in one of his poems, reproduces the denial that Jesus was Messiah, implying that the real Messiah is in fact Muḥammad.[240] Gerard Wiegers argues that a manuscript composed by Juan Alonso from Aragon (a convert to Islam) provided material for the composer of the *Gospel of Barnabas*. Alonso refers to Jesus as "the messiah of the gospel", whose mission was focused on the people of Israel, in contrast to Muḥammad whom he calls "the universal messiah".[241] Was it in this environment that the *Gospel of Barnabas* was produced in order to underline the content of the true (in an Islamic sense) Gospel of Jesus Christ? It is certainly a possibility that the enforced conversion of the Moors prior to their expulsion from Spain resulted in the latter expressing themselves thus about the religion that had been imposed upon them by the Christian authorities in Spain.

However much of a forgery the *Gospel of Barnabas* may have been, it certainly gives considerable insight into the manner in which Muslims view Jesus. It also illustrates the "power and truth" dynamic involved in Muslim–Christian relations. As Oddbjorn Leirvik concludes:

> Just as the creation of the Gospel might have been part of a strategy of resistance on the part of forcefully converted Spanish Moriscos, its polemical use by Muslims in the nineteenth and twentieth centuries may well be taken as part of an anti-colonial discourse on the part of Indian and Arab Muslims.[242]

So what about Jesus?

Are there ways in which "incarnation" might be positively expressed to Muslims? Christians certainly do not want to claim that "God is Christ", though we do want to affirm that "Christ is God". Perhaps in terms of vertical relationships – of Christ's servanthood or obedience – there might be room for conveying Jesus' origins in God. Jesus spoke of himself as being "sent" by the Father. The Qur'ân appears through "sending down". In both faith traditions, prophets are sent by God to convey his word to people on earth. Cragg suggests that the one who is sent is in some sense full of the one who sends.[243] Perhaps "incarnation" might be seen as a kind of "sentness" – equivalent to the giving of the divine word on earth as an Arabic Qur'ân, as we have noted earlier in chapter 3. Jesus is full of the one who has sent him. True submission, or "doing the works God requires", finds focus – according to this reading of Jesus' prophetic ministry – in "believing in the one he [God] has sent" (John 6:28–29).

The Qur'ân rejects the notion of "Son of God" – and rightly so if by that phrase it is understood that Jesus resulted from an act of sexual intercourse between God and Mary. In the canonical Gospels, Jesus himself was reluctant to accept the title "Son of God". Perhaps this was partly because it just miscommunicated so much with contemporary Jews. Perhaps it was also to do with the kind of person Jesus was. He wanted that aspect of who he was to be discovered and confessed, not announced and insisted upon. When a disciple got the point and confessed him as Lord and God, Jesus gladly accepted the worship being offered (as with Thomas, for example, in John 20:28–29). Jesus, meanwhile, preferred to refer to himself as "Son of Man". His life illustrated "servant" vocabulary rather than "royalty" vocabulary. In the Christological hymn preserved in Philippians 2:5–11, the name above all other names that is bestowed on Christ Jesus emerges out of obedience and humble servanthood.

Indeed, in the Gospels, Jesus never refers to himself as "Messiah", let alone "Son of God". Although the term derived from the Old Testament, "Messiah" had come by Jesus' time to carry overwhelming connotations of political liberation – Messiah was expected to bring renewed nationhood to a revived people of Israel, freed from the yoke of Rome. When Peter confessed at Caesarea Philippi that Jesus was "the Christ", Jesus insisted on silence about the issue. The "messianic secret" is to be maintained because unleashing the secret would just lead to a wrong appreciation of Jesus' aims. With Peter and the other disciples at Caesarea Philippi, Jesus ignores the messianic title in referring to himself. He goes on immediately to refer to himself as "Son of Man" (Mark 8:29, 31).

With the confession in the Qur'ân of Jesus as Messiah, there is in a sense less distance between Muslims and the truth about Jesus than there was for the contemporaries of Jesus who had such a distorted understanding of what Messiahship meant.

Heikki Räisänen reminds us of the period when Christian views about Jesus were closer to the qur'ânic view than to the definitions of the fourth-century church councils. In the New Testament there is a strand in which Jesus is presented as subordinate to God. Is it possible that the notion "Son of God" was originally conceived in a more adoptionist sense? God made Jesus his "son" or at least declared him his "son". There is certainly a strong notion of honour and shame enmeshed in the gospel story. "Honour and shame" reflect the concerns of status-oriented cultures, in which rank or position is significant. The anthropology is hierarchical in which the sent one obeys his heavenly Father, submitting to his will rather than his own, even as far as the requirement – from above – for his self-giving in death.

Whatever the cross might mean, normative Islam will not allow it to stand for vicarious suffering and redemption. The possibility of dying/failing is, however, mooted as a possible part of a prophet's experience (Sura 5:70; 2:87). Moreover, there are traces of the possibility of vicarious suffering in Islam. For all Muslims, the intended sacrifice of Abraham's son (unnamed in the Qur'ân, but assumed to be Ishmael) is what makes possible the continuing relationship of God with Abraham. In classical Shîʿa Islam, the martyrdom of Ḥussein at Karbalâ' provides the emotional and spiritual well-spring for the continuation of that expression of the Islamic faith. Christians and Muslims have shared together in suffering for a positive outcome in the experience of combating "apartheid" in South Africa and in Israel/Palestine. What is really at stake, in the Muslim denial of a historical crucifixion, is an understanding about the sovereignty of God. Can God's will embrace the seeming "failure" of his representative on earth? David Brown underlines this point:

> the difference between the Christian and the Islamic accounts of the crucifixion does not lie in the question whether Jesus was or was not crucified but in whether God displayed his sovereignty more clearly in giving Jesus to be crucified or in raising him to heaven.[244]

Which outcome gives more glory to God – a rescue from death before the mortal moment or a rescue from death after the latter has had its way? Which process, one might ask, makes of Jesus Christ the greater "sign"?

Christ is regarded as a sign both in the New Testament and in the Qur'ân (Figure 88).

Figure 88
Christ as "Sign" in Qur'ân and New Testament

Sura 21:91	Luke 2:34–35
And (remember) her who guarded her chastity: We breathed into her of Our Spirit, and We made her and her son a Sign for all peoples.	Then Simeon blessed them and said to Mary, his mother: "This child is destined to cause the falling and rising of many in Israel, and to be a sign that will be spoken against, so that the thoughts of many hearts will be revealed ... "

In the Qur'ân, the Arabic word for "sign" – *âya* – constitutes a significant word. It carries the idea of God's wonders in nature and activities in history, declaring what God has done. It refers to the miracles of the prophets and especially the wonder of the Qur'ân whose verses are labelled *âyât* (plural of *âya*). In the New Testament, the Greek word for sign – *sêmeion* – constitutes a significant word. It refers to the actions of Jesus, especially his miracles as they are received with faith. John strongly focuses on these "signs" in his Gospel account. The miraculous, for both Qur'ân and New Testament, can take on the significance of "sign". In the case of the New Testament, that significance is extended to cross and resurrection (the "sign of Jonah" in Matthew 12:39). Jesus himself introduces this notion. During his long journey to Jerusalem, he grows frustrated with the ever-increasing crowds who come out to view the spectacle of a passing prophet and healer. He complains:

> "This is a wicked generation. It asks for a miraculous sign, but none will be given it except the sign of Jonah. For as Jonah was a sign to the Ninevites, so also will the Son of Man be to this generation." (Luke 11:29–30)

What was the sign-element of Jonah for the Ninevites? Jewish commentators had concluded that the only possible explanation for the Ninevites' repentance was that they knew Jonah's story. Jonah had been swallowed by a fish as God's judgement on his disobedience. In circumstances in which a person would normally die, Jonah had been miraculously kept alive by God in the fish's stomach and had then been delivered onto dry ground on the third day. The Jewish commentators deduced that the Ninevites reasoned thus: "If God treats his special prophets so severely when they disobey him, what might we expect when our turn comes?" Jonah's state – skin, hair and clothing transformed by the gastric juices of the fish's digestive system – combined with his message to constitute an awesome "sign" to them.

Jesus responds in his day to sign-hungry contemporaries, people watching him proceed towards Jerusalem. They nag him to perform a sign that would outweigh the miracles performed by the prophets of old. Just show us, they demand in effect, a sign that will declare your Messiahship beyond any shadow of a doubt. Jesus eventually comes up with the promise of just such a sign. Matthew records this declaration by Jesus to some of the Pharisees and teachers of the Law:

> "as Jonah was three days and three nights in the belly of a huge fish, so the Son of Man will be three days and three nights in the heart of the earth." (Matthew 12:40)

Death, burial and resurrection will be conclusive proof of Messiahship. Laying down his own life, and taking it again out of death – as commanded by his Father (John 10:18) – constitutes the "Jonah-sign" that Jesus promises his critics.[245]

The "sign"-factor of Jesus' miraculous birth is mirrored by the "sign"-factor of resurrection after death at the close of his life. It is in the secret, still, "heart-of-the-earth" tomb that Jesus as sign will indicate something quite incredible. He, uniquely, has managed to overcome death! The Sent One's submission, or obedience, unto death leads to resurrection and ascension and the receiving of all authority in heaven and earth.

Retelling the "old, old story"?

Could the story of incarnation, death, burial, resurrection and ascension be retold in more hierarchical categories? The sovereign God has created angels and humankind. His honour has been compromised by the rebellion of Satan who successfully recruits humanity – God's vice-regent on earth – to his warfare against the divine creator. The God who is the kind of divine person to send guidance to deceived and damaged humanity, chooses to come himself – in his Son – to deal with the powers of darkness that have led humankind astray and to handle the consequences of humankind's going astray. The Son, full of the one who sends him, obeys his Father, his God (John 20:17) – even as far as being willing to die innocently, if that is what the Father wants. The shame of Satan's rebellion is exposed by the Son's dutiful obedience. The effect of Satan's seduction of humanity is dealt with in the self-surrender to death of the Son. In this retelling, the "battleground" image of the cross is strongly emphasized while the "mending of relationship between humankind and God" element is allowed to remain in the background.

God's own honour is restored in the divine–angelic–human relationship via Christ's willingness to obey him fully. Christ's honour is vindicated in that the powers of darkness and disobedient humans were given their hour for dealing with him – but God had a bigger "deal" being activated through their murderous treatment of his Son. The "sign" of Christ's restored honour is his resurrection from the bowels of the earth. He is now restored to God's right hand, the seat of Sonship, and has been given a new name plus unique authority over all creation. He has, through his obedience, vanquished the devil completely. Now he releases human beings from captivity to hostile spiritual powers, re-establishing them with God their creator. Again, the picture of the cross as "freeing imprisoned people" is more strongly promoted, at least initially in this telling, than the picture of the cross as "hospital" where damaged people and damaged relationships are restored.

The story is faithful to the biblical account, but carefully expressed – with integrity – in terms of the worldview of the Qur'ân. Just as the contemporary Western worldview has tended to popularize the Christ-story through the lens of John 3:16 – God loving the world – so in a more hierarchical context, that story may validly be announced through the lens of 1 John 3:8 – God destroying the devil's work.

Living beyond law?

When people seek to live by guidelines given by God – in *Torah* or *sharî*ᶜ*a* – one quick result seems to be an institutionalization of behaviour that focuses on the externals of law-keeping while ignoring the spirit of the law. After the strong Jewish renewal movement under Ezra, the Law of Moses was developed and systematized by the Jewish rabbis in their oral teaching. A few generations later, Jesus strongly challenged what the Law had come to mean. He objected, for example, to the religious leaders' interpretation of the obligation concerning sabbath observance. Jesus healed people on the day when no "work" was to be done (Mark 3:1–6; Luke 14:1–6). Jesus also broke the rules about ritual cleanliness (Luke 5:31–32). Why? He was, it seems, consistently concerned about inner motive, rather than about obedience to the letter of the Law. Such concern led Jesus strongly to attack the religious leaders of his day as hypocrites. He castigated them for employing legal arguments in order to avoid acting in mercy towards people in need, such as aged parents: "You nullify the word of God by your tradition" (Mark 7:13). Human beings, religious leaders, may "have" the word of God – in that it has been sent to them – and yet not have it; at least, not in their hearts!

We have seen that within Islam, the Ṣûfî movement arose partly in contradistinction to a hypocritical orthodoxy that would not or could not live according to the demands of *sharî*ᶜ*a*. Many Muslims have found in the mystic heritage of Sufism a means for the developing of more than a mere external observation of required duties. An emphasis on inner faith and relationship with God is given expression in many of the prayers of this heritage. The well-loved petition of Râbiᶜa al-ᶜAdawiyya al-Qaysiyya of Basra (born AD 717), one of the early mystics, constitutes a typical example of the Ṣûfî approach to living in front of God:

O God!
If I adore You out of fear of Hell,
Burn me in Hell!
If I adore You out of desire for Paradise,
Lock me out of Paradise.
But if I adore You for Yourself alone,
Do not deny to me Your eternal beauty.[246]

Getting beyond the requirements of obedience to a spiritual source for it is an overriding concern for Jesus and a personal desire for many Ṣûfî-oriented Muslims. At that level of seeking to be truly creaturely, human beings quickly come up against their need for mercy, forgiveness and salvation.

In many of the famous songs concerning Prophet Muḥammad that are sung on the remembrance of his birth and death (the same day of the year), voice is given to Muslims' need for mercy. The shame of hypocrisy and sinfulness is readily confessed and appeal made to the gracious intercession on behalf of his community that Muḥammad reputedly made during his "ascent to heaven":

So come, let us confess our sad rebellions;
With secret moan and bitter groan repenting.
Though life should last however many seasons,
Death shall one day become our sole employment.
So let us now defeat death's pangs and sadness,
By evermore entreating: God forgive us!
Our deeds have ever been of God unworthy;
We know not what may be our last condition.
Our worthless course have we not left nor altered,
No preparations made for life eternal.
Our names we make to shine before the people,
But secretly our hearts we all have tarnished.
Each breath sees us commit sins by the thousand,
Yet not once in our life repent we one sin.
Yielding to self we sin and know no limit –

What shall we do, O God, how make repentance?
No one of us but knows his heart's sedition,
Yet we have come, thy mercy to petition.
We hope for grace to make a good profession,
For Mercy's touch, and Ahmed's intercession.[247]

These lines come from Chelebi's *Mevlidi Şerif* ("Birth-song of the Prophet"), a rhymed song that is frequently chanted at celebrations in Turkey honouring Prophet Muḥammad. They are to a considerable extent similar in tone to the agonizing expressed by David in Psalm 51. They offer a poignant exposé of the sinfulness of humanity and humankind's helplessness before God but for the intervention of a mediator – Aḥmed, or Muḥammad. As I have suggested elsewhere,[248] Chelebi's moving delineation of Muslims' hypocrisy conveys in a few rhymed meters what it would take years for a Western Christian missionary to communicate. Chelebi builds on the "prone to evil" hopelessness of human beings, including Muslims, that we noticed as part of the qur'ânic story about the nature of humanity. We might also note the conviction here of Muslims that Muḥammad's merits and his intercession are happily allowed by God to have effect on behalf of others. So why should not Jesus' merits equally be seen by God as acceptable "ransom material" on behalf of others?

In many respects for Muslims, as well as for those in the Judaeo-Christian tradition, law serves as a "teacher" or "schoolmaster", leading people to know their need of rescue from the consequences of their falling short. In that sense, law might be seen as a sort of accomplice of sin. Law, however, offers no hope of rescue from the just requirements of the God who authors it. Both Prophet Muḥammad and Jesus were faced with an equivalent, delicate situation: what to do with a woman who has committed adultery?

Malik related to me from Yaqub ibn Zayd ibn Talha from his father Zayd ibn Talha that Abdullah ibn Abi Mulayka informed him that a woman came to the Messenger of Allah, may Allah bless him and grant him peace, and informed him that she had committed adultery and was pregnant. The Messenger of Allah, may Allah bless him and grant him peace, said to her, "Go away

> until you give birth." When she had given birth, she came to him. The Messenger of Allah, may Allah bless him and grant him peace, said to her, "Go away until you have suckled and weaned the baby." When she had weaned the baby, she came to him. He said, "Go and entrust the baby to someone." She entrusted the baby to someone and then came to him. He gave the order and she was stoned.[249]

Muḥammad is compassionate towards the child but requires the woman to be stoned. At all costs, the law must be upheld.

In John's Gospel, a woman caught in the act of adultery is brought before Jesus in the temple courts of Jerusalem (John 8:3). The teachers of the Law and the Pharisees seek to make use of her to entrap Jesus. The *Torah*, they declare, says that such a woman should be stoned. What would Jesus like to say? Jesus does not contradict the *Torah*. Nor, we later learn, is he approving of the act of which the woman is accused. He names her adultery as "sin" and orders her to change her way of life. But Jesus will only permit those men who are clear of conscience themselves to carry out the *Torah's* requirement for the woman to be stoned. Of course, he himself is the only person present who, on such terms, had the perfect right to implement the full weight of the Law. Jesus, however, chooses to forgive. Such forgiving is expressed as a sovereign act of his will, consistent with his character as representing a God of grace. The *Torah's* just demands are swallowed up by the spirit of the One who established them – not as an end in themselves, but as a means to lead humanity back to himself.

For those Muslims who have been "taught" by the law that they need rescuing from their own falling short, there is no real hope or sense of absolute forgiveness. The way of the law requires punishment and retribution. Justice must be seen to be completely done. That is how honour is restored. The approach of Jesus suggests that honour can be recovered another way – by the dishonoured One finding it in his divine heart to effect forgiveness. Jean-Marie Gaudeul recounts the powerful story of Ghulam Masih Naama, an underground fighter in Kashmir during the years after partition. Ghulam was involved in murder and reprisal, seeking to eliminate non-Muslims from the disputed territory. One day, when meeting with other guerrilla leaders, he came across a young female prisoner who was a friend of his family. She had been captured by a band of guerrillas and repeatedly raped. Suddenly, Ghulam began to awaken to a sense of shame for the kind of attitude to other human beings that had come to fill his heart and mind. His awakening grew acute one night when, in a raid on a village, he prepared to execute a Christian couple and their ten-year-old daughter. The child asked permission to pray with her parents. As they finished praying, Ghulam saw a wall of light rise up between him and his victims. He asked their forgiveness, which they freely gave in Christ's name, and then he fled into the night with his men.

Over a period of time, Ghulam became increasingly sensitized to his need for a kind of forgiveness that was way beyond what living by the law could offer. He had given his best years in *jihâd*, but emerged from them realizing that he needed much more than "infidel" blood on his hands in order really to please God. He began to pray:

> "My evil deeds convince me that hell is my portion, for you, O master, will judge sinners. I do not trust any religions and creeds in this world. O my Lord, show me the straight path. I do not want to go to hell. If you exist, show me the right path so that I may behold you. I am suffering, O master. I desire peace of mind and cannot find it. Help me, Lord. My consciousness of my sin pierces me like a lancet. Have mercy on me, O God, have mercy, Amen."[250]

In the waiting room of a railway station, God answered Ghulam's cry and the guerrilla experienced forgiveness, reconciliation and a sense of "union with God". Over a period of time Ghulam was discipled, baptized, commissioned as an evangelist and – a decade later – ordained in the Anglican Church.

Jesus alone is able to handle the likes of Ghulam Masih Naama. He has the authority to confront law-driven human beings and he has the will to forgive them. Jesus alone has the resources to enable those who live in fellowship with him – his disciples – to walk a path of witness that is characterized by becoming like him, even in the face of life-threatening situations. In the gospel story and in such contemporary obedience, the "cross" is the emblem, not of sword-taking and fighting, but of abandonment to the mercy and resurrection-power of God.

Interlude

If you were God, how would you convince Muslims that – all along – they had a special place in your divine heart?

God For All

After Saul of Tarsus was converted, he evidently needed some space and time to work through what had happened to him. Luke does not explicitly mention in the book of Acts the "retreat" that followed Saul's encounter with Jesus. We learn about it from Saul/Paul's letter to the Galatians (Galatians 1:12–24). The Apostle comments in that letter that, after his dramatic call, he went immediately into Arabia. The phrase "many days" in Acts 9:23 would therefore seem to refer to the time that Saul spent in Arabia, adjusting to his new calling by God.

Saul was entrusted by God with a unique task – taking the gospel to the Gentiles. He had been told so by Ananias in Damascus. Later, in Jerusalem, Paul would have that call reaffirmed directly by the Lord (Acts 22:21). Meanwhile, Saul disappeared into Gentile territory to work through what such a calling might mean. In the desert he found himself face to face with the living God, learning directly from him – as opposed to conferring with "flesh and blood" – what proclaiming the gospel to Gentiles would entail.

I imagine that Saul's crash course in the desert involved a considerable amount of rethinking or reconceptualizing. Saul had been raised as a Jew, and as a Jew he had been arrested and transformed by the Jewish Messiah, Jesus. In order to be able to communicate to Gentiles the good news that had transformed his own life, Saul would need to revise how he, as a Jew, viewed his relationship with God. Scattered throughout Paul's letters, we discover hints of the sort of rethinking he was forced to make. In a fundamental manner, out in the desert, Saul's credentials with God underwent a profound transformation (Figure 89).

Figure 89
Saul's credentials with God

Original credentials	Reconsidered credentials
an Israelite (Romans 11:1)	not all who are descended from Israel are Israel (Romans 9:6)
of the tribe of Benjamin (Romans 11:1)	neither Jew nor Gentile (Galatians 3:28)
circumcised on eighth day (Philippians 3:5)	circumcision is of the heart, by the Spirit (Romans 2:28)
a Hebrew of Hebrews (Philippians 3:5)	not a Jew if only one outwardly (Romans 2:28)
in regard to the Law, a Pharisee (Philippians 3:5)	justified by faith, not Law (Galatians 3:11)
in legalistic righteousness, faultless (Philippians 3:5)	receive the Spirit by observing the Law? No! (Galatians 3:2)

In his later letters to congregations of mixed Jewish and Gentile believers, Paul would develop the theological underpinning for his strategy of evangelism, discipleship and church growth in many communities within Asia Minor and around the seaboard of the Mediterranean. He would, with Barnabas, make strong representation at the critical council in Jerusalem, calling for the spiritual leadership there to acknowledge that the Holy Spirit was running far ahead of them in authenticating Jesus of Nazareth as Saviour of the world, not just Messiah to the Jews.

Perhaps today, we are called to rethink the kind of attitude we hold to those born Muslim in our world. A careful look at the Old and New Testaments will show the Lord God developing a relationship with human beings in a creative, generous manner. Through Abraham, God declares his wish to bless all nations with salvation if they will only count themselves in. By and large they will not, of course, and it becomes a huge fight even to hold the people of Israel to their covenant with the Lord. Hope gets squeezed smaller and smaller as both northern kingdom of Israel and southern kingdom of Judah choose to live in independence of Yahweh. Each nation is eventually punished with exile. Hope is delicately pinned on a potential, faithful remnant, and finally on Messiah.

At the same time, throughout Old Testament history, there are whisperings of faith to be found in people outside the special relationship between God and the people of Israel. Enoch and Job are examples of individuals who know an intimate relationship with their "living Redeemer", outside the Abrahamic connection. The people of Nineveh comprise a populace, contemporary with Israel, who become convicted together and repent en masse – and receive compassion from on high, much to Jonah's chagrin. Throughout Old Testament history, also, there seems to be a special concern demonstrated by God for the people of the east. They simply cannot be forgotten. They are needed. They are representative of "outsiders" whose hearts might be turned towards the Lord. Indeed, the covenant between Yahweh and his people Israel is at significant points only kept on track by the intervention or contribution of the people of the east (see Figure 90). Jethro, Ishmael, the Midianites and the Queen of Sheba are representative of other people of the east who find themselves intimately connected with God's purposes through Israel.

The same kind of engagement of God with people outside the "lost sheep of the house of Israel" may be discerned in Jesus' ministry. Who exercises the greatest faith that Jesus ever comes across? Who, uniquely, returns to render thanks to Jesus for cleansing him from leprosy? Outsiders, and those from other faiths that are historically and spiritually "connected" to Judaism (such as Samaritans), feature strongly in the story of the one sent by God who was rejected by those to whom he was sent.

There is a spiritual heritage, traceable in Old and New Testaments, that bespeaks the love of God for the children of Ishmael, the wilderness-dwellers, the easterners. Israel cannot do without them if they are to worship Yahweh appropriately. Jesus needs them to speak prophetically at his incarnation. The

Figure 90
Self-revealing God

People of faith independent of Israel	Israel	People of faith connected with Israel
Enoch		
	Abraham	
Job	Isaac	Ishmael
	Jacob	
		Midian
people of Nineveh	people of Israel	Queen of Sheba
		Ruth
	remnant	
	Messiah	magi
Roman centurion		Samaritan leper/woman

risen Christ had them as much in mind as any other peoples when he unleashed his Spirit at Pentecost. Jews and proselytes from all round the world were in Jerusalem for that feast, providentially gathered there in order to be transformed and commissioned by Jesus to represent him to the nations. Parthians, Medes, Elamites, residents of Mesopotamia, Egypt, Libya plus Arabs all heard the Galilean disciples of Jesus speaking the wonders of God in their own tongues. There is only one conclusion to draw from that assembling of people for Pentecost – God desires people from those national heritages, and more, to know that he is their God also.

Kissing Cousins?

Chapter 12 Delightful Kids

For some while, during the process of writing this book, the themes of "submission" and "intimacy with God", plus concerns about more negative aspects of "religion", tended to buzz both day and night around my head. Imagine my delight, then, in rediscovering James' strong but balanced exhortation:

> Submit yourselves therefore to God.
> Resist the devil and he will flee from you.
> Draw near to God and he will draw near to you. (James 4:7)

In his introduction to troubled believers in Jesus, James appears to have covered all the angles I was thinking about. He commands his readers to submit to God. He offers them the possibility of Christian living, free from molestation by the devil. He holds high before them the prospect of personal intimacy with God.

James begins by issuing his call for a willed submission to God. True Christian living, in a frequently hostile environment, finds its starting point in yielding to God. Alec Motyer draws out the significance of the Greek verb *hypotassô*, "to submit":

> The English translation *submit* does not do full justice to the Greek it translates, chiefly because some ways in which we use the idea of submission point to the end of struggling and the onset of passivity. In this way, we "submit" to superior forces: further resistance is useless. For the duration of the war we will stand idly by as prisoners of the enemy. But the word James uses is much more an "enlistment" word, the taking up of allegiance to a great superior in order to engage in the fight under his banner.[251]

Willed submission finds expression in active allegiance. From James' time till today, this is a word needed to be heard by Christians who too easily separate the pietistic from the secular aspect of living. Christians tend to be strong on being still and knowing God, but not so strong on allowing such worship to infiltrate daily lifestyle and living. The faith of Islam, surely, holds up a mirror or a reminder to all observers that strongly reflects this requirement of the living God. Submission, for Muslims, is the essential expression of what living before God means. Yielding to God involves active living in his will. Christians might perceive Islam's presence in the world today as part of God's reminder to them.

At the same time, James holds out the prospect of intimacy in any relationship between God and his people. Drawing near to God is possible and when sought, it provokes a counter drawing near by God to the believer. A dance of the heart may occur that brings the divine and the human together – a dance that is not only proposed as a possibility, but that is positively commended. Christian worship that centres on confessing God's "worthship" is where God commits himself to dwell. He inhabits the praises of his people and abides in the lives of those who praise him! He wants people to meet him. Sharing the knowledge of God in this sense of personal encounter is what motivated John to write his Gospel. Christians find their starting-point and goal in the awesome mystery of being allowed to "know" God. This "angle" of relating to God is weakly allowed in Islam. It is expressed in varying degrees within the mystical strain of Islam – in the Ṣûfî heritage – but it is largely eclipsed by the normative concern for knowing and doing God's will. Muslims might perceive Christianity's presence in the world today as part of God's reminder to them of what he would really like, far beyond dutiful law-keeping.

Somewhere caught up in the processes of relationship – or more accurately, non-relationship – between the divine and the human is the devil. He is not to be scoffed at, and he is constantly taking the initiative against believers. James uses a specific word to suggest how we might best respond to the devil's initiatives. This word – "resist" – is not normally utilized to describe carrying the attack into the enemy camp, but rather to give the idea of "manning the defences". The attacking is being done by the enemy and "resisting" means holding that enemy off. Such aspiring to live in an enemy-free zone is best achieved when the resisting is sandwiched between a healthy submission to God and a hunger to know him better. James' verbs are "submit", "resist" and "draw near" – he commands all three actions! Perhaps too often the devil manages to encourage human self-willedness (as opposed to submission) on the one hand, or human distancing (as opposed to drawing near) from its creator on the other, by overemphasizing either overindulgent piety or denigrating submission. Within Christianity, nearness to God can quickly degenerate into familiar, buddy-type assumptions about God being there just to please my latest fad. Within Islam, submission to God can easily turn into a fatalistic, non-relating kind of abandonment to the divine despot's will. Whatever he wills – and we have no idea what that might be – is what will come to pass. Somehow, if the devil is to be thrown out of this equation, there needs in each faith-expression to be an appropriate tension between submission and intimacy.

"Submit", "resist", "draw near" with these words James encourages the Christian believers – most likely of Jewish background – to whom he writes. In so doing, he picks up many of the themes of this book and leads us towards our conclusion.

Close cousins?

Muslims and Christians share much. They really are "cousins". They each believe that God is sole creator and sustainer of the universe. He is a God who has made himself and his will known to humankind. Humanity is, in both faiths, a special creation, different from animals and angels. Humans have the duty and honour of worshipping God, of acknowledging him for who he is, and of obeying him. People are endowed with moral responsibility for their actions, as they govern the world on God's behalf, in trust. They possess the privilege of petition. Along with Jews, Muslims and Christians gratefully acknowledge their springing from a common Abrahamic tradition. Jerusalem is venerated as a holy place in all three religions. Weekly communal prayer follows on, between them, from Friday to Saturday to Sunday. The Day of Judgement looms large in all three faiths, especially in Islam and Christianity. Moucarry suggests that Islam seems to have some emphases in common with Judaism and some with Christianity – thus potentially possessing a kind of "best of both worlds" richness (see Figure 91).[252]

Figure 91
Judaism, Islam and Christianity

Topic	Judaism	Islam	Christianity
Law	strict criminal law but lax moral code	all-embracing code of law neither too hard nor too easy	lenient criminal code but strict moral code
God	cannot name him; is one	can name him; is one	can name him; is three-in-one
Jesus	is not Messiah is not Son of God	is Messiah is not Son of God	is Messiah is Son of God
Hereafter	not a major concern	balance between life on earth and afterlife	earthly sacrifices for heavenly blessings

The Roman Catholic Church, via "Vatican II", stated its revised understanding of the common ground between Islam and Christianity in the following manner:

> The Church has also a high regard for the Muslims. They worship God, who is one, living and subsistent, merciful and almighty, the Creator of heaven and earth, who has also spoken to men. They strive to submit themselves without reserve to the hidden decrees of God, just as Abraham submitted himself to God's plan, to whose faith Muslims eagerly link their own. Although not acknowledging him as God, they worship Jesus as a prophet, his virgin Mother they also honour, and even at times devoutly invoke. Further, they await the day of judgment and the reward of God following the resurrection of the dead. For this reason they highly

esteem an upright life and worship God, especially by way of prayer, alms-deeds and fasting.

Over the centuries many quarrels and dissensions have arisen between Christians and Muslims. The sacred Council now pleads with all to forget the past, and urges that a sincere effort be made to achieve mutual understanding; for the benefit of all men, let them together preserve and promote peace, liberty, social justice and moral values.[253]

There are common features at a belief level for Muslims and Christians that give rise to shared attitudes: worship, thankfulness, asking for forgiveness, seeking to obey and so on. The idea that the future is not totally controllable, that creation reflects God's nature, that humans will be held accountable for their lives – such ideas bring Muslims and Christians together in contrast to many others in today's world. Even at the level of convictions about "salvation history", Vatican II took a fairly radical stance:

> Finally, those who have not yet received the Gospel are related to the people of God in various ways ... [The] plan of salvation also includes those who acknowledge the Creator, in the first place amongst whom are the Muslims: these profess to hold the faith of Abraham, and together with us they adore the one, merciful God, mankind's judge on the last day.[254]

As cousin-faiths, Islam and Christianity face many similar issues. This book has been deliberately constructed around some of those issues in an attempt to show that underneath the surface both faiths have had to wrestle with equivalent tensions or degrees of emphasis. So, for example, the continuity/discontinuity debate is one that is discernible in the histories of both faiths' development. How does a faith relate to the past of the people by whom it is being embraced? How do you make relevant that faith to a new community or audience? How do you decide what needs to be retained or transformed or dropped as new members join your community of faith? How do you persist with integrity in keeping unpalatable aspects of what is "on offer" in view, while trying to make as easy as possible a transition for a potential believer? At such frontiers of faith or faith-sharing, the continuity/discontinuity tension is one that both faith communities have to deal with.

Islam and Christianity each want to relate the mystery of a self-revealing God to a non-listening, human-focused world. The delicate relationship between the secular and the sacred is one that Islam has tried to maintain within a holistic view of "faith". God has a view on all of life, so that agreeing in practice with that view becomes humankind's essential expression of worship. Yet Islam has also allowed a strong mystical tradition of personal piety and non-worldliness to retain a place at the heart of its self-expression. Christianity, by contrast, has tended to separate what is God's from what is Caesar's, allowing for a deep individual piety to mould myriad different approaches to being "Christian". Yet Christianity has also constructed and paraded its concept of "Christendom", a secular society brought under the control of religious purpose and sanction. Today, Christians face the task of being "public" about this faith in a secular environment.

Islam and Christianity have both had to face up to the matter of relating "truth" to "power". "Medina" and "Milvian Bridge" constituted avenues for reconstructing growing faiths, that until then had been counter-cultural and minority-oriented, into ones that suddenly became the official religions of the politically powerful. How different was Christianity after Constantine, and how complex was the fallout from the use of imperial authority to decree resolutions to questions of faith! How different was Islam after *hijra*, and especially after Karbalâ'! The expectation that God was with the powerful promoted much unlovely behaviour in the name of religion and also left out in the cold fellow religionists who could not go along with the majority view. In both faiths, theologies seceding from "orthodoxy" seem to have become the flags of ethnic or clan-based groups trying to say: "We are not you. We will not be dictated to by you – but we are still valid Christians or Muslims!"

Of course, both Islam and Christianity are missionary faiths. The former sees the world in terms of *dâr al-Islâm* and *dâr al-Ḥarb* – the "house of Islam" where the Islamic faith holds sway and the "house of war" where power is in the hands of non-Muslims. The other sees the world in terms of Jerusalem, Judaea, Samaria and the ends of the earth. The duty incumbent upon the followers of each faith is to bring the whole world under the aegis of God's rule. For Muslims, that entails the establishment of God's law, *sharî'a*, for all people. A new "beyond nationality" community will emerge – the *umma*. For Christians, that involves the establishment of the kingdom of God among all tribes and nations. A new "beyond nationality" community will emerge – the church. And here we begin to shift into those areas where Islam and Christianity do not find themselves cosy or sharing things in common.

Cool cousins?

Christians and Muslims own faiths that are essentially constructed in ways very different from one another. Worship and obedience are highly valued in both religious expressions, but what is meant by worship and obedience is unique to each tradition. In Islam, worship and obedience tend to find focus in an *islâm* or "submission" that is expressed in living by God's laws. In Christianity, worship and obedience tend to find focus in "knowing God" and living out his desires through his direct strengthening of the believer. There are different doctrines of God in the two faiths, and contrasting interpretations as to what the expression "one" means when applied to the godhead. For Islam, God is the Master or Sovereign, infinitely powerful, whose mystery is beyond human comprehension. For Christianity, God is three-in-one, a mystery, but somehow powerfully expressive of divinity in relationship. There are alternative views concerning man's nature and relationship with his creator. Islam knows a kind of "bias to the good" and Christianity a "bias towards evil" in their different understandings of man's make-up. The Muslim is God's servant, representing his Lord in the world. The Christian is God's friend, saved by the Son's suffering on his behalf. The diagnoses of "what has gone wrong" between God and man are contrasting, and so, therefore, are the remedies put forward for effecting divine–human reconciliation. Forgiveness takes on a different nuance in each faith. "Salvation" finds its focus in different approaches to the "putting right" of humankind with God. For Muslims, knowledge leads a person to repentance and living in the way that pleases God. For Christians, conviction leads a person to repentance and renewal in a relationship with God.

Jesus is Messiah to both faiths but what that means within each construct is very different. Prophets walk onto the historical stage in both religions, but what are they there for? And how do they convey God's concerns to their contemporaries? Word of God "sent down" or "come down" produces alternative views of scripture – is the text an end in itself or does it bear witness to Another? While the cross of Christ is central and pivotal for Christianity, the divine diversion from it constitutes the action consistent with God's will in Islam. Christ is, in Christianity, the perfect Son of Man who in crucifixion becomes victimized by the sword. Muḥammad, in carrying the sword for the sake of peace, wants to finish off the enemies of his God. Maybe one could say that in Jesus Christ, peace finds expression in a bias towards mercy while in Prophet Muḥammad peace finds expression in a bias towards justice. The latter wants to put things right – with an emphasis on external acts – while the former wants to make things right – with an emphasis on internal transactions. Cragg offers the following suggestion:

> I suppose it would be right to say that the central controversy between Islam and Christianity has to do with the distancing or otherwise between the divine and the human. It is this which pervades all the themes of revelation, prophetic vocation, the ways of divine mercy, the categories of law and love, the degree of *kenosis* (or self-emptying) in creation itself on God's part, and the question of Jesus and the cross.[255]

The "cousins", by this reading, do not see "eye to eye" very much at all.

In any relating of "cousins" – of Muslims and Christians – it is important that each be true to his or her own faith. Pretending to be other than truly Muslim or Christian only confuses the opposite cousin. Duncan B. Macdonald's words, written several decades ago to address a situation in which Muslim–Christian relations were sometimes characterized by exceedingly hostile language, still convey a valid point about the manner of appropriate relating across the religious divide. Macdonald is speaking about the necessary attitude of the Christian "missionary" when faced with the "certainty" that is Islam:

> First and always, he must be explicitly and exactly Christian in his attitude and confession in every sense – theological, moral, social – of the much used and abused word "Christian." The more explicit he is that he accepts the exact Christian faith, the better the Moslem will understand him and the more he will respect him. This, the Moslem will say, is an honest and faithful enemy; no crypto-Moslem but a theologian who knows and confesses his own faith.[256]

Deceit, deliberate or mistakenly intentioned, can be no part of Christian relating to Muslim. Faithfulness to one's confession is a non-negotiable maxim in order for cousins of integrity to be able to relate honestly to one another.

At the same time, it is necessary not to idealize the other's faith. While it is right to compare the "best" with the "best", it is not helpful to domesticate the other's religious convictions to one's own way of looking at life. Christian–Muslim relationships in the world at large today are not good. Indeed they are exceedingly painful. At a political level, continuing clashes of civilizations embracing Christians and Muslims appear to be a norm in too many areas of the world. At a dialogue level, it has constantly to be asked, "Who is speaking for whom?" in such processes. Otherwise, false conclusions may be drawn from individual interpretations that do not represent the normative, historic faith-commitments of their respective constituencies. Part of the uncomfortable reality today is that Christians are frustrated by the Muslim refusal properly to engage in apologetics – especially within a Western intellectual context. And Muslims are exceedingly frustrated by the seeming world domination of a "Christian", Western, secular humanist worldview. Representatives of both faiths have questions of each other's attitude towards violence. Muslims and Christians alike have strong reservations about the role ascribed to women in the other's societal make-up. It would not be right to pretend that such frustrations, questions or reservations do not exist. Ways need to be found for representatives of each faith to be able, with respect, to hold one another accountable and to interrogate each other's unquestioned assumptions.

Cousins in trouble

One important element of both Christian and Muslim faith, at which we have not yet really looked in depth, but raised by our quotation from James' letter, is the world of the devil – or concepts of evil. I have left this matter to the final chapter for a reason. Often, in my view, the devil has been brought into the discussion far too early. Historically, and contemporaneously, language about the devil's involvement in the inspiration of Muḥammad or the actions in the world of twenty-first-century Western Christians has served as a blind. If the opposing camp is quickly demonized (literally!), then what chance is there of standing back from the disappointments and frustrations of Muslim–Christian relating and seeing the wood for the trees? Proclaiming Muḥammad as "Mahound" or the United States of America as "the Great Satan" has hardly helped to encourage mutual understanding or positive international relationships.

According to Islam, Satan was the first creature to disobey God and lead a rebellion against his creator, long before the creation of man. That disobedience of Iblîs is seen as the source of evil among humanity. Iblîs cannot bring himself to agree with God's high estimate of the worth of humankind:

> Behold! thy Lord said
> To the angels: "I am about
> To create man, from sounding clay,
> From mud moulded into shape;
> When I have fashioned him
> (In due proportion) and breathed
> Into him of My spirit,

Fall ye down in obeisance
Unto him."
So the angels prostrated themselves,
All of them together:
Not so Iblis: he refused to be
Among those who prostrated themselves. (Sura 15:28–31)

Iblîs refused to prostrate to a mortal because he saw himself as superior – being constructed from fire or light – to one made out of mere mud. Maybe also, Iblîs saw himself as superior to those other angels who did prostrate to Adam. What Iblîs misread was the fact that with the mud had been mixed God's spirit. Through God's design, the resulting "man" constituted an appropriate *khalîfa* or vice-regent to represent him on earth. Iblîs seriously miscalculated what the sovereign God intended. As a result, God rejected and cursed the "failed" angel, though at Iblîs' request God gave him respite until the day of resurrection (Sura 15:34–38). Iblîs, in the qur'ânic telling, becomes the arch-enemy of humankind from the time of creation onwards. Through a process of deceit he manages to seduce Adam and Hauwa (Eve) in the garden:

> When God settled Adam and his offspring … and forbade him the tree, it was a tree whose branches were entangled, and which has fruit which the angels eat for their eternity; this was the fruit which God had forbidden Adam and his wife. When Iblîs desired to make them slip, he entered into the belly of the serpent. Now the serpent had four legs, as if it had been a Bactrian camel, one of the most beautiful beasts God had created. When the serpent entered the Garden, Iblîs came out of its belly, took from the tree which God had forbidden Adam and his wife, and brought it to Eve. He said: "Look at this tree! How fragrant it is, how delicious it is, what a beautiful colour it has!"[257]

The progenitors of the human race are thus distracted from walking the straight path. Satan, the power of evil, is central to the whole drama of disobedience and directly responsible for the "fall". Adam and Hauwa, having realized their "sin" or "mistake", ask for forgiveness and are pardoned. Indeed, Adam is made the first messenger of God on earth. All are banned from the garden – Adam, Hauwa and Iblîs – while Iblîs and humankind are destined to be continual adversaries of one another (Sura 7:24).[258]

In Islam, Satan is not presented as a direct contestant against God. He features, rather, as a contestant against humanity. Humanity becomes the battlefield for Satan's opposing of God. Humankind is, as we have seen, composed of two elements – putrid clay and God's spirit – and Satan attacks both elements. The straight path deliberately constitutes a way that provides for the positive development of both aspects of man's make-up: it trains him, for example, in piety of spirit and it also gives him instructions for the conduct of warfare. In either area, he can be seduced by the devil into error.

For Islam, there is a strong concern to declare the contained nature of Satan's ability to oppose God. It is certainly disallowed that a mere angel could oppose what God commands and get away with it. Iblîs is limited in his sphere of activity. He does not act against God in the heavenlies, he does not meddle in the natural world. His sphere of operation is confined to humankind. But there he has a massive effect. His role is so strong that it would seem to remove a considerable degree of responsibility from Adam and Eve themselves for their falling short of what God desired for them. It is against humankind that Satan is pitted. Everywhere in the human realm one may discern the activity of Satan. Perhaps this kind of concept of "evil" explains the pervasive awareness that many Muslims have of different manifestations of (mostly evil) spiritual beings and powers.[259] Their everyday world is "peopled" with hostile spirit beings and rocked by unseen forces that constantly rob them of emotional stability and peace of mind. If humankind is designated the battlefield for Satan's opposition to God's will, then the world of folk Islam illustrates how aggressively and enthusiastically Satan has taken to battling there among the sons and daughters of Adam and Eve. In consequence, most Muslims look for rescue from an external foe far more than they sense the need for redemption from internal "sinfulness". The encroachment upon their lives of the "powers of darkness" constitutes their spiritual Achilles' heel.

The Bible, subtly but clearly, offers hints of a pre-Adamic angelic rebellion against God:

> How you have fallen from heaven,
> O morning star, son of the dawn!
> You have been cast down to the earth,
> you who once laid low the nations!
> You said in your heart,
> "I will ascend to heaven;
> I will raise my throne
> above the stars of God;
> I will sit enthroned on the mount of assembly,
> on the utmost heights of the sacred mountain.
> I will ascend above the tops of the clouds;
> I will make myself like the Most High."
> But you are brought down to the grave,
> to the depths of the pit. (Isaiah 14:12–15)

"Lucifer" (Latinized version of "light-bearer") is here described as being thrown out of heaven, disgraced and judged for his egotistic attempt to displace his creator and Lord. On the earth, and among human beings, "Satan" opposes what God would like to accomplish in the hearts and minds of those made in his image and likeness. The root of the word "Satan" in Hebrew means "one who opposes, obstructs, or acts as adversary". Its Greek counterpart, *diabolos* or "devil", literally means "one who throws something across one's path". Perhaps the most significant aspect of this personal opponent of God and meddler in God's creation is that he constitutes a former friend, a previous insider, an "intimate enemy".[260] Satan evidently encouraged other rebels, for he is spoken of elsewhere as commanding "spiritual hosts of wickedness in heavenly places" (Ephesians 6:12). Such spirit beings contrive to oppose God throughout the created realm, seeking to destroy all that is good. They target humanity, from the "serpent in the garden" episode to the cataclysmic battle of Armageddon. Yet, they and their leader have been completely disenfranchised by the cross of Christ. That was their "hour" and they thought they had won. Death for Jesus, however, was the designated pathway to resurrection and complete triumph over the worst that the devil could throw at him. So strong has been the disarming of the forces of evil that Christians "resisting" them can see them flee, Christians exorcising them from others' lives can see them depart, Christians invoking Christ's death and resurrection can see them banished.

The worldview of the Bible freely acknowledges the reality of evil, of a personal devil, of hordes of demons and powerful authorities that contest individuals and nations with God. A Christian, however, is given authority in Christ over all such evil forces, despite them being frightening and strong.

Elaine Pagels makes the suggestion that the history of "Satan" as an "intimate enemy" or former insider significantly informs the way in which the four Gospels are constructed (see Figure 92). She claims to be able to trace within them what she labels "the social history of Satan" – the manner in which the evangelists' various depictions of the devil correlate with a process of increasing conflict between Jesus and his disciples and those opposing them. Various Jewish individuals and groups are gradually and increasingly identified as being the devil's children or as even being possessed by him. Those groups constitute "intimate enemies", Jews who should really recognize Messiah, but who tragically set themselves in opposition to him. In a real sense, in Pagels' view, human beings are portrayed in the Gospels as doing the devil's work for him.

Pagels goes on to point out ways in which, after Pentecost, Gentile converts to Christ facing Roman persecution claimed to be able to discern Satan and his demonic forces at work among their persecutors and their political masters.[261] She further suggests that in succeeding centuries, "orthodox" Christian leaders tended to demonize "heretics", identifying their opponents as tools of the devil.

Pagels' analysis is intended as a "human" rationalization of language about the devil in scripture. I personally choose to believe that language about Satan reflects ontological reality: he really does exist and he really does oppose all that God is and does. The Gospels, by my reading, reflect an increasing tempo of deliberate opposition to Jesus in which the devil inspires and

Figure 92
Elaine Pagels' "social history of Satan" in the four Gospels

Gospel	"The Jews" as "intimate enemy"
Mark	at the beginning, Jesus challenges the powers of evil increasing conflict with "the scribes", then Pharisees and Herodians at the end, crowds of his own people persuade reluctant Romans to execute Jesus
Matthew	at Jesus' birth, Herod (equivalent, ironically, to Pharaoh) and "all Jerusalem" including "chief priests and scribes" are troubled Pharisees, primary antagonists of Jesus, are labelled "sons of hell" Jewish authorities are accused of bribing the Roman authorities with a false story about the disappearance of Jesus' body from the tomb
Luke	all Jesus' townspeople attempt to destroy Jesus at the beginning of his ministry Satan enters Judas and the crucifixion is set in motion. Chief priests, temple officers and elders are identified by Jesus with "the power of darkness" in Gethsemane
John	"temptations": the devil's role is taken by "the people", by members of Jesus' audience, and by Jesus' own brothers Satan appears incarnate in Judas Iscariot, then in the Jewish authorities and finally in "the Jews"

may seek to possess human beings in order to undo the Father's purposes through his Son. Pagels' careful "alternative version", nevertheless, serves as an urgent warning to all of us to resist "socializing" Satan, especially in terms of frustration with an "intimate enemy". Anti-Semitism, as it has often been expressed through the Christian centuries, might be seen as a likely result if the interraction of Jesus with "the Jews" of his day becomes recast in the manner that Pagels suggests. Certainly in the historical relationship of Christianity with Islam, the temptation to demonize the other has often been yielded to by each party. Perhaps that very fact serves to confirm the relatedness of the two faiths – the hostility is one of "intimate enemies".

Cousins in defence

There is a significant though hard-to-acknowledge way in which the faiths of Christianity and Islam are further related. They are lumped together in the perspective of those who doubt them both, who despair of them both. The cousins are seen as nuisances, maybe even as causers of awful calamity on the face of the earth. Far from bringing the "peace" that both pronounce, they have each brought the sword. Perhaps that sword-bringing has been more openly allowed as the means to justice and peace in Islam than in Christianity. But the Christian denial, throughout post-Constantinian history, of Christ's commitment to non-violence makes that faith's sword-taking the more reprehensible. What has resulted, either way, is something judged as doubt-worthy. It is with a sense of shocked disbelief that outsiders look into the source text of each religion and find recorded there the justification – in the name of God – for terrible violence:

> I doubt that God orders us to kill disobedient children, requires that we stone to death people who gather sticks on the Sabbath, sends she-bears out to maul boys who insult a prophet, or rejoices at reducing the chosen people to cannibalism, as the Hebrew Scriptures claim. I doubt that God zapped a couple who withheld a portion of their land sale, that Jesus will cast those who don't bear fruit into a fire, or that love of enemies can be reconciled with the Lamb who will return to oversee the destruction of much of humanity at the end time, as the New Testament writers claim. I doubt that those who fail to assist orphans will soon be enduring a blazing fire, that Allah punishes disobedience by causing droughts, or that Allah wants thieves to have their hands cut off, as the Quran says.[262]

This is uncomfortable territory. Especially when a lot of the religio-political violence going on in the world today is evidently motivated by interpretations of Torah, Qur'ân and Bible! Gilles Kepel, in his book *The Revenge of God*, traces the resurgence of Judaism, Islam and Christianity in their more "fundamentalist" aspects from the 1970s onwards. Kepel uncovers a common process of change, initiated by members of each of those faith communities, during the last third of the twentieth century. Such change has largely proceeded via a two-pronged strategy of seizing power "from above" (by attempting, for example, to capture the Knesset in Israel or the machinery of government in Iran or the White House in America) and promoting a sacralizing of people from below (by making religious values or ideals the new definer of "normal" society).[263] From a very different perspective, Huntington underlines the force of Kepel's conclusions with his own conviction that the twenty-first century is fated to be the period during which an intensive "clash of civilizations" will dominate world affairs. He identifies seven or eight such civilizations into which the world today is largely divided. We have earlier alluded to his claim that in the constitution of each civilization, religion plays a major role. Huntington asserts:

> Of all the objective elements which define civilizations, however, the most important usually is religion ... To a very large degree, the major civilizations in human history have been closely identified with the world's great religions; and people who share ethnicity and language but differ in religion may slaughter each other, as happened in Lebanon, the former Yugoslavia, and the Subcontinent.[264]

The *Gush Emunîm* in Israel, the Islamists of both Sunnî and Shî^c^a variety and the dispensationalist, Christian Zionists of America constitute strong, if minority, voices in their respective "civilizations". Each promote violence in the name of God.

Whether in more extreme manifestation, or just for being people with a strong allegiance to "suspect" scripture, religious cousins – Muslims and Christians – are today being tarred with the same brush. We are both subject to strong accusation in which our respective views of God are each being impugned by non-believers. Hearing this critical outside voice drives us together in a "back against the wall" sort of way. We find ourselves "in the dock" together. But does it help us take a long look at ourselves and at our constructs on faith and reality? Does it humble us at all?

> The violence-of-God traditions at the heart of the Bible and the Quran have invaded our own hearts. By sanctioning violence in "sacred" texts and in reference to them, we invariably progress along a treacherous pathway. God is powerful and proves to be God through superior violence. The God of superior violence justifies human violence in the name of God and in pursuit of God's objectives that with frightening regularity mirror our own objectives. In the end, violence replaces or becomes God.[265]

It seems to me that any desire to reply on my own behalf – and I do want to make reply as a Christian and trustee of the Bible – must push me to allow a Muslim to make reply on his behalf, from within his own view of his faith. If I want to say, "Well, really what is being expressed in these scriptures is such-and-such", then I must allow the same for a guardian of those other scriptures. The truth is that there is a debate to be had within each religious community today as to what Christianity or Islam means. Within each faith-expression, competing views as to its essence or true meaning are a mark of internal dissension and argument – that critical, internal wrestling for the "soul" of Christianity or Islam is something further that both faiths have in common at the beginning of the twenty-first century.

Cousins in the dock, as it were, might be a healthy place for us to be if we can acknowledge from within it that there truly are some issues at the heart of our own believing that are difficult to comprehend. Could we be cousins in honest doubting? "Trinity" is a concept that scripture leads us Christians to embrace, but how to understand or explain that concept is not an easy task! Similarly with the 99 divine names – do they describe God's essence or do they describe his qualities, separate from his essence? The orthodox Muslim view is that the qualities are not the essence, nor even "entities" in the essence (thus avoiding any hint of multiplicity in God), yet they are not separate from the essence of who God is. If you can follow such a contorted sentence, you'll probably agree that we are again referring to a paradox! Christian scripture is received and believed as God-sourced, and yet it is subject to frail human processes of composition, collection and passing on. There are missing fragments of sentences and words that do not make sense in what is owned as text authored by God. The uncreatedness of the Qur'ân as *kalâm Allâh* or eternal speech of God is a concept that is claimed from within that sacred text, yet how an uncreated "word" can remain disassociated from the eternal God is a mystery. Any hint in this of the sin of *shirk*, of associating something with God, is nevertheless carefully avoided. Somehow Jesus Christ is both fully divine and fully human. In explanation of that claim, the *Logos* concept is sometimes employed to describe the pre-existent Christ. Is not the relationship between *Logos* and Jesus somewhat parallel to that between *kalâm Allâh* and Qur'ân? Often, all we seem to have been able to do, as Christian or Muslim, is to say, "Well, not that ... not this ..." before such imponderables. Somehow man is made of base clay and divine spirit, yet without the end-product manifesting a likeness to God; so "what" is man like if he is no longer like mud? And how do we deal with the "violence-of-God" traditions that are endemic to our sacred texts yet unacceptable to our contemporary critics?

Cragg calls us to a humility and openness in our Christian relating to people of other faiths. After all, we all have to live with imponderables, so why not offer what we have and know, and leave the rest in God's hands? He asks whether we might find that though our "theology" cannot quite embrace all that "God" seems to be involved in, our faith can:

> Ought we to be ready for a less secured position, to be freer from moorings that reassure and more ready for the open deep? Perhaps in the end our situation calls for a capacity to hold together the finality of loyalty to Christ and the will to "concede" the other faiths, without asking for an answer how ... Would it be

better to live imaginatively with unanswered questions, rather than gather them into a commendable framework of answer that may still do violence to the ways of the Spirit?[266]

Martin Luther (original in his own day for supporting the humanist Theodore Bibliomander in publishing a Latin translation of the Qur'ân) challenged his contemporaries to think differently about the Muslims with whose imperial expansion they were having to come to terms. Luther's interpretation of the eighth commandment might be seen as especially relevant for this difficult process. That Sinaitic command forbids any bearing of false witness against a neighbour. Luther explained the import of this requirement in the following terms:

> We must fear and love God, so that we will not deceive by lying, betraying, slandering or ruining our neighbour's reputation, but will defend him, say good things about him, and see the best side of everything he does.[267]

Relating appropriately to Islam and to Muslims – our near neighbours in faith – is a serious responsibility of Christians today, just as it was in Luther's time. Such relating does not need to compromise our convictions about the authority of the Bible or the uniqueness of Christ. After all, Luther in his day was strongly "reformist" in his theological convictions! But some of us Christians today have to learn from the Spirit of God new ways of being neighbourly if the vicious cycle of mistrust and misrepresentation between Muslims and Christians in current times is to lessen. We would do well to reflect the generous spirit of that strongly "Protestant" theologian in his call to true neighbourliness.[268]

Cousins in silence

When all is said and done, it is hard to allow God to have the last word. We have spent this book analyzing what human beings mean by religion, by concepts of "God", "scripture", "prophethood" and so on. Actually, in both faiths, if one accepts that the initiator of revelation is God himself, his agenda must be allowed to take precedence. Here, I cannot speak for Islam but only as a Christian. In an Old Testament book that conveys a sense of God as "lover" and "redeemer" of a disobedient and callously unfaithful people, strong words are used about God's perspective on prophethood and scripture:

> Therefore I cut you in pieces with my prophets,
> I killed you with the words of my mouth ... (Hosea 6:5)

In the divine view expressed here, prophets are like a meat cleaver and scripture is a killing machine. Prophets and scripture are dangerous, lethal instruments. They constitute *God's* ways of communicating with fickle humanity, and they are invested with his authority and intention. They also belong only to him: "*my* prophets ... words of *my* mouth ... " This is the God of *ḥesed*-love speaking, the God of faithful, covenantal relationship. If that is how *he* speaks of prophets and scripture, how carefully do we need to come to these matters and evaluate them! The most we can do is offer some thoughts, praying that God will not find them unfaithful.

So we'll let God have the last word about "kissing". In a messianic psalm describing the enthronement of a Davidic king, God speaks to the nations, to kings and rulers of the earth. His command to them is that they serve Yahweh with fear and rejoice with trembling. In the "multi-faith" world of that day, Israel's God claims universality of sovereignty and demands due honour from all on earth. His urgent demand is that Messiah be properly greeted, appropriately acknowledged by all. "Kiss the Son," he says, "lest he be angry ... " (Psalm 2:12). Such is the desire of the creator of all: Messiah is for all.

For those of us who are sure today that we are insiders, friends or servants of the Son of God, followers of Messiah, there comes an awful warning – also wrapped up in a kiss. Ironically, those who think they know best about God, those who spend time with Jesus, can sometimes discover themselves disowning him. Perhaps they grow disillusioned that the Messiah does not exactly fit their idea of whom he should be or what he should be doing. Perhaps they get caught up in their own agenda for what faith should be about, how it should be lived and propagated. It was, after all, a convinced insider who became the target of that poignant accusation: "Judas, are you betraying the Son of Man with a kiss?" (Luke 22:48).

What kind of "kissing cousin" are you and I?

"Let us pray"

We end our exploration of Islam and Christianity with prayer – from each tradition. If such petitions mean anything, then surely it must be possible for Muslims and Christians, by the grace of God, to become less distant relatives.

O God, thou art peace.
From thee is peace and unto thee is peace.
Let us live, our Lord, in peace and receive us in thy paradise,
the abode of peace.
Thine is the majesty and the praise.
We hear and we obey.
Grant us thy forgiveness, Lord, and unto thee be our becoming.
(Prayer at the close of formal *ṣalât*)[269]

Lord, make me an instrument of thy peace.
Where there is hatred, let me bring love:
where there is injury, pardon:
where there is doubt, faith:
where there is despair, hope:
where there is darkness, light:
where there is sadness, joy:
and all for thy mercy's sake.
(Prayer attributed to Francis of Assisi)

Appendices

Appendix 1 Transliteration

A considerable number of non-English terms appear throughout this book. Italics have been used to indicate that a word is a transliteration, and does not appear as an English word in standard dictionaries. Some proper nouns have not been transliterated strictly, in order to ease reading. A glossary of all italicized transliterations is given in Appendix 3.

Most of the terms employed occur in Arabic. A standard form of transliteration, set out in Figure 93, has been used to render all Arabic expressions in English. A few words, such as "Qur'ân" and "*ḥadîth*", which do feature in some English dictionaries, are transliterated in this text.

A short list, explaining some of the more significant, historical, Muslim names and movements, is also given at the end of the glossary in Appendix 3.

Figure 93
Transliteration and pronunciation of Arabic alphabet

ARABIC NAME	SIGN USED	ENGLISH PRONUNCIATION WHERE UNCLEAR
hamza	'	glottal stop, as "a" in "apple"
âlif	*a*	
bâ'	*b*	
tâ'	*t*	
thâ'	*th*	as in "think"
jîm	*j*	
ḥâ'	*ḥ*	(aspirated)
khâ'	*kh*	as in German "Nacht"

dâl	*d*	
dhâl	*dh*	as in "this"
râ'	*r*	
zâ'	*z*	
sîn	*s*	
shîn	*sh*	as in "shoe"
ṣâd	*s*	(velarized)
ḍâd	*d*	(velarized)
ṭâ'	*t*	(velarized)
ẓâ'	*z*	(velarized)
ʿayn	ʿ	voiced counterpart of *ḥâ'*
ghayn	*gh*	similar to throaty French "r"
fâ'	*f*	
qâf	*q*	(uvular) as "k", not "kw"
kâf	*k*	(palatal)
lâm	*l*	
mîm	*m*	
nûn	*n*	
hâ'	*h*	
wâw	*w*	
yâ'	*y*	
âlif yâ	*ay*	(diphthong)
âlif wâw	*aw*	(diphthong)
tâ' marbûṭa	*a*	
unmarked (short) vowels are:	*a*	as in "had"
	i	as in "sit"
	u	as in "fruit"
vowels with a circumflex above are long:	*â*	as in "aah"
	î	as in "eee"
	û	as in "ooo"

Appendix 2 An Introductory Bibliography

ᶜAbdul-Ahad, Selim and Gairdner, W.H.T. *The Gospel of Barnabas: An Essay and Inquiry*. Henry Martyn Institute of Islamic Studies: Hyderabad, 1975.

Adelphi, Ghiyathuddin and Hahn, Ernest. *The Integrity of the Bible according to the Qur'an and the Hadith*. Henry Martyn Institute of Islamic Studies: Hyderabad, 1977.

Ahmed, Akbar S. *Living Islam: From Samarkand to Stornoway*. Penguin Books: London, 1993.

Andrae, Tor. *Mohammed: The Man and his Faith* (trans. Theophil Menzel). George Allen & Unwin: London, 1936.

Armstrong, Karen. *Muhammad: A Western Attempt to Understand Islam*. Victor Gollancz: London, 1991.

ᶜAta ur-Rahim, Muhammad. *Jesus – a Prophet of Islam*. MWH: London, 1977.

Aydin, Mehmet. "The Concepts of Man and Society in Islam." In *Newsletter*, Centre for the Study of Islam and Christian–Muslim Relations: Birmingham, no. 17/18 (1987), pp. 9–23.

Ayoub, Mahmoud M. "Roots of Muslim–Christian Conflict." In *Muslim World*, vol. 79 (1989), pp. 25–45.

Azhar, Ahmad D. *Christianity in History*. Sh. Muhammad Ashraf: Lahore, 1968.

Badawi, M.A. Zaki. *Islam in Britain (A Public Lecture 1981)*. Ta Ha Publishers: London, 1981.

Bell, Steve. *Friendship First: The Manual*. Friendship First Publications: Market Rasen, 2003.

Bijlefeld, Willem A. "Christian–Muslim Relations: A Burdensome Past, a Challenging Future." In *Word & World*, vol. 16, no. 2 (1996), pp. 117–128.

Brown, David. *The Cross of the Messiah*. Sheldon Press: London, 1969.

Bucaille, Maurice (Alistair D. Pannell trans.). *The Bible, the Qur'an and Science: The Holy Scriptures Examined in the Light of Modern Knowledge*. North American Trust Publication: Indianapolis, 1978.

al-Bukhârî, Muḥammad bin Ismâʿîl bin al-Mughîrah (Khan, Muhammad Muhsin, trans). *Al-Ṣaḥîḥ*. Vols. 1–9. Kazi Publications: Chicago, 1977–79.

Burnett, David. *Clash of Worlds*. MARC: Eastbourne, 1990.

Burton, John. *The Collection of the Qur'ân*. Cambridge University Press: Cambridge, 1977.

Butrus, Zachariah. *God is One in the Holy Trinity*. Markaz al-Shabiba: Basel, n.d.

Caetani, Leone. "Uthman and the Recension of the Koran" in *The Moslem World*, vol. 5 (1915), pp. 380–390.

Campbell, William F. *The Gospel of Barnabas: Its True Value*. Christian Study Centre: Rawalpindi, 1989.

Chair, Somerset de (trans.). *The First Crusade: The Deeds of the Franks and Other Jerusalemites (Gesta francorum et aliorum hierosolimatanorum)*. Golden Cockerel Press: London, 1945.

Chapman, Colin. *Whose Promised Land?* Lion: Oxford, 2002.

Chardri. *Vie des Set Dormanz*. Brian S. Merrilees (ed.), Anglo-Norman Text Society: London, 1977.

Christensen, Jens. *The Practical Approach to Muslims*. North Africa Mission: Marseille, 1977.

Christians Meeting Muslims. WCC: Geneva, 1977.

Christian Witness Among Muslims. Africa Christian Press: Accra, 1971.

Clair-Tisdall, W. St. *The Sources of Islam* (trans. William Muir). T & T Clark: Edinburgh (1901).

Cooper, Anne. *Heart to Heart: Talking with Muslim Friends*. Word of Life: Oldham, 1997.

Cooper, Anne (comp.). *In the Family of Abraham*. People International: Tunbridge Wells, 1989.

Cragg, Kenneth. *The Call of the Minaret*. Oxford University Press: New York, 1964.

Cragg, Kenneth. *Christianity in World Perspective*. Lutterworth Press: London, 1968.

Cragg, Kenneth. *The House of Islam*. Dickenson: Encino, 1975.

Cragg, Kenneth. *Islam and the Muslim*. Open University Press: Milton Keynes, 1978.

Cragg, Kenneth. *Jesus and the Muslim: An Exploration*. George Allen & Unwin: London, 1985.

Cragg, Kenneth. *The Mind of the Qur'ân*. George Allen & Unwin: London, 1973.

Cragg, Kenneth. *Muhammad and the Christian: A Question of Response*. Orbis: New York, 1984.

Cragg, Kenneth. *Muhammad in the Qur'an: The Task and the Text*. Melisende: London, 2001.

Cragg, Kenneth. *Sandals at the Mosque*. SCM Press: London, 1959.

Cragg, Kenneth. *The Weight in the Word. Prophethood: Biblical and Quranic*. Sussex Academic Press: Brighton, 1999.

Daniel, Norman. *Islam and the West: The Making of an Image*. Oneworld: Oxford, 1993.

Dashti, 'Ali (trans. F.R.C. Bagley). *Twenty Three Years: A Study of the Prophetic Career of Mohammad*. Mazda Publishers: Costa Mesa, 1994.

Durrani, M.H. *The Qur'anic Facts about Jesus*. Noor Publishing House: Delhi, 1992.

Elder, John. *The Biblical Approach to the Muslim*. WEC: Fort Washington, 1978.

Foss, Clive. *Ephesus after Antiquity: A Late Antique Byzantine and Turkish City*. Cambridge University Press: Cambridge, 1979.

Fulcher of Chartres. *A History of the Expedition to Jerusalem: 1095–1127* (trans. Frances Rita Ryan; ed. Harold S. Fink). University of Tennessee Press: Knoxville, 1969.

Gairdner, W.H.T. *The Muslim Idea of God*. Christian Literature Society: London, 1909.

Geisler, N. and Saleeb, A. *Answering Islam: The Crescent in the Light of the Cross*. Baker Books: Grand Rapids, 1994.

George, Ron. *Issues and Insights into Church Planting in the Muslim World*. WIN Press: Crowborough, 2000.

Gilchrist, John. *Jamᶜ al-Quran: The Codification of the Qur'an Text*. TMFMT: Warley, 1989.

Glassé, Cyril. *Jesus, Son of Mary*. Altajir World of Islam Trust: London,1998.

Goddard, Hugh. *Muslim Perceptions of Christianity*. Grey Seal: London, 1995.

Goldsmith, Martin. *Islam and Christian Witness*. Hodder & Stoughton: London, 1982.

Grossfeld, Bernard (trans.). *The Two Targums of Esther: Translated, with Apparatus and Notes*. Liturgical Press: Collegeville, 1991.

Guillaume, A. *The Life of Muhammad*. A Translation of Ibn Ishaq's *Sirât Rasûl Allah*. Oxford University Press: Oxford, 1978 (first edition 1955).

Havelaar, Henriette W. (ed.). *The Coptic Apocalypse of Peter: (Nag-Hammadi-Codex VII, 3)*. Akademie Verlag: Berlin, 1999.

Hick, John (ed.). *Truth and Dialogue. The Relationship between World Religions*. Sheldon Press: London, 1974.

Hillenbrand, Carole. *The Crusades: Islamic Perspectives*. Edinburgh University Press: Edinburgh, 1999.

Hourani, Albert. *Europe and the Middle East*. Macmillan Press: London, 1980.

Houssney, Georges. "Allah: the God of Islam". In *ReachOut*, vol. 6, nos 3 and 4 (1993), pp. 3–5.

Houssney, Georges. "Pre-Islamic Gods of the Arabs." In *ReachOut*, vol. 6, nos 3 and 4 (1993), pp. 6–7.

Houssney, Georges. "What is Allah?" In *ReachOut*, vol. 6, nos 3 and 4 (1993), pp. 11–15.

Ibn Warraq (ed.). *Leaving Islam: Apostates Speak Out*. Prometheus Books: Amherst, 2003.

Ibn Warraq (ed.). *The Origins of the Koran*. Prometheus Books: Amherst, 1998.

Ibn Warraq (ed. and trans.). *The Quest for the Historical Muhammad*. Prometheus Books: Amherst, 2000.

Ibn Warraq (ed. and trans.). *What the Koran Really Says*. Prometheus Books: Amherst, 2002.

Ipema, Peter. *The Islam Interpretations of Duncan B. MacDonald, Samuel M. Zwemer, A. Kenneth Cragg and Wilfred C. Smith: An Analytical Comparison and Evaluation*. University Microfilms International: Ann Arbor, 1972.

Jacobus de Voragine. *The Golden Legend: Readings on the Saints*. Vols. 1 and 2, William Granger Ryan (trans.), Princeton University Press: New Jersey, 1995.

Jadeed, Iskander. *Sin and Atonement in Islam and Christianity*. Markaz al-Shabiba: Basel, n.d.

Jameelah, Maryam. *Islam Versus Ahl al-Kitab: Past and Present*. Taj Company: Delhi, 1989.

Jeffery, Arthur (ed.). *Materials for the History of the Text of the Qur'an: The Old Codices*. Brill: Leiden, 1937.

Jomier, Jacques (trans. John Bowden). *How to Understand Islam*. SCM Press: London, 1989.

Kateregga, Badru D. and Shenk, David W. *A Muslim and a Christian in Dialogue*. Herald Press: Scottdale, 1997.

Kerr, David A. "The Prophet Muhammad: Toward a Christian Assessment." In *Newsletter*, Centre for the Study of Islam and Christian–Muslim Relations: Birmingham, no. 17/18 (1987), pp. 24–36.

Kritzeck, James and Winder, R. Bayly (eds). *The World of Islam: Studies in Honour of Philip K. Hitti*. Macmillan: London, 1959.

Krusch, B. (ed.). *Georgius Florentius Gregorius: Passio sanctorum martyrium septem dormientium apud Ephysum*. In *Monumenta Germaniae Historica*, Scriptores rerum merovingicarum 1:2, Berlin (1885), pp. 848–853.

Küng, Hans. *Christianity and the World Religions: Paths of Dialogue with Islam, Hinduism, and Buddhism*. SCM Press: London, 1986.

La Due, William J. *The Trinity Guide to the Trinity*. Trinity Press International: Harrisburg, 2003.

Lassner, Jacob. *Demonizing the Queen of Sheba: Boundaries of Gendered Culture in Postbiblical Judaism and Medieval Islam*. University of Chicago Press: Chicago, 1993.

Leirvik, Oddbjorn. *Images of Jesus Christ in Islam*. Swedish Institute of Missionary Research: Uppsala, 1999.

Lewis, Clive Staples. *Reflections on the Psalms*. Geoffrey Bles: London, 1958.

Lewis, Philip. *Islamic Britain: Religion, Politics and Identity among British Muslims*. I.B. Tauris: London, 1994.

Lings, Martin. *Muhammad: His Life Based on the Earliest Sources.* Unwin Paperbacks: London, 1986.

Lyonnet, Stanislas. "Le Sens deèøw en Rom 5,12 et l'Exégèse des Pères Grecs" in *Biblica*, vol. 36 (1955), pp. 436–456.

Malek, Sobhi. *Islam: Introduction and Approach.* International Correspondence Unit: Irving, 1992.

Mallouhi, Christine A. *Waging Peace on Islam.* Monarch Books: London, 2000.

Manji, Irshad. *The Trouble with Islam.* Mainstream Publishing: Edinburgh, 2004.

Mark, Brother. *A "Perfect" Qur'an.* 2000.

Marsh, Charles R. *Share Your Faith with a Muslim.* Moody Press: Chicago, 1975.

Masood, Steven. *The Bible and the Qur'an.* OM Publishing: Carlisle, 2001.

Mayer, Tobias. "A Muslim Speaks to Christians". In *Encounter*, no. 297 (2003), pp. 3–9.

McCurry, Don M. (ed.). *The Gospel and Islam: A 1978 Compendium.* MARC: Monrovia, 1979.

McGinty, Martha Evelyn (trans.). *Fulcher of Chartres: Chronicle of the First Crusade (Fulcheri Carnotensis Historia Hierosolymitana).* University of Pennsylvania: Philadelphia, 1941.

Memon, Muhammad Umar. *Ibn Taimîya's Struggle against Popular Religion.* Mouton: The Hague, 1976.

Miller, William M. *A Christian's Response to Islam.* Presbyterian and Reformed Publishing: Nutley, 1977.

Moshay, G.J.O. *Who is this Allah?* Fireliners International: Ibadan, 1990.

Moucarry, Chawkat. *Faith to Faith: Christianity & Islam in Dialogue.* Inter-Varsity Press: Leicester, 2001.

Moucarry, Chawkat. *Islam and Christianity at the Crossroads.* Lion: Tring, 1988.

Moucarry, Chawkat. *The Search for Forgiveness: Pardon and Punishment in Islam and Christianity.* Inter-Varsity Press: Leicester, 2004.

Muir, William. *The Life of Mohammed.* John Grant: Edinburgh, 1923.

Muslim, Imâm. (Siddiqi, ᶜAbdul Hamîd, trans.). *Ṣaḥîḥ*. Vols. 1–4, Sh. Muhammad Ashraf: Lahore, 1976.
Nazir-Ali, Michael. *Frontiers in Muslim–Christian Encounter*. Regnum Books: Oxford, 1987.
Nazir-Ali, Michael. *Islam: A Christian Perspective*. Paternoster Press: Exeter, 1983.
Nazir-Ali, Michael. *Understanding My Muslim Neighbour*. Canterbury Press: Norwich, 2002.
Nehls, Gerhard and Eric, Walter. *A Practical and Tactical Approach to Muslim Evangelism*. Life Challenge Africa: Nairobi, 1997.
Nehls, Gerhard and Eric, Walter. *Islam as it sees itself, as others see it, as it is*. Life Challenge Africa: Nairobi, 1996.
Nehls, Gerhard and Eric, Walter. *The Islamic–Christian Controversy*. Life Challenge Africa: Nairobi, 1996.
Neusner, Jacob. *Genesis Rabba: The Judaic Commentary to the Book of Genesis. A New American Translation*. Vols 1–3, Scholars Press: Atlanta, 1985.
Pagels, Elaine. *The Origin of Satan*. Vintage Books: New York, 1995.
Parrinder, Geoffrey. *Jesus in the Qur'ân*. Oneworld: Oxford (originally 1965), 1995.
Parshall, Phil. *Bridges to Islam*. Baker Book House: Grand Rapids, 1983.
Parshall, Phil. *The Cross and the Crescent: Understanding the Muslim's Mind and Heart*. Tyndale House: Wheaton, 1989.
Parshall, Phil. *The Fortress and the Fire*. Gospel Literature Service: Bombay, 1975.
Parshall, Phil (comp.). *The Last Great Frontier*. Open Doors with Brother Andrew: Quezon City, 2000.
Parshall, Phil. *New Paths in Muslim Evangelism: Evangelical Approaches to Contextualization*. Baker Book House: Grand Rapids, 1980.
Pawson, David. *The Challenge of Islam to Christians*. Hodder & Stoughton: London, 2003.
Pfander, C.G. *The Mîzân-ul-Haqq: Balance of Truth* (revised by W. St. Clair Tisdall). Religious Tract Society: London, 1910.

Philippides, Marios (trans.). *The Fall of the Byzantine Empire: A Chronicle by George Sphrantzes*. University of Massachusetts Press: Amherst, 1980.

Ragg, Lonsdale and Laura. *The Gospel of Barnabas*. Clarendon Press: Oxford, 1907.

Register, Ray G. *Dialogue and Interfaith Witness with Muslims*. WEC: Fort Washington, 1979.

Rickards, Donald Roland. *A Study of the Quranic References to Îsa in the Light of Tafsîr and Ḥadîth*. University Microfilms International: Ann Arbor, 1969.

Riddell, Peter and Cotterell, Peter. *Islam in Conflict: Past, Present and Future*. Inter-Varsity Press: Leicester, 2003.

Rippin, Andrew (ed.). *Approaches to the History of the Interpretation of the Qur'ân*. Clarendon Press: Oxford, 1988.

Rippin, Andrew (ed.). *The Qur'an: Formative Interpretation*. Ashgate Publishing: Aldershot, 1999.

Robinson, Stuart. *Mosques and Miracles*. CityHarvest Publications: Australia, 2003.

Runciman, Steven. *The Fall of Constantinople, 1453*. Cambridge University Press: Cambridge, 1965.

Runciman, Steven. *The First Crusade*. Cambridge University Press: Cambridge, 1980.

Samartha, S.J. and Taylor, J.B. *Christian–Muslim Dialogue*. WCC: Geneva, 1973.

Schimmel, Annemarie. *And Muhammad is His Messenger: The Veneration of the Prophet in Islamic Piety*. University of North Carolina Press: Chapel Hill, 1985.

Seale, Morris S. *Muslim Theology: A Study of Origins with Reference to the Church Fathers*. Luzac: London, 1964.

Sell, Charles Edward. *The Historical Development of the Qur'án*. Marshall: London (1923) as reprinted by People International: Tunbridge Wells (n.d.).

Shah, Idries. *The Sufis*. Doubleday: New York, 1964.

Shaikh, Anwar. *Faith and Deception*. Principality Publishers: Cardiff, 1996.

Shaikh, Anwar. *Islam, Sex and Violence*. Principality Publishers: Cardiff, 1999.

Shaikh, Anwar. *Islam, the Arab Imperialism*. Principality Publishers: Cardiff, 1998.
Sheikh, Bilquis. *I Dared to Call him Father*. STL Books: Bromley, 1978.
Shorrosh, Anis A. *Islam Revealed: A Christian Arab's View of Islam*. Thomas Nelson Publishers: Nashville, 1988.
Slomp, Jan. "The 'Gospel of Barnabas' in recent research." In *Islamochristiana*, vol. 23 (1997), pp. 81–109.
Smith, Wilfred Cantwell. *The Faith of Other Men*. Harper & Row: New York, 1962.
Smith, Wilfred Cantwell. *Islam in Modern History*. Princeton University Press: Princeton, 1957.
Smith, Wilfred Cantwell. *The Meaning and End of Religion: A New Approach to the Religious Traditions of Mankind*. Mentor: New York, 1964.
Smith, Wilfred Cantwell. *On Understanding Islam: Selected Studies*. Mouton: The Hague, 1981.
Smith, Wilfred Cantwell. *What is Scripture? A Comparative Approach*. Fortress Press: Minneapolis, 1989.
Swanson, Mark N. " 'Thinking through' Islam." In *Word & World*, vol. 22, no. 3 (2002), pp. 264–274.
Sweetman, J.W. *Islam and Christian Theology*. Part Two, vol. 2. Lutterworth Press: London, 1967.
Tames, Richard. *Approaches to Islam*. John Murray: London, 1982.
Towards Understanding the Arab Israeli Conflict. British Council of Churches: London, 1982.
Troll, Christian W. "Islam as a Missionary Religion". In *Encounter*, no. 130 (1986), pp. 3–47.
Van Dam, Raymond (trans.). *Gregory of Tours: Glory of the Martyrs*. Liverpool University Press: Liverpool, 1988.
Wansbrough, John. *Quranic Studies: Sources and Methods of Scriptural Interpretation*. Oxford University Press: Oxford, 1977.
Wansbrough, John. *The Sectarian Milieu: Content and Composition of Islamic Salvation History*. Oxford University Press: Oxford, 1978.
Watt, W. Montgomery. *The Faith and Practice of Al-Ghazâlî*. George Allen and Unwin: London, 1953.

Watt, W. Montgomery. *Muhammad at Mecca*. Oxford University Press: Karachi, 1953.

Watt, W. Montgomery. *Muhammad at Medina*. Oxford University Press: Karachi, 1956.

Watt, W. Montgomery. *Muhammad: Prophet and Statesman*. Oxford University Press: Oxford, 1961.

Wiegers, Gerard. "Muhammad as the Messiah: a comparison of the polemical works of Juan Alonso with the *Gospel of Barnabas*". In *Bibliotheca Orientalis*, vol. 52, no. 3/4 (1995), pp. 245–292.

Woodberry, J. Dudley (ed.). *Muslims & Christians on the Emmaus Road*. MARC: Monrovia, 1989.

Ye'or, Bat. *The Decline of Eastern Christianity under Islam. From Jihad to Dhimmitude: Seventh–Twentieth Century*. Farleigh Dickinson University Press: Madison, 1996.

Ye'or, Bat. *Islam and Dhimmitude: Where Civilizations Collide*. Farleigh Dickinson University Press: Madison, 2002.

Young, William G. *Patriarch, Shah and Caliph: A Study of the Relationships of the Church of the East with the Sassanid Empire and the Early Caliphates up to 820 AD with Special Reference to Available Translated Syriac Sources*. Christian Study Centre: Rawalpindi, 1974.

Zakaria, Rafiq. *The Struggle Within Islam: The Conflict Between Religion and Politics*. Penguin Books: London, 1988.

Zebiri, Kate. *Muslims and Christians Face to Face*. Oneworld: Oxford, 1997.

Zwemer, Samuel M. *Arabia: The Cradle of Islam. Studies in the Geography, People and Politics of the Peninsula with an Account of Islam and Mission-work*. Oliphant Anderson and Ferrier: London, 1900.

Zwemer, Samuel M. *The Moslem Doctrine of God. An Essay on the Character and Attributes of Allah according to the Koran and Orthodox Tradition*. Oliphant, Anderson & Ferrier: London, 1905.

Zwemer, Samuel M. *The Muslim Christ*. Oliphant, Anderson & Ferrier: Edinburgh, 1912.

Appendix 3 Glossary

Some significant terms used in the text

Aggada: Jewish folklore.

Ahmadîya movement: developed in last quarter of nineteenth century in Indian Islam, named after Mirzâ Ghulâm Ahmad; viewed as "non-Islamic" in Pakistan since the Munir Report in 1954.

al-aḥruf al-sabᶜa: "the seven modes" of reading the Qur'ân.

ᶜAlids: descendants of the Prophet's cousin ᶜAlî.

amâna: the trust of the earth delegated by God to men.

Anfâl: "Spoils of War"; title of Sura 8.

Anṣâr: "Helpers"; the Muslims in Medina who welcomed the émigrés from Mecca.

ᶜaql: "reason".

ᶜAshûrâ': "the Tenth"; 10th day of Muḥarram, the first month in the Muslim calendar. On this day, Shîᶜa Muslims bring to a conclusion their annual remembrance of Ḥussein's murder at Karbalâ' with a passion play and a procession often involving acts of self-flagellation.

al-'ismâ' al-ḥusnâ: the Beautiful Names of God.

Al-Azhar: ancient university mosque in Cairo, Egypt.

aslama: "to submit".

âya: "sign" of God's work in nature; verse of the Qur'ân.

Badr: victorious battle fought by the Prophet against Quraysh in AD 624 consolidating Muḥammad's power.

bayt-Allâh: "House of God" referring to the *kaᶜba* at Mecca.

bismillâh al-Raḥmân al-Raḥîm: "In the name of Allah, most Gracious, most Merciful."

Chishti: Ṣûfî order in India tracing their origin to Abû Isḥâq who settled at Chisht in Khurasan.

christotokos: "Christ-bearer", referring to Mary.

Companions: the *aṣḥâb* or associates of the Prophet Muḥammad. The general view is that everyone who embraced Islam, saw the Prophet and accompanied him was a "Companion".

crux: "cross"; Latin.

dâr al-Ḥarb: "the House of War"; territory not under Islamic law.

dâr al-Islâm: "the House of Islam"; lands in which Islamic law prevails.

dâr al-Kufr: "the House of Unbelief"; territory not under Islamic law.

daᶜwa: "inviting".

dhikr: Ṣûfî ritual of "remembering" the names of God.

dhimmî: a non-Muslim citizen under Islamic rule.

al-dîn: "religion"; religious practice in Islam.

El: supreme god of the Canaanite pantheon.

'êl, 'elôah, 'elôhîm: God; Hebrew.

fana': "passing away"; Ṣûfî concept of annihilation.

fard: obligatory acts under Islamic Law.

al-Fâtiḥa: "Opener", opening sura of the Qur'ân.

fatwâ: legal opinion given by a jurist-theologian.

fiqh: "understanding"; applied law.

al-fiṭra: the original pattern or state of the human soul.

al-furqân: "the criterion" referring to *Torah* or Qur'ân.

Gemara: commentaries on the *Mishna*.

Gush Emunîm: "Bloc of the Faithful"; fundamentalist Zionist group in Israel.

ḥadîth: (plural *aḥadîth*) "prophetic tradition"; a short account of some word or act of Muhammad's. In its classic form it is passed on by one authority who has received it from another. The chain reaches back to an eyewitness.

ḥajj: "setting out"; pilgrimage to Mecca and surrounding holy places.

ḥalâl: "that which is loosed"; lawful.

ḥanîf, plural *ḥunafâ'*: ascetic.

ḥarâm: "prohibited"; unlawful.

ḥesed: faithful, enduring love, as of God; Hebrew.
hijra: "migration", hejira; date of Muḥammad's flight from Mecca on the fourth day of the first month of AD 622. The Islamic calendar commences from the beginning of this year.
ḥizballah: "party of God".
Hubal: chief idol of the *kaᶜba*.
hudâ: "guidance".
hypotassô: "to submit"; Greek.
ᶜibâda: worship in servanthood.
ibn: "son".
ibn sabîl: "son of the road" or traveller.
ᶜÎd al-Aḍḥa: "Feast of the Sacrifice"; 10th of the month Dhû'l-Ḥijja.
Iesous: "Jesus"; Greek.
ijmâᶜ: "consensus"; of legal scholars or Islamic community as a whole.
ijtihâd: "exerting oneself"; individual initiative to reinterpret Islamic law or (in Shîᶜa Islam) to mediate it.
Iqraa: "Recite"; title of Sura 96.
Il: El; supreme god of Canaanite pantheon.
al-ilâh: "the god"; Arabic.
îmân: "faith"; in the sense of a formal declaration of belief in the six articles of the Muslim creed.
Injîl: "Gospel".
intifâda: "uprising"; the resistance by Palestinians to the hostile policies of the government of Israel.
ᶜÎsâ: Jesus; name used by Muslims.
islâm: "submission".
'ism: "name" or "attribute".
isnâd: chain of transmitters (of *ḥadîth*) going back to Companions of the Prophet.
al-Jamâᶜat-i Islâmî: The Islamic Organization, founded by Mawdûdî.
jihâd: "a striving"; religious war of Muslims against unbelievers or apostates.
kaᶜba: "a cube"; the cube-like building in the centre of the Sacred Mosque at Mecca. It contains the black stone.

kafara: "to reject".
kâfir: someone who rejects God's call to obedience; an infidel.
kalâm Allâh: speech of God – the Qur'ân.
kalima: "the word"; the creed of the Muslim.
kalimât Allâh: the word of God – Jesus.
kalimât al-shahâda: "the word of testimony"; the confession: "I bear witness that there is no deity but God and that Muḥammad is his apostle."
Karbalâ': city in Iraq, celebrated as the site of the martyrdom of Imam Ḥussein.
khalîfa: "caliph", possessor of *khilâfa*; successor of the Prophet and head of the Muslim community.
khilâfa: politically, the succession to the rule of the community; theologically it indicates the status of Adam, man as trustee for God in the world.
Khudâ: "Self-existing One" or God; Persian.
lâhût: al-Ḥallaj's concept of "divinity".
al-Lât: feminine form of *Allâh*.
Logos: the divine "Word"; Greek.
Mahdî: the "directed one"; a ruler to appear on earth in the last days.
al-Manât: goddess of fate.
mansûkh: verses in the Qur'ân that are abrogated.
ma^crifa: "insight"; mystical awareness of reality.
al-Masîh: "the Christ".
matn: the substance of a *ḥadîth*, as distinct from its *isnâd*.
mawlânâ: from "protector"; official versed in Islamic theology, Pakistan.
Mawlid al-Nabî: "Birthday of the Prophet"; 12th of Rabî^c al-Awwal.
may puritix: "praying into smoking oil"; ritual for praying for the spirits of the dead among Turkic peoples in Central Asia.
Mevlidi Şerif: "Birth-song of the Prophet" by Süleyman Chelebi.
midrash (plural *midrashîm*): stories that embellish incidents in the Bible in order to teach moral lessons; Hebrew.
Mishna: written down oral *Torah*.
Muddaththir: "One Wrapped Up"; title of Sura 74.

muftî: expert in Islamic law qualified to give legal opinions.

Muhâjirûn: "Emigrants"; Muslims who transferred from Mecca to Medina with Muḥammad.

mujtahid: person qualified to exercise *ijtihâd*.

mu'min: "believer" or person of faith.

muslim: "a submitted person".

nabî (plural *anbîyâ*): "the called"; a prophet.

nafs: "soul".

nâsikh: verses in the Qur'ân that abrogate other verses.

nâsût: al-Ḥallâj's concept of "humanity".

niyya: "intention" or declaration of purpose before performing one of the obligatory ordinances of Islam.

paraklêtos: "comforter"; Greek.

periclêtos: "praised one"; Greek.

pistis: "faith"; Greek.

prophêtês: a prophet; Greek.

purdah: "curtain, veil"; Persian: the practice of secluding women from the sight of men and strangers.

qalb: "heart".

qara': "to recite".

qirâ'ât: "modes" of reading the Qur'ân.

Qur'ân: "Recitation" of Muḥammad.

Quraysh: the Arabian tribe of which Muḥammad was a part and to which the majority of Meccans belonged.

Rabb: "Lord".

al-Raḥmân: "the Merciful".

Ramaḍân: the fast during the ninth month of the Muslim calendar.

rasûl (plural *rusul*): "messenger" who receives a Book from God and is sent on a mission.

rûḥ: "spirit".

ṣalât: ritual or liturgical prayer, performed five times a day.

ṣawm: fasting.

sêmeion: "sign"; Greek, especially as applied to Jesus' miracles in John's Gospel.

shahâda: Muslim confession of faith in God and his apostle.

sharîʿa: the "path" to be followed; the totality of the Islamic way of life.

shaykh: "sheikh"; Muslim religious leader, sometimes head of an order.

shaytanîya: al-Ghazâlî's concept of the "inclination to evil" of human beings.

Shî^ca: "followers"; followers of ᶜAlî, first cousin of Muḥammad and the husband of his daughter Fâṭima.

shirk: the cardinal sin of idolatry, of associating anyone or anything with God.

shubbiha lahum: "so it was made to appear to them", referring to crucifixion of Christ.

Ṣûfî : Sufi; a Muslim mystic, named after the early ascetics who wore garments of coarse wool (*sûf*).

Suhuf: (lost) "scrolls" of Abraham.

sunna: "a path, manner of life"; the custom, especially of Muḥammad, transmitted via the *ḥadîth* literature.

Sunnî: those who accept the *sunna* and the historic succession of the caliphs, as opposed to the ᶜAlîds or Shîᶜas; the majority of the Muslim community.

sura: from *sûra*, "a row or series"; chapter of the Qur'ân.

tafsîr: "explaining"; term used for commentary, especially on the Qur'ân.

taḥrîf: alteration or corruption of scripture.

Tabligh-i Jamaᶜat: pietistic Islamic reform movement.

Talmud: combination of *Mishna* and *Gemara*.

Tanakh: the written *Torah*; refers to the Law, the Prophets and the Writings.

tanzîl: movement of revelation in Islam; causing to "come down".

taqlîd: "imitation", Iran; often with sense of blind adherence to a traditional school and non-openness to renewal.

targum: a paraphrased translation of the Hebrew Old Testament into Aramaic.

ṭarîqa: "a path"; Ṣûfî term for the religious life: often describes the division of mystics into different lodges.

Taurât: "Torah" of Moses.

tawḥîd: "unity"; the oneness of God and, by implication, the holism of all creation in realizing its theocentric nature.

Taoist: follower of "Taoism", religious doctrine originally based on writings attributed to Lao-tse, Chinese philosopher (circa 500 BC).

theos: "God"; Greek.

theotokos: "God-bearer", referring to Mary.

Torah: the five books of Moses.

ᶜulamâ' (ulema): plural of *ᶜâlim*, "knower"; learned ones who are custodians of Islamic teachings.

Umayyad: Umayyad caliphate (AD 661–750) with capital at Damascus.

umma: the "community" of Islam; the whole of the brotherhood of Muslims.

al-ᶜUzzâ: goddess of east Mecca.

waḥy: inspiration.

walad: "boy" or "son".

Yahweh: the Lord; the God who reveals himself to humankind; Hebrew.

Yasûᶜa: Jesus, name used by Christians.

Yawm al-dîn: Day of Judgement.

Yathrib: Medina.

yetzer ha-ra: evil impulse endemic to humankind; Hebrew.

yetzer ha-tov: good impulse that enables an adult to feed on the *Torah* and overcome the innate evil impulse; Hebrew.

Zabûr: "Psalms" of David.

zakât: "purification"; alms-giving, one of the five pillars.

Zeus: highest of the gods in the Greek pantheon.

ẓulm: wrongdoing.

Some significant names mentioned in the text

Abû Bakr' ᶜAbd Allâh ibn Abî Quhâfa (died AD 634). An early convert and the first caliph or successor to Prophet Muḥammad.

ᶜÂ'isha: daughter of Abû Bakr and the favourite wife of Muḥammad. She died in Medina in AD 678 aged 67. Often referred to as *Ummu'l-mu'minîn* or "the mother of the believers".

Ibn al-ᶜArabi' Muhyi'l-Dîn (AD 1165–1240). Influential Ṣûfî master, born in Spain. He wrote many poems and other works, proposing a system of mystical knowledge.

Arius (about AD 250–335). Originally from Libya, he was a pupil of Lucian of Antioch. He was made a presbyter in Alexandria where he quarrelled with his bishop, Alexander. He became the central figure in the "Arian controversy".

Ashᶜari' Abû'l-Ḥasan (AD 873–935). Schooled in the theology of the Muᶜtazilî in Basra, Ashᶜari rejected his heritage and enumerated an alternative approach to theology. His school, named after him, has become the most representative in Sunnî Islam.

Athanasius (about AD 295–373). Played a major role in defining the doctrine of the Trinity during the Arian struggles. Bishop of Alexandria from AD 328.

Augustine (AD 354–430). Bishop of Hippo Regius (modern Annaba) from AD 395. Augustine was born to African parents of Romanized Berber origins in Tagaste in Numidia (modern Algeria). From childhood he was a catechumen, learning the Christian faith from his earnest mother Monica, but his baptism was delayed until AD 387 by a lengthy religious and philosophical pilgrimage, described in his *Confessions*. Augustine had unrivalled influence on the development of Christian theology in the medieval Western church.

al-Bukhârî, Muḥammad ibn ᶜAbd Allâh ibn Ismâᶜîl (AD 810–870). Major collator of *ḥadîth* whose collection is approved as a work second only to the Qur'ân itself.

Chelebi: Süleyman (died AD 1421). Author in Turkish of *Mevlidi Şerif* or "Birth-song of the Prophet".

Clement of Alexandria (died about AD 214). Became head of catechetical school in Alexandria, possibly a presbyter. He possessed a deep knowledge of Greek literature and philosophy and used the allegorical method of interpreting scripture.

Constantine the Great (about AD 274–337). Emperor from AD 306 and sole emperor from AD 324. His laws and letters are a chief primary source for the relations of Christianity and the state from AD 313 onwards.

Cyprian, Thascius Caecilius (about AD 200–258). A rhetorician from Carthage, and bishop there from AD 249. Martyred.

al-Ghazâlî, Abû Ḥamîd Muḥammad ibn Muḥammad ibn Aḥmad (AD 1058–1111). Sunnî theologian who incorporated aspects of Sufism into orthodox Islam.

al-Ḥallâj, al-Ḥusayn ibn Mansûr. Preacher-mystic of Khurasan and Afghanistan; executed in Baghdad in AD 922.

Ḥanbal, Aḥmad ibn (AD 780–855). Founder of the Hanbalite school of Sunnî law, the most strict school.

Ḥanîfa, Abû Ḥanîfa al-Nuᶜmân (AD 700–767). Founder of Hanifite school of Sunnî law.

al-Ḥussein. Second son of Fâṭima (daughter of Prophet Muḥammad) by her husband ᶜAlî, the fourth caliph. Slain at Karbalâ' by Yazîd who became seventh caliph.

Irenaeus (about AD 130–200). Originally from Asia and a student of Polycarp of Smyrna (modern Izmir), he became Bishop of Lyons from about AD 178.

Justin Martyr. Justin was a convert from paganism, but became the most notable of the second century Christian "apologists". Justin was born at Flavia Neapolis (now Nablus); he was martyred in Rome AD 165.

Khadîja: daughter of Khuwailid, a Qurayshi. After being widowed, she married Muḥammad, becoming his first wife and first convert. She died in AD 619, aged 65 years.

Mâlik, Abû ᶜAbd Allâh Mâlik ibn Anas (AD 716–796). Medinan founder of the Malikite school of Sunnî law.

Muᶜâwiya: son of Abû Sufyân. He became sixth caliph and founder of the Umayyad dynasty.

Nestorius (about AD 386–451). Bishop of Constantinople (AD 428–431). Represents the extreme of the "Antiochene" school on the nature of Christ, overemphasizing the "human aspect".

Origen (about AD 185–254). Became head of catechetical school in Alexandria from AD 203. He was a scholar, teacher, writer and preacher who lived an ascetic life.

Rumi, Jalâl al-Dîn (AD 1207–1273). Born in Balkh, he died in Konya, Turkey, where his family had settled. He is renowned for his mystical poetry and for the order of whirling dervishes, founded by him.

Shâfi'î, Muḥammad ibn Idrîs al-Shâfi'î (AD 767–820). Descendant of the Prophet and founder of one of the four schools of Sunnî law.

Ibn Taimîya, Taqî al-Dîn (AD 1263–1328). He emerged as spokesman for the traditionalists (*Ahl al-Ḥadîth*) with a programme of renewed emphasis on the *sharî'a* (Islamic law) and a vindication of religious values. He spoke out strongly against the many forms of popular practices prevalent among his peers. Ibn Taimîya's thoughts influenced the late eighteenth-century Wahhâbî movement.

Tertullian, Q. Septimus Florens (about AD 160–220). Legal background; based in Carthage. Later in life became a Montanist.

'Umar ibn al-Khattâb (died AD 644). Succeeded Abû Bakr as caliph.

'Uthmân: son of 'Affân; the third *khalîfa* of Islam (died AD 661). During his rule, a definitive text of the Qur'ân was determined and authorized, all other versions being destroyed.

Wahhâb: Muḥammad ibn 'Abdu'l-Wahhâb (AD 1703–1792) was a native of Najd in Arabia, and founded the Unitarian, conservative movement named after him. The Wahhâbî view influenced the development of the Muslim Brotherhood in Egypt, and the *Jamâ'at-i Islâmî* or Islamic Organization in Pakistan.

Waraqa ibn Nawfal ibn Asad ibn 'Abd al-'Uzzâ. Cousin of Khadîja, a Christian.

Zaid ibn Thâbit, a native of Medina; amanuensis to Prophet Muḥammad.

Appendix 4 Notes

Preface

1 Godfrey H. Jansen, *Militant Islam*, Pan Books: London (1979), p. 65.

2 Mohammed Arkoun, "Is Islam Threatened by Christianity" in *Islam: A Challenge for Christianity*, Hans Küng and Jürgen Moltmann (eds), SCM Press: London (1994), p. 49.

Chapter 1: Living Godwards

3 See Wilfred Cantwell Smith's fascinating theory on the "reification" of religion in *The Meaning and End of Religion*, SPCK: London (1978), pp. 51–79. Smith makes the further point that Prophet Muḥammad's message to his people – the Arabs – was offered, not as a reformation of their own religious tradition, but of the tradition of outsiders – Christians and Jews: "... the Islamic is the only religious movement in the world that was launched by a reformer and accepted by a people standing outside the tradition (in this case the two traditions) being reformed." In *ibid.*, p. 108. Smith's words do beg the question of whether Prophet Muḥammad should be seen as a "reformer" of Jewish and Christian traditions, a matter we shall consider in this book.

4 Hugh Latimer (AD 1485–1555) uses the term "Turks" to refer to those "evil-disposed affections and sensualities in us [which] are always contrary to the rule of our salvation". In "Sermon 1 on the Card", *The Works of Hugh Latimer*, ed. G.E. Corrie, Parker Society: Cambridge (1844), p. 12 as

quoted in *Love's Redeeming Work* by Geoffrey Rowell, Kenneth Stevenson & Rowan Williams (comps.), Oxford University Press: Oxford (2001), p. 13. Anglicans may recall the third collect for Good Friday in *The Book of Common Prayer*, part of which reads: "... Have mercy on all Jews, Turks, Infidels, and Hereticks, and take from them all ignorance, hardness of heart, and contempt of thy word ...". Church Book Room Press: Cambridge (n.d.), p. 121.

5 Chawkat Moucarry, *The Search for Forgiveness: Pardon and Punishment in Islam and Christianity*, Inter-Varsity Press: Leicester (2004), pp. 17–19. I am grateful to Chawkat for pointing out to me the inadequacy of my original manuscript in not explicitly acknowledging the diversity of various Islamic theological schools.

6 See Moucarry's summary in *op. cit.* (2004), pp. 96–101.

7 Süleyman Chelebi, *The Mevlidi Sherif*, trans. F. Lyman MacCallum, John Murray: London (1943), pp. 19–20.

8 *Saint Augustine: The Retractations*, book 1, chap. 13, part 3 (trans. Mary Inez Bogan) in Roy J. Deferrari (ed.), *The Fathers of the Church: A New Translation*, Catholic University of America Press: Washington DC (1968), vol. 60, p. 52.

Chapter 2: Voicing God's Concerns

9 At an early stage in the development of Islam, these ascetics were referred to as *ḥunafâ'*, plural of *ḥanîf*. They were Arab searchers after the truth who had become neither Jews nor Christians, yet who maintained a strict belief in one God. The word *ḥanîf* means "one who is inclined". The word occurs ten times in the Qur'ân, mostly in reference to Abraham. Abraham is looked back to as the forefather of monotheistic faith, for example in Sura 3:67. Elsewhere the word *ḥanîf* indicates a person who is sound in their faith in the one God.

10 To be found in Muḥammad bin Ismâ'îl bin al-Mughîrah al-Bukhârî, *al-Ṣaḥîḥ*, trans. Muhammad Muhsin Khan, Kazi Publications: Chicago (1976–1979), vol. 1, book 1, chap. 3, pp. 2–4.

11 We will explain in the next chapter why this "first" sura is numbered 96 and not 1.

12 To be found in al-Bukhârî, *al-Ṣaḥîḥ*, vol. 1, book 1, chap. 3, p. 5.

13 The Abyssinian Christian kingdom derived from the lives and witness of two Syrian Christians – Edesius and Frumentius – who had been shipwrecked on the Red Sea coast in the fourth century.

14 We shall meet these goddesses again in chapter 4.

15 The Septuagint constitutes the earliest version of the Old Testament scriptures that is extant; its Greek text was translated from the Hebrew at Alexandria in the third century BC.

16 See W. Montgomery Watt's survey of the earlier Muslims and his lists of Meccan Muslims and pagans, to be found in *Muhammad at Mecca*, Oxford University Press: Karachi (1953), pp. 88–96 and pp. 170–179 respectively.

17 Yathrib was also known as *al-Madina*, an Aramaic word meaning "the city" (probably introduced by the local Jewish population); hence Medina. After the *hijra*, Yathrib was referred to as *Madînat al-Nabî* (the City of the Prophet).

18 The *hijra* or "emigration" in AD 622 became the starting point for the Islamic lunar calendar which dates events as AH – from the year of *hijra*.

19 The question of whether or not Muḥammad "changed character" in shifting from Mecca to Medina is a delicate one. Samuel Zwemer, for example, saw no change in character, just an emergence of what was already present but unexpressed in the Meccan years. Duncan Macdonald and others saw in the emigration the beginning of degeneration in the moral character of Muḥammad. For Kenneth Cragg, the *hijra* provoked and constituted a major decision by Muḥammad to employ human skill, ingenuity and might to implement God's message. Cragg consistently rues the Medinan expression of Islam for it makes much harder his task of "retrieving" a Christian message from within the Islamic milieu. In his view, the opting for power in Medina

by Muḥammad is the exact antithesis of Jesus opting for the cross in Jerusalem.

20 Quoted in 'Ali Dashti, *23 Years*, Mazda Publishers: Costa Mesa (1994), p. 92.

21 In Badru D. Kateregga and David W. Shenk, *A Muslim and a Christian in Dialogue*, Herald Press: Scottdale (1997), p. 81.

22 See W. Montgomery Watt's complete list of expeditions and battles in *Muhammad at Medina*, Oxford University Press: Karachi (1956), pp. 339–343.

23 Watt names 13 wives or concubines, another 16 women who were thought of at various times as being his wives (perhaps some of the names in this list are variants of the same name), and a further 7 women about whom there was talk of marriage with Muḥammad. His list is found in *Muhammad at Medina*, pp. 393–399. 'Ali Dashti names 20 women as a "more or less" complete listing of Muḥammad's wives, in Dashti, *op. cit.*, pp. 123–125.

24 Elaine Pagels, for example, argues strongly for this perspective in *Adam, Eve, and the Serpent*, Vintage Books: New York (1988), pp. 11–13. The paramouncy of procreation, however, does not appear to be the only consideration involved in the defining of legitimate sexual relations within Israel. Leviticus 18 prohibits sexual relations between certain (related) adults not because they would not lead to procreation but because they would undermine the stability and health of Israelite society.

25 Gerhard Friedrich on *prophêtês* in *Theological Dictionary of the New Testament*, Eerdmans: Grand Rapids (1968), vol. 6, p. 832.

26 Quoted in Jean-Marie Gaudeul, *Encounters & Clashes: Islam and Christianity in History*, vol. 2, "Texts", Pontificio Istituto di Studi Arabi e Islamici: Rome (1990), p. 242. See also William G. Young, *Patriarch, Shah and Caliph*, Christian Study Centre: Rawalpindi (1974), pp. 202–203. We should note that Patriarch Timothy is firm, however, in his rejection of the case put forward by Caliph al-Mahdî that the "paraclete" prophesied by Jesus in John's Gospel equates to Muḥammad. A more contemporary evaluation of

Muḥammad in such a positive mode is found in Robert Charles Zaehner's assessment. He asserts: "That Muhammad was a genuine prophet and that the authentic voice of prophecy made itself heard through him, I for one find it impossible to disbelieve on any rational grounds." In *At Sundry Times: An Essay in the Comparison of Religions*, Faber & Faber: London (1958), p. 27.

27 Mark A. Gabriel (name taken at baptism), *Islam and Terrorism: Bringing the Gospel to Muslims*, Charisma House: Lake Mary, Florida (2002), p. 201. Gabriel also insists on a public denial from would-be converts to Christ of the Qur'ân as the word of God.

28 Kenneth Cragg, for example, admits that "prophethood as finalized in Muhammad is in crucial senses discontinuous with prophethood as operative in Isaiah and Jeremiah". In *Sandals at the Mosque: Christian Presence amid Islam*, SCM Press: London (1959), pp. 91–92. He expands on this admission in a later work:

> The contrasts give the whole clue to the dissimilarities of biblical and Quranic prophets. Muhammad was set to become "head of state", in the formula: "Obey Allah and obey the Prophet." It was never so with the sequence from Amos to Malachi. These prophets were never "kings", only their mentors, emissaries from God within an establishment already launched via Moses and David and requiring to be addressed in its given identity as Yahweh's realm of covenant.

In *The Weight in the Word. Prophethood: Biblical and Quranic*, Sussex Academic Press: Brighton (1999), p. 6.

29 See Jacques Jomier's discussion on these three positions: pragmatic, maximalist and minimalist in *How to Understand Islam* (trans. John Bowden), SCM Press: London (1989), pp. 142–143.

30 *Witness to God in a Secular Europe*, Conference of European Churches: Geneva (1985), p. 56. See Kenneth Cragg's helpful summary of the "too much" and the "too little" made of

Muḥammad by Christian onlookers in *The Call of the Minaret*, Oxford University Press: London (1956), pp. 92–93.

31 See Willem A. Bijlefeld, "A Prophet and More than a Prophet" in *The Muslim World*, vol. 59 (1969), pp. 1–2.

Chapter 3: Words Perfectly Spoken

32 Theodor Nöldeke, whose suggestion concerning chronology of revelation is given in Figure 18, set the tone for this kind of research in his *Geschischte des Qorâns*, Georg Olms Verlag (1981), a reprint of the Dieterich'sche edition (1909). Sell gives a table comparing the chronological orders proposed by Jalâlu'l-Dîn al-Suyûti, Theodor Nöldeke and William Muir in Charles Edward Sell, *The Historical Development of the Qur'án*, Marshall: London (1923) as reprinted by People International: Tunbridge Wells (n.d.), pp. 203–204.

33 Further details may be found in G. Margoliouth's "Introduction" to *The Koran* as translated from the Arabic by J.M. Rodwell, Everyman: London (1909), pp. 3–4.

34 *Midrashîm* (plural of *midrash*) constitute stories that embellish incidents in the Bible in order to teach moral lessons or suggest principles for law-making. A simplified summary of various Jewish terms, mentioned in this chapter, is offered in Figure 94.

35 For example, "Obey God, and obey the Apostle, and beware (of evil)" in Sura 5:95.

36 Recorded in al-Bukhârî *al-Ṣaḥîḥ*, vol. 6, book 61, chap. 7, trad. 518, p. 485.

37 Leone Caetani questions the reliability of the claim (from tradition) that during Abû Bakr's caliphate a first compilation of the Qur'ân was thus made. He asks why, if the death of so many Muslims at al-Yamama endangered the preservation of the text, would Abû Bakr practically conceal the copy commissioned by him from Zaid ibn Thâbit, entrusting it to the guardianship of a woman? Caetani suggests that "Ḥafṣa's copy" is an invention made to justify the corrections of the compilation subsequently compiled under ᶜUthmân. Nonetheless, Caetani allows the possibility of a

Figure 94
A summary of terms for relevant Jewish material

Explanation	Term	Details
	Torah	strictly refers to the five books of Moses can refer to entire Jewish Bible
written *Torah*	*Tanakh*	acrostic of *Torah* (the Law), *Nevi'im* (the Prophets) and *Ketuvim* (the Writings)
	oral *Torah*	tradition explaining what the *Torah* means and how to interpret and apply it Orthodox Jews believe God taught the oral *Torah* to Moses; it was maintained in oral form until the second century AD
written-down oral *Torah*	*Mishna*	*Mishna* completed AD 220. Over next centuries, additional commentaries elaborating on the *Mishna* were written down in Jerusalem and Babylon
commentaries on *Mishna*	*Gemara*	completed in fifth century AD
Mishna + *Gemara*	*Talmud*	Jerusalem *Talmud* completed AD 430 Babylonian *Talmud* completed AD 530 i.e. completed at least a century before Muḥammad
	Midrashîm	stories expanding on incidents in the Bible to derive principles of Jewish Law or to teach moral lessons
	Responsa	from the Middle Ages local rabbis made their own interpretations of Talmudic passages, which were collected together and printed

copy of the Qur'ân being prepared at Medina during the time of Abû Bakr and ᶜUmar – a copy in which no verse of the text was accepted which was not authenticated by at least two witnesses who could declare that they themselves had heard it from the Prophet. Caetani's investigation is prompted by his assumption that the official canonical redaction undertaken at ᶜUthmân's command was due to uncertainty at the time with regard to the text of the Qur'ân. Caetani is interested in the tensions that existed between champions of the provincial copies of the text (copies that would be destroyed after ᶜUthmân's redaction was completed) and the caliph in al-Kufa with his promotion of a Medinan text. Caetani also investigates the role of the *qurra*, or Qur'ân-readers, and their relationship with the emerging central authority of the caliphate. He reads ᶜUthmân's commissioning of an "authentic" text as an open challenge to the *qurra* and a successful attempt to end the monopoly on the sacred text that they claimed. See his article "Uthman and the Recension of the Koran" in *The Moslem World*, vol. 5 (1915), pp. 380–390.

38 In Abû Bakr ᶜAbdullâh ibn Abî Da'ûd, *Kitâb al-Masâhif* (ed. Arthur Jeffery), Cairo (1936), p. 21 and quoted in John Burton, *The Collection of the Qur'ân*, Cambridge University Press: Cambridge (1977), p. 143.

39 The alleged comparison with "Ḥafṣa's copy" is sometimes disputed because no mention is made of that copy in the descriptions given of the collection and consultation process. Difficulties also remain in reconciling seemingly incompatible contentions concerning the development of a single text of the Qur'ân. The contentions include the following: the Qur'ân was first collected by Abû Bakr; the Qur'ân was first collected by ᶜUmar; the Qur'ân's collection was begun by Abû Bakr and completed by ᶜUmar; the Qur'ân's collection was begun by ᶜUmar and completed by ᶜUthmân; the Qur'ân was solely collected by ᶜUthmân. See Burton, *op. cit.*, p. 225.

40 Recorded in al-Bukhârî *al-Ṣaḥîḥ*, vol. 6, book 61, chap. 8, trad. 527, p. 489.

41 Burton, *op. cit.*, p. 154.

42 This process is described in al-Bukhârî *al-Ṣaḥîḥ*, vol. 6, book 61, chap. 3, trad. 510, p. 479.

43 Arthur Jeffery, for example, records the known differences of readings in qur'ânic codices that were destroyed under ᶜUthmân: see Arthur Jeffery (ed.), *Materials for the History of the Text of the Quran*, Leiden: Brill (1937). Jeffery presents in this comprehensive list of codices the *Kitâb al-Masâhif* of Ibn Abî Da'ûd, plus a collection of variant readings from the codices of Ibn Masᶜûd, Ubai, ᶜAli ibn ᶜAbbas, Anas, Abû Mûsâ and other early qur'ânic authorities. The codices provide evidence of texts that were different and earlier than ᶜUthmân's canonical text. John Burton comments on the significance of later proponents of the "legal sciences" of Islam in their appeal to such codices: "it soon becomes apparent that, far from being identical with the so-called ᶜUthmânic text, the *suhuf* of Ḥafṣa, like the *suhuf* of ᶜÂ'isha or the *suhuf* of a third widow of the Prophet, Umm Salama, played a role analogous to that conferred upon the *mushaf* of ᶜAbdullâh, of Abû Mûsâ, of Ubayy, of Miqdâd (or Muᶜâd). Like all of these, Ḥafṣa's codex had occasional exegetical value in the scholars' attempts to decide issues left 'unclear' in the ᶜUthmân text." Burton, *op. cit.*, p. 227. See also Arthur Jeffery, "The Textual History of the Qur'an", a lecture delivered in October 1946 at a meeting of the Middle East Society of Jerusalem and published in *The Qur'an and Scripture,* R.F. Moore: New York, 1952. John Gilchrist offers a summary of the process of codification of the qur'ânic text in his *Jamᶜ al-Quran: The Codification of the Qur'an Text,* TMFMT: Warley, 1989.

44 Recorded in al-Bukhârî, *al-Ṣaḥîḥ,* vol. 6, book 61, chap. 5, trad. 514, p. 482.

45 In Muslim *al-Ṣaḥîḥ,* vol. 2, chap. 289, trad. 1782, pp. 389–390.

46 *Ibid.*, trad. 1785, p. 390. N.J. Dawood, in the introduction to his translation of the Qur'ân into English, makes the point: "owing to the fact that the kufic script in which the Koran was originally written contained no indication of vowels or

diacritical points, variant readings are recognized by Muslims as of equal authority." In N.J. Dawood, *The Koran*, Penguin Books: London (1983), p. 10.

47 John Burton and others question whether the different modes of reading can simply be explained as a linguistic issue. In *op. cit.*, p. 152.

48 Adrian Brockett makes the following comment arising from his comparison of the transmission of Hafs with that of Warsh: "The simple fact is that none of the differences, whether vocal (vowel and diacritical points) or graphic (basic letter), between the transmission of Hafs and the transmission of Warsh has any great effect on the meaning. Many are differences which do not change the meaning at all, and the rest are differences with an effect on meaning in the immediate context of the text itself, but without any significant wider influence on Muslim thought. One difference (Q. 2/184) has an effect on the meaning that might conceivably be argued to have wider ramifications." In "The Value of the Hafs and Warsh Transmissions for the Textual History of the Qur'an" in Andrew Rippon (ed.), *Approaches to the History of the Interpretation of the Qur'an*, Clarendon Press: Oxford (1988), p. 37. Muhammad Fahd Khaaruun has collected together all the known variants from among ten accepted "Readers" [the seven we have referred to, plus Abu Jaᶜfar, Yaᶜqub al-Hashimi and Khalaf al-Bazzar] and printed them alongside the text of the Qur'ân in the Hafs transmission. His book's title translates into English as *Making Easy the Readings of What Has Been Sent Down*, Dar Beirut: Beirut, n.d.

49 For example, the word "trusts" in Sura 23:8 can be read as either "trust" (singular, *li-amânatihim*) or "trusts" (plural, *li-amânâtihim*) according to the consonantal text without vowels.

50 Aḥmad, another name for Prophet Muḥammad.

51 Muḥammad is called *al-nabî al-ummî*, meaning "the Gentile prophet" (Sura 7:157–158) – *ummî* being the adjectival form of *umma* or "nation". The reference is to someone being of the nations as opposed to being Jewish. Traditional Muslim

exegesis tends to interpret *ummî* here as meaning "illiterate", in order to heighten the miraculous nature of the Qur'ân. Other qur'ânic passages using *ummî* (such as Suras 2:78, 3:20, 75 and so on) make best sense with the word meaning "Gentile".

52 Wilfred Cantwell Smith, *The Faith of Other Men*, Harper & Row: New York (1962), pp. 65–66.

53 John Wansbrough, formerly of the School of Oriental and African Studies though not, of course, a Muslim, certainly proposed an alternative construct concerning "Muḥammad" to Islam's own sacralized story of origins and early history. He argued in his *Quranic Studies*, for example, that the *Sunna* at least was more valuable as a historical source for the theological and legal debates of the early centuries of Islam than as a source for the life of Muḥammad. Other Western scholars have built upon Wansbrough's researches. See Ibn Warraq (ed. and trans.), *The Quest for the Historical Muhammad*, Prometheus Books: Amherst, 2000.

54 On Saturday 21 October 1995, the *Daily Sadaqat* newspaper, published in Lahore, demanded the extradition to Pakistan and execution there of Anwar Shaikh. Anwar Shaikh – Muslim turned humanist – had written material against Islam from his safe base in Wales. His books and manuscripts include an exposé of alleged inconsistencies in the Qur'ân, a criticism of Muslim attitudes towards women and a condemnation of Islam's espousal of violence. See the bibliography for details of Shaikh's published material. The case of Anwar Shaikh is highlighted by Ibn Warraq in *Leaving Islam: Apostates Speak Out*, Prometheus Books: Amherst (2003), p. 425. Another contemporary Muslim to receive death threats is Irshad Manji. She describes herself as a "Muslim refusenik" and, as journalist and public speaker, has dared to raise questions about Muslims' anti-Semitism, the Muslim view of women and, critically, the nature of the Qur'ân. Her latest book will undoubtedly bring further threats to her well-being and safety: *The Trouble with Islam*, Mainstream Publishing: Edinburgh, 2004. Bat Ye'or (pseudonym) is an Egyptian-born European

scholar who has sought to expose Islam's ideology of discrimination against Jews and Christians. She made use of the term "dhimmitude" to describe this hostile attitude towards People of the Book living in Muslim societies. See the work born out of her postgraduate research: *The Decline of Eastern Christianity under Islam. From Jihad to Dhimmitude: Seventh–Twentieth Century* (Miriam Kochan and David Littman trans.), Farleigh Dickinson University Press: Madison, 1996.

55 The Arabic word for "Proclaim" is *iqra'*. It derives from *qara'* and could equally well be translated "Recite!" The whole sura is named *Iqra'*.

56 Tobias Mayer, "A Muslim Speaks to Christians" in *Encounter*, No. 297 (2003), p. 7. Mayer goes on to press the parallelism further, positing the uncreatedness of the Word in both cases (Sura 7:54 and John 1:3). He suggests a further parallel between Muḥammad and Mary as bearers of the Word. Mary is a virgin, prerequisite for her function of bearing the Word made man. Muḥammad is illiterate, prerequisite for his function of bearing the Word made book. Wilfred Cantwell Smith has also written about a parallel existing between the incarnation of God in Christ and the incorporation of the transcendent word in history through Muḥammad. The points of comparison in this parallel are Qur'ân/Christ, Prophet Muḥammad/Paul (or the twelve apostles), and *ḥadîth*/Bible (or the four Gospels). In "Some Similarities and Differences in Christianity and Islam: an Essay in Comparative Religion" in *The World of Islam. Studies in Honour of Philip K. Hitti* (eds Kritzeck and Winder), Macmillan: London (1959), p. 52.

57 Wilfred Cantwell Smith, *Islam in Modern History*, Princeton University Press: Princeton (1957), footnote 13, pp. 17–18.

58 Fazlur Rahman, *Islam*, Weidenfield and Nicolson: London (1966), p. 29.

59 A. Yusuf Ali (trans), *The Glorious Qur'an*, American Trust Publications, 1977, p. 1117, note 3723.

60 Quoted in 'Ali Dashti, *op. cit.*, p. 132.

61 *Ibid.*, p. 133.

62 We need to note that some Muslims have abandoned this traditional understanding of "abrogation". Instead, they claim, the process of abrogation refers to the replacement by verses in the Qur'ân of verses in previous scriptures. This more polemical interpretation of "abrogation", however, remains without support in the Qur'ân itself, in the *ḥadîth*, and in classical commentaries.

63 For a summary of the early development of the Muᶜtazilî theological school(s) of theology, see Ira M. Lapidus, *A History of Islamic Societies*, Cambridge University Press: Cambridge (1988), pp. 105–108. For a brief synopsis of Muᶜtazilî theology, see Moucarry, *op. cit.* (2004), pp. 341–342. The challenges proposed by some of the excesses of Muᶜtazilî rationalism helped lead to the emergence of al-Ashᶜari's distinctive theologizing. Abu'l-Ḥasan al-Ashᶜari began as a disciple of the Muᶜtazilî school but went on to produce his own distinctive school of theology. That school, named after him, has become the most representative within Sunnî Islam. Major theologians of its persuasion have included Abu'l-Maᶜali al-Juwayni, Abu Ḥamid al-Ghazâlî and Fakhr al-Dîn al-Razi.

64 Wilfred Cantwell Smith, *Questions of Religious Truth*, Gollancz: London (1967), pp. 48–49.

65 A targum is a paraphrased translation of the Hebrew Old Testament into Aramaic. For centuries, the Jews were pressurized to assimilate to the ways of foreign nations that exiled them and ruled their land. Study and observance of the *Torah*, for example, was specifically outlawed by Antiochus Epiphanes in 168 BC. After the return of the people of Israel from exile, an oral explanation of the Hebrew text was offered in Aramaic to the people gathered for worship on sabbaths. Such targums were not supposed to be written down, but they eventually came to be recorded – probably for private use or study. There are targums to all the canonical books of the Old Testament except Daniel, Ezra and Nehemiah; for some books there are several targums. Figure 95 summarizes the various targums that have been identified.

Figure 95
Targums

Type	Name	Details
Major targums	*Targum of Onkelos*	official targum to the Pentateuch
	Targum of Jonathan	targums to the Prophets (comprising the historical and prophetic books), ascribed to Jonathan ben Uzziel [most noted pupil of the elder Hillel]
The Jerusalem targums *more accurately* The Palestinian targums	*Targum Yerushalmi I*	on Pentateuch, often mistakenly called *Targum of Jonathan* or *Targum of Pseudo-Jonathan* because in first printed edition it was cited under the name of Jonathan ben Uzziel; the targum could not, however, have appeared in its present form before AD 650 because it mentions a wife and daughter of Muḥammad
	Targum Yerushalmi II	on Pentateuch, also called the *Fragmentary Targum* because not all of it has been preserved; it is possible that *Targums Yerushalmi I* and *II* are both to be traced back to different recensions of an older Jerusalem targum
	Targum Yerushalmi III	on Pentateuch only small fragments preserved
Targums on Hagiographa [12 books of the Hebrew scriptures not included under Law and Prophets]	Targums …	to Proverbs, Psalms, Job
	Targums …	to Ruth, Esther, Lamentations, Ecclesiastes, Song of Solomon
	Targums …	to the Books of Chronicles

66 The Bible does not mention what happened to Abel's body (Genesis 4:10–11). According to early oral tradition, Cain did not expect Abel's death (this was a new experience for human beings) and, shocked by the silent body, fled from the site of the crime. Abel's parents, Adam and Eve, found the corpse. Several questions arising from this early tradition were answered in various literary Midrashic versions. Why did Abel's body not deteriorate in the hot, sunny garden of Eden? Why did beasts not devour it? What was the reaction of Adam and Eve on finding their son? How did they dispose of the body? Professor Dov Noy (M. Grunwald chair of folklore at the Hebrew University of Jerusalem) suggests that the main literary text is preserved in Rabbi Eleazar's narrative, whence it was taken over by two medieval Midrashic compilations – those of *Yalkut Shimeoni* and *Midrash Haggadol*. Answers to the questions are given in these texts: birds, flying over Abel's body shadowed it from the hot sun. The dog that had guarded Abel's flocks during his lifetime kept preying beasts away. Adam and Eve mourned their son, sitting over the corpse. The mourning parents observed a raven disposing of a dead bird of its own kind by burying it in the ground. Following the example of the raven, Adam (Eve is not mentioned) buried Abel's body in the ground. See Dov Noy, "The Story of Abel's Burial: The Interrelationship of Myth and Custom" in *Folklivsgransking*, vol. 21, Oslo (1978), pp. 129–140.

67 The explanation given in Parashah 38:13 is that Terah was an idol-manufacturer. Once he went off on a trip, leaving Abram in charge of his store. Abram challenged the customers about their idolatry when they came to purchase idols; he even ended up breaking some himself! When his father returned and discovered what Abram had been doing, he was angry and took him to Nimrod. Nimrod tested Abram's faith and will, trying to get him to bow down before fire or water or clouds or wind. Abram resisted each suggestion, so Nimrod eventually threw him into a fire: "let your God whom you worship come and save you from the fire," he angrily shouted. Haran was present

observing all this. Nimrod turned to Haran and asked him whose side he was on? Haran thought to himself: "If Abram wins I'll say I am on Abram's side, and if Nimrod wins, I'll say I'm on Nimrod's side." Abram was miraculously saved from the fire. Nimrod then asked Haran for his verdict. Haran opted for his brother's side. So Nimrod threw Haran into the fire, "and his guts burned up and came out, and he died in the presence of his father." In Jacob Neusner, *Genesis Rabba: The Judaic Commentary to the Book of Genesis. A New American Translation*. Scholars Press: Atlanta, vol. 2 (1985), pp. 55–56.

68 In chapter 1:2 of the *Targum Sheni of Esther*, Xerxes' rule is compared with Solomon's. In that comparison, mention is made of the Queen of Sheba's visit to Solomon: "Then Benayahu [Solomon's servant] brought her [the Queen of Sheba] before King Solomon. Now when King Solomon heard that she was coming to him, King Solomon arose and went to sit down in a bathhouse. When the Queen saw that the king was sitting in a bathhouse, she thought to herself the king must be sitting in water. So she raised her dress in order to wade across. Whereupon he noticed the hair on her leg, to which King Solomon responded by saying: 'Your beauty is the beauty of women, but your hair is the hair of men. Now hair is beautiful for a man but shameful for a woman.' Whereupon the Queen of Sheba answered, saying to him: 'O lord, King, I will cite you three riddles; if you will solve them for me I will acknowledge that you are a wise man, but if not, (you are) like the rest of mankind'." The queen asks her three riddles, which Solomon successfully answers. He then escorts her to his palace: "Now when the Queen of Sheba saw the greatness and glory of King Solomon, she offered praise to the One Who created him, saying: 'Blessed be the Lord, your God who has chosen you to place you on the throne of his kingdom to do righteousness and justice!'" She then plies the king with gold and other gifts. In Bernard Grossfeld (trans.), *The Two Targums of Esther: Translated, with Apparatus and Notes*, Liturgical Press: Collegeville (1991), pp. 116–117. Louis Ginzberg links

this incident with an Arabic legend suggesting that the jinn want to hinder the marriage of Solomon and the Queen of Sheba, so they call Solomon's attention to the hair on the queen's legs. Such hair indicates that she is a *jinnî*. In *The Legends of the Jews*, vol. 6, Jewish Publication Society of America: Philadelphia, footnote 41 (1928), p. 289. Jacob Lassner helpfully brings together all the texts about the Queen of Sheba and King Solomon in his *Demonizing the Queen of Sheba*, University of Chicago Press: Chicago, 1993. He suggests that the Muslims learned the gist of the Jewish post-biblical material via oral culture. He concludes that the point of the story is that "left to their own devices, dangerous female characters would change the nature of the universe as we know it ... " (*Ibid.*, p. 34).

69 Genesis 6:2 announces that "the sons of God saw that the daughters of men were beautiful, and they married any of them they chose". The earliest rabbinic interpretations of this verse explained that the term "sons of God" refers to princely angels. Stories about the angels Shemhazai and/or Azazel consorting with human women are found in *Yalkut Shimeoni* (section 44) and are alluded to in the Talmud (e.g. *Yoma* 67b) and by the *Targum Yerushalmi I* to Genesis 6:4. The angels also impart to humankind secret knowledge and magical arts. In the *Targum Yerushalmi I* to Genesis 6:4, Shemhazai and Azazel are named as the source of the "Nephilim" or "giants". The *First Book of Enoch* (chapters 6–19) contains a detailed account of how 200 angels led by Shemhazai and including Azazel were enticed by the beauty of the human women, suggesting that Mount Hermon became the site of their debauchery. It is likely that some such understanding of these verses in Genesis lies behind Paul's instruction in 1 Corinthians 11:10 that a woman ought to have a veil on her head "because of the angels". Rabbi Shimon ben Yohai preferred an interpretation that saw the "sons of God" not as angels but as human judges. He cursed all who said they were angels. Since him, the "judges" interpretation has become the standard Jewish one. It has been argued that the names Hârût and Mârût

derive from the Avestan (Iranian) Haurvatâ and Amûrtât. Al-Tabarî in his *tafsîr* reasons that after lusting for women, becoming intoxicated with wine and committing murder, Hârût and Mârût were imprisoned in a well, suspended by the feet with their tongues sticking out through thirst. Abdullah Yusuf Ali, in his note on Sura 2:102, admits that the verse might contain an allusion to Jewish traditions about fallen angels. He himself, however, prefers to follow an Islamic interpretative tradition that identifies Hârût and Mârût as wise men of Babylon. The good things learned from such wise men were turned to bad ends by "evil ones".

70 Mar Jacob of Saruq wrote in Syriac. Other Syriac versions of the Seven (or eight) Sleepers are preserved in manuscript form or as included in other works, such as Procopius' *Anecdota* or *Secret History*. The story was popularized in the West by Gregory of Tours (died AD 594) in his late sixth-century collection *De Gloria Martyrium* or *Glory of the Martyrs*, chapter 94. Gregory evidently translated the story from Greek into Latin, "with the assistance of a Syrian". See Raymond Van Dam (trans.), *Gregory of Tours: Glory of the Martyrs*, Liverpool University Press: Liverpool (1988), pp. 117–119. Gregory gave a longer account of the same story in his *Passio sanctorum martyrium septem dormientium apud Ephysum*. At the end of the *Passio*, Gregory named his Syrian assistant as Johannes. Simeon Metaphrastes (died *c.* AD 1000) was a civil servant who became a monk in later life. He collected the lives of saints from oral traditions and written collections, publishing his rewrite of them in Greek in ten volumes (the *Menologion*). He mentions the Seven Sleepers of Ephesus in his entry for the remembrance of saints on July 27. The Seven Sleepers were included in the *Golden Legend* of Jacobus de Voragine (died AD 1298), Archbishop of Genoa. Written in simple, readable Latin, this volume became very popular and editions quickly appeared in every major European language. It was one of the first books that William Caxton printed in English. An easily accessible version of the legend in English can be found in Brian S. Merrilees' translation from Chardri's

Anglo-Norman text, entitled *La vie des set dormenz*. Mar Jacob's original homily referring to the Seven Sleepers was published in the *Acta Sanctorum* (*Acts of the Saints*) – a huge text in 68 folio volumes of documents examining the lives of Christian saints, organized and published by the Societé des Bollandistes between AD 1643 and AD 1940. A feast day was observed on 27 July for the "sleepers" who were named as Maximianus, Malchus, Martinianus, Dionysius, Johannes, Serapion and Constantinus – until 1969 when the story of the Seven Sleepers was judged to be mythical. The Eastern Orthodox feast, celebrated on 22 October, however, remains in that church's calendar of saints. The outline of the legend is that during the persecutions of Decius (around AD 250), seven young men are accused of being Christians. Given some time to recant, they give away their worldly possessions and retire to a mountain to pray, where they fall asleep. The emperor finds them and orders the mouth of the cave – in which they were sleeping – to be sealed. At some later time (usually during the reign of either Theodosius I or II), the current landowner decides to open the cave to use it as a cattle pen. Inside the cave's mouth he discovers the sleepers. They awaken, imagining that they have just slept for one day. One of them returns to Ephesus. There he is astounded to discover buildings with crosses attached to them. Merchants are shocked to find a man trying to spend old coins from the reign of Decius! The bishop is summoned to interview the sleepers. In some versions, the emperor also appears in Ephesus to meet them. The sleepers tell their story, and die praising God. For details about the archaeology of the "Grotto of the Seven Sleepers" in Ephesus, see Clive Foss, *Ephesus after Antiquity: A Late Antique Byzantine and Turkish City*, Cambridge University Press: Cambridge, 1979.

71 The incident with the palm tree occurs, according to the *Gospel of Pseudo-Matthew*, chapter 20, during the journey of the holy family to Egypt: "And it came to pass on the third day of their journey, while they were walking, that the blessed Mary was fatigued by the excessive heat of the sun

in the desert; and seeing a palm tree, she said to Joseph: Let me rest a little under the shade of this tree. Joseph therefore made haste, and led her to the palm, and made her come down from her beast. And as the blessed Mary was sitting there, she looked up to the foliage of the palm, and saw it full of fruit, and said to Joseph: I wish it were possible to get some of the fruit of this palm. And Joseph said to her: I wonder that thou sayest this, when thou seest how high the palm tree is; and that thou thinkest of eating of its fruit. I am thinking more of the want of water, because the skins are now empty, and we have none wherewith to refresh ourselves and our cattle. Then the child Jesus, with a joyful countenance, reposing in the bosom of His mother, said to the palm: O tree, bend thy branches, and refresh my mother with thy fruit. And immediately at these words the palm bent its top down to the very feet of the blessed Mary; and they gathered from it fruit, with which they were all refreshed. And after they had gathered all its fruit, it remained bent down, waiting the order to rise from Him who had commanded it to stoop. Then Jesus said to it: Raise thyself, O palm tree, and be strong, and be the companion of my trees, which are in the paradise of my Father; and open from thy roots a vein of water which has been hid in the earth, and let the waters flow, so that we may be satisfied from thee. And it rose up immediately, and at its root there began to come forth a spring of water exceedingly clear and cool and sparkling. And when they saw the spring of water, they rejoiced with great joy, and were satisfied, themselves and all their cattle and their beasts. Wherefore they gave thanks to God."

72 For example, the *Arabic Gospel of the Infancy of the Saviour*, chapter 36 relates: "Now, when the Lord Jesus had completed seven years from His birth, on a certain day He was occupied with boys of His own age. For they were playing among clay, from which they were making images of asses, oxen, birds, and other animals; and each one boasting of his skill, was praising his own work. Then the Lord Jesus said to the boys: The images that I have made I will order to

walk. The boys asked Him whether then he were the son of the Creator; and the Lord Jesus bade them walk. And they immediately began to leap; and then, when He had given them leave, they again stood still. And He had made figures of birds and sparrows, which flew when He told them to fly, and stood still when He told them to stand, and ate and drank when He handed them food and drink. After the boys had gone away and told this to their parents, their fathers said to them: My sons, take care not to keep company with him again, for he is a wizard: flee from him, therefore, and avoid him, and do not play with him again after this."

73 Ernest Renan makes this point in his article "Muhammad and the Origins of Islam" in Ibn Warraq, *The Quest* (2000), p. 154.

74 C.S. Lewis, *Reflections on the Psalms*, Geoffrey Bles: London (1958), p. 86. Lewis suggests that "where ancient Gentile literature (in some measure) anticipates the nature poetry of the Jews, it has also (in some measure) anticipated their theology" (*Ibid.*, p. 85). Akhenaten, according to Lewis, did not identify God with the sun; the visible disc was only God's manifestation. For Lewis, of course, Plato provides the strongest evidence of God revealing himself through "pagan religion": in Plato, he discerns "a clear Theology of Creation in the Judaic and Christian sense" and suggests that the one who is the "Father of lights" assisted Plato in conceiving such a view (*Ibid.*, pp. 79–80).

75 Maurice Bucaille, *The Bible, the Qur'ân and Science* (trans. Alastair D. Pannell), North American Trust Publishers: Indianapolis (1978), p. 250. See Ahmed Deedat's pamphlet, *Is the Bible God's Word?*

76 The exposure of textual and other problems in the Old and New Testaments tends to confirm Muslims in their common assumption that differences to be found between the Qur'ân and the Bible are due to the text of the latter being "corrupted". The qur'ânic suggestion about former scripture being "changed" arises in several places. Sura 2 contains specific accusations against the Jews in this regard:

Then woe to those who write
The Book with their own hands,
And then say: "This is from God,"
To traffic with it
For a miserable price! –
Woe to them for what their hands
Do write, and for the gain
They make thereby. (Sura 2:79)

"The Book" most likely refers to the Torah. This verse occurs in a passage in which the immediate argument applies to some Jews of Medina. They are accused of changing (*ḥarrafa*, whence *taḥrîf*) the text of their scripture in order to fool people and make financial gain. Does such a verse permit the view that the Jews (all of them) connived in deliberately and successfully corrupting all copies of the genuine text of the Torah? Or does it simply refer to the underhand activity of a group of greedy Jews in Medina? It might be concluded, moreover, that in the context of Sura 2, "The Book" could refer to the Qur'ân. In Sura 5, also, the Jews are charged with changing (*ḥarrafa*) words from their text and forgetting a part of what they had received from God:

They change the words
From their (right) places
And forget a good part
Of the Message that was
Sent them ... (Sura 5 :14)

Christians are also found at fault in this sura:

From those, too, who call
Themselves Christians,
We did take a Covenant,
But they forgot a good part
Of the Message that was
Sent them ... (Sura 5:15)

The Christians are accused of "forgetting" a good part of the message – the Gospel – entrusted to them. The charge is one of forgetfulness, not of altering any text. Indeed, the plain reading of verses 44 to 52 of this same sura conveys the assertion that the Jew does in fact have the genuine Torah in his possession and the Christian has the genuine Gospel in his possession. So what does the Qur'ân mean by its accusation against the Jews (especially) of *taḥrîf*? There does not appear to be any charge against the Jews of conspiracy to alter the original texts of the Torah but rather of concealing them, hiding them behind their backs or writing down a substitute text in order to make financial gain. There are different degrees of *taḥrîf*, of which the most serious is known as *taḥrîf al-lafzî*. This amounts to directly altering a written text so that the true text is void. Less serious are various forms of *taḥrîf al-maᶜnawî*, or corruption of the meaning. Such forms include making arbitrary alterations while reading aloud a correct text, omitting parts of the correct text, inserting extraneous interpolations in a correct text or wrongly expositing a correct text. It would seem fair to conclude that qur'ânic references to *taḥrîf* can at the most amount to accusations of *taḥrîf al-maᶜnawî*, and not the more serious charge of deliberately altering the text of Torah or Gospel. See the helpful exposition of this important issue in Ghiyathuddin Adelphi and Ernest Hahn, *The Integrity of the Bible according to the Qur'an and the Hadith*, Henry Martyn Institute of Islamic Studies: Hyderabad, 1977.

77 The argument is that this prophecy fits Muḥammad because the Ishmaelites are brothers of the Israelites and Muḥammad is in so many ways like Moses. Christians, of course, prefer to interpret this verse in its context where "brothers" refers to the tribes of Israel. They are also aware that Peter specifically refers to Jesus as fulfilling this prophecy in Acts 3:20–23. They would probably also argue that there are more similarities between Moses and Jesus than between Moses and Muḥammad.

78 Again, Christians argue that there is no textual evidence for such an alteration of the Greek word, nor does the word *periclêtos* make any sense in the context of the passage. The description of the person and work of the *paraclêtos* in the verses following show that an ordinary human being cannot be being referred to.

79 W. St Clair-Tisdall, *The Sources of Islam* (trans. William Muir), T. & T. Clark: Edinburgh (1901), p. 2.

80 Brother Mark, *A "Perfect" Qur'an or "So it was made to appear to them"*, (2000), pp. 382–383. This material is served up as "A response to Islamic allegations concerning the Gospel, the Qur'an and Islam". It is presented in a highly polemical manner, with a final conclusion that the Qur'ân and Islam amount to "phantasmagoria" (p. 384). Interestingly, the anonymous author offers in his introduction an apology for "any departure from an appropriate attitude of heart" (p. k). I suppose my question would be whether the will to indulge in polemic does not too easily – almost inevitably – run the risk of involving an inappropriate attitude of heart? The outstanding example of the Christian polemical approach to Islam is provided in Carl Gottlieb Pfander (d. 1865). Pfander was a German Lutheran missionary to India with the Church Missionary Society. He engaged in public Christian–Muslim debates in India, most celebratedly at Agra in 1854. He wrote *Mîzânu'l-Haqq* or *Balance of Truth* in Persian in 1835. A later revision by St Clair-Tisdall (made in 1910) is still available in English translation today.

81 Steven Masood, *The Bible and the Qur'an: A Question of Integrity*, OM Publishing: Carlisle (2001), pp. 209–210.

82 Kenneth Cragg, *The Mind of the Qur'ân*, George Allen & Unwin: London (1973), p. 185.

83 From Austin M. Farrer, "Biblical Inspiration and the Rendering of Scripture" in *Interpretation and Belief*, SPCK: London (1976), p. 11.

Chapter 4: And Who Exactly is God?

84 "How Nasrudin created Truth" may be found in Idries Shah, *The Exploits of the Incomparable Mulla Nasrudin*, Picador: London (1966), p. 23.

85 The theological term for this facet of Christian appreciation of the Bible is "progressive revelation".

86 *kaᶜba*: "a cube"; the cube-like building in the centre of the Sacred Mosque at Mecca. It contains the black stone.

87 This table is found in J.A. Naudé, "The Name of God", in *Journal for Islamic Studies*, vol. 6 (1986), p. 28 where the statistics derive from J. Chelhod, "Note sur l'emploi du mot Rabb dans le Coran" in *Arabica*, vol. 5 (1958), pp. 161–163.

88 In G. Johannes Botterweck & Helmer Ringgren (eds; John T. Willis trans.): Frank M. Cross on "*ēl*" in *Theological Dictionary of the Old Testament*, vol. 1, William B. Eerdmans: Grand Rapids (1974), p. 253.

89 Cross, *op. cit.*, p. 260.

90 Found in al-Bukhârî, *al-Ṣaḥîḥ*, vol. 4, book 55, chap. 18, trad. 605, pp. 395–396. In another tradition emanating from cÂ'isha, Waraqa is described as Khadîja's cousin "who, during the pre-Islamic period became a Christian and used to write the writing with Hebrew letters. He would write from the Gospels in Hebrew as much as Allah willed him to write". In al-Bukhârî, *al-Ṣaḥîḥ*, vol. 1, book 1, chap. 3, p. 4. Ibn Isḥaq records of Waraqa that he "attached himself to Christianity and studied its scriptures until he had thoroughly mastered them". In A. Guillaume, *The Life of Muhammad: A translation of Ibn Ishaq's Sirat Rasul Allah*, Oxford University Press: Oxford (1955), p. 99. Ibn Isḥaq was born in AH 85 and grew up in Medina; his is one of the earliest full-length biographies of Prophet Muḥammad.

91 Steve Bell, for example, concludes that "Allah is the God of the Bible semantically", basing his argument on linguistic, semantic and historical evidence. He does not, however, discuss whether the semantic heritage came directly from the previous use of the word in Arabic or via an importation from Syriac. Bell's thoughts on "Allah – God of the

Bible?" may be found in *Ordinary Christians discussing good news with ordinary Muslims*, Friendship First Publications: Market Rasen (2003), p. 82.

92 From al-Bukhârî, *al-Ṣaḥîḥ*, vol. 4, book 55, chap. 9, trad. 583, pp. 378–379.

93 Ghulam Sarwar, *Islam: Belief and Teachings*, Muslim Educational Trust: London (1980), p. 19.

94 Abul A'la Mawdudi, *Towards Understanding Islam*, Islamic Foundation: Leicester, (1981), p. 62.

95 In Kateregga and Shenk, *op. cit.*, pp. 120–121.

96 Kenneth Cragg, *The Call of the Minaret*, p. 36.

97 The problem has been that of whether or not the singular God of Islamic theology can possess "attributes" that are eternal as part of his essence. A positive assertion would seem to imply multiformity. Maybe the names reveal, not God's nature or essence, but his will – his choice of action at any specific moment.

98 Moucarry, *op. cit.* (2004), p. 41.

99 See Moucarry's exposition of God as "Most-Returning" in *op. cit.* (2004), pp. 68–78. From Adam onwards, God has turned graciously towards his human creation: "God turns to people when he accepts their repentance." *Ibid.*, p. 70.

100 Katie Morris, for example, tries to "have her cake and eat it" in "Challenge to the True Church", an article in the periodical *Prophetic Vision*, no. 30 (2003), pp. 2–4. She argues that "Mohammed's Koran is a forgery of what is real, the Bible. It is a corruption of the Old and New Testaments which Mohammed often heard told him by traders in the market place, and into this he introduced his own completely new 'revelations'" (p. 2). Morris asserts the influence of Old and New Testaments in the formulation (via corruption of them) of the Qur'ân. Yet she also claims that there is no common ground at all between Islam and Christianity. She warns that "Christians who do not recoil from Islam are bankrupt theologically" (*Ibid.*, p. 2). Samuel Zwemer similarly argued, though in much less inflammatory language, that Muḥammad understood very well the Christian doctrine of the Trinity and deliberately rejected it: "...

Muhammad's idea of God includes a deliberate rejection of the Christian idea of the Godhead ... " The travesty put forth is that Christians are tritheists, worshipping a family of deities: father, mother and son gods. In *The Moslem Doctrine of God: an Essay on the Character and Attributes of Allah according to the Koran and Orthodox Tradition*, Oliphant, Anderson & Ferrier: London (1905), p. 92. Tor Andrae, on the other hand, argues in favour of common ground because, in his view, Muḥammad was strongly influenced by the Nestorian church in both theology and piety. He begins his study of the life and faith of Muḥammad with some strong assertions: "That the fundamental ideas of Islam were borrowed from the biblical religions is a fact which requires no further discussion. As we shall see later, the religion of the Prophet, both in its form of expression and in its spirit, is related, even more closely than has hitherto been assumed, to the dominant piety of the Syrian churches." See his *Muhammad: The Man and his Faith* (trans. Theophil Menzel), George Allen & Unwin: London (1936), p. 11. Dr Baby Varghese argues that the Greek text of the anaphora of St James was translated from Greek into Syriac before the end of the sixth century. Part of the motivation for doing so, he suggests, was that the "non-Chalcedonians were actively involved in evangelization among the pagans of Mesopotamia and the Arab tribes, most of whom understood Syriac better than Greek". He notes that in about AD 542, Jacob Baradaeus and Theodore of Bostra were consecrated as missionary bishops: Theodore served the Ghassanid Arabs. The "non-Chalcedonians" came to include both the Nestorians who were expelled from Antioch by the emperors Justin I and Justinian, and the monophysite-oriented church leaders in Edessa who developed their theology in opposition to the incoming Nestorians. Perhaps the missionary zeal of both groups of Christians in Syria ensured that Muḥammad and his contemporaries became equally aware of the Nestorian tradition (which proved attractive in that it overstressed the human element of Christ's nature) and the monophysite tradition (which proved unattractive in its overemphasis of Christ's divinity via a recognition of Mary as "God-bearer").

101 Moucarry, *op. cit.* (2004), *passim.*

102 Adapted, with permission, from Colin Chapman, *Cross and Crescent*, Inter-Varsity Press: Leicester (1995), p. 218. In speculation over the development of Muslim theology, especially during the early centuries, some commentators believe that Muslim theologians were dependent upon earlier Christian discussions. Thus, Christian debate about the nature of the divine *Logos* is held to have influenced later Muslim views on the uncreated nature of the Qur'ân. See Morris S. Seale, *Muslim Theology: A Study of Origins with Reference to the Church Fathers*, Luzac: London (1964), p. 66. If there is truth in this view, one could reasonably expect there to be considerable overlap of meaning with regard to Muslim and Christian concepts of God.

103 Moucarry, *op. cit.* (2004), pp. 325–326.

104 Wilfred Cantwell Smith, "Mission, Dialogue, and God's Will for Us", in *International Review of Mission*, vol. 78, no. 307, pp. 360–374 (1988), p. 367.

105 Prophet Muḥammad evidently had a dream in which he saw ᶜAmr bin Luhayy "dragging his intestines in hell". This was interpreted as punishment for his infidelity: "He was the first to change the religion of Ishmael, to set up idols, and institute the custom of the *bahîra, sâ'iba, wasîla*, and *hâmî*." This "custom" (comprising superstitions about the birth of certain kinds of animals) was the subject of a revelation in Sura 5:106. Guillaume, *op. cit.*, p. 35.

106 Guillaume *op. cit.*, p. 68.

107 Gerhard Nehls and Walter Eric, *Islam – as it sees itself, as others see it, as it is*, SIM: Nairobi (1996), p. 91.

108 Samuel M. Zwemer in *Arabia: The Cradle of Islam. Studies in the Geography, People and Politics of the Peninsula with an account of Islam and Mission-work*, Oliphant, Anderson and Ferrier: London (1900), p. 171. Zwemer does somewhat qualify his criticism, suggesting that the Qur'ân reveals that Muḥammad "had in a measure a correct knowledge of the *physical* attributes of God but an absolutely false con-

ception of his *moral* attributes" (*Ibid.*, p. 175). However, Zwemer's firm conclusion is that "This is *not* 'the only True God' whom we know through Jesus Christ and so knowing have life-eternal ... Islam knows no Godhead, and Allah is not love" (*Ibid.*, p. 176).

109 Samuel M. Zwemer in "The Allah of Islam and the God Revealed in Jesus Christ", in *The Moslem World*, vol. 36 (October, 1946), pp. 308–309.

110 Georges Houssney, "What is Allah like?" in *ReachOut*, vol. 6, nos 3 and 4 (1993), p. 14.

111 *Ibid.*, p. 15.

112 In Phil Parshall, *The Cross and the Crescent: Understanding the Muslim's Mind and Heart*, Tyndale House: Wheaton (1989), p. 24.

113 Bell goes on to say: "Yes there is darkness within the Islamic system but to conclude that Allah is therefore a demonic entity is both confusing for Muslims and only makes the gulf between us bigger. Patient discussion based on the Bible is the only way." In Steve Bell, *op. cit.*, p. 83.

114 Kenneth Cragg, *The Call of the Minaret*, p. 36.

115 Steven Masood, *Into the Light*, STL/Kingsway: Bromley, 1986.

116 G.J.O. Moshay, *Who is this Allah?*, Fireliners International: Ibadan, 1990.

117 Henri Blocher. "A Biblical Response to the Challenge of Islam (John 1:1–18)" in paper presented to EUROM '91 (De Bron, 1991), p. 12.

118 Vincent J. Donovan, *Christianity Rediscovered: An Epistle from the Masai*, SCM Press: London (1982), pp. 63–64. Paul argues strongly in Romans 1:20 that all people are without excuse (in their rejection of God) precisely because God's "invisible qualities" have been clearly on display to all through his creation.

Chapter 5: "Befores" and "Afters"

119 Tobias Mayer suggests that the "Christianity" that heralded Islam "is in practice probably specifically identifiable with Ebionitism, a self-consciously Judaic form of religion". In

op. cit., p. 4. Samuel Zwemer, whose basic assumption was that Muḥammad took an anti-Christian position, concedes that "Muhammad's conception of Christian doctrine betrays a relationship to the Ebionitic-Manichaean teaching which cannot be accidental". In *The Cross above the Crescent: The Validity, Necessity and Urgency of Missions to Moslems*, Zondervan: Grand Rapids (1941), p. 66; as quoted in Peter Ipema, *The Islam Interpretations of Duncan B. MacDonald, Samuel M. Zwemer, A. Kenneth Cragg and Wilfred C. Smith: An Analytical Comparison and Evaluation*, University Microfilms International: Ann Arbor (1972), p. 87. The Ebionites, while not denying the divinity of Christ, construed it as a special dignity conferred upon him (maybe at Jesus' baptism). The Ebionite conception was that, really, of a deified man.

120 "Monism" describes the conviction that only one ultimate principle or being exists. Philosophical monists tend to seek a reduction of substances to a single substance (as, for example Spinoza with his *Deus sive Natura*) or of attributes to a single attribute (as materialists who assert that there is only one kind of substance).

121 Tobias Mayer acknowledges that "the forms of Trinitarianism explicitly condemned in the Qur'ân are heterodox even within Christianity – for example the Collyridian elevation of Mary to the Godhead and the teaching that God is 'the third of three'." In *op. cit.*, p. 8. The Collyridian heresy originated in Thrace but spread to the area north of the Black Sea and to Arabia. The designation "Collyridian" derives from a Greek word signifying "a little loaf". The Collyridians appear to have worshipped Mary, offering her small cakes in an alternative version of the Eucharist. Epiphanius writes against the Collyridians in the late fourth century: "Some women decorate a sort of bench or rectangular litter, spreading a linen cloth over it, on an annual feast day, placing on it a loaf and offering it up in the name of Mary; then all communicate in that loaf ... They tell us that certain women, come here from Thrace, from Arabia, make a loaf in the name of the Ever-Virgin, assem-

ble together in one selfsame place and carry out quite irregular actions in the name of the Blessed Virgin, undertaking to do something blasphemous and forbidden and performing in her name, by means of women, definitely priestly acts." In *Panarion*, chap. 79, paragraph 1. Archpriest Zachariah Butrus refers to the Collyridians as "Mariamists". He suggests that prior to their conversion to Christianity, they worshipped Venus. As Christians, they came to identify Mary as "queen" or "goddess" of heaven, instead of Venus. They were evidently still around until the seventh century and believed in three gods: God, Mary and Christ. In *God is One in the Holy Trinity*, Markaz-al-Shabiba: Basel (n.d.), p. 30. Muḥammad's reaction against "Trinity" was aimed at such a kind of distortion. Meanwhile, Mayer boldly suggests that an "esoteric" interpretation of Sura 17:85 might offer the hint of a properly Trinitarian substrate within the Qur'ân:

> They ask thee concerning
> The Spirit (of inspiration).
> Say: "The Spirit (cometh)
> By command of my Lord ... "

The "Lord", the "Command" (to be equated with the *Logos*) and the "Spirit" provide for Mayer a possible bridge to Christian intention in speaking of "Trinity". Mayer is quite clear that his kind of interpretation of Sura 17:85 is strictly off-limits in the normative teachings of Islam, but he wants to offer his thoughts because – in line with the positive witness elsewhere given in the Qur'ân concerning Christianity (Sura 5:47) – he feels that he has uncovered a clue enabling Muslims to affirm "the intrinsic rectitude of Christian faith" (*Ibid.*, p. 8). Butrus seeks to construct an equivalent – though, to my mind, less convincing – bridge from Sura 4:171:

> Christ Jesus the son of Mary
> Was (no more than)
> An apostle of God,

And His Word,
Which He bestowed on Mary,
And a spirit proceeding
From Him ...

Butrus suggests that this verse makes clear that God has "a personality", "a word", and "a spirit". Despite the fact that the verse goes on to specifically deny the possibility of "Trinity", Butrus declares that "this testimony of the Kurân for the creed of the Trinity is what we Christians proclaim and no more." In *op. cit.*, p. 18.

122 Lapidus, *op. cit.*, p. 194.

123 Bill Musk, *Holy War: Why Some Muslims Become Fundamentalists*. Monarch: London, 2003. This book offers an in-depth look at Islamism and demonstrates the dependence of recent Islamists on the theological views of Ibn Taymiya.

124 *Majmû^c^at ar-rasâ'il wa'l-masâ'il*, al-Manar: Cairo, vol. 1 (1922–1931), p. 62, quoted in Muhammad Umar Memon, *Ibn Taimîya's Struggle against Popular Religion*, Mouton: The Hague (1976), p. 30.

125 *Ibid.*, p. 30.

126 See Moucarry, *op. cit.* (2004), pp. 233–268 for an exposition of some of the major themes with which Ibn al-^c^Arabi deals in his various works.

127 From Abû Ḥâmid Muḥammad al-Ghazâlî, *Al-Munqidh min al-Dalâl* (*Deliverance from Error*, trans. W. Montgomery Watt) in W. Montgomery Watt, *The Faith and Practice of Al-Ghazâlî*, George Allen & Unwin: London (1953), p. 21. Al-Ghazâlî also acknowledges a tradition according to which Prophet Muḥammad declared: "Everyone who is born is born with a sound nature; it is his parents who make him a Jew or a Christian or a Magian" (*Ibid.*, p. 21). We shall consider the significance of this tradition in chapter 10.

128 Kenneth Cragg, *The Call of the Minaret*, p. 63.

129 Kenneth Cragg, *Sandals at the Mosque*, p. 94.

130 Archbishop David Penman, *A Garden of Many Colours: The Report of the Archbishop's Committee on Multicultural Ministry*

and Mission presented to the Synod of the Anglican Diocese of Melbourne (March 1985), p. 159.

131 John Travis, "The C1 to C6 Spectrum" in Parshall (comp.), *The Last Great Frontier: Essays on Muslim Evangelism*, Open Doors with Brother Andrew: Quezon City (2000), pp. 97–100.

132 Joshua Massey, "The Amazing Diversity of God in Drawing Muslims to Jesus" in Phil Parshall (comp.) (2000), *op. cit.*, p. 117.

133 Elizabeth Brooks (pseudonym), "May Puritix: Praying into Smoking Oil", in *International Journal of Frontier Missions*, vol. 17, no. 4 (2000), p. 41.

134 Anwar al-Jundî as quoted by Mahmoud Ayoub, *op. cit.*, p. 38.

135 Kenneth Cragg, *Sandals at the Mosque*, p. 92.

Chapter 6: Set Free or Set Fast?

136 John Bright, *The Kingdom of God*, Abingdon Press: Nashville (1953), p. 28.

137 Taken from Lewis Pelly's translation of the miracle play as quoted in Thomas Patrick Hughes, *Dictionary of Islam*, Premier Book House: Lahore (originally 1885), p. 186.

138 Kenneth Cragg, *Islam and the Muslim*, p. 66.

139 Kenneth Cragg, "Contemporary Trends in Islam" in J. Dudley Woodberry (ed.), *Muslims and Christians on the Emmaus Road*, MARC: Monrovia (1989), p. 40.

140 Kenneth Cragg, *Islam and the Muslim*, Open University Press: Milton Keynes (1978), p. 19.

Chapter 7: Do It in Public?

141 Ghulam Sarwar, *Islam Beliefs and Teachings*, Muslim Educational Trust: London (1987), p. 13.

142 A.A. Maududi, *Towards Understanding Islam*, Idara Tarjuman ul-Qur'an: Lahore (n.d.), pp. 95–96.

143 Kenneth Cragg, *Islam and the Muslim*, p. 49.

144 Gérard Prunier, *The Rwanda Crisis: History of a Genocide*, Hurst: London (1997), p. 253. One such testimony can be

found in *Rwanda: Death, Despair, Defiance*, African Rights Organisation: London (1994), p. 419.

145 See Musk, *Holy War* (2003).

146 John L. Esposito, "Islam and Muslim Politics" in *Voices of Resurgent Islam*, Oxford University Press: New York (1983), pp. 10–11.

147 Callum G. Brown, *The Death of Christian Britain: Understanding Secularisation 1800–2000*, Routledge: London (2001), p. 1.

148 *Ibid.*, p. 10.

149 *Ibid.*, p. 193.

150 Shabbir Akhtar, *Be Careful with Muhammad: The Salman Rushdie Affair*, Bellew: London (1989), p. 130.

151 *Ibid.*, p. 131.

152 Stuart Robinson, *Mosques and Miracles*, CityHarvest Publications: Australia (2003), p. 23.

153 A submission by the Muslim College to the parliamentary select committee on religious offences in England and Wales, made in October 2002, identified only a "small Afro-Caribbean and white convert group (10,000)".

154 Quoted in Robinson, *op. cit.*, p. 24.

155 From an interview with Sheikh Omar Bakri Muhammad by *Al-Hayat* newspaper, as quoted by Katie Morris in *op. cit.*, p. 4.

156 *Ibid.*, p. 4.

157 Jay Smith, "Is it Time to Confront?" in *Bulletin*, Centre for Islamic Studies, London Bible College (2003), pp. 13–14. The Muslim Council of Britain, by contrast, claims that "Sheikh Omar represents no more than a thousand Muslims out of the country's two million." As quoted in Manji, *op. cit.*, p. 223.

158 Ron George, *Issues and Insights into Church Planting in the Muslim World*, WIN Press: Crowborough (2000), p. 46.

159 The April 2001 census gives the following percentage breakdown for a total of 1,546,626 Muslims in England and Wales (see Figure 96). Source: Office for National Statistics.

160 Jorgen S. Nielsen, "Muslim Immigration and Settlement in Britain" in *Research Papers*, no. 21 (March 1984), p. 8.

161 Examined by Danièle Joly in "Ethnic Minorities and Education in Britain: Interaction between the Muslim

Figure 96
Muslims by ethnic group according to 2001 census

Ethnic group	Detail	%
White		**11.62**
	British	4.08
	Irish	0.06
	Other White	7.49
Mixed		**4.15**
	White & Black Caribbean	0.09
	White & Black African	0.68
	White & Asian	1.97
	Other Mixed	1.42
Asian or Asian British		**73.65**
	Indian	8.51
	Pakistani	42.52
	Bangladeshi	16.79
	Other Asian	5.82
Black or Black British		**6.88**
	Black Caribbean	0.29
	Black African	6.22
	Other Black	0.37
Chinese or Other Ethnic Group		**3.70**
	Chinese	0.05
	Other Ethnic Group	3.65

Community and Birmingham Schools." In *Research Papers*, no. 41 (March 1989), pp. 1–28 (p. 17).

162 Joly, *op. cit.*, p. 17.

163 Ghulam Sarwar, *Islam Beliefs and Teachings*, Muslim Educational Trust: London (1987), p. 173.

164 Khalda, "A Personal Reflection" in *Good News for Muslims*, Global Connections: Oswestry (2002).

165 *Ibid.*

Interlude: Eastern Relatives

166 Gleason L. Archer, Jr. in *A Survey of Old Testament Introduction*, Moody Press: Chicago (1974), p. 458.

167 O. Michel on "Melchizedek" in *Theological Dictionary of the New Testament*, Gerhard Kittel (ed.), Geoffrey W. Bromiley (trans.), vol. 4, Eerdmans: Grand Rapids (1967), pp. 568–571.

Chapter 8: A Tainted Past

168 Albert Hourani, *Europe and the Middle East*, Macmillan: London (1980), p. 4.

169 Irshad Manji, *op. cit.*, p. 67.

170 Kate Zebiri, *Muslims and Christians Face to Face*, Oneworld: Oxford (1997), p. 25. See William Montgomery Watt, *Muslim–Christian Encounters: Perceptions and Misperceptions*, Routledge: London (1991), p. 83.

171 Steven Runciman, *The Fall of Constantinople, 1453*, Cambridge University Press: Cambridge (1965), p. 145. An eyewitness account of the pillage is preserved by Makarios Melissenos, the Metropolitan of Monemvasia, in "The Chronicle of the Siege of Constantinople, April 2 to May 29, 1453". In Marios Philippides (trans. and ed.), *The Fall of the Byzantine Empire: A Chronicle by George Sphrantzes*, University of Massachusetts Press: Amherst (1980), pp. 96–136. Melissenos, for example, records: "As soon as the Turks were inside the city, they began to seize and enslave every person who came their way; all those who tried to offer

resistance were put to the sword. In many places the ground could not be seen, as it was covered by heaps of corpses. There were unprecedented events: all sorts of lamentations, countless rows of slaves consisting of noble ladies, virgins, and nuns, who were being dragged by the Turks by their headgear, hair, and braids out of the shelter of churches, to the accompaniment of mourning. There was the crying of children, the looting of our sacred and holy buildings ... There were lamentations and weeping in every house, screaming in the crossroads, and sorrow in all churches; the groaning of grown men and the shrieking of women accompanied looting, enslavement, separation, and rape." *Ibid.*, pp. 130–131. After the three days of licence, an amnesty was declared by Sultan Mehmet II for citizens who had managed to escape detection during the blood-letting.

172 Fulcher was present at the Council of Clermont and heard Pope Urban's message. See Martha McGinty (trans.), *Fulcher of Chartres: Chronicle of the First Crusade*, University of Pennsylvania Press: Philadelphia (1941), pp. 12–17. Fulcher travelled to the Middle East with the Crusade and never returned to Europe. He remained in the east, possibly as the prior of the Mount of Olives.

173 The anonymous author of *Gesta francorum* – probably a cavalry officer – records first-hand the Crusaders' taking of Jerusalem: "At this moment one of our knights, Lethold by name, climbed the wall of the town. At once, even as he ascended, all the defenders of the town fled from the walls through the city, and our people followed them and chased them, killing and sabring them as far as Solomon's Temple, where there was such a slaughter that our people were walking up to their ankles in blood! ... The following morning our people climbed the roof of the Temple, attacked the Saracens, men and women, and decapitated them with drawn swords." In Somerset de Chair (trans.), *The First Crusade: The Deeds of the Franks and Other Jerusalemites*, Golden Cockerel Press: London (1945), pp. 87–88. Fulcher of Chartres, though not present himself, relates that within the temple area "about ten thousand were beheaded" – a

note is included in the text indicating that Albert of Aix said that the number was 300. Fulcher also comments that the Crusaders spared neither women nor children. In McGinty (trans.), *op. cit.*, p. 68. See Steven Runciman's summary of the slaughter of Muslims at al-Aqsâ Mosque on the temple mount and the incineration of Jews in the chief synagogue of Jerusalem. In *The First Crusade*, Cambridge University Press: Cambridge (1980), p. 229.

174 Kate Zebiri, *op. cit.*, pp. 23–24.

175 Mahmoud Ayoub, *op. cit.*, pp. 29–30.

176 Sayyid Qutb, *Fî Zilâl al-Qur'ân*, Dâr al-Shurûq: Beirut, 1973–74, vol. 1, p. 108, quoted in Yvonne Y. Haddad, "Sayyid Qutb: Ideologue of Islamic Revival" in John L. Esposito (ed.), *Voices of Resurgent Islam*, Oxford University Press: New York, 1983, p. 80.

177 For details of the march see Lynn Green, *The Reconciliation Walk: Defusing the Bitter Legacy of the Crusades*, YWAM, Procla Media Productions (1995), video cassette. For a discussion about the appropriateness of the walk, see Colin Chapman, "Living through the 900th Anniversary of the First Crusade: To Apologise or Not to Apologise?" in *The Faith to Faith Newsletter*, no. 1 (November 1998), pp. 1–3.

178 Philip K. Hitti, *The Arabs: A Short History*, Macmillan: London (1968), p. 129.

179 Akbar S. Ahmed, *Living Islam: From Samarkand to Stornoway*, Penguin Books: London (1993), p. 73. Ahmed refers to this scar as "the Andalus syndrome". It resulted from a rich Muslim civilization being abruptly killed off. While "the contours of Muslim civilization" remained visible in places like the fortress palace of Alhambra, loss of political power for Muslims brought physical expulsion and cultural annihilation.

180 His italics. Gerard A. Wiegers, "Muhammad as the Messiah: a comparison of the polemical works of Juan Alonso with the *Gospel of Barnabas*." In *Bibliotheca Orientalis*, vol. 52, parts 3–4 (1995), p. 245. Other concepts in common between Alonso's material and the *Gospel of Barnabas* are the denial that Jesus is the Son of God, the idea that Jesus is a mani-

festation of Elijah, and the central role given to Psalm 110 in proving the Messiahship of Muḥammad. Wiegers cites other parallels between the two works. He also identifies some differences, the most major of which is found in the identity of the persons who underwent the crucifixion instead of Jesus. In the *Gospel of Barnabas* this is Judas, while in Alonso's manuscript BNM MS 9655 it is King Jesus of Damascus (*Ibid.*, pp. 280–286).

181 In Peter Riddell and Peter Cotterell, *Islam in Conflict: Past, Present and Future*, Inter-Varsity Press: Leicester (2003), p. 103.

182 Mahmoud Ayoub, *op. cit.*, p. 35.

183 Quoted in Bell, *op. cit.*, p. 8.

184 Parshall (comp.) (2000), p. 378.

185 Mahmoud Ayoud, *op. cit.*, p. 37.

186 Bell, *op. cit.*, p. 32.

187 For a brief analysis of this Christian fundamentalist view, see Bill Musk, *Holy War: Why Do Some Muslims Become Fundamentalists?*, Monarch: London (2003), pp. 259–263.

188 David Grossman, "Where Death is a Way of Life" in *Guardian Weekly*, 17–23 June 2001, quoted in Colin Chapman, *Whose Promised Land?*, Lion: Oxford (2002), p. 13.

189 Rafiq Zakaria, an Indian Muslim, sums up the feelings of Muslims over the existence of Israel in such graphic language, in *The Struggle Within Islam: The Conflict Between Religion and Politics*, Penguin Books: London (1988), p. 295. Zakaria makes the point that the creation of the State of Israel led to a strong anti-West feeling on behalf of Arabs. That feeling, he suggests, gave an openness towards the Islamization of the Palestinian struggle for justice.

190 Richard W. Rousseau (ed.), *Christianity and Islam: The Struggling Dialogue*, Ridge Row Press: Montrose (1985), p. xiv.

191 Bell, *op. cit.*

192 Margaret Burness, *What Do I Say to my Muslim Friends?* Church Missionary Society: London, 1989.

193 Michael Moore, *Stupid White Men*, Penguin Books: London, 2001.

194 *Ibid.*, pp. 176–184.
195 Chapman (2002), *op. cit.*, p. 244 – emphases his.

Chapter 9: Meeting Head-on

196 Zebiri, *op. cit.*, p. 5.
197 Figures adapted from David Burnett and Todd Johnson, "Annual Statistical Table on Global Mission: 2002" in *International Bulletin of Missionary Research*, vol. 26, no. 1 (January 2002), p. 23. The table reveals that, currently, "Muslims are growing far faster than all other major religions"; *ibid.*, p. 22.
198 M.A. Zaki Badawi, *Islam in Britain (A Public Lecture 1981)*, Ta-Ha Publishers: London (1981), p. 26.
199 See Andrew Wingate's article "Converting Away from Christianity" in *Theology, News and Notes*, Fuller Theological Seminary: Pasadena (Spring 2003), pp. 16–18.
200 *Ibid.*, p. 17.
201 Reprinted in *Courier International*, no. 531 (4–10 January 2001), p. 29 and translated by Ibn Warraq in *Leaving Islam* (2003), p. 92.
202 al-Bukhârî, *al-Ṣaḥîḥ*, vol. 4, book 52, chap. 149, trad. 260, pp. 160–161.
203 Published by Barnabas Fund, November 2003.
204 Kateregga and Shenk, *op. cit.*, p. 112.
205 Samuel P. Huntington, *The Clash of Civilizations and the Remaking of World Order*, Free Press: London (1996), p. 255.

Chapter 10: Dust and Divinity

206 Maurice Bucaille, *op. cit.*, p. 203.
207 My thought here finds a wonderful illustration in C.S. Lewis' book, *Perelandra*, John Lane The Bodley Head: London, 1943. In the climax of that novel, set in Perelandra or Venus, the protagonist – a man pointedly named Ransom – is involved in a desperate struggle to protect the innocence of the "Queen" and "King" of the planet. The novel tells the imaginary story of an Eden-like world being

enabled to retain its purity because the tempter or "Un-man" is frustrated in his attempts to cause the Perelandran equivalent of the biblical Eve to "fall". After a successful, heel-wounding defeat of this enemy, Ransom is brought to a meeting with the King/Adam and Queen/Eve of Perelandra. Later he recounts the details of that encounter to the author of the novel (Lewis!), and Lewis tries to pass on to the reader the import of Ransom's recollection. The King/Adam's face, it seems, looks so like the one in whose image it is made that it is hard to keep in mind that the "human" is only an image, not the original: "You might ask how it was possible to look upon it and not to commit idolatry, not to mistake it for that of which it was the likeness" (p. 210). So with the Islamic concept of human createdness – humankind's uniqueness from the rest of creation is only due to the spirit of God being mixed with clay to produce us. How can we not help, then, but display the likeness of the non-earthly contribution to our make-up?

208 al-Bukhârî, *al-Ṣaḥîḥ*, vol. 8, book 74, chap. 1, trad. 246, p. 160. Muhammad Muhsin Khan (trans.) comments on this tradition: "'His picture' means that Adam has been bestowed with life, knowledge, power of hearing, seeing, understanding, etc., but the features etc. of Adam are different from that of Allah, only the names are the same" (*Ibid.*, p. 160). The tradition does seem to suggest, however, that in some manner at least, the divine attributes are applicable to people.

209 An equivalent version of angelic reluctance to do obeisance to humankind is found in *Vita Adae et Evae*, a Jewish apocryphal tale of the life of Adam and Eve. In this account, God, having created Adam in his own image, sends Michael to gather the angels together to admire what he has made. God orders the angels to bow down to their younger sibling. Michael obeys but Satan refuses. Because of his refusal, Satan is cast down to earth, from where he sets about to get his revenge on Adam. Later, after successfully engineering Adam's "fall", Satan explains to Adam in his own words why he hates him so much:

> ... And Michael went out and called all the angels saying: "Worship the image of God as the Lord God hath commanded." And Michael himself worshipped first; then he called me and said: "Worship the image of God the Lord." And I answered, "I have no (need) to worship Adam." And since Michael kept urging me to worship, I said to him, "Why dost thou urge me? I will not worship an inferior and younger being (than I). I am his senior in the Creation; before he was made was I already made. It is his duty to worship me." (*Vita Adae et Evae*, 14:1–3).

210 Kateregga and Shenk, *op. cit.*, p. 52.
211 Iskander Jadeed lists some of the more significant words used in the Qur'ân to denote sin in *Sin and Atonement in Islam and Christianity*, Markaz al-Shabiba: Basel (n.d.), pp. 3–8. His description is summarized in Figure 97.
212 Kateregga and Shenk, *op. cit.*, p. 45.
213 al-Bukhârî, *al-Ṣaḥîḥ*, vol. 6, book 60, chap. 230, trad. 298, p. 284.
214 In James Alison, *The Joy of Being Wrong: Original Sin through Easter Eyes*, Crossroad Publishing: New York (1998), pp. 153–154. Alison seeks to comprehend "original sin" from the vantage point of redemption. He makes use of René Girard's mimetic model of the origin and structure of human behaviour, building on Girard's concept of "mimetic desire" (people imitating each other or wanting what the other is or has) and his insight into the processes of communal victimization (rivalry, conflict, collective violence) and the significance of scapegoating. Alison argues that original sin is fully and radically known only through redemption and resurrection – by being seen "through Easter eyes". If human beings are those who, through mimesis, are beings "being-constituted-by-another", the key question becomes that of identifying what sort of relationship to which "other" is being formed or expressed. Alison suggests that Christ-as-victim, yet raised from the dead, offers the possibility to humankind of a new pacific mimesis instead of the old, rivalistic mimesis into which

Figure 97
Sin as described in the Qur'ân

Arabic	English	Reference
al-dhanb	offence, crime, misdeed	"... faults of the past ... " (Sura 48:2)
al-faḥshâ'	vile deed, crime, adultery	"... shameful deeds ... " (Sura 6:151)
al-wizr	sin as a heavy load, burden	"... thy burden ... " (Sura 94:2)
al-ḍalâl	straying, to be lost	"... found thee wandering ... " (Sura 93:7)
al-kufr	godlessness, atheism	"... unbelief ... " (Sura 49:7)
al-ẓulm	injustice, unfairness	"... people of iniquity ... " (Sura 26:10)
al-ithm	crime, misdeed, offence	"Eschew all sin ... " (Sura 6:120)
al-fudjûr	immorality, depravity	"... the wicked ... " (Sura 82:14)
al-khaṭi'a	sin, offence	"... a fault ... " (Sura 4:112)
al-sharr	evil	"... an atom's weight of evil ... " (Sura 99:8)
al-sayyi'a	offence, misdeed	"... if any do evil ... " (Sura 27:90)
al-sû'	evil, misfortune	"... whoever works evil ... " (Sura 4:123)
al-fasâd	corruption	"... to spread mischief ... " (Sura 2: 205)
al-fisk	viciousness, moral depravity	"... those who are perverse." (Sura 2:99)
al-buhtân	slander, lying	"... a most serious slander!" (Sura 24:16)

we are all locked outside of Christ. His is a highly creative, orthodox Catholic revisiting of the doctrine of original sin.

215 Elaine Pagels, *Adam, Eve, and the Serpent*, pp. 98–126, in a chapter entitled "The Politics of Paradise".

216 Book 1, chapter 9, part 3 in *St Augustine: The Retractations*, Mary Inez Bogan (trans.), Catholic University of America Press: Washington DC (1968), p. 44.

217 Elaine Pagels, *Adam, Eve, and the Serpent*, p. 150. The provincial Council of Carthage (AD 418), the Second Council of Orange (AD 529) and eventually the Council of Trent (AD 1545–1563) promulgated canons defining and defending Augustine's views on original sin. The earlier councils were concerned in that process with confounding Pelagian and Manichaean interpretations, and the last with addressing issues raised by Lutheranism.

218 Moucarry gives a helpful summary of these theological debates in *op. cit.* (2004), pp. 81–94. The issue is an important one because Muslims need to know whether, in committing a sin, they might be committing a major sin, thus deserving eternal punishment unless they repent. Also, if the sin in question comprises an offence (such as adultery or theft), what kind of punishment in this life is required? A major sin of robbery (however defined) would carry a far stronger punishment than a minor sin of robbery.

219 The qur'ânic punishment for adultery is actually one hundred lashes (Sura 24:2). This text has been considered by Muslim commentators to be abrogated by "the verse of the stoning" – a verse found not in the Qur'ân but in the *ḥadîth*. See Moucarry, *op. cit.* (2004), p. 275 for an explanation.

220 By repenting *and* killing themselves, the sinful Israelites would show that their repentance was genuine. They would have accepted the punishment that they truly deserved, namely death.

221 Abû Jaᶜfar al-Tabarî, *The Commentary on the Qur'an* (*Jamiᶜ al-Bayân ᶜan Ta'wîl ây al-Qur'ân*, trans. and ed. J. Cooper), Oxford University Press: Oxford (1987), p. 251. Al-Tabarî is dealing here with the interpretation of "*fa-azalla-huma 'l-shaitânu ᶜan-hâ*" from the beginning of verse 36 of Sura 2:

"Then Satan caused them to slip therefrom." The words of Wahb ibn Munabbih are quoted from ᶜUmar ibn ᶜAbd al-Raḥmân ibn Muhrib whose opinion al-Tabarî records.

222 See Moucarry, *op. cit.* (2004), pp. 106–116 for an illustration of some of the arguments about the nature of repentance by Islamic theologians of different schools.

223 al-Bukhârî, *al-Ṣaḥîḥ*, vol. 6, book 60, chap. 3, trad. 3, pp. 3–5.

224 From "Poem 14" in John Donne, *Selections from Divine Poems, Sermons, Devotions, and Prayers*, ed. J. Booty, Mahwah: New York (1990), p. 83.

Chapter 11: Made-up Messiah

225 Jesus is referred to once in the Gospels as "son of Mary" in Mark 6:3. Certainly the intent of that reference is to remonstrate that Jesus is nobody special, only Mary's son. The speakers are people from Jesus' home town who are offended by Jesus' flouting of social and religious conventions.

226 Carol Ann Duffy, "The Virgin Punishing the Infant", in *Selling Manhattan*, Anvil Press Poetry: London (1987), p. 42.

227 From "Let us go to Bethlehem" in Rhys Prichard, no. 82, "Crist sydd oll yn oll" in *Gogoneddus Arglwydd, Henffych Well! Detholiad o ryddiaeth a barddoniaeth Gristnogol Gymraeg drwy're Canrifoedd*, ed. Gwynn ap Gwilym, (1999), p. 152, trans. R.D. Williams; quoted in Rowell et al., *op. cit.*, p. 154.

228 Gulshan Esther, *The Torn Veil* (Thelma Sangster ed.; Noble Din trans.), Marshalls: Basingstoke (1984), p. 59.

229 Irenaeus' summary of Cerinthus on the crucifixion may be found in J. Stevenson (ed.), *A New Eusebius*, SPCK: London (1957), p. 96. The quotation from Irenaeus on Basilides may be found in Henry Bettenson (ed.), *Documents of the Christian Church*, Oxford University Press: Oxford (1963), p. 36. The excerpt from the *Coptic Apocalypse of Peter* may be found in Henriette W. Havelaar (ed.), *Nag Hammadi Codex VII, 3*, Akademie Verlag: Berlin (1999), pp. 47 and 49.

230 Kenneth Cragg, *Jesus and the Muslim*, pp. 169–176.

231 Sobhi Malek, *Islam: Introduction and Approach*, International Correspondence Institute: Irving (1992), p. 224.

232 Tobias Mayer, *op. cit.*, p. 5.

233 Sobhi Malek, *op. cit.*, p. 223.

234 Ahmad D. Azhar, *Christianity in History*, Sh. Muhammad Ashraf: Lahore (1968), p. 23. Azhar's aim in distinguishing the two is, of course, to permit his polemic against the "Jesus Christ" presented in the New Testament. His view is that the Christian Jesus is not the historic Jesus. Rather, the "'Risen' Christ, the 'Redeemer' and the 'Son of God' are, as will gradually emerge, Pauline concepts, unknown to the historic Jesus himself" (*Ibid.*, p. 22).

235 Quoted in John Travis, "Is It Fitting for Christians to Use the Name *Isa Al Masih*?" in Parshall (comp.), *op. cit.* (2000), p. 363.

236 *Ibid.*, pp. 359–367. Travis's article was originally written in 1990. In a footnote at the end of the article as it is reproduced in Parshall's compilation, Travis notes: "Although *Yesus Kristus* is still the most commonly used term for Jesus in Bible translations [in Indonesia], from 1994 onward there have been a number of Bibles published using the name *Isa Al Masih*" (p. 367).

237 In 1992, Luis F. Bernabé Pons presented his thesis on the Morisco origin of the *Gospel of Barnabas* in Alicante, Spain. He suggests that the genre used by the author lies somewhere between that of the New Testament Gospels and that of the *ḥadîth*. Bernabé Pons demonstrates parallels to the *Gospel of Barnabas* in other Morisco authors of the same period (Ahmad al-Hayari Bejerano of Granada/Morocco and Ibrahim al-Taybili of Toledo/Tunis) and especially cites al-Taybili as referring to the *Gospel of Barnabas* directly, plus reproducing its denial that Jesus is Messiah. Luis F. Bernabé Pons, *Edición y estudio del manuscrito Espanol del Evangelio de Bernabé. Evangelio hispano-islámico de autor morisco*, 5 vols, PhD thesis: Alicante, 1992. Summarized in Oddbjorn Leirvik, *Images of Jesus Christ in Islam*, Swedish Institute of Missionary Research: Uppsala (1999), p. 138.

238 Luis Bernabé Pons describes in his thesis the "plot" leading to the discovery of the *Gospel of Barnabas*. In March 1588, workers discovered a lead box under the ruins of a minaret in Granada where a church was about to be constructed. The lead box contained a bone (reputedly of Stephen) plus a painting and parchment supposedly written by the patron saint of Granada (Caecilio) containing a text in Latin, Arabic and Castilian that included a prophecy of John the Apostle intended for Granada. The Morisco, Miguel de Luna (official translator for King Philip II), was asked to translate the Arabic. Pope Sixtus V (in whose library the Italian version of the *Gospel of Barnabas* would later be found) gave permission for the investigation on the authenticity of the text to continue. In February 1595, 22 lead boxes were found in Granada. The texts in these boxes related to the arrival of St James in Spain along with his disciples. One book from these boxes, about the "Truth of the Gospel", is attributed to the mother of Jesus, who had received it from Gabriel in a splendid light. The champion of this Gospel will be a conqueror king of the Arab kings (an Ottoman, by whom the Moriscos expected to be rescued?) who will call a council on the island of Cyprus (Barnabas' island) and have the book "The Truth of the Gospel" accepted by it. Bernabé Pons goes as far as to suggest that one of three possible candidates is responsible for the composition of the *Gospel of Barnabas*: Miguel de Luna, Ahmad al-Hayari Bejarano or, most likely in his opinion, Ibrahim al-Taybili. Bernabé Pons suggests that the *Gospel of Barnabas* was not distributed simply because the Spanish authorities took measures between AD 1609 and 1614 to expel all Moriscos from the country. A syncretistic Gospel might have been of use to the Moriscos in Spain but it was irrelevant to Moriscos already in exile in Morocco, Tunis or Turkey. Various suggestions are made as to why copies of the *Gospel* in both Spanish and Italian were deemed necessary.

239 A few Muslim authors have rejected the *Gospel of Barnabas* as a forgery. They include Yahya al-Hashimi of Syria, who contends that the Gospel was written by a Jew who wanted to incite hatred between Muslims and Christians, ʿAbbas Mahmud al-ʿAqqad of Egypt and Mahmoud Ayoub.

240 Bernabé Pons, *op. cit.*, p. 174 and pp. 151–152. Gerard Wiegers describes a specific manuscript (BNM MS 9655) dating from this same period (AD 1602 to 1612) that shows a number of parallels to the *Gospel of Barnabas* though without mentioning that work (see Note 180 above). From other contemporary Muslims sources, Wiegers deduces that the author of this manuscript is Juan Alonso from Aragon, a child of Christian parents and master of theology who became a Muslim and left for Tetuan. Several works designed for the Morisco community were composed by Juan Alonso. Wiegers notes that the concept of Muḥammad as the Messiah in both this manuscript and in the *Gospel of Barnabas* is closely linked with the denial that Jesus is the Son of God. Wiegers proposes that BNM MS 9655 had an influence on the composition of the *Gospel of Barnabas*. See G.A. Wiegers, *op. cit.*, p. 287. Wiegers believes that the *Gospel of Barnabas* itself was originally written, in Italian, in Istanbul. There also, he suggests, the Spanish translation was composed by Mostafa de Aranda, a Muslim from Aragon. He deems it likely that Mostafa de Aranda is in reality the author of the *Gospel* and wonders whether Juan Alonso's Muslim name was Mostafa de Aranda.

241 In Wiegers, *op. cit.*, p. 252.

242 Oddbjorn Leirvik, *op. cit.*, p. 139.

243 Kenneth Cragg, "Islam and Incarnation" in *Truth and Dialogue: The Relationship between World Religions*, edited by John Hick, Sheldon Press: London (1974), pp. 126–139. In this paper, Cragg investigates qur'ânic "sentness" and "sentness" in Christ. He concludes that "the human has to be known in its divine credentials: the divine must be authenticated in its human locus. Traditional minds, in either faith, may see this common issue of the 'rightness' of association as infinitely disparate and contrasted. The pre-

sent case is that, in 'association' itself, in 'sentness' with its divine fiat and its human aegis, we have a potentially recognisable affinity, beyond and beneath all else, however abiding and exacting the disparities" (*Ibid.*, p. 135).

244 David Brown, *op. cit.*, pp. 39–40.

245 See John Gilchrist's booklet *What Indeed was the Sign of Jonah?*, Qur'an and Bible Series, no. 2, South Africa.

246 In Charles Upton (trans.), *Doorkeeper of the Heart: Versions of Rabi'a*, Threshold Books: London (c. 1988), p. 45.

247 Süleyman Chelebi (F. Lyman MacCullum trans.), *The Mevlidi Sherif*, John Murray: London (1943), pp. 38–39.

248 Bill Musk, *Touching the Soul of Islam*, Monarch: London (2004), p. 178.

249 Imâm Abû ᶜAbd Allâh Mâlik ibn Anas (716–795) was the founder of the Malikite school of Sunnî law. His authority concerning the *ḥadîth* or traditions is generally quoted as decisive. The *Muwatta'* (meaning "that which has been compiled") contains his collection of *ḥadîth*. It constitutes the earliest compilation of *ḥadîth*. The tradition quoted here is found in book 41, chap. 1, trad. 5.

250 Jean-Marie Gaudeul (1999), *op. cit.*, pp. 164–165.

Chapter 12: Delightful Kids

251 Alec Motyer, *The Message of James*, Inter-Varsity Press: Leicester (1985), p. 151.

252 Chawkat Moucarry, *Islam and Christianity at the Crossroads*, trans. David Monkcom, Lion: Tring (1988), p. 13.

253 Austin P. Flannery (ed.), from "Nostra Aetate" in *Documents of Vatican II*, Eerdmans: Grand Rapids (1975), p. 740.

254 From "Lumen Gentium" in *ibid.*, p. 367.

255 Kenneth Cragg, "Foreword II" in Kateregga and Shenk, *op. cit.*, p. 15.

256 Duncan B. Macdonald, "The Christian Message is Peace", in *The Moslem World*, vol. 23, no. 4 (1933), p. 327.

257 From al-Tabarî's commentary on the Qur'ân (*op. cit.*), p. 251.

258 Though see a different interpretation of the plural verb in this verse in chapter 10.

259 See Bill Musk, *The Unseen Face of Islam*, Monarch: London, 2003 for a detailed analysis of the cosmology of folk Islam.

260 "Intimate enemy" is the phrase used by Elaine Pagels in her powerful and disturbing study, *The Origin of Satan*, Vintage Books: New York (1995), p. 49.

261 Elaine Pagels has further developed this latter theme in *Adam, Eve, and the Serpent* (1988). In her chapter "Christians Against the Roman Order", she quotes Justin Martyr and Clement of Alexandria especially, illustrating their contention that "Christians had discovered a terrible secret: the powers behind the Roman magistrates – and, in particular, behind the emperors themselves – are not gods, nor are they mere appearances, as the Platonists said, but demons, active evil forces bent upon corrupting and destroying human beings, determined to blind people to the truth that there is only one God, creator of all, who made all humankind alike" (p. 39).

262 Jack Nelson-Pallmeyer, *Is Religion Killing Us? Violence in the Bible and the Quran*, Trinity Press International: Harrisburg (2003), p. 97.

263 Gilles Kepel, *The Revenge of God* (trans. Alan Braley), Polity Press: Cambridge, 1994.

264 Huntington, *op. cit.*, p. 42.

265 Nelson-Pallmeyer, *op. cit.*, p. 146.

266 Kenneth Cragg, *Christianity in World Perspective*, Lutterworth Press: London (1968), p. 83.

267 Martin Luther, *The Small Catechism* (1529) as translated by Robert E. Smith for *Project Wittenberg*, Concordia Theological Seminary: Fort Wayne (1994). See Mark Swanson's comments on Luther as part of a gracious minority in medieval Europe whose views on Islam contrasted with the standard, polemical attitude. In Mark N. Swanson, "'Thinking through' Islam" in *Word & World*, vol. 22, no. 3 (2002), p. 268.

268 The outstanding Roman Catholic example of an eirenic approach to Islam is provided, of course, in Francis of Assisi. At the time of the infamous Crusades, Francis entered the camp of the Muslim "enemy" in Egypt during

the autumn of AD 1219 to share the gospel with the sultan, al-Kamil. See Christine A. Mallouhi's challenging account of Francis of Assisi's approach to Muslims in *Waging Peace on Islam*, Monarch: London (2000).

269 Taken from Kenneth Cragg (ed. and trans.), *Common Prayer: A Muslim–Christian Spiritual Anthology*, Oneworld: Oxford (1999), p. 69.

Appendix 5 Index

Aaron 53, 98–99, 250, 315
ᶜAbbassid 190–191, 257
Abd al-Rahman III 266–267
Abdul Aziz ibn Saud, King 289
ᶜAbdullah ibn Masᶜud 91
Abdul Majid II 289
Abdu'l-Muṭṭalib 142
Abel 108, 315, 433
Abraham, Abram 12–13, 27, 29, 31, 39–43, 73, 81–82, 96, 108, 127, 129–131, 155, 159, 211, 248–250, 300, 327–329, 356, 367, 369, 376–377, 400, 414, 420, 433–434
abrogation 103, 104, 105, 431
Abû Bakr, Caliph 57, 62, 69, 72, 90, 189, 191, 207, 415, 418, 424, 426
Abû Ḥamza 93, 236, 245
Abû Mûsâ Ashᶜari 91
Abû Ṭâlib 47–48, 187–188, 190, 207
Abyssinia 52, 69, 72, 109, 187, 256
Acta Sanctorum 437
Acts, book of 21, 56, 146–147, 155–157, 178, 185, 215, 366, 441
Adam 26–27, 77–78, 96, 108, 196, 212, 306–308, 311–319, 324, 330–331, 333, 350–351, 383–385, 412, 433, 444, 459–460
Adam, Eve, and the Serpent (Pagels) 422, 462, 468
Adoptionism 197
adultery 64, 320, 322–323, 362–363, 461–462
Afghanistan 173, 278, 417
Against Heresies (Irenaeus) 167
Ahmadîya 115, 345, 409
al-aḥruf al-sabᶜa 93, 409
ᶜÂ'isha 49, 55, 62, 69, 71–72, 128, 207, 415, 427, 443
Akhenaten, Pharaoh 109, 111, 439
Akhtar, Shabbir 233–234, 452
ᶜAlawiyya Order 242
Alexander, Bishop 197, 416
Alexandria 109, 165–166, 193–195, 197–201, 203, 205–206, 295, 316, 351, 416–417, 421, 468
Alfonso VI 266, 268
Alfonso VIII 267, 269
Alfonso XI 269
ᶜAlî, Caliph 48, 62, 90, 190–191, 207–209, 211–212, 294, 409, 414, 417
Alison, James 315, 460
Allâh 34, 99, 118–131, 133–135, 137, 140–143, 145, 147–149, 295, 328, 348, 391, 409, 412
Almohad dynasty 267–268
Almoravid dynasty 257, 266–269
amâna, trust 309–310, 409
Amenhotep IV, Pharaoh 109
Amos 57–59, 423
ᶜAmr ibn Luhayy 142, 446
A Muslim and a Christian in Dialogue (Kateregga and Shenk) 403, 422
Ananias 366
Andalusia, *see* Spain 257
Andrae, Tor 399, 445
angel 26, 42–43, 47, 49–50, 54–57, 62, 77, 83, 89, 108, 187, 216, 307–308, 330, 333–334, 336, 338–340, 352–353, 359, 375, 382–385, 435–436, 459–460
annunciation 333, 336
Anṣâr 61–62, 88, 91, 409
Antioch 21, 156–157, 185, 193–195, 198, 202–203, 205–206, 260, 344, 416, 445
Apollinarians 202
Apollinarius, Bishop 200–202
Apology (Justin Martyr) 166
al-Aqṣâ 456
Arabia 43, 47, 60–61, 66, 79, 83, 107, 109, 130, 134, 142, 150, 159, 189–190, 208, 248–249, 263, 278, 366, 413, 418, 448
Arabia: The Cradle of Islam (Zwemer) 408, 446

Arabic Gospel of the Infancy of the Saviour 108–109, 338, 438
Arafat, President Yasser 281
Aragon 267–270, 353, 466
Aramaic 107, 125–126, 134, 158, 249, 414, 421, 431
Aratus 147
Archer Jr., Gleason L. 249, 454
Areopagus 146
Arian controversy 196, 200, 416
Arianism 195, 197, 199–200
Arius 168, 197–200, 416
Armageddon 385
Armenia 193–195, 197, 205, 255
aslama 24–25, 409
Assyria 59, 78, 187, 194
Atatürk 222
Aten 109–110
Athanasius, Bishop 199–201, 416
Athens 81, 146–147
Augustine, Bishop 165, 167–168, 196, 314–319, 330, 416, 462
Aws 61
âya, *see* sign 357, 409
Ayoub, Mahmoud 262, 399, 451, 456–457, 466
al-Azhar 79, 289, 295, 409
Azhar, Ahmad 348, 399, 464

Babylonia 39, 59, 187, 213, 425
Badajoz 266, 268
Badawi, Zaki 273, 399, 458
Badr, Battle of 65, 67, 72, 217, 345, 409
Baghdad 171, 173, 175, 206, 256–257, 267, 417
Balfour Declaration 274
Balkans 199, 255, 258, 276–278
Bangladesh 183, 226, 239–240, 453
al-Banna', Hasan 226
Baptist Missionary Society 285
Barcelona 267
Barelwi 242
Barnabas 146, 156–157, 350–351, 367, 465
Baruch 98
Basilides 344, 463
Basra 91, 93, 361, 416
bayt-Allâh 121–122, 409
Beautiful Names of God, the 124, 135–136, 409
Bell, Steve 144, 275, 280, 399, 443, 447, 452, 457
Berber 265, 268, 416
Bernabé Pons, Luis F. 353, 464–466
Bevan Jones, L. 349
Bible 15, 34–35, 42, 54, 71, 73, 75, 80, 82, 85–88, 98–100, 107, 109, 111–113, 115–116, 118–119, 126, 128–129, 131–132, 137–142, 144, 148–149, 164, 182, 192, 249, 276, 281, 297–298, 301, 314–315, 320, 329–331, 336, 348–349, 385–386, 389–390, 392, 412, 424–425, 430, 433, 439, 443–444, 447, 464, 467
The Bible and the Qur'an (Masood) 115, 404, 442
The Bible, the Qur'an and Science (Bucaille) 400
Birmingham 241, 243, 399, 403, 454
"Birth-song of the Prophet" (Chelebi) 26, 362, 412, 416
bismillâh 134, 409
The Book of Common Prayer 420
The Book of Wisdom of Amenemope 111
Bradford 234, 237, 241
Brierley, Peter 237–238
Bright, John 188, 451
British and Foreign Bible Society 285
Brockett, Adrian 428
Brooks, Elizabeth 183–184, 451
Brother Mark 114–115, 442
Brown, Callum 229–230, 233, 452
Brown, David 356, 400, 467
Bucaille, Maurice 113, 306, 400, 439, 458
al-Bukhârî, Muḥammad 55, 91, 128, 323, 328, 400, 416, 420–421, 424, 426–427, 443–444, 458–460, 463
Burness, Margaret 280, 457
Burton, John 91, 400, 426–428
Bush, President George W. 264
Butrus, Zachariah 400, 449–450
Byzantium, *see* Constantinople 192, 256, 260

Cadiz 269
Caesarea 156, 198, 201
Caesarea Philippi 355
Cain 108, 315, 433
Cairo 79, 107, 257, 289, 409, 426, 450
caliph 48, 90, 170–171, 174, 189–190, 208–209, 211, 235, 256–257, 266–267, 291, 307, 412, 414–415, 417–418, 426
The Call of the Minaret (Cragg) 134, 400, 424, 444, 447, 450
Camel, Battle of the 207
Cappadocian Fathers 201
Carthage 165–167, 417–418, 462

Castile 266–270
Catalonia 268–269
Catholicism 197
Cerinthus 344, 463
Chalcedon, Council of 193–194, 203–205, 342
The Challenge of Islam to Christians (Pawson) 234–235, 405
Chapman, Colin 16, 138–139, 275–276, 281, 400, 446, 456–458
Chelebi, Süleyman 26, 362, 412, 416, 420, 467
Christendom 255–256, 261, 378
Christian Zionism 263
Christianity 12, 21–23, 28–29, 31–38, 47, 99–100, 116–118, 128, 134, 142, 144, 155–156, 158–159, 163–164, 165–167, 186, 192–194, 197–198, 207–208, 213, 217–218, 229, 238, 245–247, 255, 257–258, 261, 264, 271, 278–279, 283–286, 293–298, 319, 326, 332, 341, 347, 374–380, 388–390, 394, 416, 419, 430, 443–444, 447–449, 458
Chrysostom, John 316, 317
Church Missionary Society 285, 442, 457
Clair-Tisdall, William St 114–115, 400, 442
Clement (of Alexandria) 165–167, 316, 416, 468
Clermont 260, 455
The Collection of the Qur'ân (Burton) 400, 426
Commission for World Mission and Evangelism 287
Commonwealth Immigration Act 241
Constantine, Emperor 36, 164, 190–193, 198–200, 285, 378, 416
Constantinople 192–195, 200, 202, 204–206, 258–261, 267, 271, 314, 417, 454
Constantinople, Council of 194, 198, 201, 205
Constantius, Emperor 200
contextualization 179–186
continuity 35, 79, 143–147, 156, 160, 163, 166–167, 185–186, 377–378
conversion, convert 48, 52, 57, 65–66, 69, 88, 128, 143–145, 157, 159, 164, 166, 175, 182, 184, 187, 190, 192, 206, 227, 235–236, 256, 260, 265, 269, 271, 285–286, 288, 293–297, 324, 353–354, 366, 386, 415, 417, 423, 449, 452, 458
Coptic Apocalypse of Peter 402, 463
Copts 256, 288
Cordoba 256–257, 266–267, 269, 271
Cotterell, Peter 271, 406, 457
Cragg, Kenneth 115, 134, 144, 177, 179, 184, 211, 217–218, 222, 343, 345, 354, 380, 391, 400–402, 421, 423, 442, 444, 447, 450–451, 463, 466–469
Creed of Nicaea 198–199
Crete 80–81
crucifixion 32, 182, 216, 329, 341, 343–347, 351, 356, 380, 387, 414, 457, 463
crusade 258, 261–264, 268
Crusades, the 37, 255, 258–264, 278, 280, 455–456, 468
Cyprian 29, 165–167, 417
Cyprus 156–157, 465
Cyril, Bishop 203, 205

Damascus 91, 93, 155, 170–171, 174, 190, 208–209, 249, 366, 415, 457
dâr al-Ḥarb 378, 410
dâr al-Islâm 378, 410
Dashti, 'Ali 70, 103, 401, 422, 430
David, King 27, 44, 71, 76, 80, 85–86, 95–96, 189–190, 302, 332, 334, 336, 362, 393, 415, 423
daʿwa 37, 235, 237, 288–290, 410
Dawood, N.J. 427–428
The Death of Christian Britain (Brown) 229, 452
Declaration of the Rights of Man and Citizen 228
Deedat, Ahmed 113, 237, 439
"definition" of Chalcedon 203–205
Delhi 287, 291–292
Deliverance from Error (al-Ghazâlî) 175–176, 450
Deobandi 242, 292
Deuteronomy 44, 56, 68, 73, 114, 132, 164, 315, 323
dhikr 177, 410
dîn 22, 410
discontinuity 35, 144–147, 156, 162–163, 167, 186, 377–378
Donatist controversy 196
Donne, John 330, 463
Duffy, Carol Ann 336–337, 463

Ebionite 158, 202, 448
ecumenism 287
Edict of Milan 191
Edinburgh 287
Egypt 41, 53, 62, 72, 74, 84, 108, 188, 195, 199, 203, 205, 227, 255–256,

259, 262–263, 275, 295, 297, 300–302, 369, 409, 418, 437, 466, 468
El 125–127, 129, 410–411
'êl 126–127, 129, 131, 410, 443
'elôah 126, 249, 410
'elôhîm 29, 126–127, 164, 249, 410
Enlightenment, the 22, 28, 225, 258, 272
Enoch 29, 77, 248, 368–369
Ephesus, Council of 193–194, 203–204
Epimenides 80–81, 83, 147
Epistle of Barnabas 350
Eric, Walter 142, 405, 446
Esau 43–44, 138
Ethiopia 52, 150, 193–194, 205
Eusebius 191, 198
Eutyches, Abbot 203–205
Eutychians 202
Eve 26, 311–313, 315, 318–319, 324, 330–331, 350, 383–384, 433, 459
evil 25, 81, 127, 177, 211–212, 249, 278, 309–316, 324, 326–327, 330, 334, 343, 362, 364, 379, 382–384, 386–387, 414–415, 419, 424, 436, 461, 468
exodus 20, 54, 62, 69, 74, 187–188, 225, 230, 249
Ezra 98, 342, 360, 431

faith 12–16, 20–38, 41, 49, 62–63, 82, 85, 87–88, 100–101, 106, 112, 114–115, 117, 129, 132, 136, 138–142, 144–145, 155, 158–160, 163–164, 166–167, 169–170, 176, 178, 180, 183–186, 188, 191–192, 197–198, 200, 205, 211–213, 217–218, 220–221, 223–225, 227, 229–232, 235–237, 243–247, 251–252, 255–256, 261, 271–273, 279, 282–285, 287–288, 291–298, 302, 306, 310, 313, 316, 320, 329, 331, 351, 354, 356–357, 360, 367–369, 374–382, 388–394, 411, 413, 416, 420, 433, 445, 449, 466
Faraj, ʿAbd al-Salâm 173
Farrer, Austin 116–117, 442
Fâtiḥa 22, 219, 410
Fâṭima 48, 69, 212, 414, 417
Fâṭimid 257, 260
fatwâ 213, 263, 410
Fernando II 267, 269
Finsbury Park Mosque 236
First Book of Enoch 435
al-fiṭra 176, 410
frankincense 150–152
Friendship First (Bell) 280, 399
Fulcher of Chartres 260, 401, 455–456
al-furqân 95, 410

Gabriel 47, 50, 54–55, 77, 83, 89, 93, 99, 114, 207, 333, 336, 338, 340, 350, 352, 465
Gaudeul, Jean-Marie 363, 422, 467
Gaul 165, 167, 350
Genesis 39–44, 73, 88, 108, 126–127, 164, 248–250, 300–301, 314–316, 318–319, 324, 433, 435
Genesis Rabba (Neusner) 405, 434
Gentile 35, 81, 155–158, 163, 178–179, 185, 216, 281, 366–367, 386, 428–429, 439
George, Ron 237, 401, 452
Gesta francorum 400, 455
Gethsemane 216, 387
al-Ghazâlî, Muḥammad 172, 175–177, 268, 313, 414, 417, 431, 450
Ginzberg, Louis 434
Glory of the Martyrs (Gregory of Tours) 407, 436
Glucharev, Makary 286
gnostic 165–166, 344
God is One in the Holy Trinity 400, 449
god, supreme 121, 123, 125–126, 128, 410–411
god, tribal 120–123, 130
Gospel 19, 29, 35, 73–75, 95–96, 99–100, 109, 113, 128, 143, 148, 152, 155–158, 161, 178–180, 184–186, 213, 216, 236, 246, 322, 336–338, 343–344, 346, 349–351, 353–357, 363, 365–366, 374, 377, 386–387, 411, 413, 422, 430, 441–443, 463–466, 469
Gospel of Barnabas 270, 348–354, 399–400, 406–408, 456–457, 464–466
Gospel of Pseudo-Matthew 108, 335, 437
Gospel of the Nativity of Mary 334
Gospel of Thomas 108, 338
Granada 266–270, 464–465
Greek 31, 35, 44, 67, 75, 80–81, 99, 114, 128, 146, 156–158, 163–167, 178–179, 197–199, 205, 256–257, 317, 333, 348, 357, 373, 385, 411–413, 415–416, 421, 436, 442, 445, 448
Greek Orthodoxy 197

Gregory of Tours 436
Gregory VII, Pope 268
Grossfeld, Bernard 402, 434
Guidelines on Meeting the Religious and Cultural Needs of Muslim Pupils 243
Guillaume, A. 402, 443, 446
Gulf War 278
Gush Emunîm 389, 410

ḥadîth 41, 89, 92–93, 100, 130–131, 135, 169, 171, 208, 212, 294, 307, 323, 327, 340, 346, 397, 410–412, 414, 416, 430–431, 462, 464, 467
Hafs 93–94, 428
Ḥafṣa 71, 90–91, 424, 426–427
Hagar 40–43, 130
ḥajj 72, 221, 292, 410
ḥalâl food 243, 410
al-Ḥallâj, al-Ḥusayn ibn Mansûr 172–174, 413, 417
Ḥanbal 23, 169, 172, 417
ḥanîf 124, 410, 420
Ḥanîfa 169, 417
Ḥasan, son of ʿAlî 207, 209, 212
Ḥasan al-Basrî 106, 171
Hauwa, *see* Eve 311, 383–384
hijra 20, 48, 62–63, 86, 88, 187–188, 217, 237, 378, 411, 421
Hindu 21, 80, 231, 288, 290–291, 298
Ḥirâ 48, 50, 187
Ḥizbollah International 263
Holy Spirit 75, 99, 112, 134, 148, 155, 158–159, 164, 168, 186, 199, 295, 339–340, 367
Houssney, Georges 144, 402, 447
Hubal 120, 142–143, 411
Ḥudaibiya, Treaty of 66–67, 207
humankind 15, 24, 26, 28, 32–33, 37, 39, 47, 54, 95–97, 100–101, 108, 127, 133, 170, 217, 220, 305–307, 311–314, 316, 325–326, 330–331, 339, 359, 362, 375, 378, 380, 382–384, 415, 435, 459–460, 468
Huntington, Samuel P. 298–299, 389, 458, 468
Ḥussein, son of ʿAlî 207, 209, 211–213, 329, 356, 409, 412, 417
Hymn to Aten 109–110

"I am a Little World" (Donne) 330
ʿibâda 220, 222, 306, 411
Iblîs 311–312, 327, 331, 382–384
ibn 342–343, 411
Ibn ʿAbbas 55, 93, 130, 294, 323, 427
Ibn Isḥaq 107, 142, 402, 443
Ibn Rushd 257, 268
Ibn Sina 257
Ibn Warraq 402, 429, 439, 458
Ihya' ʿUlum al-Dîn, see The Revivification of the Religious Sciences 176
ijtihâd 169, 212, 411, 413
Il, see El 125, 411
al-ilâh 121–123, 125, 411
imam 90, 212–213, 241
îmân 23, 310, 411
incarnation 30, 32, 75–76, 99–100, 133, 152, 182, 201–202, 204, 217, 340, 347, 354, 359, 368, 430, 466
India 21, 150, 159, 193–194, 212, 224, 226, 233, 238–239, 242, 271, 288, 290–291, 293, 345, 410, 442
indigeneity 184
Indonesia 293, 299, 351, 464
Injîl, see Gospel 95–96, 350, 411
Innocent III, Pope 259, 268
inspiration 33, 49, 54–55, 75–78, 80, 88, 95, 99, 101, 117, 159–160, 291, 312, 382, 415, 442, 449
intention 26, 30, 33, 94, 299, 301, 313, 327–330, 343, 345, 393, 413, 449
International Missionary Council 287
intifâda 274, 411
Iqraa (Sura 96) 51, 411
Iran 175, 212–213, 223, 278, 389, 414
Iraq War 237, 278, 280
Irenaeus 165, 167, 316, 344, 417, 463
ʿÎsâ 140, 333, 348–349, 411
Isaac 40–42, 44, 127, 129, 248, 300, 328, 369
Isabel I 269
Isaiah 29, 44, 54, 58, 76, 385, 423
Ishmael 27, 40–44, 79, 130–131, 151, 301, 356, 368–369, 446
Ishmaelite 44, 300, 441
islâm 23, 25–29, 32, 171, 178, 224–227, 326, 379, 411
Islam 12–13, 16, 21–28, 32–37, 47, 51–52, 62, 64–66, 72, 76, 78–79, 81, 84–85, 90, 98–101, 103–104, 112, 114–118, 122, 125, 129–130, 132, 134, 138–139, 141–142, 144, 159, 162–163, 169–173, 175–177, 181–182, 184, 186, 191–192, 197, 206, 208, 211–213, 217–225, 227, 233–238, 241–242, 244, 247, 256–257, 261–265, 269, 271–273, 277–279, 281, 283, 288–296, 298–299, 307, 311, 313, 321, 325–326, 328, 343, 347, 353, 356, 360, 374–382, 384, 388–390,

392–394, 399, 402, 407, 409, 410–411, 413–421, 427, 429–431, 439, 442, 444–445, 447, 449, 451–452, 466, 468
Islamic Broadcasting Service Organisation 290
Islamic Council of Europe 290
Islamic Development Bank 290
Islamic Organization 235, 291, 411, 418
Islamic Solidarity Fund 290
Islamic World Congress 289
Islamism, Islamist 104, 132, 172–174, 218, 223–224, 226–227, 235–236, 238, 242, 244–245, 262–264, 274, 277–279, 295, 351, 389, 450
al-'ismâ' al-ḥusnâ, see the Beautiful Names of God 135, 409
Israel, kingdom of 57–58, 71, 189, 191, 368
Israel, State of 265, 273–276, 457

Jaᶜfar al-Ṣâdiq 212
Jacob 71, 127, 129, 138, 300–301, 336, 369
Jacobite 205
Jadeed, Iskender 403, 460
Jalâlu'l-Dîn 103–104, 424
al-Jamâᶜat-i Islâmî, see Islamic Organization 411
James, Apostle 157, 215, 373–375, 382
James, epistle of 334, 373
Jeddah 289
Jeffery, Arthur 403, 426–427
Jeremiah 54, 96, 98–99, 423
Jeroboam II, King 57–58
Jerusalem 13, 57, 59, 63, 73, 98, 105, 107, 127, 155–158, 162, 187, 193–194, 205–206, 213, 215, 226, 235, 250, 259–261, 264, 334, 336, 357–358, 363, 366–367, 369, 376, 379, 387, 422, 425, 432, 455–456
Jesuits 285
Jesus Christ 15–16, 19–21, 23, 27, 29–32, 34–37, 44, 57, 73–76, 78–79, 83, 87, 95–97, 99–100, 108–109, 113–114, 116–117, 128, 132, 134, 140–148, 152, 155–159, 161, 164–165, 174–175, 178–186, 192–193, 195–197, 199, 201–204, 206, 213–218, 245–246, 250–252, 256, 264, 273, 279, 282–283, 286, 294–295, 297, 307–308, 314–315, 318, 320–322, 324, 326, 329, 331–333, 335–364, 366–369, 373, 376, 380, 385–388, 391–393, 410–415, 417, 422–423, 430, 438–439, 441, 445–449, 451, 456–457, 460, 462–466
Jethro, the Midianite 188, 250, 301–302, 368
jihâd 64–65, 84, 105, 173, 218, 235, 277, 364, 411
jinn 52, 88, 220, 306, 326, 435
Job 97, 126–127, 248–249, 368–369, 432
John, Apostle 19, 31, 75–76, 158, 251, 344, 357, 374, 387, 465
Jonah 357–358, 368
Joseph 87–88, 300, 327
Josephus 250
The Joy of Being Wrong (Alison) 315, 460
Judah, kingdom of 58–59, 191, 368
Judaizer 185
Julian of Eclonum, Bishop 314, 318–319
Justin I, Emperor 205, 445
Justin Martyr 158, 165–166, 179, 417, 468
Justinian, Emperor 205, 445

kaᶜba 52, 63, 66, 120–123, 130–131, 142–143, 409, 411, 443
kafara 24–25, 412
kâfir 24–25, 412
Karbalâ' 209, 213, 329, 356, 378, 409, 412, 417
Kashmir 246, 363
Kateregga, Badru 62, 133, 297, 311, 313, 403, 422, 444, 458, 460, 467
Kepel, Gilles 389, 468
Keturah 40–42, 300
Khadîja 48–50, 60, 69–70, 72, 109, 128, 161, 207, 417–418, 443
khalîfa, see vice-regent 307, 383, 412, 418
Kharijîs 208, 320
Khazraj 61
Khomeini, Imam 212, 223, 237
Khudâ 140–141, 412
knowledge 14, 66, 77, 79, 116, 133, 148, 162, 170, 176–177, 212, 214, 217, 222, 227, 261, 292, 306, 308–310, 325, 330, 374, 380, 416, 435, 446, 459
The Koran (Dawood) 428
Kosovo 258, 276–277
Kufa 91, 93, 209, 426

Ladin, Usama bin 263
Lady Macbeth 150
Lahore 107, 292
Laodicea 200
Lapidus, Ira 170, 431, 450
al-Lât 52, 120, 123, 412
League of Nations 274
The Legends of the Jews (Ginzberg) 435
Leo, Pope 204–205
Leon 266–269
Lewis, C.S. 109, 439, 458–459
Licinius, Emperor 191, 193
The Life of Muhammad (Ibn Ishaq) 402, 443
logos 99, 166–167, 197–198, 201–202, 338, 391, 412, 446, 449
London 231, 235, 238, 241, 346
Lucian 198, 416
Luther, Martin 258, 392, 468
Lystra 146

Macdonald, Duncan B. 380–381, 421, 467
Maghreb 257
Magi 313, 450
Mahdi 212, 347
"Mahound" 79, 85, 382
Malaysia 141
Malek, Sobhi 345–346, 404, 464
Mâlik 169, 417, 467
Mamluk 171
al-Manât 52, 120, 123, 412
Mandate for Palestine 274
Manji, Irshad 256, 404, 429, 452, 454
mankind, *see* humankind 95, 114, 219, 292, 309, 313, 377, 434
mansûkh 103, 412
Manzikert 259–260
Margoliouth, G. 86, 88, 424
Marrakesh 268
Martel, Charles 265
Mary, the Virgin 19, 108, 113, 152, 161, 201–204, 206, 333–336, 338–343, 345–347, 350, 353, 355, 357, 410, 415, 430, 437–438, 446, 448–450, 463
Masai 148
al-Masîh, see Messiah 140, 333, 348, 412
Masood, Steven 115, 404, 442, 447
Massey, Joshua 183, 451
Massignon, Louis 174
Materials for the History of the Text of the Quran (Jeffery) 403, 427
Matthew 19, 29, 73–75, 152, 158, 213–216, 357–358, 387
Mawdûdî, Abû'l-ʿAlâ' 132, 221, 224, 226, 235, 291, 351, 411
Maxentius 190–191
may puritix 183–184, 412
Mayer, Tobias 99, 346, 404, 430, 447–449, 464
The Meaning and End of Religion (Smith, W.C.) 407, 419
Mecca 20, 33, 36, 47–48, 52, 57, 59–63, 65–67, 69–70, 80, 86–87, 91, 93, 95, 105, 119–121, 124, 130, 142, 161–163, 187–188, 190, 207–208, 217, 221, 225, 227, 289, 327, 329, 409–411, 413, 415, 421, 443
Medina 20, 33, 36, 48, 60–66, 69–70, 80, 86–87, 89–91, 93, 95, 161–163, 188–189, 207–209, 217, 225, 333, 378, 409, 413, 415, 418, 421, 426, 440, 443
Mediterranean Sea 150
Melchizedek 250, 454
Menologion (Metaphrastes) 436
Messiah 20, 134, 155, 157, 181, 212, 270, 302, 332–333, 339, 352–355, 366–369, 376, 380, 386, 393, 408, 456, 464, 466
Metaphrastes, Simeon 436
Mevlidi Şerif, see "Birth-song of the Prophet" 26, 362, 412, 416
Michel, O. 250, 454
Midian, Midianite 40, 42, 44, 188, 250, 300–302, 368, 368–369
midrash 88, 107, 412, 424–425
Midrash Pirkei Rabbi Eleazar 108
Midrash Rabbah 108
Midrash Yalkut Shimeoni 108, 433
Milvian Bridge 191, 378
Minakshipuram 293
Mirpur 245–246
Mishna 410, 412, 414, 425
mission 37, 47, 59, 76, 84, 119, 141, 146, 148, 155, 166, 175, 179–180, 186, 235–236, 264, 272, 283–285, 287–288, 290–291, 293, 297, 299, 307, 310, 339, 353, 413, 446
Moab 142
monarchianism 167–168
Mongol 171, 173
monophysitism 195, 197
Moor, Morisco 265, 267–270, 353–354, 464–466
Moore, Michael 281, 457
Moses 27, 32, 36, 53–54, 56–57, 67, 69, 73–76, 80, 85, 87, 95–96, 98–100, 111–112, 114, 124, 127, 151, 159, 161, 188, 191, 249–250,

301–302, 315–316, 320, 323, 325, 332, 360, 414–415, 423, 425, 441
The Moslem Doctrine of God (Zwemer) 408, 445
mosque 65, 105, 181–182, 185, 223, 225, 227, 233, 236, 238–239, 242, 271, 277, 291, 409, 411, 443, 456
Motyer, Alec 373, 467
Moucarry, Chawkat 16, 24, 137–139, 376, 404, 420, 431, 444, 446, 450, 462–463, 467
Muᶜâwiya 170, 190–191, 207–209, 417
Muddaththir (Sura 74) 51, 412
Muhâjirûn 62, 413
Muhammad at Mecca (Watt) 408, 421
Muhammad at Medina (Watt) 408, 422
Muhammad Ilyas, Mawlânâ 291–292
Muḥammad, Prophet 26–27, 32–36, 47–55, 57, 59–66, 69–73, 76–83, 85–92, 94–107, 109, 113–114, 119–124, 128–132, 134–135, 137, 142, 159–163, 169–171, 175–176, 185, 187–191, 207, 209, 211–213, 217–218, 225, 237, 256, 270, 279, 288, 291–292, 294, 310, 320–322, 327, 332–333, 337, 340–343, 345, 349–353, 361–363, 380, 382, 409–415, 417–419, 421–425, 428–430, 432, 441, 443–446, 448–450, 457, 466
Muhammad: The Man and his Faith (Andrae) 445
Mulla Nasrudin 118
mu'min 23, 413
al-Munqidh min al-Dalâl, see Deliverance from Error 176, 450
Murad, Khurram 235
Murphy-O'Connor, Cardinal Cormac 238
muslim 25, 27–29, 81, 332
Muslim 12–16, 19–28, 32–39, 42, 52, 61–63, 65–67, 70, 72, 78–81, 84–85, 88–92, 94, 96–97, 100–101, 104, 106–107, 112, 114–115, 118, 129, 132–134, 137–147, 149–150, 162–163, 169, 171, 173, 175–186, 188, 190, 192, 206, 208, 211–212, 217–218, 220, 222–228, 231–248, 255–285, 288–300, 311–313, 319–322, 325, 327–330, 332, 340, 345–346, 348–349, 351, 353–356, 360–364, 366–367, 374–382, 384, 389–392, 394, 397, 399, 404, 409–415, 418, 421, 424, 427–431, 435, 439, 442, 446–447, 449, 451–453, 456–458, 462, 466, 468–469
The Muslim News 236
Muslim World League 289–290
Muᶜtazilî 23, 104, 106, 138, 320, 416, 431
myrrh 150–152, 300

Naama, Ghulam Masih 363–364
Nabatieh 209
nabî 73, 76–77, 413
Najrân 109
nâsikh 103, 413
Nasser 84, 262
Navarre 266–269
Nazareth 19, 31, 75, 215, 334, 336, 350, 367
The Necessity of the Straight Path against the People of Hell (ibn Taymiya) 173
Nehls, Gerhard 142, 405, 446
Nestorian controversy 206
Nestorianism 195, 197
Nestorius 202–203, 205, 417
Neusner, Jacob 405, 434
New Paths in Muslim Evangelism (Parshall) 183, 405
Nicaea, Council of 193–194, 199
Nineveh 59, 368–369
North Africa 93, 150, 174, 227, 255–256, 265, 270, 316
Nubia 256

O'Donovan, Vincent 148–149
Omar Bakri Muhammad, Sheikh 236, 245, 452
Organization of the Islamic Conference 289–290
Origen 165–168, 198, 417
Ossius, Bishop 198
Ottoman Empire 258, 271, 274, 278

Pagels, Elaine 316, 319, 386–388, 405, 422, 462, 468
Pakistan 102, 180, 226–227, 235, 239, 291–292, 409, 412, 418, 429, 453
Palestine, Palestinians 74, 215, 250, 273–276, 278, 280–281, 290, 314, 350, 356, 411, 432, 457
Pantenus 159
Parshall, Phil 144, 183, 273, 405, 447, 451, 457, 464
Paul, Apostle 31, 76, 81, 83, 117, 143, 146–147, 155–158, 217, 315–317, 349–351, 366–367, 430, 435, 447

Pawson, David 234, 238, 405
Pelagian controversy 196
Pelagius 313–314, 316, 318
Penman, David 180, 450
Pentarchy 193–194
Pentecost, Day of 155, 369, 386
Persia 193–194, 205–206
Peter, Apostle 75–76, 155–157, 178, 251, 344, 355, 441
Pharaoh 41, 53–54, 74, 87, 96, 188, 217, 300–302, 325, 387
Pharisee 147, 213–214, 358, 363, 367, 387
Philip III 269
Philistine 189
Plato 81, 165, 439
polygamy 13, 64, 71
power 13–14, 29, 31, 36, 47, 83, 104, 134, 136, 148, 162, 171, 189, 191–192, 196, 205–208, 212–218, 225–226, 228, 230, 232, 237, 255–256, 258–259, 271–272, 275, 278–280, 285, 288, 308, 316, 325, 331, 336, 340, 343, 354, 359, 365, 378, 383–384, 387, 389, 409, 421, 456, 459, 468
Praxeas 167
Prichard, Rhys 337, 463
Protevangelium of James 334
Psalm 104 109–110
Punjab 241
purdah 241, 413

Qâsim ibn Ibrâhîm 346
Queen of Sheba 108, 152, 368–369, 434–435
Qur'ân 19, 21–25, 27, 32, 34–35, 50, 55, 62, 65–66, 69, 76–77, 84–87, 89–108, 112–116, 118–119, 121, 123–125, 127–129, 131–134, 137–142, 145, 148–149, 160–162, 169, 171–173, 185, 207, 210–212, 218–220, 239, 246, 262–263, 283, 291, 294, 297, 305–306, 308, 310–311, 321, 323–325, 327, 328–330, 332–334, 336–337, 339–343, 345–351, 353–357, 360, 389, 391–392, 397, 409–410, 412–414, 416, 418, 420, 423–424, 426–431, 439–442, 444, 446, 448–449, 460–462, 467
Quraysh 47, 50–51, 57, 61, 91, 120–122, 190, 208, 345, 409, 413, 417
Qutb, Sayyid 84, 173, 226, 262–263, 456

Rabb 124–125, 413
Râbi^ca al-^cAdawiyya al-Qaysiyya 360–361
Ragg, Lonsdale and Laura 349, 406
Rahim, Muhammad ^cAta ur- 351, 399
al-Rahmân 124
Räisänen, Heikki 355
Ramaḍân 55, 63, 89, 105, 221, 225, 227, 413
Ramiro II 266, 268
ransom 328–329, 362
Reconquista, the 265–266
Red Sea 65, 150, 421
Reflections on the Psalms (Lewis) 403, 439
Refutation of the Christians (al-Tabarî) 206
The Retractations (Augustine) 318, 420, 462
revelation 20, 24, 32, 34, 48, 50–51, 54–56, 62, 79–80, 82, 85–86, 89–90, 94–95, 97, 99–101, 104, 111–112, 116–117, 119, 123, 129, 130–132, 142, 148, 160–162, 164, 167–168, 184, 214, 222, 306, 332–333, 338, 380, 393, 414, 424, 443–444, 446
The Revenge of God (Kepel) 389, 468
The Revivification of the Religious Sciences (al-Ghazâlî) 176
Riddell, Peter 271, 406, 457
Rio Salado 269
Robinson, Stuart 235, 406, 452
Roman Empire 164, 191–193, 200, 256
Romans, epistle to 147, 315–318, 367, 447
Rome 165, 167, 190–191, 193–195, 204–206, 313–314, 355, 417
Rousseau, Richard 279–280, 457
Rumi, Jalâl al-Dîn 172, 417
Runciman, Steven 406, 454, 456
Rushdie, Salman 52, 79, 85, 233–234
Ruth 302, 369, 432

Sabellianism 167–168
Sabellius 167
al-Ṣaḥîḥ (al-Bukhârî) 55, 323, 420–421, 424, 426–427, 443–444, 458–460, 463
Saladin 259, 261
ṣalât 221, 337, 394, 413
Saljuq 175, 257, 259–260
Samaria 58–59, 187, 226, 379
Samaritan 31, 178–179, 368–369

Sandals at the Mosque (Cragg) 401, 423, 450–451
Santiago de Compostela 267
Sarah, Sarai 40–43
Satan 52, 85, 123, 142, 144, 249, 257, 312, 324, 330–331, 350, 352, 359, 382–387, 459, 463
"Satan, the Great" 84, 382
The Satanic Verses (Rushdie) 79, 85
Saul, King 73, 86, 189, 191
Saul, *see* Paul 155–157, 366–367
ṣawm 221, 413
scripture 14–15, 32–34, 76, 82, 85, 95–96, 112–113, 117, 128–129, 137, 147, 155, 160–161, 164–165, 167, 169, 176, 183, 281, 326, 337, 351, 380, 386, 388–393, 414, 416, 421, 431–432, 439–440, 442–443
secularization 222, 229–230, 233, 246, 272, 322
sêmeion, see sign 357, 413
Septuagint 56, 128, 248, 421
Seville 266–268
Shaddai 127, 249
Shâfiʿî 169, 418
Shah Wali Allah 291
shahâda 185, 221, 351, 413
sharîʿa 169–172, 175–177, 222–224, 360, 379, 413, 418
Shenk, David 297, 403, 422, 444, 458, 460, 467
Shîʿa 23, 140, 169, 171, 208–209, 211–212, 329, 356, 389, 409, 411, 414
shirk 132, 320, 391, 414
Siffin, Battle of 208
sign, Jesus as 336, 339, 356–359, 413
sin 29, 58, 77, 106, 132, 137–138, 196, 204, 211, 217, 264, 307, 313–325, 328, 330, 347, 361–364, 383, 391, 414, 460–462
Sinai 34, 56, 68, 74, 124, 188, 302, 323
Sin and Atonement in Islam and Christianity (Jadeed) 403, 460
Smith, Jay 237, 452
Smith, Wilfred Cantwell 97, 100, 107, 141–142, 407, 419, 429–431, 446
Solomon, King 71, 80, 108, 151–152, 155, 189, 191, 434–435, 455
Somalia 150, 298
Son of God 155, 195, 197, 199, 216, 250, 333, 336, 338, 340–341, 351, 355, 376, 393, 456, 464, 466
Son of Man 355, 357–358, 380, 394
Spain 174, 255–257, 260, 265–271, 278, 280, 285, 354, 416, 464–465
Stephen 155–156, 465
Stupid White Men (Moore) 281, 457
subordinationism 168
Ṣûfî, Sufism 143, 170–177, 190, 211, 236, 242, 268, 288–289, 291, 360–361, 374, 410, 414, 416–417
Suhuf 96, 414
sunna 291, 325, 328, 414, 429
Sunnî 23–24, 106, 138, 140, 169, 171, 177, 208, 211–212, 320, 389, 414, 416–418, 431, 467
sura 21–22, 25, 48, 50–52, 55, 63–66, 70, 76–77, 82, 85–89, 91–92, 94–98, 101, 103–104, 106–108, 112–114, 122–124, 128, 130–131, 133–135, 137, 159–162, 172, 211, 217, 219–220, 283, 292, 294–295, 305–307, 309–313, 319, 321, 323–325, 327–328, 332–343, 345–346, 351, 353, 356–357, 383–384, 409–412, 414, 420–421, 424, 428–430, 436, 439–441, 446, 449, 461–462
Sylhet 240–241
syncretism 184–185
Syria 91, 195, 200, 206–207, 249, 255, 259–260, 445, 466

al-Tabarî, ʿAlî ibn-Rabbân 206
Tabligh-i Jamaʿat 242, 291–293, 414
Tafsîru'l-Jalâlayn 103
taḥrîf 32, 414, 440–441
Ṭa'if 59–60, 120
Talmud 107, 414, 425, 435
Tanakh 414, 425
tanzîl 95–97, 100–101, 338, 414
targum 107, 414, 431–432
Targum of Jonathan ben Uzziel 108, 432
Targum Sheni of the Book of Esther (Grossfeld) 108, 434
Targum Yerushalmi I 108, 432, 435
Taurât, see Torah 96, 414
tawḥîd 106, 132, 173, 414
al-Taybili, Ibrahim 464–465
Taylor, Hudson 285
Taymiya, Ahmad ibn 171–173, 450
Tertullian 165–168, 316, 418
theocracy 36, 63, 67, 73, 188–189
Theodore of Mopsuestia 201–202, 205
Theodosius I, Emperor 200–201, 437
Theodosius II, Emperor 203–205, 437

theos 118, 146, 415
theotokos 201–204, 206, 341, 415
Thoughts on the Methods to be Followed for a Successful Dissemination of the Faith among Mohammedans, Jews and Pagans in the Russian Empire (Glucharev) 286
Timothy, Patriarch 78, 422
Tome of Leo 205
Torah 54, 68, 96, 315, 324, 360, 363, 389, 410, 412, 414–415, 425, 431, 440–441
Towards Understanding Islam (Mawdûdî) 132, 444, 451
Travis, John 180–182, 349, 451, 464
Trench, Battle of the 65–67
Trinity, the 32, 35, 82, 106, 132, 134, 141, 164, 166–169, 178, 195, 206, 340–341, 347, 390, 416, 444, 449–450
The Trouble with Islam (Manji) 404, 429
truth 19, 35–36, 49, 58, 66, 80–83, 88, 95–97, 111, 118, 122, 130, 136, 139, 142, 144–145, 147–148, 160, 162, 165–166, 174–175, 192, 201, 206–207, 212–213, 216–218, 221, 258, 288, 310, 349, 351, 354–355, 378, 390, 420, 443, 446, 465, 468
Turkey 222, 260, 348, 362, 417, 465
Tyre 151–152

Ubai ibn Kaᶜb 91
Uḥud, Battle of 67, 217
ᶜUmar 57, 72, 90, 92–93, 189, 191, 207, 323, 418, 426, 463
Umayyad dynasty 267, 417
umma 226, 288, 297, 379, 415, 428
United Nations 274, 278, 288
The Unseen Face of Islam (Musk) 468
Urban II, Pope 259–260
ᶜUthmân, Caliph 57, 90, 92, 94, 190–191, 207–208, 418, 424, 426–427
al-ᶜUzzâ 52, 120, 123, 415, 418

Valencia 268
Vatican II 376–377
Venice 258
vice-regent 307–308, 330–331, 359, 383
Vienna 258, 349
"The Virgin Punishing the Infant" (Duffy) 337, 463
Visigoth 200, 265
Vita Adae et Evae 459–460

Wahb ibn Munabbih 324, 346, 463
walad 342–343, 415
Wansbrough, John 407, 429
Waraqa ibn Nawfal 50, 109, 418
Warsh 93, 428
Wâsil ibn ᶜAtâ 106
What Do I Say to my Muslim Friends? (Burness) 280, 457
White Fathers 285
Whitehouse, Jerald 14
Whose Promised Land? (Chapman) 276, 400, 457
Wiegers, Gerard 270, 353, 408, 456–457, 466
Word (of God) 34, 104, 106, 114–115, 200, 203, 339, 380
The Works of Hugh Latimer (Corrie) 419
World Council of Churches 279, 287
World Islamic Call Society 290
World Missionary Conference 287
World War II 225, 229, 239, 273–274, 287
worldview 27, 35–36, 178, 180, 224, 229–230, 240, 243–246, 262, 276, 286, 346, 360, 381, 386

Yahweh 29, 39, 41, 44, 53–54, 59, 67–69, 73, 118, 124, 126–127, 131, 134, 137, 141, 152, 165, 188, 249, 368, 393, 415, 423
Yalkut Shimeoni 435
Yasûᶜa 140, 348, 415
Yathrib, *see* Medina 48, 60, 188, 415, 421
Yazîd 209, 417
Yemen 109, 134

Zabûr 96, 415
Zaid ibn ᶜAmr ibn Nufail 124
Zaid ibn Thâbit 90–92, 418, 424
zakât 64, 221, 337, 415
Zamzam 130–131
Zaynab 69, 71–72, 102–103
Zebiri, Kate 257, 261, 408, 454, 456, 458
Zeus 80–81, 125, 147, 415
Zwemer, Samuel 143, 184, 408, 421, 444, 446–448